# Bessie
# Blount

# ABOUT THE AUTHOR

ELIZABETH NORTON gained her first degree from the University of Cambridge, and her Masters from the University of Oxford. Her other books include *England's Queens: The Biography*, *Anne Boleyn: Henry VIII's Obsession*, *Jane Seymour: Henry VIII's True Love*, *Anne of Cleves: Henry VIII's Discarded Bride*, *Catherine Parr* (all published by Amberley Publishing) and *She Wolves: The Notorious Queens of England*. She lives in Kingston Upon Thames.

Praise for Elizabeth Norton

*Catherine Parr*
'Scintillating' *THE FINANCIAL TIMES*
'Cuts an admirably clear path through tangled Tudor intrigues'
JENNY UGLOW
'Wonderful... a joy to read' *HERSTORIA*

*Anne Boleyn*
'Meticulously researched and a great read'
*THEANNEBOLEYNFILES.COM*

# Bessie Blount

## Mistress to Henry VIII

ELIZABETH
NORTON

AMBERLEY

Cover illustrations: Front: Hans Holbein portrait of a lady c.1540 © Stephen Porter. Front flap: Bessie Blount from the side of her parents' tomb. © Elizabeth Norton. Back: Hans Holbein mural of Henry VIII. © Elizabeth Norton.

This edition first published 2013

Amberley Publishing
The Hill, Stroud
Gloucestershire, GL5 4EP

www.amberley-books.com

British Library Cataloguing in Publication Data.
A catalogue record for this book is available from the British Library.

ISBN 978 1 4456 1385 7

Typesetting and origination by Amberley Publishing
Printed in Great Britain

# Contents

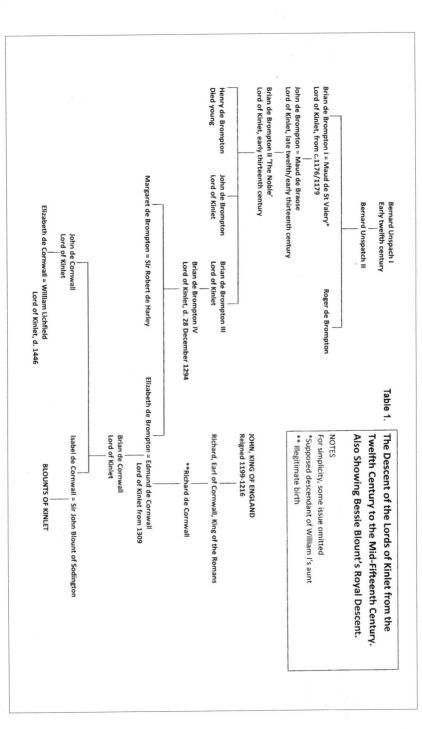

**Table 1. The Descent of the Lords of Kinlet from the Twelfth Century to the Mid-Fifteenth Century. Also Showing Bessie Blount's Royal Descent.**

NOTES

For simplicity, some issue omitted

\* Supposed descendant of William I's aunt

\*\* Illegitimate birth

Bernard Unspach I
Early twelfth century

Bernard Unspatch II

Brian de Brompton I = Maud de St Valery\*
Lord of Kinlet, from c.1176/1179

Roger de Brompton

John de Brompton = Maud de Braose
Lord of Kinlet, late twelfth/early thirteenth century

Brian de Brompton II 'The Noble'
Lord of Kinlet, early thirteenth century

Henry de Brompton
Died young

John de Brompton
Lord of Kinlet

Brian de Brompton III
Lord of Kinlet

Margaret de Brompton = Sir Robert de Harley

Brian de Brompton IV
Lord of Kinlet, d. 28 December 1294

Elizabeth de Brompton = Edmund de Cornwall
Lord of Kinlet from 1309

JOHN, KING OF ENGLAND
Reigned 1199-1216

Richard, Earl of Cornwall, King of the Romans

\*\*Richard de Cornwall

John de Cornwall
Lord of Kinlet

Brian de Cornwall
Lord of Kinlet

Elizabeth de Cornwall = William Lichfield
Lord of Kinlet, d. 1446

Isabel de Cornwall = Sir John Blount of Sodington

BLOUNTS OF KINLET

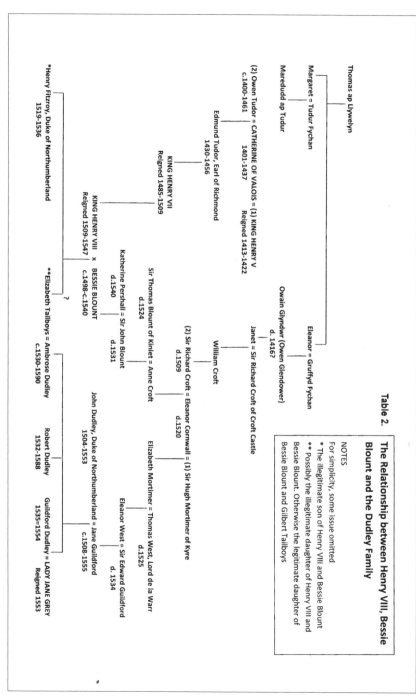

## Table 2. The Relationship between Henry VIII, Bessie Blount and the Dudley Family

**NOTES**

For simplicity, some issue omitted

\* The illegitimate son of Henry VIII and Bessie Blount

\*\* Possibly the illegitimate daughter of Henry VIII and Bessie Blount. Otherwise the legitimate daughter of Bessie Blount and Gilbert Tailboys

Thomas ap Llywelyn

Margaret = Tudur Fychan

Maredudd ap Tudur

(2) Owen Tudor = CATHERINE OF VALOIS = (1) KING HENRY V
c.1400-1461      1401-1437      Reigned 1413-1422
              Reigned 1413-1422

Edmund Tudor, Earl of Richmond
1430-1456

**KING HENRY VII**
Reigned 1485-1509

Owain Glyndŵr (Owen Glendower)
d. 1416?

Eleanor = Gruffyd Fychan

Janet = Sir Richard Croft of Croft Castle
d. 1416?

William Croft

**KING HENRY VIII** x **BESSIE BLOUNT**
Reigned 1509-1547   c.1498-c.1540
                 ?

Katherine Pershall = Sir John Blount
d.1540                  d.1531

Sir Thomas Blount of Kinlet = Anne Croft
d.1509

(2) Sir Richard Croft = Eleanor Cornwall = (1) Sir Hugh Mortimer of Kyre
d.1520

Elizabeth Mortimer = Thomas West, Lord de la Warr
d.1525

John Dudley, Duke of Northumberland = Jane Guildford
1504-1553                              c.1508-1555

Eleanor West = Sir Edward Guildford
d. 1534

\*Henry Fitzroy, Duke of Northumberland
1519-1536

\*\*Elizabeth Tailboys = Ambrose Dudley
c.1530-1590

Robert Dudley
1532-1588

Guildford Dudley = **LADY JANE GREY**
1535-1554          Reigned 1553

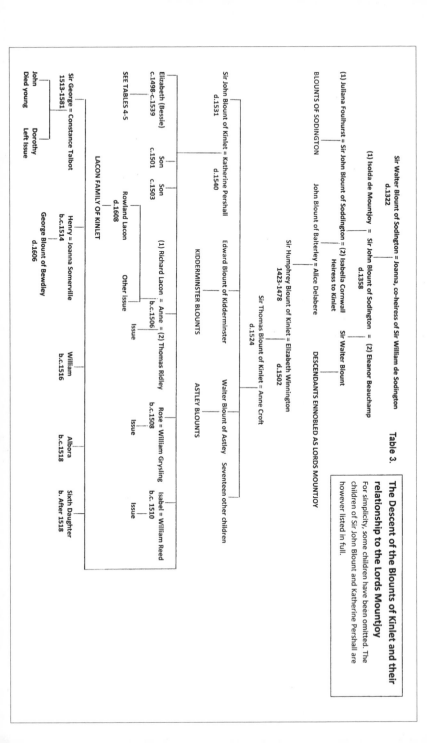

# Table 3.

## The Descent of the Blounts of Kinlet and their relationship to the Lords Mountjoy

For simplicity, some children have been omitted. The children of Sir John Blount and Katherine Pershall are however listed in full.

Sir Walter Blount of Sodington = Joanna, co-heiress of Sir William de Sodington
d.1322

**BLOUNTS OF SODINGTON**

(1) Isolda de Mountjoy    =    Sir John Blount of Sodington    =    (2) Eleanor Beauchamp
d.1358

(1) Juliana Foulhurst = Sir John Blount of Soddington = (2) Isabella Cornwall
Heiress to Kinlet

John Blount of Balterley = Alice Delabere         Sir Walter Blount

**DESCENDANTS ENNOBLED AS LORDS MOUNTJOY**

Sir Humphrey Blount of Kinlet = Elizabeth Winnington
1423-1478                                              d.1502

Sir Thomas Blount of Kinlet = Anne Croft
d.1524

Sir John Blount of Kinlet = Katherine Pershall
d.1531                                    d.1540

Edward Blount of Kidderminster    Walter Blount of Astley    Seventeen other children

**KIDDERMINSTER BLOUNTS**         **ASTLEY BLOUNTS**

Elizabeth (Bessie)    Son       Son
c.1498–c.1539        c.1501    c.1503

**SEE TABLES 4-5**

(1) Richard Lacon = Anne = (2) Thomas Ridley    Rose = William Grysling    Isabel = William Reed
b.c.1506              b.c.1506                      b.c.1508                      b.c.1510

Rowland Lacon    Other issue              Issue                        Issue
d.1608

**LACON FAMILY OF KINLET**

Sir George = Constance Talbot
1513-1581

Henry = Joanna Somerville    William    Albora    Sixth Daughter
b.c.1514                          b.c.1516    b.c.1518    b. After 1518

George Blount of Bewdley
d.1606

John              Dorothy
Died young       Left issue

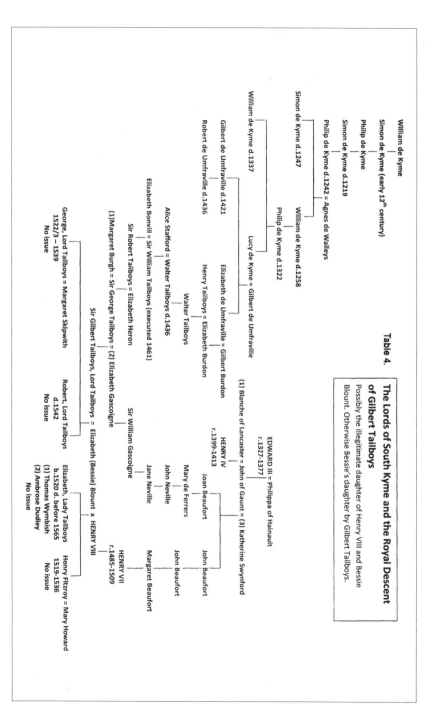

Table 4.

## The Lords of South Kyme and the Royal Descent of Gilbert Tailboys

Possibly the illegitimate daughter of Henry VIII and Bessie Blount. Otherwise Bessie's daughter by Gilbert Tailboys.

William de Kyme

Simon de Kyme (early 12th century)

Philip de Kyme

Simon de Kyme d.1219

Philip de Kyme d.1242 = Agnes de Walleys

Simon de Kyme d.1247

William de Kyme d.1258

Philip de Kyme d.1322

William de Kyme d.1337

Lucy de Kyme = Gilbert de Umfraville

Gilbert de Umfraville d.1421

Robert de Umfraville d.1436

Elizabeth de Umfraville = Gilbert Burdon

Henry Tailboys = Elizabeth Burdon

Walter Tailboys

Alice Stafford = Walter Tailboys d.1436

Elizabeth Bonvill = Sir William Tailboys (executed 1461)

Sir Robert Tailboys = Elizabeth Heron

(1)Margaret Burgh = Sir George Tailboys = (2) Elizabeth Gascoigne

Sir William Gascoigne

Sir Gilbert Tailboys, Lord Tailboys = Elizabeth (Bessie) Blount × HENRY VIII

George, Lord Tailboys = Margaret Skipwith
1522/3 – 1539
No Issue

Robert, Lord Tailboys
d.1542
No Issue

Elizabeth, Lady Tailboys
b.1520 d. before 1565
(1) Thomas Wymbish
(2) Ambrose Dudley
No Issue

EDWARD III = Phillippa of Hainault
r.1327-1377

(1) Blanche of Lancaster = John of Gaunt = (3) Katherine Swynford

HENRY IV
r.1399-1413

Joan Beaufort

Mary de Ferrers

John Neville

Jane Neville

Margaret Beaufort

John Beaufort

John Beaufort

John Beaufort

HENRY VII
r.1485-1509

Henry Fitzroy = Mary Howard
1519-1536
No Issue

# Table 5.

## The Clinton Family and the Marriages of Bessie's Younger Daughters

NOTE
* Illegitimate Daughter

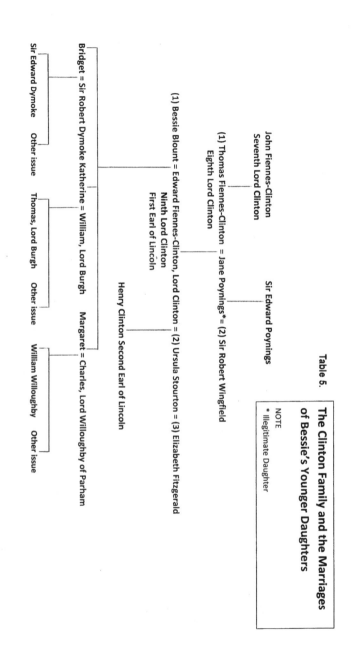

John Fiennes-Clinton
Seventh Lord Clinton

Sir Edward Poynings

(1) Thomas Fiennes-Clinton = Jane Poynings* = (2) Sir Robert Wingfield
Eighth Lord Clinton

(1) Bessie Blount = Edward Fiennes-Clinton, Lord Clinton = (2) Ursula Stourton = (3) Elizabeth Fitzgerald
Ninth Lord Clinton
First Earl of Lincoln

Henry Clinton
Second Earl of Lincoln

Bridget = Sir Robert Dymoke    Katherine = William, Lord Burgh    Margaret = Charles, Lord Willoughby of Parham

Sir Edward Dymoke    Other issue    Thomas, Lord Burgh    Other issue    William Willoughby    Other issue

# PART 1
# BESSIE BLOUNT OF KINLET,
## *c*.1498–1512

# 1
# THE BLOUNTS OF KINLET

Elizabeth, or Bessie Blount as she is more famously known, is one of the few mistresses of Henry VIII whose name is remembered today. She was a love of Henry VIII's youth – before he met Anne Boleyn and decided to end his first marriage to take her as his wife. Bessie would have had no conception that there was any possibility that the king might choose to make her his queen and she was happy to accept the role of royal mistress. It was the birth of her son, Henry Fitzroy, the only acknowledged illegitimate child of the king, that brought her to prominence. As her son aged and the king's first and second marriages failed to provide him with the male heir he craved, Bessie came to increasing prominence as the mother of the king's son. At one point her son's accession as Henry IX looked a virtual certainty and there were even rumours that Henry VIII might take her as his bride in order to increase the standing of their child. These hopes came to nothing and Bessie died in obscurity, but, for a few brief years, the future must have looked glittering.

Any attempt to write a biography of Bessie Blount is hampered by the fact that she left so little behind her. No letters written by her survive and there are few examples of her writing. There are no recorded instances of her speech and, whilst the records for her family (both by birth and marriage) are reasonably complete, she is strangely absent. Bessie Blount was an independent woman and acted in defiance of convention, ending her life married to the (considerably younger) man of her choice. This is an attempt to reconstruct her life. As such, it can never be a full biography. We do not know what Bessie thought at any one point or even, often, where she was. In spite of this, the real Bessie can be glimpsed through an analysis of surviving documents surrounding both her and her family and a consideration of the lifestyle that a woman of her class and station would have enjoyed. Much has been written about Bessie Blount which is inaccurate. This is an attempt to bring out the real woman for the first time: the story of the first woman to arguably truly capture the heart of Henry VIII.

Bessie's story begins with her family background and she, like all her contemporaries, was a product of both her upbringing and her class. Both paternal and maternal kin were important in Tudor England and both sides of an individual's family would take an interest in their advancement. Bessie was the daughter of Sir John Blount of Kinlet and his wife, Katherine Pershall, or Peshall. The Blounts were solid members of the gentry whose ancestors had held the manor of Kinlet in Shropshire since around the time of the Norman Conquest. The family, who were reputedly descended from the third Count of Guisnes and his wife, the daughter of the Count of St Pol, came to England with William the Conqueror, settling at Sodington.[1] They followed a tradition over the next few centuries of marrying well, with one John Blount marrying Isolda, heiress of Sir Thomas de Mountjoy, a substantial landowner. It was their son, another John, who brought the family to Kinlet in the fourteenth century through his marriage to the heiress Isabella Cornwall. Generously, if somewhat short-sightedly, this John Blount, considering that his paternal inheritance and the lands he inherited from his wife were sufficient, passed his mother's Mountjoy inheritance over to his half-brother, Walter Blount.[2] Walter was the founder of the more successful line of Blounts, with his descendants eventually joining the peerage as Baron Mountjoy. Although only distantly related to the Kinlet Blounts by Bessie's time, the Mountjoy Blounts remembered the debt that they owed their less prosperous kin, actively supporting Bessie's family in the Tudor period. By the sixteenth century the family name of Blount was reputed to have been 'taken first from their Golden Locks' and, from an early period, the family was considered to be unusually good-looking in an age when blond hair was highly valued.[3]

The Blount family home of Kinlet, in Shropshire, had belonged to Edith Godwin, the wife of King Edward the Confessor at the time of the Norman Conquest.[4] It was recorded in the Domesday Book as a substantial estate with 111 hides of land and fields sufficient for eight ox teams. Following Edith's death, Kinlet passed to the powerful marcher lords, the Mortimers, and they in their turn granted the manor to a man named Richard, who also held lands in nearby Brampton Brian.[5] By the reign of Henry I in the early years of the twelfth century, the manor was held by a Norman named Bernard Unspach.[6] His son Brian succeeded him and the Brian de Brompton who was recorded as being in possession of Kinlet between 1176 and 1179 can be identified as either Brian Unspach or his son.

The Brompton family were locally very prominent and firmly identified with their Mortimer overlords. French annals record that at the foundation of Wigmore Abbey in 1179:

Hugh de Mortimer laid the first stone. Brian de Brompton laid the second, and promised 100 s. in aid of the work: but he gave no money, though he granted the canons all the easements of his lands, which easements were of great avail. John, son of the said Brian, laid the third stone and neither gave nor promised anything, but what he did not then do in promise he performed fully afterwards in deed, for by him was the Church of Kinlet given to the Abbey.[7]

The Brompton family was a pious one and, along with the grant of the church at Kinlet to Wigmore Abbey, records confirm that, in 1185, Brian de Brompton and his brother, Roger, granted 24 acres of land in Kinlet to the monastery of St John of Jerusalem for the annual rent of four shillings.[8] In a second grant both Brian and Roger confirmed 'the donation of their ancestors to the abbey of Lira in Normandy of one man with his land in the manor of Kinlet, & two parts of the tithes of that lordship'.[9] This was, once again, a generous grant, although the feelings of the peasant thus granted, who effectively became the Abbey's property, went unrecorded. The Brompton family was a prosperous one and the Brian de Brompton who made the two donations to religious houses married Maud, daughter of Sir John de St Valery, allowing the family at Kinlet to claim distant kinship to the royal family.[10] Maud was wealthy in her own right as her father's heiress, as well as, reputedly, a descendant of an aunt of William the Conqueror. In recognition of this, the Brompton family quartered the arms of St Valery with their own. Their son, John, made an equally prominent marriage to Maud, the daughter of the powerful Norman lord William de Braose. It was perhaps due to this grand lineage that their son, Brian, obtained his nickname of 'the Noble'. He was so well known that, in 1233, he delivered his young son Henry to the king as a hostage for Ralph de Mortimer's loyalty.[11] Young Henry died in captivity and his brother, John, succeeded their father. He was succeeded by his brother, Brian, who died young, passing Kinlet to his son, Sir Brian de Brompton. This Sir Brian would prove to be the last male member of his family. He had died by 28 December 1294, leaving two infant daughters as his heirs.[12] Margaret, the eldest, married Sir Robert de Harley and took the more prosperous estates at Brampton Brian and the surrounding area. Elizabeth, the younger daughter, inherited Kinlet.

Bessie was a direct descendant of Elizabeth de Brompton and would almost certainly have been familiar with the life of this ancestress. Elizabeth was married in her youth to Edmund de Cornwall, of whom a representation as a knight in armour survives in a stained-glass window in Kinlet church. The window, in one of the side chapels in the church, would have been prominent in Bessie's time and it is almost certain that Edmund, who brought the family its only drop of royal blood, would have been pointed out to her proudly.

Edmund de Cornwall was the eldest son of Richard de Cornwall, an illegitimate son of Richard, Earl of Cornwall and King of the Romans, the younger son of King John and brother to Henry III.[13] In spite of his family's illegitimacy, Edmund was recognised as a kinsman by the royal family and it was the king, Edward I himself, who granted Edmund the custody of Brian de Brompton's lands in 1300, until his daughters came of age. Edmund and Elizabeth had married by 7 December 1309 when Edmund did homage for her property and, at the same time, Kinlet was formally allotted to her.[14] Elizabeth bore her husband three sons and the couple were succeeded by the second, Brian de Cornwall of Kinlet.[15] Brian de Cornwall's son, John, succeeded him in his turn and died leaving a daughter, Elizabeth, or Isabel, as his heir. A sad memorial to Elizabeth de Cornwall survives in Kinlet church, below the window displaying the image of her great-grandfather. Her effigy shows a young woman in fine medieval dress with a swaddled baby lying at her side. This implies that she died in childbirth and the child with her, a common but tragic fate. Following her death, Elizabeth's husband enjoyed the revenues of Kinlet until his own death in 1446, when it passed to the only remaining Cornwall heiress, Elizabeth's aunt, Isabel, the wife of Sir John Blount of Sodington. This Sir John was succeeded by his son, another John. He, in turn, was succeeded by his eldest son, Sir Humphrey Blount. Kinlet then passed to Humphrey's son, Sir Thomas Blount, and finally to Bessie's father, another Sir John Blount.

The Blount family of Kinlet were prominent locally and can be considered to have been of gentle rather than noble rank. The term 'gentleman' was a fluid one in fifteenth-century England, with one recent historian commenting that, whilst knights and esquires formed a recognisable group, for example, 'to be a "gentleman" could mean either that one was claiming membership of the whole class of people, including knights and esquires, occupying the social space between the peerage and the free peasantry, or, more narrowly, that one was from the lower range of this group, ranking above a mere yeoman or franklin, but not aspiring to the title of knight or esquire'.[16] The term was used in a number of ways during the period, with knights sometimes included or, alternatively, placed in a higher rank, distinct from a mere gentleman. Such distinctions mattered in fifteenth-century England. It has been pointed out that the famous Paston family of fifteenth-century Norfolk, who had peasant origins, were at pains to claim a noble root at odds with their actual ancestry when they obtained their patent of gentle status. It is not impossible that the rumours of Norman origins for the Blounts arose in a similar way, as they sought to define their gentle status. Even their dash of royal blood through the Cornwall family was rather lacking and, whilst all of Henry VIII's six wives (including the lowly Jane Seymour) could claim legitimate descent from Edward I, or his grandson, Edward III, Bessie was only able to claim a blood link through an illegitimate son of the earlier King John. At a time when most of the nobility and gentry had royal blood, this was far from impressive. In spite of this, the Blounts were important locally in Shropshire and members of the family regularly served as sheriffs, a common role for members of the gentry.[17] Laws put in place in 1371 held that a sheriff was required to have lands in the county in which they served worth at least £20, which ideally suited the numerous gentlemen of England. From the latter half of the fifteenth century, the Blounts were able to lay claim to links with the nobility through the marriage of Bessie's grandfather, Thomas Blount, to Anne Croft.

The Crofts were considerably better connected than the Blounts, with strong links to the Yorkist royal dynasty in England. They were also a long-lived family and Bessie's great-grandparents were an active presence in the advancement of her parents, and of herself.

Although not of royal descent, the Crofts of Croft Castle on the Welsh border were, following the accession of the Welsh Henry VII, able to claim kinship with the reigning monarch. It was well known in the fifteenth century that Henry VII's grandfather, Owen Tudor, had been a Welsh squire who had had the good fortune to attract the attention, and capture the affections, of the queen dowager of England, Catherine of Valois. Owen took his surname from his grandfather, Tudur, a Welsh gentleman who married one of the daughters of the prominent Thomas ap Llywelyn.[18] Thomas's other daughter, Eleanor, was the mother of Owain Glyndwr (or, using his Anglicised name, Owen Glendower), who rebelled against the English king, Henry IV, in 1400. His three cousins, the sons of Tudur, supported him and were outlawed by the king in 1406. The youngest brother, Maredudd ap Tudur, survived the rebellion to father Owen Tudor. Owain Glyndwr's daughter, Janet, married Sir Richard Croft of Croft Castle in Herefordshire. The couple's grandson, another Sir Richard Croft, was Bessie's great-grandfather and this connection served both to provide her with a romantic descent from the famous Welsh prince Owain Glyndwr, and to make her a distant cousin of Henry VIII through his Welsh family.[19] The family retained firm interests in Wales and, as late as the reign of Henry VII, Bessie's great-grandfather, Sir Richard Croft, was involved in a dispute over a manor in the lordship of Dynas in Wales.[20]

In spite of their Welsh connection, the Crofts were solidly English in their outlook. Croft Castle, although heavily modified, still stands and commands an imposing outlook across the hills of the Welsh border. It had been the seat of the Croft family since the time of Edward the Confessor and remained in their possession into the nineteenth century, with one later member of the family being famous as the doctor who, in 1817, attended Princess Charlotte, the only child of the future George IV, during the birth of her first child. Sadly, the princess and her child both died, causing her physician to take his own life.[21] In the Domesday Book, it was recorded that Croft was held by Bernard de Croft, the first named ancestor for the family.[22] Some generations later, a Sir Hugh de Croft was made a Knight of the Bath by Edward I, a great honour. Later members of the family also came to some national prominence, with Bessie's great-great-grandfather, William Croft, for example, serving in the French wars of Henry VI's reign.

At the time of Bessie's birth, the head of the family was her long-lived great-grandfather, Sir Richard Croft, and his wife, Eleanor. Sir Richard died in 1509, when Bessie was approaching adulthood and her great-grandmother survived longer. Croft Castle lies only a few short miles from Kinlet and it is certain that Bessie would have known her great-grandparents. Certainly, Sir Richard showed an interest in his Blount descendants in his will, making a bequest to one of his Blount granddaughters, Bessie's aunt, Joyce, on the condition that she marry only on the advice of his wife, his two sons and her father.[23] The couple's images survive on their fine monumental tomb in the chapel at Croft Castle and show a kindly-looking elderly couple in late fifteenth-century dress. This is how Bessie would have known her great-grandparents, who were reputedly parents to twenty children. The couple were noted for their exceptionally high number of descendants even in their own time, with one sixteenth-century manuscript recording of Lady Croft that 'it is truly reported this lady lived so long and had such increase of issue that she had, before she died, seventeen score and odd people descended from her body: whereof the Duke of Richmond, base son to Henry VIII was one, and the late Duchess of Northumberland, mother to Ambrose Earle of Warwick and to Robert Earle of Leicester was another'.[24]

Sir Richard Croft used his strong royal connections to benefit his Blount kin. Following the accession of Henry VII, he was appointed to the prominent position of comptroller of the king's household, as well as other important offices.[25] He also had strong links to the Yorkist royal family, who, through the marriage of Anne Mortimer to the Yorkist Richard, Earl of Cambridge, were the heirs to the great marcher Mortimer family. Bessie's great-grandmother was described in a contemporary manuscript as 'lady governess' to the young princes at Ludlow and, whilst this has generally been interpreted to have referred to the Princes in the Tower, the future Edward V and his brother, in reality it almost certainly refers to the young princes' father, the future Edward IV (then Earl of March) and his brother, Edmund, Earl of Rutland.[26] Richard, Duke of York, the younger brother of Edward V, is not recorded to have ever lived with his brother in the Welsh Marches, whilst the boys' father and uncle certainly did reside with Sir Richard Croft at Ludlow during their boyhood, as two letters of complaint to their father, the elder Richard, Duke of York, attest.

The two princes, Edward and Edmund, arrived at Ludlow, the ancient seat of their Mortimer ancestors, in 1454, shortly before their father was appointed as Protector and Defender of the Realm to rule in the place of the unstable Henry VI. Sir Richard and his wife were diligent in ensuring that their young charges attended to their education, with the two princes writing to their father to inform him that:

> And where ye command us by your said letters to attend specially to our learning in our young age that should cause us to grow to honour & worship in our old age Please it your highness to wit that we have attended our learning since we come hither. And shall hereafter by the which we trust to God your gracious lordship and good fatherhood shall be pleased.[27]

Sir Richard was evidently a strict guardian, with the boys complaining in a subsequent letter:

> Please it your highness to wit that we have charged your servant William Smyth bearer of these for to declare unto your nobility certain things on our behalf, namely concerning and touching the odious rule and demeaning of Richard Croft and of his brother. Wherefore we beseech your gracious lordship and full noble fatherhood to hear him in exposition of the same, and to his relation to give full faith and credence.[28]

The Duke of York's response to these accusations unfortunately does not survive. Although his two young charges evidently railed against the strict rule of their governors, it is certain that Sir Richard and his wife had a beneficial effect on them. Although Edmund died young, Edward IV went on to become an avid collector of books, an interest for which the groundwork may well have been laid by Bessie Blount's great-grandfather.[29] The adult Edward IV did not bear a grudge against his old guardian and he appointed Sir Richard as general receiver for the earldom of March in the shires of Hereford and Shropshire, in addition to other important local offices.[30]

Sir Richard remained a staunch supporter of the Yorkist dynasty and was knighted by Edward IV. He was able to be of particular service to Edward IV in 1471 during the Battle of Tewkesbury: a battle that saw the final defeat of Margaret of Anjou, the wife of the deposed Lancastrian king, Henry VI, and the near-annihilation of the Lancastrian cause. Edward IV had been briefly deposed in favour of

Henry VI in 1470 but had returned in the following year and reclaimed his crown. Unaware of the Yorkist king's return, Margaret of Anjou and her only child, Edward of Lancaster, Prince of Wales, had sailed from France to rejoin Henry VI and they were dismayed to learn on landing that the Lancastrian king was once again a prisoner in the Tower. Undaunted, the pair raised an army and met with the Yorkist king's forces at Tewkesbury, where they sustained a heavy defeat. Edward of Lancaster's exact fate is uncertain, with some accounts recording that he fell in battle and others that he was captured and then murdered. Whatever the truth, it is clear that Sir Richard Croft played some role in his death. The Tudor chronicler Edward Hall claimed that Edward IV tricked Croft, 'a wise and valiant knight', into handing over the prince, whom he had taken prisoner, assuring him that he would spare his life.[31] This proved to be a trick, with the king ordering the murder of the prince.[32] Whether Croft was so easily duped by the king is debateable: it seems improbable that he could have believed that Edward would simply allow the Lancastrian heir to walk free. Bessie's great-grandfather also continued to be prominent throughout the reigns of Edward IV, his son Edward V, and brother Richard III, regularly serving as sheriff of Herefordshire, for which he once received the substantial sum of £50 from the king.[33] This may, perhaps, have been a reward for his role in the dispatch of the last Lancastrian Prince of Wales.

Bessie's great-grandfather retained his prominence following the accession of Henry VII, the last remaining Lancastrian claimant to the throne, in 1485. This may, in part, have been due to the role of Henry's queen, Elizabeth of York, the daughter of Edward IV, who remembered her father's fondness for his old guardian. By the time of Bessie's birth, Croft – who, as the evidence of his will shows, enjoyed a close friendship with his son-in-law, Sir Thomas Blount – was the most prominent member of the family and well placed to ensure the advancement of his grandson, John Blount, and his wife, Katherine Pershall.

# 2

# BESSIE'S PARENTS

By the time of Bessie's birth, her family enjoyed a great deal of prominence in Shropshire and surrounding counties, with the marriage of her parents increasing the family's standing.

Bessie Blount's great-grandfather, Sir Humphrey Blount, died in 1478.[1] His son, Thomas, would later erect a fine stone tomb to both his parents in Kinlet church. It is clear that, at the time of Humphrey's death, the family was prosperous. In his will, Humphrey was able to bequeath an expensive black velvet gown to the church at Kinlet to be made into a cope or religious ornament.[2] A gold chain was ordered to be sold to pay for masses in the same church for the good of his soul. Sir Humphrey was a pious man and he made bequests to pay for the repair of a number of churches in the local area. The rector of Sudbury was singled out for particular favour in his will, receiving a fine long gown of London cloth. The vicar of Kinlet and his servants also received cash bequests, as did the church at Worcester and the friars in the monastery there. Sir Humphrey had made Worcester his home for the last years of his life and was close enough to the friars at Worcester and the church there to be aware of their particular needs. He left money for the repair of the bell tower at All Saints church in the city, as well as leaving to the friars 'as many rails [i.e. fence posts] as will suffice to enclose their garden called the friar's orchard'. Although Sir Humphrey died many years before Bessie's birth, his wife, Elizabeth Winnington, was an early influence on her great-granddaughter. She shared her husband's piety, remaining with him until the end and receiving the compliment of being appointed as his executor alongside a family friend, Humphrey Cotes, Esquire of Woodcote.

Sir Humphrey Blount evidently had a good relationship with his many children and his most valuable chattels were divided between them. His eldest son, Thomas, received a black horse, his best gilt sword, a gilt saddle and other horse trappings in silver gilt, as well as a gold collar.

For his second son, John, there was a rich furred gown and a doublet of red damask, as well as his second best gilt sword and a gold cross. Sir Humphrey evidently possessed only two swords, as a further son, William, received only a gilt wood knife, alongside a more valuable bequest of a furred gown made of tawny cloth. His daughters each received a cash bequest to be paid on their marriages. He also made more substantial provision for his two younger sons, directing that they should share all the lands and tenements that he had purchased within the counties of Staffordshire, Shropshire and Worcestershire, excepting only those that lay within the manor of Kinlet which passed to Thomas Blount. Thomas Blount's two brothers settled locally and remained in contact with their eldest brother, ensuring that, as she grew up, Bessie was surrounded by kin.[3]

Sir Humphrey Blount was a well-loved figure in both the local community and amongst his family. His eldest son, Thomas, was of a somewhat different character, enduring a troubled relationship with his eldest son, Bessie's father, John. Thomas Blount and his wife, Anne Croft, eventually went on to have twenty children, a substantial number even for the late fifteenth century, although only five sons and six daughters survived to adulthood.[4] At the time of his father's death, Thomas was a simple Esquire, although he was knighted by Henry VII in 1487 for his participation in the Battle of Stoke against the Yorkist pretender Lambert Simnel.[5] At the same time, his father-in-law, the noted soldier Sir Richard Croft, obtained the rank of knight banneret.

By 1491 Thomas Blount's family was far from complete, although it is likely that most of those then living, as well as his brother John, to whom he was close,[6] journeyed to the manor of Bewdley in Worcestershire, only a few miles from Kinlet to celebrate the wedding of his eldest son, John Blount, with Katherine Pershall of Knightley.[7] Arrangements for the wedding had been finalised at Kinlet in February and some of the bride's family viewed her future home at that time.[8] They would, however, have returned home to prepare for the wedding before travelling to Bewdley in time for the ceremony on 1 August 1491.

Bewdley was an interesting place for the wedding to take place. The manor had originally been in the possession of the monks of Worcester but, by the reign of Edward III in the fourteenth century, had passed to the Mortimer family.[9] With the accession of Edward IV (the Mortimer heir) to the throne in 1461, the manor passed into crown ownership although there is evidence that it was regularly let to tenants. In 1601, for example, it was leased to a Sir Edward Blount, presumably a descendant of one of Bessie's uncles, great uncles or more distant kin. He may have been the Sir Edward Blount buried in Kidderminster church, the grandson of Bessie's uncle, Edward Blount. A number of 'Blunts', a corruption of the surname 'Blount', were living in the locality at the time of the 1831 census, demonstrating a continuing presence in the area.[10] Given its choice as the location of Bessie's parents' wedding, it is likely that property there was already let to the Blount family in 1491. Certainly, Bessie's younger brother, Henry Blount, lived there in the sixteenth century with his wife Joanna, daughter of John Somerville of Edreston in Warwickshire.[11] Their son, George Blount of Bewdley, also settled there, making his will in the town in 1606 in which he referred to Sir Edward Blount as his 'beloved kinsman'.[12] Bessie's brother, Sir George Blount, who became the head of the family on the death of their father, is recorded to have owned land in Bewdley, suggesting again a connection there.[13] Bessie's grandfather, Thomas Blount, also made a specific bequest of lands and tenements that he held in Bewdley in his will, again evidence that the family had a significant presence in the town.[14] It appears that part of the terms of the lease was the agreement that, when the manor was required by a royal visitor, the tenants would make themselves scarce.[15] It is known to have been occupied by Arthur, Prince of Wales, for a time towards the end of the fifteenth century, as well as by the future Mary I and Elizabeth I in the early sixteenth century. Alternatively, the property occupied by members of the Blount family may have been a subsidiary building. Certainly, the family were closely associated with the building. In 1525–26, for example, Bessie's uncle, Edward Blount, was appointed to act alongside Thomas Fowler as 'deputy overseers of the works' on the manor, in order to ensure that it was a fitting home for Princess Mary during her visit to the Welsh Marches.[16]

The manor was already a fine building and dominated the surrounding area with its hilltop location.[17] It had originally been built by Richard, Duke of York, before being extended in the reign of his son, Edward IV.[18] By the sixteenth century the manor house was only one of a complex of buildings, with, for example, a new building being erected in 1473–74 on the south side of the manor house, which was one hundred feet long and built over two storeys. The manor was remodelled further by Henry VII and was the finest building in the area during Bessie's time. It was also noted for its park, which was locally famous for its fine spreading oak trees.[19]

Bewdley may, perhaps, have been chosen as the site for the wedding due to its convenient location: it had the only bridge over the Severn until Worcester. The bridge was a recent stone structure and an impressive landmark, with five arches and a number of wooden buildings.[20] Alternatively, the name Bewdley was derived from the name 'Beaulieu' or 'beautiful place', which may account for why it was considered an excellent location for a wedding. The sixteenth-century antiquary John Leland recorded only a few decades after the marriage that:

> The Town self of Bewdley is set on the side of an Hill, so comely, a man cannot wish to see a Town better. It riseth from Severn bank

by East upon the hill by West; so that a man standing upon a Hill trans pontem by East may discern almost every house in the town, and at the rising of the Sun from East the whole Town glittereth (being all of new Buildings) as it were of gold.[21]

The town, which by 1602 had a population of approximately 2,450 people, was a substantial one and made up of three main streets. It had one parish church, although it is unlikely that the marriage ceremony took place there. Instead, Katherine Pershall would have been led to the manor house which, according to a survey of 1612, was bounded by the town to the south and also the River Severn, as well as meadows and a park containing over 3,000 trees and 400 acres of heath land. It was a beautiful place and, although few details of the old manor house survive, it is known to have had a fine chapel.[22] The manor house was nearly destroyed during the Civil War in the seventeenth century. It was rebuilt and Tickenhall House survives today on the site on a hill just outside the town, marking the spot where Bessie's parents were married. The old Tudor building was apparently of timber and stood within the bounds of its park. It also had a great court and formal gardens, as well as a number of outbuildings. The marriage ceremony would have taken place there, surrounded by Blount family members and, in all likelihood the mother of the bride. Although the marriage took place in beautiful surroundings, it would have seemed an unusual ceremony in many respects, for the bride and groom were still very young children.

Bessie's father, John Blount, was, according to the *Inquisition Post Mortem* for his father, Sir Thomas Blount, aged 'forty years and upwards' in 1524.[23] Based on this, in 1491, Bessie's father could have been as young as seven and he was certainly no more than around ten years of age. His bride, Katherine Pershall, was around a similar age. According to the *Inquisition Post Mortem* for her grandfather, Humphrey Pershall, which was held in 1502, she was then aged '21 and more', placing her birth date at no later than 1481.[24] This was exceptionally young for marriage as medieval canon law placed the age of consent at twelve for girls and fourteen for boys.[25] Child marriages certainly did occur, but these tended to be reserved for the higher nobility. Margaret Beaufort, the heiress of the Duke of Somerset and eventual mother of Henry VII, for example, was married in 1450, at the age of six, to the young son of the Duke of Suffolk.[26] This marriage ended in an annulment, something that was entirely possible before the age of consent when a marriage could be consummated. It was more usual for English girls in the late medieval period to marry in their late teens or early twenties. One recent historian has pointed out that, whilst early marriage did occur amongst gentry classes or higher, it could not be considered the norm and that 'even where such early marriage did occur, anxieties expressed about the youth of the girls concerned indicates that early marriage does not necessarily indicate the absence of a notion of a phase intervening between childhood and adulthood for girls, but rather that family, political or economic interests could sometimes override that notion'.[27] Whilst the Blount and Pershall families had no political prominence, it is clear that family and economic interests did, indeed, dictate the early marriage of John Blount and Katherine Pershall.

Katherine Pershall would, as her later correspondence bears out, prove to be a remarkable and forthright woman and she almost certainly inherited these characteristics from her mother, the redoubtable Isabel Stanley. It was Isabel who arranged the marriage, ensuring that the only child of her first marriage was deposited away from the control of her paternal family and bestowed in a position of her mother's own choosing.

Bessie's mother was the only surviving child of Isabel and her first husband, Sir Hugh Pershall or Peshall. Hugh was the only surviving son of the marriage of Humphrey Pershall of Knightley in Staffordshire and Agnes Egerton.[28] Hugh enjoyed a scandalous private life, fathering, either before his marriage or after, a number of illegitimate children. A visitation of Staffordshire in 1583 recorded that Hugh fathered two daughters: Alienora and Alicia, both of whom were referred to as *filia bastarda*. Illegitimate daughters Isabella, who married Richard Fane of Tunbridge in Kent, and Jocosa, who married Humphrey Wolrych of Dulmaston in Shropshire, are also recorded.[29] Hugh expected his wife, Isabel Stanley, to attend to the upbringing of his four illegitimate daughters.[30] According to the visitation in 1583, Katherine also had a full sister, Eleanor, who died young.

As well as his scandalous private life, Hugh Pershall was a violent and turbulent individual. In 1466, for example, he was one of a number of men sued by the Countess of Shrewsbury 'for collecting together a great body of malefactors and disturbers of the peace, and breaking into her closes and houses at Whitchurch and Blakemere, and so threatening her servants and tenants that for fear of their lives they were unable to attend to their business or perform their duties to her'.[31] Some years later, in 1477, Hugh, along with seventy-two others, was accused of breaking into the house of Sir William Young and severely beating his servants.[32] Hugh's violent behaviour was considered to be out of the ordinary even by the standards of the lawlessness of the late fifteenth century. Later in the same year, both Hugh and his father were accused in the Star Chamber of leading the group of twenty men who attacked one Richard Berell at Gnosall, breaking his skull and causing such injuries that 'by them he is utterly maimed and destroyed'.[33] The Pershall family, as a whole, had a reputation for lawlessness. In a postscript added to a suit brought by one John Delves in the third year of the reign of Edward IV, Delves appeared in person to comment that:

Since the process had begun one Humfrey Pesehale, arminger, had been appointed Sheriff of co Stafford, and that Humfrey had married Anne, the sister of Elena, the wife of the said John, and he asked, therefore, that a writ might be addressed to the Coroner to summon a jury in place of the sheriff.[34]

Evidently a family feud had marred relations between the two brothers-in-law to such an extent that John Delves could not rely on Humphrey's fair judgement.

Hugh Pershall was the heir to substantial estates in Staffordshire. The family had been prominent in Staffordshire for centuries, with one member of the family, Robert de Peshale, recorded as having fought with William the Conqueror at the Battle of Hastings.[35] According to family legend, Robert married a descendant of the Anglo-Saxon king Aethelred II, bringing a drop of royal blood to the family and, in all probability, serving to endear the Norman family to their English tenants.[36] Whilst the Pershalls had always been well known in Staffordshire, they were relative latecomers to Knightley, their principal estate, obtaining it only in 1436 following a grant to Hugh's grandfather, Richard Pershall, from his cousin, Joan de Pershall, daughter of Joan de Knightley.[37] Joan also granted her manor of Little Wyrley to her cousin. These lands, in addition to the Pershall family manors of Hopton, Teyne, Little Onn, Blythewood, Caldon and Waterfall, as well as property in Stafford, ensured that the family became one of the most prominent in the county. Hugh's father, Humphrey Pershall, served as sheriff of Staffordshire on a number of occasions. He sat as the member of parliament for Knightley in 1484.[38]

Hugh was raised at Knightley, his father's seat, and, whilst the house there has long since disappeared, it is known to have had a chapel and to have been reasonably substantial.[39] Knightley itself was a small settlement, part of the parish of Gnosall. Gnosall church – at which the Pershall family would, on occasion, have worshipped – still stands as a Norman cruciform building with a central tower of pale sandstone. Its parish register survives from the latter years of the sixteenth century, and between 1572 and 1580 there were only 175 baptisms and 129 burials for the entire parish, something that, for a parish which encompassed seven manors, indicates that the settlements were only sparsely populated.[40] The records of court hearings held in the parish also demonstrate a rural community with distinctly local and, to modern eyes at least, rather trivial concerns. A great court held on 10 April in the seventh year of Henry VII's reign, for example, was primarily concerned with complaints about parishioners failing to enclose their fields. One case stated:

Thomas Broun is presented that he sufficiently fence the ditch, which is an annoyance to his neighbours, between the Wall meadow and John Banaster's croft, before the feast of Pentecost next coming, under pain 12d. Agnes More is presented that she sufficiently make her enclosure, and also cleanse her ditch round the said enclosure, before the feast aforesaid, under pain 12d.[41]

During the same session of the court, one Robert London was fined for keeping five more cows in the common fields than he was permitted. Gilbert White and Roger Sterke were similarly censured for overburdening the common land. Humphrey Pershall was of great importance to the parish and local affairs, with the record of a great court held after his death stating that his estate owed a heriot, or death duties, of a spotted cow and a red cloak. In his lifetime Humphrey was just as concerned with local, small-scale affairs as his tenants and, at Easter 1464, he sued two men for the theft of three of his heifers, appearing personally before the court.[42] In a similar case he also sued four men for pasturing their cattle on his grass.[43]

Humphrey Pershall also had some degree of national prominence. According to the sixteenth-century chronicler John Stow, he was in the service of the Duke of Buckingham at the time of Edward IV's death in 1485. It was Humphrey that Buckingham trusted to ride to York to meet with the deceased king's brother, Richard, Duke of Gloucester, and assure him of his support.[44] Buckingham assisted Gloucester in the coup that saw him take the throne as Richard III and it is certain that Bessie's great-grandfather was deeply involved in affairs. He already had some association with the Yorkist royal family. In 1469, Gloucester's elder brother, George, Duke of Clarence, sued him for abducting one of his wards, something that led to Humphrey's arrest.[45]

Hugh Pershall made an excellent marriage to Isabel Stanley. By the late fifteenth century the Stanleys had become one of the most powerful families in England. The head of the family, Thomas Stanley, second Lord Stanley and later first Earl of Derby, married as his second wife Margaret Beaufort, Countess of Richmond, the mother of the future Henry VII.[46] The Stanley line went back to the twelfth century, with one branch coming to particular prominence through its marriage to the heiress of Lathom in Lancashire, which brought the family an extensive power base in the county.[47] This branch of the family became the senior one and the head of the family joined the peerage as the first Baron Stanley in 1456. Isabel Stanley, the daughter of Sir John Stanley of Pipe, was only distantly related to the senior branch of the family, through the son of the first Sir John Stanley, who married the heiress Isabel de Lathom.[48] Their son, who was also called Sir John Stanley, married three times and it was the son of his third marriage who founded the Stanleys of Pipe.

Isabel Stanley's family resided at Elford in Staffordshire and, whilst only distantly related to the senior branch of the Stanley family, they

enjoyed prestigious links with them.[49] Isabel's brother, Sir John Stanley
of Pipe, entertained the future Henry VII at Elford when he met with
his stepfather, Lord Stanley, in the days before the Battle of Bosworth
Field.[50] Lord Stanley, who had a remarkable talent for keeping his
troops and person out of any battle of the Wars of the Roses, was, at
first, reluctant to listen to his wife's demands that he assist her son,
who was considered by many to be the heir to the house of Lancaster.[51]
Stanley was, for the most part, a loyal Yorkist and had family links
to the royal family. He played no part in a rebellion in 1484 against
Richard III which was led by the Duke of Buckingham and in which
his wife and stepson were heavily involved. He could, however, see the
benefits of being the stepfather to a king. By the summer of 1485, when
an invasion by Henry Tudor from France was planned, Stanley left
court for his own lands in Lancashire, reluctantly leaving behind his
eldest son, Lord Strange, as a hostage of Richard III. Soon afterwards,
the king ordered Stanley to join him at Nottingham, 'for the king was
afraid lest that, as it really turned out, the mother of the said Earl
of Richmond [Henry Tudor], whom the Lord Stanley had married,
might induce her husband to go over to the party of her son'.[52] Stanley
feigned illness but was unable to openly show his support due to his
son's presence with the king. Instead, when, in August 1485, Henry
Tudor sailed for England with a troop of foreign mercenaries, Stanley's
brother, Sir William Stanley, moved with his own troops to join him.

Lord Stanley left his home at Lathom in Lancashire on 15 August and,
on 21 August, he and his brother met with the young pretender outside
Lichfield, most likely at Bessie's grandmother's family home. Certainly, both
her brother, Sir Humphrey Stanley, and her husband, Sir Hugh Pershall,
were present. The *Ballad of Bosworth Field*, a song which, although it
only survives as a version produced during the reign of James I in the early
seventeenth century, is likely to be near contemporary, was composed by
a member of Lord Stanley's retinue. The *Ballad* states that Lord Stanley
agreed to support his stepson at their meeting, although he refused to
commit his troops. He did make one small concession to the pretender,
offering him four knights and their men to support his vanguard. According
to the *Ballad*, Lord Stanley called four of his best knights to him:

>He bade array them with their chivalry,
>& go to the vanguard with our king:
>Sir Robert Tunsall, a Noble knight,
>& come of royal ancestry;
>Sir John Savage, wise & wight,
>Sir Hugh Persall; there was 3:
>
>Sir Humphrey Stanley the 4th did be,
>That proved noble in everything;

They did assay them with their chivalry,
& went to the vanguard with our king.[53]

The choice of Bessie's grandfather and great-uncle as two of the four knights was a mark of singular favour from their kinsman, Lord Stanley, and demonstrates that the Stanleys of Pipe remained firmly aligned with their more prominent kin. The Battle of Bosworth Field was fought on 22 August 1485 in a field outside Atherstone near Leicester. Again according to the *Ballad*, Bessie's grandfather acquitted himself bravely:

> Sir Hugh Persall, with shield & spear
> Full doughtily that day did he;
> He bare him doughtily in this war,
> As a man of great degree.

Sir Hugh was rewarded for his support of Henry VII by being appointed a knight of the king's body alongside his brother-in-law and friend Sir Humphrey Stanley.[54] In the first year of the king's reign, Sir Humphrey was appointed as sheriff of Staffordshire and, perhaps at his request, Hugh Pershall was included with his brother-in-law in the Commission of the Peace issued soon after the Battle of Bosworth Field.[55] Within a year of the king's accession, Hugh received two separate pensions of £20 per annum each as evidence of the king's gratitude.[56] He served on at least one occasion as sheriff of Staffordshire.[57] Shortly before his death, he also received a grant from the king of £100.[58] His early death in 1488 limited the rewards that he received and it was Isabel, in the year of her daughter's marriage, who received the greatest reward. Henry VII's patent roll for 1491 survives and it includes a pardon for Isabel:

> The king, of his especial grace, certain knowledge and mere motion, has pardoned, remitted and relaxed to Isabel, late the wife of Hugh Persale, late sheriff of the county of Stafford, administratix of the goods and chattels which were the said Hugh's and tenant of the lands and tenements which were hers and the said Hugh's or which were the said Hugh's or otherwise granted to him or her, and all debts, accounts, profits, arrearages and sums of money whatsoever due to the said king by the same Hugh, in virtue of his office of sheriff of Stafford or otherwise, and all actions, executions and demands which may be brought against the said Isabel for the same Hugh for any cause touching the said office of Sheriff, and statute or order to the contrary notwithstanding.[59]

It appears that Hugh's accounting whilst sheriff may not have been entirely above board and the pardon was a lucrative grant. It also

demonstrates that Isabel continued to be remembered and well thought
of by the king. This may, in part, have been helped by her kinship
by marriage to the king's powerful mother, Margaret Beaufort. It is
probable that Hugh died in London due to the fact that he was buried
in Grey Friars church in the capital.[60]

As a widow with a young child, Isabel Stanley would have expected
to receive support from her husband's family. Isabel and her father-
in-law, Humphrey Pershall, had a poor relationship which would, as
the years progressed, turn openly hostile. Humphrey, who was left
without any living sons following Hugh's death, had no intention of
accepting his son's daughter as his heir, perhaps due to a reluctance
to see Knightley and his other estates pass out of the Pershall family.
Alternatively, he may already have been estranged from his son in his
lifetime as it appears that Hugh fully identified with his wife's family,
perhaps at the expense of his own family; for example, he appointed
his brother-in-law, Sir Humphrey Stanley, as one of the executors in
his will and made a bequest to him.[61] Soon after Hugh's death, the
aged Humphrey took the surprising step of remarrying twice, and
fathering a son, Richard, who was aged three at the time of his father's
death in 1498 and for whom his father attempted to disinherit his
granddaughter.[62] Although this was some years in the future at the time
of Hugh's death, Isabel Stanley would have been aware of a distinctly
hostile atmosphere and she instead sought protection from her own
family and, in particular, her two brothers: Sir John Stanley of Pipe
and Sir Humphrey Stanley.

Isabel's brother, Sir Humphrey Stanley, was involved in arranging
the marriage of Katherine Pershall with John Blount.[63] Sir Humphrey
Stanley has been described by one nineteenth-century writer as a 'man of
turbulent spirit' and, whilst he was shown royal favour and appointed
as one of the knights of the body to Henry VII, he was frequently in
trouble.[64] According to one story, recorded by the eighteenth-century
antiquary Thomas Pennant, Humphrey was responsible for a murder
only two years after his niece's wedding. In his description of Tixall
Heath in Staffordshire, he recorded that:

In 1493,[65] an infamous assassination was committed on this heath;
which shews how little the vindictive spirit of the feudal times was
subdued. A family emulation had subsisted between the Stanlies of
Pipe, in this county, and the Chetwynds of Ingestre. Sir Humphrey
Stanley was one of the knights of the body to Henry VII; Sir
William Chetwynd one of his gentlemen-ushers. The former, as
is said, through envy, inveigled Sir William out of his house, by
means of a counterfeit letter from a neighbour; and while he was
passing over this common, caused him to be attacked by twenty
armed men, and slain on the spot; Sir Humphrey passing with a

train at the instant, under the pretence of hunting, but in fact to glut his revenge with the sight.[66]

This account is corroborated by a contemporary petition made by the deceased's widow, Alice, who claimed that a letter was sent to her husband, purporting to be from the county sheriff, asking him to meet with him at 5 a.m. the next morning.[67] As the widow related to the king himself, this letter was, in fact, 'feigned and craftily by the ungodly disposition of Sir Humphrey Stanley', whose servants hid in a pit on the heath to await the arrival of their victim. Dame Alice asserted that, in the aftermath of the murder, Stanley was unable to resist gloating over the killing, arriving in its wake dressed for hunting and claiming to have passed that way by chance although, tellingly, it was a place 'where no deer was seen there xi years before'. In spite of his clear involvement, Katherine Pershall's uncle received no punishment due to the powerful support of his kinsman, the king's stepfather, Thomas Stanley, Earl of Derby.[68] Alternatively, it has been suggested that the murder may have been carried out with the king's connivance, perhaps due to Chetwynd's suggested support for Perkin Warbeck, a pretender to the throne.[69] This seems an unlikely task for the somewhat impetuous Sir Humphrey, who had previously only been employed by the king in the inspection of weirs and water wheels.[70] It is clear that Humphrey Stanley's lawlessness engaged the king's suspicions.[71] Regardless of this, Humphrey remained in nominal royal favour until his death in 1505, receiving the singular honour of burial in Westminster Abbey. His grave is marked by a funeral brass on which he is shown bare-headed and wearing plate armour and a long sword.[72] This uncle would have been a familiar figure to Katherine Pershall and, perhaps, also her daughter, Bessie Blount. If vengeance visited the family for the murder of Sir William Chetwynd, it certainly did not touch his killer, instead turning on his son, Sir John Stanley of Pipe, who succeeded to both his father's possessions and the main family estates of his uncle, the senior Sir John Stanley of Pipe. In the south aisle of Lichfield Cathedral lies a badly mutilated tomb effigy depicting a knight naked to the waist and wearing a skirt, which was formerly noted to be decorated with the Stanley family arms, and with legs encased in armour.[73] The figure was traditionally known as 'Captain Stanley' and his curious dress explained by the fact that he had been excommunicated for an offence against the Church and had only been allowed Christian burial on the agreement that his tomb should mark his disgrace. The nature of Sir John's offence is lost but his penance and the rumours about his father are evidence of the remarkable and unorthodox family from which Bessie's grandmother sprang.

Isabel Stanley showed something of the spirit of her family in arranging her daughter's marriage with only limited involvement from the child's paternal family.[74] According to John and Katherine's own later testimony, it came to Thomas Blount's attention that Katherine Pershall was the sole heir to the estates of Humphrey Pershall, which were then valued at 200 marks per year. In the late fifteenth century, before the rapid inflation of the mid-Tudor period, this was a substantial sum.[75] It was certainly enough for Thomas to hope that 'John Blount then being his son and heir might marry with the said Katherine'. Thomas sent a message to Isabel, broaching the question of the marriage, to which she responded favourably. She was not, however, inclined to sell her daughter's valuable marriage cheaply and extracted a promise from Thomas that he would create a settlement, allowing him to enjoy Kinlet and his other manors during his lifetime, but entailing the reversion on John, Katherine and their heirs. This was duly drawn up into a marriage settlement, of which Isabel, her father-in-law Humphrey Pershall, and her brother Sir Humphrey Stanley, acted as trustees. To further ensure that the young couple were protected, Thomas passed the deeds to his manors to his kinsman, William Blount, Lord Mountjoy. It is clear from this that Thomas was anxious to secure Katherine's lands for his son as the settlement, which he later evidently came to regret, was a very generous one. Whilst Hugh Pershall's will had stated that Katherine should remain with her mother until she reached her majority, it is certain that she and John had begun to live together long before she turned twenty-one. Given the fact that the couple were married in Shropshire, so close to the Blount family seat, it is probable that Katherine remained with the Blounts to be raised by them. Safe in the knowledge that her daughter was financially secure, Isabel, who would eventually bury three husbands, left Katherine with her new husband at Bewdley before returning to London, where she made her own second marriage.

# 3

# BESSIE BLOUNT OF KINLET

As a child bride, Katherine Pershall would not have been expected to consummate her marriage to John Blount immediately. Equally, however, it is unlikely that she would have continued to live with her mother, who was embarking on her second marriage in London. Instead, she doubtless returned to Kinlet with her young husband and his family following the marriage ceremony, to pass into the custody of her mother-in-law, Anne Croft, who was still busy raising her own expanding family.

The Blount family spent much of their time at their principal manor of Kinlet and members of the family demonstrated a great attachment to the place in their wills, frequently requesting burial in the parish church that lay next to the manor house.[1] Katherine Pershall herself, many years in the future as an independent and wealthy widow, often chose to stay at Kinlet, using it as one of her two principal residences.[2]

Kinlet remains a small settlement in Shropshire close to the border with Worcestershire and near the River Severn.[3] The name had Welsh origins, denoting its connection with the principality.[4] Few details survive of the village in Bessie's time but it is possible to surmise what it would have been like. A survey of Shropshire was undertaken early in the nineteenth century when Kinlet was assessed to be made up of eighty-seven houses, with 552 inhabitants.[5] The population remained stable, with 536 residents recorded just under a century later in 1911.[6] The parish registers survive from the seventeenth century. Between 1657 and 1700 there were 766 baptisms in the parish, 588 burials and 91 marriages.[7] Infant mortality was high; for example, 21 February 1661 saw the baptism of Elizabeth, daughter of Roger and Elizabeth Carpenter. Sadly, this was followed on 28 April 1661 by the child's burial. That same year Charles, son of Charles and Anne Howell, was baptised in October and buried in November. As with the later data, the seventeenth- century records support the contention that the parish was always a small and sparsely populated one.

The seventeenth-century parish registers record that Kinlet contained a number of houses distinct from the manor house, including a Moore Hall, Foxcott, Moor's Ground, Norton's End, Tippers, Elliotts and Crump's End.[8] Usual country occupations were recorded, including labourers and smiths. An early nineteenth-century account supports this, with the vicar at the time stating that 'the inhabitants consist entirely of persons employed in husbandry, with the exception of a wheelwright, blacksmith, & the like necessary profession'.[9] It is certain that, in the fifteenth and sixteenth centuries, the village would have been similarly populated.

Kinlet is now little more than a hamlet, with the church and eighteenth-century hall (which is now used as a school) situated on a hillside far away from the other buildings in the village. It has always been a quiet place. Amongst the few wider references to the village in medieval sources, the one of most note dates to 1282 when Wharton's *Anglia Sacra* recorded that:

> Three suns were seen at Kinlet in the Ides of March, one in the East, one in the West, and one in the South, in the presence of the Prior of the Order of St Augustine in Ludlow, Sir Bryan de Brompton, and many others.[10]

In 1290 the settlement was graced by a visit from the Bishop of Hereford, who wrote a letter to the pope from the manor. Few other events were noted in even local sources.

Nothing now remains of the manor house in which the Blount family lived. In 1727 William Childe, a descendant of Bessie's sister Anne, and the then owner of the manor, had the old house destroyed and replaced with the substantial building that still stands on the hill close to the church.[11] Few details survive of the original hall although it is known to have stood next to the church. It was built by the Cornwall family and their arms are recorded to have been displayed on the building.[12] The parlour window was decorated with the arms of Sir John Blount, quartering those of the Cornwall family and impaling those of Pershall, something that indicates both Bessie's father's pride in his wife's lineage and that he carried out his own improvements to the hall during his brief ownership.

The only building remaining in Kinlet that would have been familiar to Bessie is the church, which dates to the late Anglo-Saxon or early Norman period. Its interior is dominated by the fine tombs of members of Bessie's family although, at the time of her parents' marriage, only the tomb of her great-grandparents, Sir Humphrey Blount and the then still living Dame Elizabeth Blount (née Winnington), can even have been contemplated.

Between 1800 and 1815, the vicar of Kinlet was a former lawyer, the Reverend J.B. Blakeway.[13] As his obituary recorded, Blakeway was not a natural countryman and his move to Shrewsbury following the end of his tenure at Kinlet facilitated 'unquestionably a kind of life much more suited to his habits and disposition than the retirement of a country village'.[14] However, during his time at Kinlet, Blakeway was studious in his attempts to record its history and his manuscript account of the history and topography of the village is invaluable in attempting to reconstruct how the seat of the Blounts would have been in the late fifteenth century and early years of the sixteenth. In his manuscript, Blakeway documented a parish that measured three and a half miles from the turnpike road to a bridge below Kinlet Common.[15] He described a rural parish that is likely to have remained relatively unchanged for centuries. According to Blakeway 'the soil contains almost every variety, (except gravel) often within a very small compass of ground. It is well adapted for the growth of corn, but still better for the pasturage of sheep.' In an 1801 enquiry, 1,403 of the 6,384 acres in the parish were found to be arable, another indication that, even in Bessie's time, Kinlet was essentially rural. The farms in the parish were also, in Blakeway's time, known for their orchards and the cider that was produced by them, something that was, perhaps, enjoyed by Bessie and her family. It was, and still is, a hilly parish. The main landmark in Bessie's time, apart from the church and the hall, would almost certainly have been a bridge which was described by Blakeway as 'the new bridge, – as a bridge now very ancient & almost ruinous continues to be termed'.[16]

Bessie's parents spent the latter parts of their childhoods at Kinlet. The age of consent in the late medieval and early Tudor period was twelve for a girl and fourteen for a boy and the couple would certainly not have started to live together as husband and wife before, at least, 1495: approximately the earliest date at which John Blount could have turned fourteen. He may well have been younger still – the latest date that John could have turned fourteen was 1498. No portrait of Bessie's parents survives, but their images are preserved in their fine tomb monument in Kinlet church. The tomb, which shows the couple reclining, depicts them in their youth. John Blount is shown wearing armour of the early Tudor period, whilst his wife, who was a striking-looking woman, wears a dress and jewellery of an approximately similar date. Katherine is shown wearing an English gable hood: a fashionable piece of headwear that entirely concealed the hair and was favoured by the early Tudor queens Elizabeth of York and Catherine of Aragon, as well as the later Jane Seymour. Judging from their appearances on their tomb, Bessie's parents were well matched and they passed their good looks down to their daughter.

The year of 1495 is the earliest date at which John Blount and Katherine Pershall could have consummated their marriage. In all likelihood, it would have been later and early consummation was generally frowned upon due to the dangers that early pregnancy could pose to a girl. It is therefore more probable that the couple began to live together as husband and wife in the last years of the fifteenth century.

The tomb of Bessie's parents, in accordance with late medieval and early Tudor tradition, is decorated with small carved depictions of their children around its base, showing them as mourners for their parents. On the panel directly beneath Sir John, there are depicted five adult male figures, all wearing armour of a style similar to their father, with scrolls that would originally have contained their names beside their heads, and are now worn entirely smooth. The panel beneath Katherine contains a similar tableau, although, in this case, it depicts six young women, all standing in different poses and dressed in a similar style to their mother. Once again, the figures were originally identified by their names carved into scrolls next to their heads. Like their brothers' scrolls, the daughters' names have also been worn away through the passage of time. Unlike their brothers, however, the panel with the six daughters faces the wall of the church and is considerably harder to view or to touch. The names are therefore not entirely obliterated.

The five sons and six daughters of Sir John Blount and Katherine Pershall will, almost certainly, be depicted in their birth order (although, of course, grouped according to their sex). The identification of Bessie amongst the daughters is therefore crucial to determining her age and position in the family. The names of eight of John Blount and Katherine Pershall's children survive: George, William, Henry, Elizabeth, Anne, Rose, Isabel and Albora.[17] The eldest surviving son, George, is known to have been born in 1513,[18] although no other birth dates are known. Elizabeth, who came to court in 1512, was clearly some years her brother's senior and must rank as one of the eldest daughters on the tomb. It appears that two sons and one daughter died in infancy. In court papers listed at some point between 1514 and 1518, the couple confirmed that they had 'iii sons and v daughters between them lawfully begotten which yet be alive'.[19]

There is some contention over the sixth daughter. It not impossible that a sixth daughter might indeed have been born after the above court papers were written, allowing for the survival of all six daughters. In the late nineteenth century, one historian claimed that one Robert Pigot of Chetwynd in Shropshire 'married Margaret, daughter of Sir John Blount of Kinlet (who, it will be remembered, had married Katharine, daughter and heir of Sir Hugh Peshale, and brought in the Patshull, Wyrley, and other properties) and had issue Thomas, father, by Elizabeth Oneley, of Robert Pigot, sheriff of Shropshire in 1574'.[20] This comment is worthy of further investigation. The Robert Pigot who married Margaret Blount was a member of a neighbouring gentry family and was sheriff of Shropshire in 1517. In a visitation carried out in Shropshire in 1623, it was noted that Robert Pigott of Chetwynd married 'Margaret da. To Sir John Blount'.[21] No mention was actually made here of this John Blount being 'of Kinlet', although a number of nineteenth-century writers later stated this with certainty.[22] There were, of course, other branches of the Blount family in Shropshire which could have produced a Margaret Blount. However, there is no mention of her in the visitation carried out in Shropshire as a daughter of a John Blount of any other branch of the family, such as John Blount of Yeo (or Eye, near Leominster), a cousin of Bessie's father.[23] Margaret was a name commonly used in the Blount family. For example, Thomas Blount's brother, John Blount of Bitterley, had a daughter named Margaret. She can, however, be discounted due to the fact that she married a foreigner named Jasper Balthazar.[24] A Margaret Blounte, widow of Netleye, who was a kinswoman of the Blounts and died during the reign of Elizabeth I, can also be discounted due to the fact that her will contains no mention of any members of the Pigott family, instead showing links to another local family, the Corbetts.[25] This Margaret Blounte can probably be identified with Bessie's aunt, Thomas Blount's daughter, who married John Corbet of Leigh. One possibility is that, in the 1623 visitation, the commissioners noted that Mary, daughter of Sir John Blount of Kinlet, the father of Bessie's great-grandfather Humphrey Blount, married a gentleman named Pigott, although no first name was given. However, it is certain that she cannot have been the wife of a man who was sheriff of Shropshire in 1517. Mary Blount's father, Bessie's great-great-grandfather, died in 1442 and, even accounting for the possibility that Mary was some years older than her husband, it is highly unlikely that a woman born before 1442 would have had a husband who was still alive and active enough to take on public office nearly eighty years later. Equally, Mary's 'son', whose own son served as sheriff in the 1570s, would have needed to be an extremely elderly father. Whilst marriages between an elderly woman and a young man did occasionally occur in the fifteenth century – for example in the case of twenty-year-old John Woodville, the brother of Edward IV's queen, who married the wealthy dowager duchess of Norfolk ('a slip of a girl of about eighty years old')[26] – such matches caused comment. Mary Blount cannot be considered to be the Margaret Blount who married Robert Pigott. It appears from other works that her husband's Christian name was John.[27] Mary had a sister called Margaret, but she was also not the Margaret Blount in question as she is known to have married a John Oteley.[28]

There is good evidence that Margaret Pigott was, indeed, a member of the Kinlet branch of the Blount family. The will of her grandson survives, dated 1584, which refers to a younger son named George, a name that could, perhaps, have been chosen as a tribute to his great-uncle, George Blount, if, indeed, Margaret can be considered to be Bessie's sister.[29] In 1573 Bessie's nephew, Edward Lacon, as well as a Lancelot Ridley, who was presumably a kinsman of Lacon's stepfather, Thomas Ridley, were witnesses to a marriage settlement prepared between Thomas Pigott of Chetwynd, the great-grandson of Margaret, and Dorothy Eyton, again suggesting links between the Pigotts of Chetwynd and the Blounts of Kinlet.[30] Finally, conclusive proof of the link is provided by evidence of the now lost east window in the parish church of Stottesdon. In the seventeenth century, amongst other coats of arms decorating the window, were the arms of Blount of Kinlet, Croft and Pigott. In addition to this, there was an inscription which stated: 'Pray for S'r Tho' Blount, Knight, and Dame Anne, his wife, which made this window in the yeare 1414: orate pro bono statu Tho' Pigott et Isabella ux'.[31] The date 1414 is a mistake and the window almost certainly originally referred to 1514. Stottesdon belonged to the Pigott family, with the Thomas Pigott referred to in the inscription, who was the son of Margaret Blount, being referred to as of Chetwynd and Stottesdon on a number of occasions. There is no doubt, from this inscription, that Margaret Blount was indeed a member of Bessie's family.

However, this is still not proof that she was Bessie's sister and it is apparent from the evidence that she was not. No birthdates survive for members of the Pigott family and, whilst Robert Pigott must have been considerably older than any sister of Bessie's to have been sheriff in 1517, it is not impossible that, if Margaret had been born in around 1500, she could have borne Thomas Pigott in around 1520. He in turn could have become a father at around 1540, meaning that it was entirely possible for her grandson to have been sheriff of Shropshire in 1574. However, whilst there are no birthdates for members of the immediate Pigott family, it has been possible to trace other members of the family. Margaret Blount's grandson, Robert Pigott, took as his second wife Elizabeth Gatacre of Gatacre.[32] Her father, who succeeded to his father's estates in 1509, died in 1577. It is therefore possible that his daughter could have been young enough to be a granddaughter-in-law to Bessie's sister, although her father would have been middle-aged when she was born. Conclusive proof is provided by the fact that the younger Robert Pigott's first wife, Jane Pontisbury, was the daughter of Thomas Pontisbury of Aldbrigetlee, who died on 26 March 1514.[33] His wife had died the previous year. Jane Pontisbury was a widow when she married Margaret Blount's grandson but, even allowing for the fact that she may have been some years older than him, she would certainly not have been so close in age to his grandmother. The Margaret Blount who married the elder Robert Pigott can certainly not be identified as Bessie's missing sister and the sixth daughter of John and Katherine Blount must have died in infancy. Almost certainly, the visitation made a mistake in calling Margaret Blount a daughter of Sir John Blount, and instead meant that she was the elder Sir John Blount of Kinlet's granddaughter. Few records survive of the children of Bessie's great-grandparents, Humphrey Blount and Elizabeth Winnington, but Margaret Blount can almost certainly be identified as one of their daughters.[34] She was certainly not a daughter of their grandson.

Bessie's earliest biographer, William Childe-Pemberton, who was a descendant of her sister Anne, referred to Bessie as the second daughter of the family, and this is something that appears to have been accepted without further consideration by more recent historians, including the author of a recent biography of Bessie's son, Henry Fitzroy.[35] Childe-Pemberton, however, admitted that the names of the daughters were no longer legible in his time, something that modern lighting has demonstrated is not entirely correct. Childe-Pemberton appears to have based his assertion that Bessie was the second daughter solely on the fact that it was Rowland Lacon, the son of Bessie's sister Anne, who succeeded their brother George to the family estates.[36] This would indeed usually imply that Anne was the eldest sister. However, it is clear in this case that George Blount was not motivated by strict heredity. Although Sir George Blount had no living sons at the time of his death, he did leave a daughter, Dorothy, the wife of John Purslowe of Sidbury.[37] He also passed over the claims of Dorothy's children and his nephew, George Blount, the son of his younger brother, Henry, who was alive at the time of his uncle's death in 1581. From this younger George Blount's will, it is clear that Sir George Blount's settlement caused no ill feelings in the family. The younger George referred repeatedly, and fondly, to his cousin, Rowland Lacon, as well as leaving bequests to Rowland's younger brother, William, and William's daughter, Ellen, who was the younger George's goddaughter.[38] Given the younger George Blount's hereditary seniority, it is clear that Kinlet and the other Blount estates were widely recognised, and accepted, as Sir George Blount's property to bequeath as he wished. It is therefore entirely likely that Sir George would also have ignored some of his sisters and their children. Bessie was long since dead by 1581 and was survived only by daughters. George wanted a male heir and so his selection of Anne's son as his heir should in no way be taken as necessarily confirming that she was also the oldest sister.

The argument that Anne was not the eldest daughter of John Blount and Katherine Pershall is supported by the evidence of the tomb itself. Although the scrolls next to the six daughters are considerably worn, they are not entirely illegible. The scroll for the second daughter clearly reads 'Anne' and that for the fifth daughter, although much less distinct, appears to say 'Albora'. The first daughter's scroll, although no longer legible, is considerably longer and suggests a longer name. In contrast, the third daughter's scroll is as short as that for Anne, implying a shorter name.

From the evidence of the tomb it therefore appears that Anne was, in fact, the second of the six daughters, rather than the eldest. This would mean that Bessie must be either the first daughter or the fourth or sixth (assuming that the name 'Elizabeth' is too long to have been contained on the short third scroll). Given that the very earliest date for the birth of a child to Bessie's parents can only have been around 1496 (and probably later) and that Bessie joined the court in 1512 to serve Queen Catherine of Aragon, a post for which the minimum age was twelve, it is improbable that she was the fourth daughter of her parents. The earliest that she can have been born is 1500 and, whilst it is possible that her mother produced one daughter a year from the consummation of her marriage, it seems unlikely given that she was still so young. It is also entirely likely that Bessie was older than twelve when she first came to court as, whilst the earliest age for a court appointment was twelve – as the considerably better connected Lady Lisle (the wife of an illegitimate son of Edward IV) found in the 1530s – it could take a substantial amount of time to secure such a coveted position for a daughter.[39]

Further evidence that supports the contention that Bessie was the eldest daughter can be found in the lives of her other sisters. Whilst it appears that one of the six sisters died in infancy or childhood, the others all survived to adulthood. Anne, who, from the evidence of the tomb, appears to have been the second daughter, married twice. Her youngest child by her first husband, a son named Edward Lacon, was christened in 1541.[40] Surprisingly, this was not to be her youngest child and, in late 1554, the vicar of Much Wenlock – a town with which Anne's second husband, Thomas Ridley, had links – recorded that 'here was buried out of Willey, George a sucking child, the son of Mr Thomas Rydley Bailiff of the Franchises and Liberties of this Borough of Much Wenlock'.[41] A 'sucking child' must refer to a child still nursed by its mother.[42] Based on this, the dead child can have been, at most, three years old but, in all probability, was somewhat younger. It is clear that Anne was the child's mother, both from his location at Willey (an estate that had belonged to her first husband and in which she retained a life interest) and from his name, George, which was that of Anne's eldest surviving brother. For Anne to have borne a child in around 1552, she must have been a considerably mature mother. It is simply not possible that she can have been older than Bessie, who, at the absolute latest, must have been born in 1500 due to her court appointment in 1512. The earliest Anne can have been born, based on the birth of George Ridley, must have been around 1504. The birth of the youngest child of her first marriage, Edward Lacon, in 1541, also suggests a later birthdate, as does the fact that a daughter, Cecily, was born during her second marriage to Thomas Ridley.[43] Final evidence for Anne's comparative youth in relation to Bessie can be seen in the fact that she survived her second husband, who died in 1580.[44]

Bessie's sister, Rose, had married a William Gryslyng by the mid-1530s at the latest, when he was mentioned by Bessie's son, Henry Fitzroy, in a letter dated to around 1534.[45] Given the fact that the third scroll on the tomb is notably short, Rose was probably the third daughter. Isabel married William Reed of Shepperton in a marriage arranged by her father in 1528.[46] This was nearly ten years after Bessie had her first child and must imply that Isabel was the younger sister. She was already of childbearing age by that date as the will of her husband William, which showed great esteem for Isabel and named her as executor, was drafted in 1534, shortly before his death.[47] In his will, Reed referred to children named Henry, Anthony, Elizabeth, Anne and Joan, as well as a child that his wife 'now goeth with'. He had been married before and Elizabeth appears to have been already married, suggesting that she was not Isabel's daughter. His son and heir, John, was also the son of the previous wife. The other children appear to have been Isabel's, however, and she must have been pregnant for much of her brief marriage, indicating a birthdate of at least approximately 1512, if not earlier.

The final sister, Albora, who appears from the tomb to have been the fifth sister, was unmarried at the time of her mother's death in 1540. In her will, Katherine Pershall made detailed provision for Albora's inheritance, to be paid in the event of her marriage, something that again suggests that she would have been one of the younger children. Katherine took care to ensure Albora's future, requiring that she 'be ordered and advised by my executors and by my daughter Anne Lacon in her marriage'. Further evidence of Albora's youth is given by the terms of her grandmother Isabel Stanley's will, dated 1519, in which she bequeathed to Albora 'the small bed upon which I raised my daughter'.[48] Clearly, in 1519, Albora was still tiny enough for this small bed to be of use to her. As the fifth daughter (with the unnamed daughter as the sixth), she must have been born by 1514–18, when her parents referred to their five daughters in a court case. However, using the evidence of her grandmother's will, her birth was probably around 1517 or 1518. The latest year for Katherine Pershall's birth is 1481, meaning that she is likely to have reached the menopause in around 1521–26, with a decline in her fertility from a few years earlier. Albora appears to have been the youngest child at the time of Isabel Stanley's death, suggesting that the sixth daughter was born between 1519 and 1521. She had certainly died by 1540 as she was not mentioned in Katherine's will.

It is certain that Bessie was the eldest daughter of her parents. It would usually have been the eldest daughter who was given the prestigious post of serving the queen, and there is also a clue in the names which Sir John Blount and his wife gave to their daughters. At the time of the births of their eldest children the most senior lady living in the household at Kinlet was Sir John's widowed grandmother, Dame Elizabeth Blount (née Winnington), who died in 1503.[49] After Dame Elizabeth, the next most senior lady was Anne Croft, John Blount's mother. Bessie was not the first member of the family to be named after her great-grandmother as her father's cousin, Elizabeth Otteley of Shrewsbury, was named for her.[50] From Katherine Pershall's point of view, there may also have been an added incentive. The names 'Isabel' and 'Elizabeth' have the same etymological origins and were often used interchangeably. Katherine's mother, Isabel Stanley, used the name Elizabeth on occasion and, by naming her eldest daughter Elizabeth, Katherine may also have intended to honour her own mother.[51] Naming their eldest daughter after the queen, Elizabeth of York, might also have been desirable: Bessie's still-living great-grandfather, Sir Richard Croft, had royal links and had helped to raise the queen's father, Edward IV. It is true that George, the eldest son, was not given a family name and this could therefore be taken as evidence that Bessie need not necessarily have been the eldest daughter. However, his late birth in 1513 suggests that he may well have been preceded by the two unnamed sons depicted on the tomb, who presumably died in infancy. They might, perhaps, have borne the names Thomas and John in honour of their grandfather and father, although it is now impossible to read their names from the tomb. Childe-Pemberton, writing in the early twentieth century, noted that the scrolls naming the children on the tomb had been legible in recent memory. A nineteenth-century drawing of the tomb, when the scrolls may still have been legible, is no help, however, providing no clue to what they actually said.[52] It is almost certain, based on all the evidence, that Bessie was the eldest daughter of her parents. Given the age gap between her and her next eldest sister, Anne, it would seem probable that she was the eldest child, with her birth being followed by two brothers who died in infancy. A birth date of *c*.1498, rather than a later date of around 1500 or 1501 which is often stated by historians, is highly probable. Bessie's birth would have been followed by two brothers born in around 1500 and 1502. Anne followed between 1504 and 1507. Then Rose in perhaps 1508 and Isabel in around 1510. George was born in 1513, then William in *c*.1514–15. Henry followed in *c*.1515–16 and Albora in *c*.1517–18. The final daughter followed in *c*.1519–20.

As her parent's likely eldest child, Bessie would have been born at Kinlet. The birth would have been awaited with interest by the family and servants as, if it were a boy, it would have been a future heir to Kinlet. However, Katherine Pershall's confinement would not have been a particularly remarkable event in the household as her mother-in-law, Anne Croft, was still enduring near annual pregnancies to build a family that would ultimately number approximately twenty children. Births were a regular event at Kinlet, and it is likely that Katherine would already have been expected to assist in them.

Giving birth came to take on a great ceremonial importance during the Tudor period. Henry VII's mother, Bessie's own distant kinswoman by marriage, Margaret Beaufort, addressed the issue herself by producing a set of ordinances for the ceremony to accompany a royal birth.[53] These included considerable minutiae, such as the furnishings and decorations for the birthing chamber, with the chamber to be 'hanged with rich Clothe of Arras, Sides, Roof, Windows and all, except one Window, which must be hanged so as she may have light when it please her'. It was felt that fresh air was dangerous to both mother and child and the birthing chamber must have been a stuffy and uncomfortable place to be. Margaret Beaufort set out details of the bed that should be used and ordered that the floor should be carpeted. Even the type and number of cushions were dictated. A queen was expected to retire, with great ceremony, to a female world approximately a month before the expected birth, with the king's mother expressly dictating that:

> None to come unto the great Chamber but Women; and Women to be made all Manner of Officers, as Butlers, Panters, sewers, & c. and all Manner of Officers shall bring them all needful Things unto the great Chamber Door, and the Women Officers shall receive it there of them.

That such ceremony for a royal birth existed even before the Tudor period is suggested by an illustration in the fifteenth-century Beauchamp Pageant, which depicts the birth of the future Henry VI and shows his mother, Catherine of Valois, lying in her bed wearing her crown.[54]

Katherine Pershall's own lying-in would not have been as elaborate as that required for a queen and would have had more in common with the birth of Richard Beauchamp, future Earl of Warwick, in 1389, which is depicted in the Beauchamp Pageant. The Beauchamp Pageant is a remarkable manuscript, drawn in the late fifteenth century, which depicts the life of the Earl of Warwick from his birth to death. Warwick was of considerably higher status than Bessie and was born over a century before she was. However, the images do provide a useful source in their depictions of major events in a late medieval person's life and there is much that would have been similar for Bessie's own life. The scene showing Warwick's birth, for example, shows his mother sitting up in bed, apparently naked having just given birth, with the sheets pulled up over her for warmth.[55] Four other ladies are also present in the room. One holds the swaddled baby to her, showing the mother her son for the first time. Another woman kneels beside an open fire close to the bed, preparing food in a pan, whilst a third stands beside the bed offering food to the mother in a bowl. Finally, another woman kneels before an open chest at the foot of the bed. The birthing chamber itself is small and crowded, with a roaring fire and curtains covering the windows.

Although caution should be maintained when using the Beauchamp Pageant as evidence of Bessie's own birth, it is useful. Almost certainly, Katherine Pershall's own lying-in would have been similarly the preserve of women, with her mother-in-law (if she was not at that time busy with her own lying-in), sisters-in-law, other female relatives of her husband, and servants assisting her. Her own chamber would have been similarly stuffy due to the prevailing belief in the harmfulness of fresh air to both mother and child. In his will, Sir Thomas Blount left a bequest of a fine bed to his wife Anne, describing it as a 'bed of damask with the curtains and hangings to the same and a feather bed of down with a pair of the best sheets and the best board clothe'. His daughter Eleanor also received a bed, with the will describing it as having 'coverings and hangings two pair of sheets a pair of blankets a bolster and a pillow'.[56] Further bequests of beds were made to Thomas's favourite son, Edward, two of his younger sons, Arthur and Robert, and his daughter Joyce. A bed was a high-value item and one of these may, perhaps, have been the actual bed in which Bessie was born. If not, it would have been similarly comfortable and prepared with warm, clean sheets for the confinement. With the rates of infant mortality and maternal deaths in childbirth so high, the teenaged Katherine Pershall cannot but have been anxious as she approached her own confinement. The birth of a healthy daughter must have been a relief, although the sex was almost certainly something of a disappointment to both her parents and her wider family.

Following her birth, Bessie would have been swaddled tightly and laid in a crib. She is likely to have been cared for both by servants and by her mother in the crowded household. Within a few days of her birth she was christened in the parish church next to the hall. The christening scene from the Beauchamp Pageant shows the baby dipped naked in the font whilst the godparents and other guests stand around.[57] Whilst no details of Bessie's christening survive, the choice of the name Elizabeth suggests that her aged great-grandmother, who was resident in the household, acted as her godmother. Dame Elizabeth was evidently well regarded in the family as a whole as she was appointed to act as executor of the will of her son-in-law, Thomas Otteley of Shrewsbury, a mark of his esteem for her.[58] It is unclear when the child's name was shortened familiarly to 'Bessie', and it is possible that this was a later invention by the populace of England when she became well known as the mistress of the king. Alternatively, it may have been adopted in childhood to differentiate her from her great-grandmother and a number of other relatives, including an aunt, another Elizabeth Blount.[59] This could also account for the choice of the name 'Isabel' for her younger sister, a name which is etymologically the same as Elizabeth and was still used interchangeably at that time: a Bessie and an Isabel living in the same household would not have been confused, whilst an Elizabeth and an Isabel may have been. What Bessie thought of her nickname is not recorded. Interestingly, a considerably later king's mistress, the twentieth-century Wallis Simpson, was also given the first name Bessie but she abandoned it in favour of Wallis, declaring, 'I always hated the name Bessie, for, as I told my aunt, "So many cows are called Bessie".[60] Perhaps Bessie felt the same. That Bessie was indeed known by her nickname during childhood is suggested by the fact that her sister Anne was known by a nickname, to distinguish her from their grandmother, Anne Croft. In a number of sources, Anne is referred to as Agnes, particularly those sources written by those who knew her personally.[61] This is the name by which she was known to Bessie and her other siblings.[62]

Assuming that Katherine Pershall was born in 1481, she probably continued to bear children up to her mid to late thirties (with the evidence of a court document dating from around 1517 suggesting that she had, by then, nearly ceased to bear children).[63] In a period of around twenty years, she therefore produced eleven children which, although it by no means matched the record of her mother-in-law, would mean a birth approximately every two years. Bessie would not have been an only child for long, therefore. Her birth must have been quickly followed by those of her two younger brothers, who died in infancy. In addition to this, the household was crowded with her grandparent's children. Bessie's aunt Joyce, for example, was still unmarried in 1524 although – according to the will of her father, Sir Thomas Blount – of marriageable age.[64] She later went on to have two husbands in Worcestershire, something that suggests that she married in her late teens or early twenties, the usual age for girls.[65] She is therefore likely to have been younger than her niece. Thomas Blount and Anne Croft's fourth son, of five surviving boys, was named Arthur, presumably after Arthur, Prince of Wales. This would suggest a birthdate of between 1499 and 1502, when the prince was a regular visitor to the Welsh Marches and had contact with the Blounts – these are dates which suggest that both Arthur Blount and his younger brother were born after Bessie, their niece.[66] The household would have been impossibly crowded.

Bessie's parents may well have had another reason for wanting to leave the household at Kinlet. Bessie's grandfather, Sir Thomas Blount, although widely admired in the county, was a difficult and irascible figure. In his will, drafted in 1478, Thomas's father, Sir Humphrey Blount, was described as 'Sir H. Blunt of the parish of all saints Worcester'.[67] This was a few years after his son's marriage, and it is possible that Humphrey moved from Kinlet to allow more space for his eldest son's growing family. Sir Thomas Blount had no intention of repeating this precedent for his own eldest son – although, with such a large and still-growing family of his own, it would hardly have been prudent to have done so. Sir Thomas may also have had personal reasons for not assisting his eldest son and the evidence of his own will, in which he attempted to disinherit John in favour of his second son, Edward, suggests that there was little love lost between father and son. Thomas Blount was content, at least in his son John's youth, to associate with him and, in

1503, the pair jointly became indebted to a London merchant for the substantial sum of £200.[68] Thomas evidently lived somewhat beyond his means and the following year it was recorded that he owed another London merchant £80.[69]

Thomas Blount also had an acquisitive streak as his own mother, Dame Elizabeth Blount, was forced to take her case to the king's court in 1488 to ensure that she received sufficient dower from the lands inherited by her son for her to live on. Elizabeth obviously made a good case and was able to obtain a

> Writ to the escheator in the county of Stafford, for the assignment of reasonable dower to Elizabeth, widow of Humphrey Blounte, Knt., and tenant in capite, deceased, of all lands and tenements in the said escheator's bailiwick that belonged to the said Humphrey on the day of his death; the said Elizabeth taking oath not to marry without the king's licence.[70]

She obtained similar writs against her son in the counties of Hereford, the Welsh Marches and Oxfordshire. In spite of this, she was forced to take money that had been entrusted to her care by her son-in-law, Thomas Otteley, at the time of his death for the marriage of his daughter, Mary. Dame Elizabeth promised to return the sum of £100 to Mary when her granddaughter 'came to lawful age'. Notwithstanding this, she made use of the money as if it were her own, lending it out without Mary's permission on the security of some gold plate.[71] Whether Dame Elizabeth did, in fact, ever intend to return the funds to her granddaughter is not clear. Certainly Mary, on reaching adulthood, was forced to take her two uncles, John and William Blount, who were acting as their mother's executors, to court to attempt to obtain the plate since there were apparently insufficient sums to repay the sum in cash from Dame Elizabeth's estate.

Dame Elizabeth appears as an active figure in her suits against her son and this may, perhaps, have had its roots in her own youth. Her mother, Margaret Norwood, has been described as 'formidable', a trait that her daughter apparently emulated.[72] Margaret managed to make her way through four husbands, making her a wealthy woman. She was largely responsible for her daughter Elizabeth Winnington's complicated relationship history with men. At the age of three in 1428, Bessie's great-grandmother had been married to the nine-year-old Richard Delves, the son of a prominent landowner, a child who promptly became her step-brother when her mother married, and was soon widowed by, her husband's father. Nine years later, in the midst of a bitter inheritance battle between Margaret, her own eldest son Richard Winnington and her young stepson and son-in-law Richard Delves, the young couple gathered before the Bishop of Coventry and Lichfield only for Dame

Elizabeth to suffer the humiliation of giving her confirmation of the match shortly before her young husband withheld his consent, leading to the marriage being annulled. Dame Elizabeth soon found a second husband in Humphrey Blount, but her youthful experience must have coloured her character. It is possible that Katherine Pershall, who arrived at the manor of Kinlet as a child bride herself, found an ally in her husband's grandmother, something that can again be suggested by the compliment of Bessie being named for her great-grandmother. However, it is more likely that relations between the pair were hostile: Richard Delves had been aided in his repudiation of his marriage to Dame Elizabeth by his friend and neighbour, Ralph Egerton of Wrinehill, who participated in the kidnap of her mother and stepfather, as well as the 'liberation' of another young Delves stepbrother from her mother's control.[73] Ralph Egerton's granddaughter, Anne, was the mother of Hugh Pershall and thus Katherine's grandmother. Given other surviving evidence of Dame Elizabeth's tenacious memory and courage, it seems impossible that she could have allowed herself to forget the slight done to her and her mother by the family of her new granddaughter-in-law, whatever the financial advantages of the match.

The antagonism between Dame Elizabeth and her eldest son is apparent from her will, in which she made no mention of her eldest son, instead naming her three younger sons. She was able to leave bequests of an embossed silver bowl, two silver cups and other goods, including beds and furnishings. There was no evidence of great wealth and it does not appear that she was ever able to resolve her dispute with her eldest son.[74]

Thomas Blount was not a man to give anything away when he could help it. This was something Katherine Pershall's own family would later find to her cost; her half-sister, Mary Judd, and Mary's husband Thomas Judd of Wickford, took Thomas Blount to court for the return of certain chains of gold and other property that Isabel Stanley, Katherine and Mary's mother, had entrusted to his custody.[75] Isabel obviously expected this property to be returned to her and made bequests to Mary in her will of the chains and a cash sum held by her eldest daughter's father-in-law. Isabel evidently had little else to bequeath to her younger daughter, although it is perhaps Mary Judd who received the gift of six equal bundles of flax in her mother's will.[76] She also left a feather bed and linen to other beneficiaries, but there appears to have been little else of value in her estate at the time of her death in 1519.

Given the overcrowding and John Blount's difficult relationship with his father, as well as a frosty relationship between Katherine and her grandmother-in-law, the couple had every reason to try to conceive their first child as soon as possible. Their marriage settlement provided that within one year of the birth of the couple's eldest child, Thomas would provide Katherine with lands to a yearly value of £20 for the duration of her lifetime, something which would enable them to set up their own household.[77] Unfortunately, it has proved impossible to locate the couple with any certainty during the years of Bessie's childhood. The Reverend Blakeway, in his manuscript account of Kinlet, believed that the family settled at Bitterley.[78] At first glance, this does indeed seem logical. Thomas Blount is known to have been associated with a John Blount of Bitterley during the early years of the sixteenth century.[79] Bitterley is in Shropshire and approximately twelve miles from Kinlet: a convenient place for Bessie's family to settle.[80] Unfortunately, it is clear that John Blount of Bitterley – who had a wife called Elizabeth, a daughter called Margaret and a son called John – was not Bessie's father.[81] He can almost certainly be identified as Thomas Blount's younger brother.

Katherine Pershall was the heir to her grandfather, Humphrey Pershall of Knightley, apparently very much against his will. At some point before 1476 her maternal grandfather, Sir John Stanley, paid Humphrey Pershall £100 in return for his confirmation that all his lands would pass to Katherine's parents.[82] This was a response to Humphrey's second marriage to Margaret Chadworth and the fear that it would produce a second son. These fears proved groundless but, at some point after his eldest son's death, Humphrey took a third wife, Leticia Harcourt.[83] Leticia bore the couple's only child, a son call Richard, in 1495, a birth that led Humphrey to attempt to disinherit his granddaughter. According to the *Inquisition Post Mortem* carried out after Humphrey's death on 26 May 1498, when his son was only three years old:

> The jurors say he was seized of the Manors of Knightley, Hopton, Theyne, Blythwood and Little Onne and the advowson of Chekkeley Church, and Manors of Baldon, Waterfall and one-third part of Manor of Astonfeld, co. Staff. and so seized by charter conveyed the same to trustees to the use of himself and his wife Letice and the survivor and Letice still survives. He confirms the same by his will here quoted and dated 8 April 13, Henry VII.[84]

To have borne a child in 1498, Leticia must have been considerably younger than her husband and, in all likelihood not much older than his granddaughter. When, during his lifetime, Humphrey attempted to settle his lands on her for life, he effectively disinherited Katherine. Katherine's mother, Isabel Stanley, and stepfather, John Russhe, a merchant of London, immediately took Humphrey to court, complaining that he acted in breach of the terms of the marriage settlement agreed at the marriage of Katherine's parents in that, 'for a marriage to be had and solemnised between the said Hugh and your said Oratrix the foresaid Humphrey faithfully promised amongst other things that he should not alienate discontinue nor put assay' his lands and manors.[85] They further complained that Humphrey 'intendith utterly to disinherit the said Katherine heir of the said Hugh thereof contrary to all right and conscience and contrary to the said trust and promise that the said Humphrey made'. According to the couple, at the time of Hugh and Isabel's marriage, in return for the payment of £100 by Isabel's father, Humphrey undertook to pass all his lands, save a small jointure for his wife, to his eldest son and his heirs in remainder, retaining only a life interest for himself.[86] Evidence of this promise did not deter Humphrey and he reiterated his settlement in his will before his death. In addition, his son Richard inherited some cottages and other property in the town of Stafford outright and was usually referred to as his father's heir in official documents, in preference to his niece.[87] It was agreed in Humphrey's *Inquisition* that Katherine should only succeed to the lands not entailed by Humphrey's settlement.

Even during the lifetime of her grandfather, Katherine launched her own legal claim for lands and tenements in Knightley.[88] Her actions to obtain her inheritance continued after Humphrey's death and, whilst she was unable to obtain possession of Knightley and Little Onne during Leticia's lifetime, she did succeed in wresting back control of the other manors.[89] In 1504 Katherine, acting with her husband and father-in-law, was able to secure the bulk of her inheritance during Richard's minority, in return for payments for her young uncle's upkeep.[90] By 1511 John Blount was able to describe himself in a legal document as 'of Knightley', demonstrating that the couple had, at last, obtained full possession of Katherine's inheritance.[91]

It appears that Katherine and her step-grandmother and young uncle were entirely estranged. Richard Pershall died at the young age of twenty-five in 1520 and the jurors at his *Inquisition Post Mortem* were entirely unaware of Katherine's relationship to him, recording that his next of kin were Richard Appleby and Alice Littleton, children of Humphrey Pershall's sisters. They further complained that 'John Blount Esq. has taken the issues and the profits of the lands since Richard's death, but by what right the jurors know not'.[92]

It is possible that John and Katherine settled with their family at one of the Staffordshire manors that Katherine was able to secure. However, most of the manors that she claimed were a considerable distance from John's family and financial interests in Shropshire. Katherine's manor of Hopton, for example, was around fifty miles from Kinlet. It was also usually let by the Pershall family, implying that it would not have been available for occupation.[93] Tean was even further distant from Kinlet at sixty miles and Waterfall and Cauldon further still, both being approximately seventy miles away. Alternatively, it has been suggested that they settled on the Blount family's Staffordshire lands.[94] Certainly, these Staffordshire manors remained of importance to the family and it is known that the son of an earlier Sir John Blount and Isabel de Cornwall was in possession of the manors in his father's lifetime in 1428. However, it seems difficult to posit from this that the Staffordshire lands 'often seem to have been employed as residences for the eldest son upon his marriage'.[95] If anything, the son of Isabel de Cornwall – who was, after all, the heiress to Kinlet – may well have enjoyed a greater prominence in the family estates than would usually be expected during the lifetime of his father, due to local loyalties to the Cornwall family. It seems more likely that Bessie's parents remained in Shropshire, at least for most of her childhood, and one likely candidate for their location does emerge amongst the Blount family documents.

Bewdley, where they married and where their third son, Henry, would later settle, is certainly a possibility and it may be that Bessie spent much of her childhood there. This is supported by the fact that her grandfather, Thomas Blount, had the power to appoint one Walter Blount as the rector of the parish within which Bewdley stood in 1507, something that suggests considerable influence there.[96] In addition, he had also been appointed as steward of the park and manor of Bewdley, implying that he, or his family, had a right to occupy the royal manor there.[97] In 1519 Bessie's father and grandfather were granted the joint stewardship of the manor by the king, again suggesting a close connection.[98] There are very few records about the whereabouts of Bessie's immediate family during her childhood. However, there is just one hint that this speculation may indeed be correct. According to a mid-nineteenth-century account, the author had come across an old manuscript that stated that the church at Wolverhampton had been robbed in 1529 and that the churchwardens took steps to discover the location of the church's goods. The robbers offered the plate to an unsuspecting Lady Blount, who purchased it for the church at Bewdley. According to the account, the church at Bewdley was then forced to pay £10 12s 6d to the churchwardens at Wolverhampton when it was discovered that the plate was theirs.[99] The year 1529 fell after Thomas Blount's death, when Bessie's family can have been expected to have moved to Kinlet. However, the Lady Blount referred to is almost certainly Bessie's mother, Katherine Pershall. This suggests close links with Bewdley and the possibility that the family resided there for much of the time before Katherine Pershall inherited her own manor at Knightley and before Thomas Blount's death.

A move by the family to Bewdley at around the turn of the century would have allowed Bessie's parents to be well established for the arrival in Shropshire of Arthur, Prince of Wales and his bride, Catherine of Aragon.

# 4

# BESSIE'S CHILDHOOD

It appears that Bessie was born in around 1498 at Kinlet Hall and that the family then moved to the neighbouring manor of Bewdley in her early childhood. As with so much of her life, few details survive of her childhood, but it is possible to reconstruct something of her upbringing in rural Shropshire.

Some evidence of Bessie's character in childhood, and that of her siblings, survives. It was Anne's son who eventually succeeded to the family estates. His mother also appears to have been the most forceful character amongst the siblings, something which is supported by her portrayal on the side of her parents' tomb. Whilst Bessie was depicted demurely, with downcast eyes, Anne looks directly outwards with a bold and lively expression, suggesting a dominance amongst the siblings.[1] It is notable that the images of the five sons of John Blount and Katherine Pershall are all identical and do not appear to have been intended as true representations of their subjects. The panels containing the six daughters are, however, entirely different. Whilst the six daughters are all dressed in simplified versions of their mother's clothes, they are also all placed in very different poses. The face of the third sister is damaged, but the faces of the remaining figures show enough differences to suggest that true likenesses were attempted. Stylistically, although Katherine Pershall's sleeves on the tomb have been described as approaching an Elizabethan form, they are also consistent with a date in Henry VIII's reign.[2] The rest of Sir John's and Katherine's costumes are also consistent with a date in the reign of Henry VIII and it is likely that work on the tomb began soon after John's death in 1531, or even during his lifetime. It is therefore entirely possible that the images of the daughters were intended to be true likenesses. The difference between the faces of the eldest daughter (Bessie) and the second (Anne) are particularly striking, and it is clear that some attempt was made to differentiate them. Whilst it is unlikely that, given the wide age difference between them, the sisters were ever all together as adults, it is possible that the sculptor attempted true likenesses based on memory and drawings of the sisters. The fact that the sixth, unnamed sister, who apparently died in infancy, is also represented as an adult should not be considered too prejudicial to this, as it was common for infant children to be portrayed as adults when depicted as mourners on a tomb and the sculptor may simply have created a representation based on the mother or other daughters. It therefore appears that something of the character of Bessie and her younger sister Anne survives in their depictions on the tomb: Bessie was the quieter, more demure sister, whilst Anne was firmly in charge.

This can be seen from Anne's later life when she was appointed as executor for their brother, William Blount, in preference to his other surviving sisters.[3] After she was widowed, Anne worked with William, encouraging him to purchase the wardship of her young son, Rowland Lacon, to ensure that the Blount family were able to control his marriage and lands.[4] She was not afraid of the law courts and, as executor for her husband, took action to secure the return of a 'cup of byrrall set in silver', a 'glass' (i.e. a mirror) and other high-value household goods that had belonged to him.[5] She was similarly sued by her associate, George Wood, for the price of twenty yards of broad cloth and twenty yards of black cloth, perhaps for use in mourning clothes, which he had purchased on her behalf and for which she had, according to Wood, 'faithfully promised' to pay.[6] George Wood, who acted as an agent for William, appears to have particularly disliked her, complaining that a suit that she made against him was designed 'to put the said Defendant [Wood] wrongfully to cost and expenses'.[7] Anne's dominance over her siblings may also account for the long-held belief that she was the eldest daughter, which was passed down by her family at Kinlet.[8]

The upbringing of daughters in the late medieval and early Tudor period was usually left entirely to the mother. Katherine was responsible for preparing her daughters for their futures as wives, as well as their educations.[9] The education of women in the late fifteenth and early sixteenth centuries was by no means a foregone conclusion, but there is clear evidence that Katherine could write. Four of Katherine Pershall's letters, all addressed to Henry VIII's chief minister, Thomas Cromwell, survive from the 1530s. The letters are detailed and well composed and appear to have been written out in Katherine's own hand rather than by a scribe.[10] It is therefore apparent from this correspondence that Katherine had received a good education. Given her youth at the time of her marriage, much of this would have been arranged for her by Thomas Blount and Anne Croft. Thomas was interested in education and was a benefactor to Brasenose College, Oxford, from the time of its foundation.[11] In 1516, for example, he gave £6 13s 4d to the college, as well as generous sums at other times. He left the college a legacy in his will, a sign of his commitment to education. It is likely that tutors were still employed at Kinlet during Bessie's childhood for her grandparents' younger children. Alternatively, it is possible that the parish priest was employed to teach the Blount children their lessons. The vicar of Kinlet between 1486 and 1509 was a William Spencer and he was succeeded by a Thomas Mason, who evidently was on friendly terms with Thomas Blount as he was appointed an executor of his will.[12] These priests can perhaps be identified as Bessie's early tutors. It is certainly clear that she was later known to value education. Her son's tutor later wrote to her to ask her to intercede with Henry VIII and Cardinal Wolsey on his behalf, so that they might 'perfectly understand my diligent labours taken with my lord of Richmond's grace [Bessie's son], and his great furtherance in good learning by reason of the same'.[13] Two books which belonged to Bessie survive as testaments to her interest in learning and are discussed later. There are also sufficient examples of her writing to demonstrate that she was literate.

Bessie's family also had another connection to learning which must have helped influence her own education. Details of a lawsuit between the early book printer Richard Pynson and Dame Isabelle Grey and John Wellis, the executors of a merchant, John Russhe, were published for the first time in 1909.[14] The author of the article, H.R. Plomer, tentatively identified the merchant as a John Russe of Great Yarmouth who, on 18 November 1479, was granted a patent to act as a deputy to Anthony, Earl Rivers, the brother of Queen Elizabeth Woodville, in the port of Great Yarmouth.[15] Rivers was an important early patron of the printer William Caxton, something that added weight to this identification. John Russe of Great Yarmouth was a prominent local figure. He is recorded to have been appointed to act as a bailiff of Great Yarmouth on a number of occasions.[16] He also served as one of the burgesses of the town who attended parliament in 1472. He was further known to be literate and appears regularly in the Paston Letters, the correspondence surviving between members and acquaintances of a Norfolk gentry family, as a friend of John Paston.[17] In 1462 John Paston went so far as to procure for him an official post in the port of Yarmouth which was the first advancement in an active and successful local career. He left a widow named Elizabeth who was a claimant in a lawsuit in the last years of the fifteenth century concerning land at Maltby in Norfolk.[18] Given that the names 'Elizabeth' and 'Isabel' share the same etymological origins, it is not impossible that this Elizabeth could have been the Isabelle Grey of Pynson's lawsuit. However, it is clear that she was not. The *Inquisition Post Mortem* for John Russe of Suffolk held in 1492–93 refers to John Russe of Great Yarmouth and conclusively proves that he died in 1492.[19] Pynson's John Russhe died in 1499.

Richard Pynson's debtor was, in fact, Bessie Blount's step-grandfather: the second husband of Isabel Stanley. It was Isabel, then married to her third husband, Sir Thomas Grey, who was one of the parties to the lawsuit. In his will, probate for which was granted in May 1499, Russhe appointed his wife, Isabel Stanley, and a friend, John Wellis, as his executors.[20] Russhe's funeral brass in the church of All Hallows by the Tower shows a prominent and wealthy merchant, dressed in furs. He was a wealthy man who left substantial sums of money and other property, including lands at Walthamstow in Essex. Bessie's grandmother, who received little on the death of her first husband, Hugh Pershall, since he died in the lifetime of his father, was left comfortably off with a life interest in her second husband's lands and all his goods and chattels not otherwise disposed of in his will. Whilst John Russhe left Isabel wealthy, she never took his name. As a merchant, however wealthy, Russhe ranked below Isabel, the widow and daughter of a knight. According to one of the many fourteenth-century books of etiquette designed to educate the gentry as to the proper manners with which to socialise with their social betters, some people were puzzled by the fact that it was possible for lords of royal blood to be poor, whilst others, who were not royal, were rich.[21] Blood was considered to be of more importance than money: a lady of royal blood who married a commoner kept her own rank, whilst a lady of low blood took her husband's rank when she married a prince. Similarly, Isabel, although not wealthy, brought John Russhe status and links to the great Stanley family. She maintained her own rank, keeping her first husband's name during her second marriage and only taking her third husband's name due to his similar rank. Sir Hugh Pershall was, evidently, still a higher-status husband than Sir Thomas Grey, in spite of their similar ranks, as, after Grey's death, Isabel reverted once again to the name of 'Dame Isabell Pursell'.[22]

It is possible that Isabel first became acquainted with John Russhe through his links to her distant kinswoman, Lady Margaret Beaufort, and her husband, Lord Stanley. The sixteenth-century antiquary John Stow, who had access to documents now lost, recorded that, soon after the controversial accession to the throne of Richard III (who became king after deposing his young nephew, Edward V, and imprisoning him in the Tower with his brother, Richard, Duke of York), some Londoners wrote to the future Henry VII in his exile in Brittany to inform him that they 'purposed to have set fire on divers parts of London, which fire, whilst men had been staunching, they would have stolen out of the Tower, the prince Edward [Edward V], & his brother the Duke of York'.[23] Whilst this plot was a failure and the leading figures were executed, it is interesting to note that one of the leaders was a Robert Russe, sergeant of London. It has recently been asserted that Lady Margaret Beaufort played a role in this plot.[24] She certainly played a role in a second, greater conspiracy against Richard III later in the year, led by the Duke of Buckingham. Buckingham's rebellion, which involved an invasion from Brittany led by the future Henry VII, was an abject failure. Buckingham was executed, whilst other leaders of the rebellion, including Margaret Beaufort, were attainted for treason.[25] Amongst the men attainted for treason in an Act of Parliament alongside the Duke of Buckingham and the Bishop of Ely (a leading conspirator) was, interestingly, 'John Rush late of London, merchant'.[26]

Further details of the John Rush who was the subject of the attainder can be found in a grant made by the king to Sir John Everyngham regarding 'the manors lands & tenements late belonging unto our Rebel & traitor John Russhe within our Counties of Essex and Suffolk'.[27] The John Rush in question evidently survived his disgrace as, shortly afterwards, he received a licence for a ship of his that was docked at St James's.[28]

It has recently been suggested that the John Russhe who was involved in the rebellion should be identified as John Russe of Great Yarmouth.[29] This is possible as he was a retainer of Earl Rivers, whose sister, Queen Elizabeth Woodville, was deeply involved in Buckingham's Rebellion, alongside her eldest son, Thomas Grey, Marquis of Dorset. The reference to lands in Suffolk belonging to the attainted John Rush might also suggest that he was John Russe of Great Yarmouth. John Russe of Great Yarmouth also did not hold the post of Bailiff of Great Yarmouth again until 1485, the year that Henry VII came to the throne, something that could be used to suggest that he had incurred the king's disfavour.[30] It must be noted, however, that he had not held the position since 1477 and it therefore appears to have been unconnected with any involvement in a rebellion against Richard III.

It is therefore possible to make a case for the attainted John Rush being John Russe of Great Yarmouth. However, it is more plausible that he can be identified with John Russhe of London, the husband of Isabel Stanley. In the attainder, John Rush is referred to as a merchant of London, a description that fits Pynson's patron. The grant to Sir John Everyngham also refers to lands in Essex and Russhe is known, from his will, to have owned land in Walthamstow in Essex, as well as making a bequest to the church of Little Wakering in that county. It is not impossible that the wealthy merchant would have owned land in the neighbouring county of Suffolk. It has recently been suggested that the John Rush who was attainted may have been the father of the aforementioned Robert Russe, who was executed for his attempt to free the princes from the Tower.[31] This is possible. Hugh Pershall died in 1490 and Russhe and Isabel therefore cannot have been married before 1491 at the earliest. In a chancery case dated to some point between 1504 and 1515, John Russhe of London, the son and heir of Isabel Stanley's second husband, took her to court concerning lands in Walthamstow.[32] He was, presumably, an adult by the time of the case and, whilst it would have been possible for him to be born in 1491 and to have then sued his mother in 1515, it seems more plausible that he, and Robert Russe if he was indeed the elder John Russhe's son, were the children of Russhe's first marriage. In his will, the elder John Russhe mentioned a number of children, including a daughter who had already become a nun. By the late fifteenth century, it was unusual for children to be dedicated to the church in their early childhood. If this daughter was Isabel's, she could not have been more than eight years old at the time of her father's death. More plausibly, she could have been the child of an earlier wife. It is, however, possible that Katherine Pershall did, indeed, have some maternal half-siblings. One of Russhe's daughters, Mary, the wife of Thomas Judd of Wickford, took Thomas Blount to court after Isabel's death for the return of some property which Isabel had bequeathed to her.[33] Thomas Judd of Wickford died in 1535, leaving three sons and an unmarried daughter.[34] The younger two sons, William and Edward, were noted in their father's will to then be aged under twenty-one and the fact that the daughter was still unmarried also suggests that she was young. Mary survived her husband and the children referred to were likely to be hers, with her husband requesting that she 'be good to my children as she shall find cause at her pleasure'. The youth of her children in 1535 suggests that it was entirely possible that Mary Russhe was born after 1491. The bequest to her from Isabel suggests that she was her daughter.

Isabel Stanley's continuing links with Thomas Blount, as well as the legal case that she and John Russhe instigated against Humphrey Pershall on Katherine's behalf, indicates that mother and daughter remained in contact, and relatively close, even following Katherine's early marriage. This is interesting because of Isabel and Russhe's connections to Margaret Beaufort and the court. On a more domestic level, the subject of the lawsuit brought by the printer Richard Pynson is informative about the type of education that Katherine was able to give to Bessie and her younger children.

In his claim against Russhe's executors, Pynson claimed that Russhe caused him to print a number of books, including persuading him to prepare, and print, an edition of the popular religious work *Dives and Paupers*, to the value of 1,000 marks.[35] In return, Russhe promised to bear half the cost of the printing. In order to ensure that the books were saleable, Russhe further requested that Pynson supply copies of other popular books, such as Chaucer's *Canterbury Tales* and an edition of Aesop's Fables. For Russhe, a wealthy merchant, the books made up only a part of his sales stock. Many would have been distributed to local booksellers outside London, as well as sold at fairs.[36] According to Pynson, in his claim, his relationship with Russhe almost immediately began to break down as Russhe failed to pay the agreed sum, leaving the printer 100 pounds out of pocket.[37] Russhe also refused to make an advance payment for books supplied, instead promising the printer that he would pay him the amount due once they had been sold. Following

Russhe's death, Pynson launched a suit for sums outstanding, as well as amounts due for other items, such as household goods and horse harnesses, which he claimed to have supplied. At the same time, Isabel Stanley and John Wellis launched a counterclaim, stating that Pynson had received goods to the value of 300 pounds from Russhe. The dispute dragged on for several years. There appears to have been something of a personal grudge between the parties, with Pynson complaining that Wellis made his counterclaim 'of his pure malice which he beareth toward your Supplicant [Pynson] for other causes intending to undo and utterly to destroy him'.[38] Isabel took a personal interest in the proceedings, giving her own statement to the court. She similarly took an active role in other proceedings brought against her husband's estate, including a case by a tailor for sums owing in which she declared to the court that Russhe was a man 'of good substance and trust' and a 'gentleman'.[39]

The books that John Russhe received from Richard Pynson were a mixture of genres and calculated to appeal to the largest possible number of his customers. As well as the *Canterbury Tales*, *Dives and Paupers* and Aesop's Fables, they included unnamed chronicles (presumably works of history), books of grammar and religious primers. Russhe also requested, at the more popular end of the market, copies of a romance which he sold for only 10 pence each.[40] Russhe himself is believed to have supplied Pynson with the original manuscript for *Dives and Paupers*, indicating that he was well educated and well read.[41] The surviving documentary records indicate that Katherine and her stepfather, Russhe, enjoyed friendly relations and stayed in contact. In an age when it was becoming fashionable for women to patronise printers and to possess books themselves, it is entirely possible that Katherine benefited from her stepfather's stock by acquiring some of the titles herself.[42] If this was the case, Bessie could also have made use of the wide library of titles available for sale by her step-grandfather. Her signature appears in two books which she acquired before her marriage, attesting to her ability to read and her literary interests. The first of these books, Chaucer's *Troilus and Criseyde*, was a romance popular with young ladies of her class and also suggests that she may indeed have taken an interest in her step-grandfather's edition of Chaucer's more well-known work, the *Canterbury Tales*.[43]

The late fifteenth century was an age when the gentry sought to improve themselves and to mingle with their social superiors. It was, very much, the age of the self-help book, with improving works produced on a wide range of topics. As well as ensuring that her daughters could read and write, Katherine would have insisted that they learned the equally important skills of deportment, dancing and embroidery, as well as religious education.[44] One historian has recently pointed out that the ideal for a young, later medieval woman was that of the virgin-martyr – a select class of highly popular saints.[45] The most popular virgin-martyr was St Katherine of Alexandria, whose life was described in the very popular early fifteenth-century work, the *Red Book of Bath*, which presented the saint explicitly as a model young lady: 'beautiful, yet soberly dressed, not affected by worldly vanities such as dancing; intelligent, yet reserved and demure'.[46] Books such as this, with their emphasis on what constituted an ideal woman, began to reach a wide audience with the development of printing in the later fifteenth century and were widely followed.[47] It is almost certain that the Blounts, members of the upper gentry, would have been aware of at least some of these books.

Fifteenth-century self-help books covered a wide range of topics. One particularly popular one was *The Book of the Knight of the Tower*, written by a French knight, Geoffrey de la Tour Landry, in the 1370s as a book of instruction for his daughters.[48] This book, which was made up of a number of stories to demonstrate the virtues that the girls should acquire and the vices that they should avoid, was extremely popular and translated into English twice in the fifteenth century. It was printed by Caxton in 1483 and still used in the 1530s. *The Book of the Knight of the Tower* set out the behaviour and demeanour that a well-born girl should aspire to and was followed avidly by Bessie's class. In his book, the knight set out his aims for writing, stating of his work that 'I would have collected the memorable instances of admirable women, and of their carriage; so as to show, by their patter, what was true feminacy and good conduct; and also how, by their virtues, they were held in honour and estimation, and will ever continue to be so'.[49] He desired to show his daughters, and his female readers, 'the contempt that is the meed of wicked and unseemly women, so as to serve as a warning, of all the mischief which may befall those who are reflected on, blamed, or defamed'.[50]

The book is a cautionary work and one which set out the standards that young women were expected to adhere to. In one story, the knight related the story of two sisters who were the daughters of the Emperor of Constantinople.[51] One was very pious and would pray all night, earning her the protection of heaven. A knight attempted to enter her bedchamber at night. At the same time, another knight entered the room of her sister, who had proven herself less devout. This sister was more willing and became pregnant, to her shame. The moral of this story, as far as the author and his readers was concerned, was that it was necessary to pray both on going to bed and on rising in the morning. Another story dealt with gluttony, detailing a greedy wife who would rise in the night to empty the larder, eventually losing her eye when, on being discovered, her husband beat a servant who assisted her and a splinter flew from the stick. The moral of this was that, until they married, girls should fast three days a week and dedicate themselves to

God.[52] If this proved too difficult for them, they should at least fast on Fridays 'and if you cannot support yourselves on bread and water, at any rate abstain from anything which had life'.

In addition to piety and ensuring that they did not overeat, the book made it clear that women were expected to be courteous and unassuming.[53] They should show condescension to the poor. It set out that what a man wanted in a wife was not necessarily the most beautiful, nor the most witty, but a retired and subdued wife who spoke little and with deliberation; a man wanted 'a safe wife; one to be relied on, and of a good presence'.[54] From their earliest childhood, Bessie and her sisters were aware that they were being raised to be wives and were expected to behave themselves accordingly. As the knight said:

> And from this, you see, my lovely daughters and my noble maids, how all gentlewomen of conditions ought to be of retiring manners, self-respectful, unassuming, small-talkers. They should rejoin with diffidence, nor should they be too ready to understand, or yet anxious, or allow their eyes to be seen about. For, to end the matter, no good comes of it. Many have lost their chances through too much readiness, and of whom one would have expected very other things.[55]

Bessie's own future conduct indicates that she did not entirely adhere to the ideals of feminine conduct set out by the knight. However, she, along with her sisters, would have been very aware that to lose their reputation was a dangerous thing. They were not heiresses, nor from a particularly influential or wealthy family. The sisters therefore would have been raised to understand that they must be pleasing to a husband and accord, as much as possible, with expected feminine ideals. With the births of their three surviving brothers between 1513 and 1518, the sisters had little hope of inheriting the family estates and therefore knew that, to a large extent, they would have to attract a husband using their own personal attributes. Not all were successful in this, even with the help of Bessie's later royal connections. Her younger sister, Albora, never married.[56] As one sixteenth-century book on manners, 'The Schoole of Vertue', recorded, a woman was required to conform to the rules set by a paternal society: 'ye wives, to your husbands be obedient always, For they are your heads, and ye bound to obey'.[57]

Bessie was raised by her mother to be proficient at the traditional feminine pursuits of dancing, singing and needlework. Katherine would also have attended to her daughters' religious education, ensuring that they were, at least, conventionally pious. Bessie's childhood occurred before the break with Rome and her education would have been a traditional Catholic one. However, even in the years before the Reformation, religious reform (which eventually developed into

Protestantism) was a rising movement and it is useful to speculate on Bessie's own personal faith both in her childhood and later life.

The Blount family was divided on matters of religion: a not uncommon position in the sixteenth century. Bessie's father died in 1531 when the religious reform movement was still in its infancy and England still firmly under the sway of the pope. It is therefore not possible, or even helpful, to consider Bessie's father's religious beliefs. They were almost certainly traditional. However, John's longer-lived brothers did leave better evidence of their own responses to the religious changes in England. Thomas Blount's third son, Walter, settled at Astley in Worcestershire, where the fine tombs of him and his wife, and that of his eldest son and daughter-in-law, can still be seen. Walter Blount died in 1561 whilst his son Robert lived on until 1575 in the town which is only a few miles from Bewdley.[58] The Astley Blounts were Catholic recusants and were fined for their refusal to attend Protestant church services. Robert Blount, Bessie's first cousin, maintained a close relationship with his siblings and children, who are depicted on the sides of the tombs of their respective parents.[59] One sister, Joyce, married twice. Her eldest son lived in Stratford-upon-Avon, where he was a well-known Catholic. He and his wife paid fines to avoid having to attend Protestant services and are known to have sheltered a Jesuit priest at one point.[60] Margaret Reynold's, Joyce Blount's daughter-in-law, was charged with not receiving communion at Easter in 1606 and her son, William Reynolds, appeared before the Star Chamber some years later for rioting against the Puritans in Stratford and threatening to flay the local vicar. In 1619 he was accused of continuing to practise the Catholic faith with the evidence against him being a maypole set up near his house. A further member of the Astley family, Thomas Blount, found himself involved in a conspiracy to depose Elizabeth I by the Earl of Essex at the turn of the seventeenth century. An official report to the queen's council which recommended sending Thomas for questioning also advised that he be sent for secretly and with an assurance of his safety as 'otherwise, being a recusant, he may be fearful and keep out of the way. He is of an honest, loyal disposition as any of his sort may be.'[61] There is no doubt that the Astley Blounts were Catholic.

Bessie's brother George Blount, the Catholic Walter Blount of Astley and Edward Blount of Kidderminster (Thomas Blount's second son) were all associated with their kinsman, the great John Dudley, Duke of Northumberland, during his ascent to power as the leading counsellor of the boy king Edward VI in the 1550s.[62] Although, during Edward VI's lifetime, Northumberland portrayed himself as a staunchly Protestant nobleman, following his failed coup against the accession of Queen Mary where he attempted to place Lady Jane Grey on the throne, he reconverted to Catholicism in the vain hope that it would save his life.[63] Whilst Northumberland's religious beliefs were lightly held, those of his comptroller, Bessie's first cousin, Thomas Blount of Kidderminster, were more strongly held, with the Protestant Bishop Sandys for one commenting in 1564 that he was a favourer of the Protestant religion.[64] This was in stark contrast to his cousin, George Blount, who was considered by his contemporaries to be either neutral or hostile to the Protestant religion during the same period.[65] This Thomas Blount was an active dignitary of Kidderminster during the years of the Reformation; for example, he was one of the men of the town who administered justice to Miles Denison, a tailor of the town, who had been arrested for his comments about the clergymen invited to preach in the town, declaring of one that 'there is a foolish knave priest come to preach of the New Learning, which I set not by'.[66] He further declared that 'my Lord hath sent a foolish puppy and a boy to make a sermon of the New Law' and complained during the sermon. Bessie's cousin wasted no time in reporting the tailor to the king.

Thomas Blount of Kidderminster was a particular favourite of Northumberland's son, Robert Dudley, Earl of Leicester, who made him the steward of his manor of Kenilworth in 1563. It was to this 'Cousin Blount' that the earl also turned following the death of his wife in suspicious circumstances in 1560 when he asked his cousin to investigate the death as 'the greatness and the suddenness of the misfortune doth so perplex me until I do hear from you how the matter standeth, or how this evil should light upon me, considering what the malicious world will bruit, as I can take no rest'.[67] Thomas Blount of Kidderminster's son served with the earl in his expeditionary force to the Low Countries in 1585 and was one of the gentlemen prominent at his patron's funeral a few years later.[68] Whilst Leicester's precise religious beliefs are unclear, he was a prominent nobleman in the reign of the Protestant Elizabeth I and it appears that the Kidderminster Blounts were sincere in their reformist beliefs. Bessie's father John had a deeply hostile relationship with his younger brother, Edward Blount of Kidderminster, and it is not impossible that this feud could have had its roots in religious differences as the younger brother took an interest in reform at odds with the elder's beliefs. Regardless of what caused the quarrel, there is considerable evidence to suggest that Bessie's branch of the family followed its Astley cousins' beliefs more closely than those held by the Kidderminster branch of the family.

Bessie lived through a period of great religious turmoil, experiencing the Protestant Reformation firsthand. In spite of this, there are no direct references to her personal religious beliefs and it is likely that she always conformed with the king's own religious beliefs. There are some indications that she might have adhered more to the traditional, Catholic faith than to the religious reform movement, the followers of which would later be called Protestants. Her mother appears to have had traditional beliefs. A new vicar of Kinlet, appointed in the years following the break with Rome, was Alan Clyp, a former monk, who was presented to the parish by Katherine and her son-in-law, Richard Lacon.[69] The appointment of an ex-monk suggests sympathy with traditional beliefs, as does Katherine's gift of plate to the church at Bewdley detailed in the previous chapter. Bessie's nephew, Rowland Lacon, the eventual heir to Kinlet, would later find his name mentioned in relation to an apparent Catholic conspiracy against Elizabeth I in 1573. Rowland's servant, Avery Kellet, was arrested by the Earl of Shrewsbury, the gaoler of the Catholic Mary, Queen of Scots.[70] Although Kellet at first denied any wrongdoing, after a period of 'sharper imprisonment', he admitted using magic to help find hidden treasure, heal the sick and, ominously, 'to have certain knowledge also touching the state of the realm' which presumably, given the circumstances of his arrest, related to his hopes for the succession of the Catholic Mary. Whilst no charges were brought against Rowland, Kellet's presence in his household is indicative of his own religious sympathies. He was the favoured nephew of Bessie's brother, George Blount, and chosen to succeed him, suggesting that he approved of his nephew's beliefs. It is likely that the entire family sympathised with the traditional, Catholic religion, something that was not uncommon amongst the gentry of the mid-Tudor period. This was very much the mood of the local area. One local churchman, John Brome, the vicar of Stanton Lacy and curate of the chapelry of Ludford, was accused in September 1535 of failing to erase the pope's name from his services books.[71] Apparently considering the religious changes to be temporary, Brome had enterprisingly only covered the offending names with small strips of paper lightly glued in place. When they were removed the books proved to be entirely undamaged, something that strongly suggests a mood of acceptance of religious changes but hardly active support.

Bessie's daily life in childhood would have been very prescribed. Religion was very much a part of daily life, with one manuscript on child raising, dating to around 1500, stating that, when a child rose, they should pray, wash their hands and face and comb their hair before going to the church to hear mass.[72] Only then could they go to breakfast. Another similar work from around half a century later confirmed that prayers must be said first thing in the morning, with the child repeating the Lord's Prayer both on waking and before bed at night.[73] They were to ensure that they did not oversleep, for too much sleep was commonly held to cause illness, as well as pain that would dull the wits. Once they had packed away their bed, the child would go downstairs to greet their parents, with another work declaring that they must remember to say 'God speed' to the head of the household, who would usually be their father, as well as kneeling in their presence or standing until they were told to sit.[74] They would wash and dress before attending to their lessons. Dinner, which was eaten in the morning, was preceded by grace and a child of the household would be expected to help serve if they were old enough. Certainly Bessie, as the eldest child, would have been expected to assist her parents, pouring out water for them with a curtsey at their meals.[75] A child was required to be silent at the table and to be obedient to their parents at all times.

In the late medieval period and early Tudor period, there was a very fine line between service and those who were served. For example, one fifteenth-century courtesy book, which was widely followed, was written to instruct a young gentleman in the service of a lord.[76] Life in the late fifteenth century and early sixteenth century was very communal, with servants and gentlewomen sharing the same spaces in the house. Henry VIII's fifth wife, Catherine Howard, for example, is known to have spent much of her childhood sleeping in a dormitory room amongst both servants and girls of noble birth like herself. During Bessie's childhood, her home, although considerably more elaborate than those of people below gentry rank, would have seemed spartan. For meals, boards were laid on trestles to make tables, with stools for seats.[77] The hall was the main room of the house and the boards were stored away in the corners of the room when not needed. The house must have been dirty and crowded, with one job of the marshal of the household being to ensure that no dogs got into the hall in the day. In the morning the groom was responsible for carrying away 'all other filth of the hall'. Important rooms were lit with wax candles but, in general, the household would have been dark.[78] It would also have been cold. In winter, it was the groom of the household's responsibility to fetch wood and coal for the hall every morning. In *The Book of the Knight of the Tower*, the author considered that it was necessary for girls to dress up warmly, to ensure that the chill did not cause the loss of their beauty.[79]

Although life could be spartan and cold, it was very far from cheerless. Meals in the late medieval period could be elaborate. On special occasions, the entire household would gather, with the marshal watching closely to ensure that there was sufficient meat, bread, ale and wine in the hall. Numerous courses could be served, with the tables laid with salt, bread, trenchers (old bread to be used as plates), carving knives, spoons and napkins.[80] The menus for a number of great feasts of the fifteenth and sixteenth centuries have survived. For one which was held during the reign of Edward IV in the honour of the Archbishop of York, over 300 tuns of ale and 100 of wine were required.[81] 104 oxen and six wild bulls were also served, along with 1,000 sheep and 400 swans. More exotically, porpoises and seals found their way to the table, along with quails, peacocks and other birds. Such a feast would only have been seen in the houses of the upper nobility, but the Archbishop of York's dinner was attended by much of the nobility and the local gentry. Something of a similar character, although on a considerably lesser scale, was attempted in the households of the gentry in England.

Such occasions were highly stratified, with the head of the household served the freshest bread, other honoured guests receiving one-day-old bread, and the servants and lesser members of the household getting bread that had been baked three days before.[82]

Feasting was not the only entertainment available to Bessie and her family during childhood. Her likely childhood home of Bewdley was also a prominent town in the early sixteenth century due to the good transport links provided by its bridge. The town had been granted a charter to hold a market on Wednesdays, as well as two annual three-day fairs to be held in November and July in 1376.[83] This was confirmed in 1446, with an additional fair in February added to the town's calendar. Saturday markets were allowed by at least 1507. The twice-weekly markets would have provided interest for the young Blount children, and by at least the end of the sixteenth century it is known that card-makers, hosiers and weavers rented regular stalls. The annual fairs saw the arrival of more exotic and interesting wares. The April fair appears to have been particularly for the sale of horned cattle, horses, cheese, linen and woollen cloth, whilst the July fair displayed more seasonal wares. Games and entertainments were held alongside the stalls, with one particularly popular game known as 'shin-kicking' involving two men locking their shoulders against the other's as they attempted to knock their opponent over. Bewdley is so close to Kinlet and other Blount estates that, even if it was not in fact the main home of Bessie's family, it is highly likely that the family would have taken the time to attend at least some of the fairs, enjoying the highlights of the annual social calendar.

During her childhood, Bessie would have spent most of her time at home with her siblings. Although her mother was ultimately responsible for her upbringing, servants must also have been employed to help raise the Blount children, the usual practice for a family of her class.[84] Both John and Katherine led active local lives. They might also, on occasion, have travelled to London to visit Katherine's mother and, perhaps, attend court, where Isabel Stanley had family connections. Bessie's grandfather, Thomas Blount, was appointed a squire to the body of Richard III, a prestigious appointment which may have been acquired through the Yorkist connections of his father-in-law, Sir Richard Croft.[85] The family remained prominent into the Tudor period and, notably, the proxy wedding of Arthur, Prince of Wales, to the Spanish Princess, Catherine of Aragon, took place at Bewdley in 1499.[86] Whilst the bride, who was still in Spain, was necessarily absent from the ceremony, the prince and much of his household were in residence there, remaining at the manor for some time afterwards. Records demonstrate that he was resident at the manor in 1500, when he met with the Bishop of Lincoln there, and again in August 1501, when he signed a letter to Oxford University at the manor.[87] If, indeed, Bessie's parents had already made

Bewdley their home, it is possible that the infant Bessie was herself in attendance during the marriage ceremony although, as an infant, she would not actually have been allowed to witness the ceremony. It has been suggested that her grandfather, Thomas Blount, who had connections in the early Tudor court and had been knighted by Henry VII at the Battle of Stoke, may well have been privileged to be present at this important local event.[88] Prince Arthur was the probable godfather of Thomas's fourth son, Arthur Blount.

The marriage of Prince Arthur to Catherine of Aragon was a major event of Bessie's early childhood. The sixteen-year-old princess landed at Plymouth for her wedding in the winter of 1501.[89] The king, Henry VII, left Richmond Palace on 4 November to meet his new daughter-in-law, being met along the route by his eldest son, Prince Arthur, who was fifteen. The first meeting was not entirely a success; the king, at first denied access to the princess, was informed that she was in bed. To this, Henry VII replied 'that if she were in her bed, he would see and common [talk] with her, for that was the mind and the intent of his coming'.[90] This was enough to see Catherine rise swiftly from her bed. The following day she resumed her journey towards London, making her ceremonial entry to the city on 12 November. The couple were married with great ceremony in St Paul's Cathedral shortly afterwards. Once the celebrations had finished, the couple travelled to Ludlow to set up a court at the castle there, in order to allow Arthur to rule over his principality in person.

Today Ludlow is a picturesque town, dominated by the castle which stands on the edge of the market square. Much of the medieval and later Tudor buildings survive, including the ruin of the tower in which Catherine and Arthur spent their brief married life. Whilst Bessie spent much of her childhood at her family estates, if she did venture to a large town, it would have been Ludlow. The town was described by the late sixteenth- and early seventeenth-century antiquary William Camden as 'a place of greater beauty than antiquary'.[91] Until Bessie came to London, it would have been the largest place that she visited. Early in the sixteenth century, during Bessie's own lifetime, another antiquary, John Leland, provided a more comprehensive description, recording that:

> The town of Ludlow is very proper, well walled and gated, and standeth every way eminent from a bottom. In the side of the town as a piece of the enclosing of the wall is a fair castle. Within the town even in the middle is one parish church. Without the walls be aliquot sacella, and ii houses of Friars Augustines and Carmelites. Among other gates of the town there is Corve-Gate and Galford-Gate.[92]

The parish church was the second most notable building in the town, standing away from the castle to the other side of the market place. Its popularity was such that, at some point in the medieval period, regulations were made allowing the grant to an individual or family of a piece of ground measured out on the floor of the church.[93] On this, the parishioner would build their own pew, which was their private property and could be sold or bequeathed in their will. This led to competitive pew-building as families sought to outdo each other in conspicuous displays of wealth. The rights to a pew could be hotly contested and the surviving church accounts note a case from 1540 where 'it is ordered and agreed be the said bailiffs that the foresaid Richard Langford from henceforth shall peaceably have, occupy, and enjoy the pew or seat in church late in the tenure of Alice Lane deceased'.[94] The funds raised from the sale of the pews helped to ensure that the church at Ludlow was one of the finest in the county. The churchwarden's accounts for the 1540s and later make it clear that the church was well maintained, with sums spent on repairs to a clock, bells and an organ, amongst other items.

Bessie was too young to have had any involvement in the arrival of Prince Arthur and Catherine of Aragon early in 1502, but her family helped to welcome them. Bessie's great-grandfather, Sir Richard Croft, was given the important post of steward of the prince's household, becoming one of Arthur's most important advisors.[95] Croft found a role for his son-in-law, Thomas Blount, who was prominent in the household. Before leaving London, Catherine had been upset by the king's insistence that most of her Spanish attendants return to Spain, leaving her instead with a household primarily composed of English ladies.[96] It has been suggested that Katherine Pershall, as one of the highest ranking ladies local to Ludlow and with her family links to the still living and active Lady Margaret Beaufort, was one of the ladies chosen to attend her in the Welsh Marches.[97] There is no evidence to confirm that such a prestigious appointment was made but it is very likely that Katherine and her husband were frequent visitors to the young princess and her husband.[98] Unfortunately, this privileged access to royalty was not destined to last long and Prince Arthur died suddenly at Ludlow on 2 April 1502 of the sweating sickness, a dreaded disease which had apparently been first brought to England with the foreign mercenaries in the employ of the future Henry VII when he claimed the English crown.

Bessie's family played a prominent role in the funeral for the young prince. The body was embalmed and then placed in a coffin covered by a black cloth decorated with a white cross. Arthur was laid in his chamber beneath hangings of rich cloth of gold and with wax tapers set in silver candlesticks.[99] Members of the prince's household kept a constant vigil over his body until St George's Day, when he was carried in procession from the room by yeomen of the chamber. As they walked, a bishop threw incense and holy water onto the corpse. The prince's body was attended by 'many noble men', including Bessie's great-grandfather, the prominent Sir Richard Croft. The Earl of Surrey walked behind as the chief mourner, attended by the earls of Shrewsbury and Kent. A role was found for Bessie's grandfather, Sir Thomas Blount, who carried over the prince's coffin a banner depicting a pious image. The prince was then taken into the parish church, where a funeral service was held for him, attended by all the members of his household.

Even after this opulent ceremony, the funeral rites of the deceased heir to the throne had not come to an end. Arthur was placed on a rich chariot and the entire company set out on horseback on 'the foulest, caudle, windy, and rainy day and the worst way' that one observer had seen.[100] Interestingly, the soaked and cold procession moved first to Bewdley, the royal manor likely to have been occupied by Bessie's family. Bessie was aged around four at the time of Prince Arthur's death and the memory of his funeral would have remained with her for the rest of her life as her first exposure to court spectacle. The body spent the night in the chapel at Bewdley whilst its attendants tried to make themselves as comfortable as possible in the cramped house, drying their soaked clothes as best they could. The following day they all set out again, with Sir Richard Croft and his colleague Sir William Oredall, the controller of the prince's household, riding on ahead to Worcester to ensure that the way was clear. A second funeral service was held in the cathedral there, with Croft once again prominent, before the corpse was finally laid in its grave. It was an emotional moment for those who had been appointed to attend and assist the young prince who had been seen as the living embodiment of the union between the houses of York and Lancaster and a symbol of the end of the civil war, now known as the Wars of the Roses, which had blighted England during the latter half of the fifteenth century. According to one contemporary account, as the body was placed in its grave Croft and other officers ceremonially threw their staves of office onto the coffin in what was considered 'a piteous sight'.[101] Bessie's great-grandfather's role was not entirely over and he spent the next day arranging for the payments of Arthur's debts. Katherine Pershall's role was also not quite at an end. Catherine of Aragon, who had contracted sweating sickness at the same time as her husband, was too ill to attend any of the funeral ceremony. Her ladies remained with her at Ludlow until a litter, hung with black velvet and black cloth and commissioned by the queen in London, arrived to take the princess back to the capital city.[102]

Katherine Pershall did not travel with her mistress to London, instead returning to her own family. Her time with Catherine of Aragon was brief and Catherine, a childless widow, would in 1502 have seemed to have little possibility of any future influence in England. Bessie's own future would later prove to be linked to Catherine's own, and her mother's brief role with the Spanish princess provided links with which Bessie Blount's own career was forged.

# PART 2
# BESSIE BLOUNT, THE KING'S MISTRESS
## 1512–1522

# 5
# MAID OF HONOUR TO THE QUEEN

As with so much of Bessie's life, knowledge of her whereabouts during her early teenage years is scant. However, we do know, with certainty, that by the autumn of 1512 she had established herself at court as a maid to Queen Catherine of Aragon.

Both Bessie's father and grandfather continued to enjoy local prominence following the accession of Henry VIII in April 1509, receiving appointments to a commission of the peace for Staffordshire on 8 July 1509.[1] This commission was renewed later in November. At the same time, Thomas Blount also received an appointment as sheriff of Herefordshire.[2] The two men were successful in these roles and continued to be regularly appointed in commissions of the peace for some years.[3] Thomas Blount also received an appointment to a similar commission for Shropshire in February 1510.[4] John Blount's interests did not entirely lie in Shropshire and Staffordshire and he managed to attain some reputation at court, as evidenced by his appointment as an esquire of the body at the funeral of Henry VII in 1509.[5] It may have been at the funeral that he first came to the attention of the king and, by the time of Henry VIII's coronation, he had been appointed as one of the king's Spears, appearing at the ceremony in the Spears' uniform of 'cloth of gold, silver, and goldsmiths work', with their servants 'richly apparelled also'.[6]

The king's Spears were intended to be an elite force of noblemen and gentlemen and functioned both for a ceremonial purpose and as the king's bodyguard. They were founded soon after Henry's accession in 1509 in an attempt by the king to boost his international prestige, with the Spears consciously emulating similar bodies in France.[7] For Henry, one of their main functions was for display, as set out in the official document recording the creation of the force:

Forasmuch as the king our sovereign lord of his great nobleness wisdom and prudence considereth that in this his realm of England be many young gentlemen of noble blood. Which have no exercise in the feats of Arms in handling and running the spear and other feats of war on horseback like as in other realms and countries be daily practised and used to the great honour and laud of them that so doeth, his highness hath ordained and appointed to have a retinue daily of certain spears called men of arms to be chosen of gentlemen that be come and extract of noble blood to the intent that they shall exercise the said feat of arms and be the more meet and able to serve their prince as well in time of war as otherwise.[8]

That John Blount was chosen to join the king's Spears was a flattering appointment and demonstrates that he had come to the attention of the king for his martial prowess and his solid gentry background. Although a full list of his fellow Spears does not survive, there were some prominent members of the court included amongst their number, including the king's friend Charles Brandon (the future Duke of Suffolk) and Arthur Plantagenet, the illegitimate son of Edward IV (the future Lord Lisle) and therefore also the king's uncle.[9] The Spears formed a select group of around fifty gentlemen and minor noblemen, with the Earl of Essex as their captain. As one of the Spears of Honour, John had to live by the statutes set out by the king himself when the troop was formed. For example, the Spears were expected to keep their arms and other equipment in good order in case they were required in time of war. Each Spear had to employ a page, a mark of their rank, and both Spear and page were called upon to have horses and other equipment 'convenient and necessary for a man of arms'. Unsurprisingly, given the name chosen for the order, a javelin was an essential piece of equipment. The circumstances behind John Blount's appointment do not survive but he would have viewed it as a privilege. The wages may have been part of the attraction but, in addition to this, the Spears enjoyed their own pageantry and rules which served to set them apart from everyday men and gave them something of an aura of mystique. For example, on the death of any of the Spears, the survivors in the troop were empowered to nominate a successor (although the final approval lay with the king). An oath was required of every new Spear in which the gentleman in question swore that 'I shall be true and faithful subject and servant unto our sovereign lord king Henry the VIIIth and to his heirs kings of England and diligently and truly give mine attendance in the room of one of his Spears'.

The Spears were required to be ready for war, or some other duty, at a moment's notice and it was ruled that 'they shall make their abode in such place as the king's grace shall appoint them or the said captain or the Deputy lieutenant in the kings names. Whether it be in place nigh his person or otherwise upon pain for any such default to lose six days wages.' Once settled in the lodgings ordered by the king, the Spears were required to stay there, unless they received the licence of the king or his deputies. Evidently the Spears were to be given no autonomy at all in their choice of abode, with a further statute declaring that 'none of the said Spears shall presume to take his lodging by his own authority'. As Henry's bodyguard, the Spears were required, not unnaturally, to remain close by him. Given that, for the most part, the court remained in or around London, this would have brought John Blount frequently to court. Since John and Katherine continued to produce children with considerable regularity after his appointment, it would seem reasonable to assume that Katherine accompanied her husband to London, although she would not necessarily have been able to share his lodgings. In addition to this, it is not implausible that they may also have brought Bessie, their eldest daughter by some years. Bessie would also have spent some time at her mother's principal manor of Knightley in Staffordshire, which the family were finally able to move to by at least November 1511.[10]

Although there is no definite evidence for Bessie's arrival in London, it does seem probable that she arrived before her appointment in 1512. Bessie would have turned twelve in around 1510, the youngest possible age for a girl to take up an appointment as a maid of honour. Although no formal portrait of Bessie survives, the king himself later stated that he required the ladies around his wives to be fair.[11] There is good evidence that Bessie was particularly good-looking, something which, coupled with his success in becoming a Spear, may have encouraged John Blount to try to find a position for Bessie at court. Different nationalities had different ideas of attractiveness. The Italians reputedly sought thick, well-set and plump women, whilst the Germans looked for strength as their ideal of beauty.[12] The Spanish apparently liked their women to be lean, whilst the French looked for delicate features. It has been pointed out that a surviving portrait of Bessie's brother, George, shows him to have had fair skin, blonde hair and blue eyes, something that, assuming a family likeness between the siblings, would suggest that Bessie also conformed to the sixteenth-century English ideal of beauty.[13] In addition to this, it is suggested that John Blount must have been tall, with a strong build, and handsome in order to have obtained his position as one of the ceremonially important king's Spears, again implying that Bessie might have been notably attractive.[14] In contemporary sources Bessie was commonly referred to as a beauty, with the Dean of Westbury stating, when she was aged around thirty, that she was more beautiful than the king's second wife, Anne Boleyn.[15]

Although no formal portrait survives of Bessie, two representations of her do exist: the image on the side of her parents' tomb at Kinlet and her funeral brass. It is therefore possible to make some comments on her appearance from those. As already discussed, an attempt is likely to have been made at a likeness in Bessie's depiction on her parents' monument. The second surviving image of Bessie, from her funeral brass, was commissioned by her and is therefore very likely to be a true representation. It is lucky that it is recognised to be a representation of Bessie at all. The British Museum, which displays Bessie's brass, has a small collection of approximately sixty English brasses, dating to between the fourteenth and seventeenth centuries.[16] These brasses were largely acquired in a haphazard manner and, by early 1990, the museum possessed a brass known to have been in a private collection since at least 1861, which was described only as 'kneeling lady in heraldic mantle, barry nebuly, with ermine collar, *c*.1540, local, probably Lincolnshire work; palimpsest, on reverse a portion of canopy work with the crowned head of the Virgin, Flemish, *c*.1400–20'.[17] In 1990, it was noted by Anne Dowden that the figure fitted a description of Bessie's funeral brass, recorded from a time before her monument was broken up.[18] In order to confirm this, Dowden matched the position of the rivet holes on both the surviving slab of Purbeck Marble (on which the brass had originally been fixed) in South Kyme church, with those on the brass itself. The positions fitted exactly, confirming that the brass, which has been described as 'clumsily executed', was indeed Bessie's. As Dowden described, the brass is poorly carved, with, for example, Bessie's right hand being twice as large as her left. In addition to this, she seems to have two right eyes, giving the face a slightly uneven look. In spite of that, the brass is of use as a depiction of how Bessie chose to depict herself and can be taken to be an attempt at a true likeness, even if it is not entirely accurately rendered. Fittingly, an excellent replica of the original brass has now been affixed to the remaining monument in South Kyme church.

The representation of Bessie on her parents' tomb shows a modest-looking young woman, with downturned eyes and a serene expression which contrasts with the more lively depiction of her sister, Anne. Bessie's features are regular and pleasing. In the second depiction of Bessie, produced when she was in her early thirties, the young girl from her parents' tomb has visibly aged, but the fact that she chose to be depicted in a French hood, rather than the more modest English gable hood that she wore on her parents' tomb, is interesting. The French hood was considered more daring than the bulkier English gable hood and allowed a view of the wearer's hair. Henry VIII's sister, Mary Tudor, Queen of France, was one of the earliest Englishwomen to be depicted wearing one and they rapidly became fashionable during Bessie's years at court and later.[19] They were so popular that Catherine of Aragon ordered one for her daughter in 1520 and Anne Boleyn was famous for her love of the headwear. By the time that Bessie's funeral brass was made, a French hood was the height of fashion. For example, in 1540 Henry VIII's fourth wife, Anne of Cleves, on noting the king's disappointment in her appearance, attempted to appear more pleasing to him at a joust following their marriage by wearing a French hood that 'so set forth her beauty and good visage, that every creature rejoiced to behold her'.[20] French hoods were all but banned in the household of Henry VIII's third wife, Jane Seymour, who sought to present a virtuous and sober image in contrast to that of her predecessor, Anne Boleyn. When she appointed a new maid, the French-educated Anne Bassett, in 1537, Jane insisted that the girl replace her French hoods with English gable hoods, in spite of the fact that the new hood 'became her nothing so well as the French hood'.[21] Bessie's decision to be depicted in the hood demonstrates that she maintained an interest in her appearance and would have appeared well dressed and striking during her later years.

Bessie's arrival in London is unrecorded although, given the difficulties that families could have in securing places in the queen's household for their daughters, it could have been some months, or even years in advance of her appointment at court in 1512. It seems likely that Bessie had never journeyed far from Shropshire and Staffordshire before 1512 and London must have seemed impossibly large. In around 1500, a traveller in England noted that the countryside was very sparsely populated and that 'all the beauty of this island is confined to London'.[22] According to the observer, the city was as populous as Florence or Rome and the citizens lived comfortably in their brick and timber houses in a city which 'abounds with every article of luxury, as well as with the necessaries of life'. London in the early sixteenth century was considerably smaller than it is now, with various areas which are now considered to be part of the capital forming separate settlements. A traveller in the mid-seventeenth century, for example, commented that 'Greenwich is a fair sized market town with some nice streets and many fine houses'.[23] The city was dominated by the mighty Tower of London, which had been first built by William the Conqueror, the other royal palaces and by London Bridge. In Bessie's time the medieval bridge, which was a massive undertaking made up of nineteen arches, formed something of a shopping arcade, with the top storeys of the shops that lined the bridge touching to form a tunnel through which shoppers strolled.[24] Small gaps between the buildings allowed glimpses of the river and daylight managed to find its way through, lightening the gloom to some extent. Beneath the bridge the arches formed a barrier to the progress of the water, causing a 'great roar' as the river dropped six or seven feet from one side to the other, ensuring a hair-raising descent for anyone brave enough to pass under in a boat. Young gentlewomen often browsed in the markets and shops of the capital accompanied by a servant. The river itself was also a feature of the city and a late sixteenth-century visitor commented that, although it was only 'tolerably broad', it was home to many tame swans.[25] The city was bustling and bigger than anything else Bessie would ever have experienced. A visitor in 1592, less than a century after Bessie arrived, marvelled that:

> London is a large, excellent, and mighty city of business, and the most important in the whole kingdom; most of the inhabitants are employed in buying and selling merchandise, and trading in almost every corner of the world, since the river is most useful and convenient for this purpose, considering that ships from France, the Netherlands, Sweden, Denmark, Hamburg, and other kingdoms, come almost up to the city, to which they convey goods and receive and take away others in exchange. [26]

The city was populous and one could 'scarcely pass along the streets, on account of the throng'.[27] Bessie's lodgings before she took up her court appointment are unknown. She perhaps stayed with her parents in the lodging appointed to her father in his role as a Spear. Alternatively, her grandmother, Isabel Stanley, still lived in London. John Blount's sister, Katherine, and her husband, Robert Smythe, also lived nearby in Thames Ditton, close by Hampton Court Palace. Smythe was later paid to lodge members of the royal court at his home when the king was resident at Hampton Court, with one entry in the king's privy purse expenses for February 1530 recording that he was paid two shillings apiece 'for the board of the kings iij Riding boys by the space of an fortnight after'.[28] Evidently, he did not provide the boys' meals, and these were obtained from a Thomas Ogull.[29] The boys, who were furnished with doublets of Bruges satin and fustian, were young gentlemen and expected a reasonable standard of lodging, which Bessie's uncle evidently provided.[30] Smythe would certainly have had room to take some of his brother-in-law's family if they had accompanied him to the capital.

Since the earliest age that a girl could take up an appointment as a maid of honour was twelve, it would seem likely that Bessie's parents began their campaign to place her in the queen's household from around 1510. Although no details of the attempts to secure a place for Bessie survive, some comparison can, perhaps, be made in relation to the appointment of Anne Basset, the daughter of Lady Lisle, as a maid of honour to Henry VIII's third wife, Jane Seymour, in 1537. Although Anne Basset was, effectively, a generation younger than Bessie, some conclusions can be drawn and it is clear that it could take considerable time for an appointment to be secured, even when a girl was well connected. Anne Basset's mother, Lady Lisle, began her campaign to secure an appointment for one of her daughters whilst Anne Boleyn was queen, and transferred her attentions to her successor, supplying both queens with presents in the hope that it would win her daughters favour. Lady

Lisle also enlisted her relatives and friends at court, finally receiving the good news in July 1537 that:

> My Lady Rutland and my Lady Sussex being waiters on her Grace, her Grace chanced, eating of the quails [given as a gift by Lady Lisle], to common of your ladyship and of your daughters; so that such communication was uttered by the said ij ladies that her Grace made grant to have one of your daughters; and the matter is thus concluded that your ladyship shall send them both over, for her Grace will first see them and know their manners, fashions and conditions, and take which of them shall like her Grace best.[31]

Apart from Katherine's possible brief service to Catherine of Aragon during her time at Ludlow, neither she nor John had direct connections with the queen and they must have relied on intermediaries, as Lady Lisle did, in order to bring Bessie to the queen's attention.

John Blount's position as one of the king's Spears was a prestigious one, but this alone would not have been enough to secure for Bessie one of the coveted places in the queen's household. A more prominent patron must have been involved in Bessie's appointment. One likely candidate is William Blount, Lord Mountjoy, who, although a very distant kinsman of the Blounts of Kinlet, had been a trustee of the marriage settlement of Bessie's parents and sought to advance the family where he could.[32] The Mountjoy branch of the Blount family had risen rapidly during the second half of the fifteenth century, with Walter Blount, the first Lord Mountjoy, marrying the widowed duchess of Buckingham in 1467, who was herself a descendant of Edward III.[33] Walter's grandson, William, was an exceptionally well-educated man and, with his humanist leanings, played host to the famous scholar Erasmus when he visited England during the reign of Henry VII. Mountjoy had connections in the queen's household. His wife, Agnes, was one of the Spanish ladies who had attended Catherine of Aragon when she first came to England. He was also well known to the king, for example making an offering on the king's behalf at the wedding of Sir Nicholas Carew in December 1514.[34] He was made master of the mint in 1509 and, significantly for Bessie, was appointed as the queen's chamberlain in May 1512,[35] only a few months before Bessie secured her own place. Although the familial relationship between the Kinlet and Mountjoy branches of the Blount family was distant by the early sixteenth century, it was the first John Blount of Kinlet who had founded his kinsmen's fortunes when he passed his mother's Mountjoy inheritance over to his paternal half-brother. This was a debt that the Mountjoy Blounts well remembered and Lord Mountjoy is a particularly likely candidate for Bessie's patron in 1512 and, also, perhaps, in recommending John Blount to be one of the king's Spears.

Mountjoy is not the only candidate for promoting Bessie, and a considerably nearer kinsman, Sir Edward Darell of Littlecote, had been appointed as vice-chamberlain to the queen by November 1517, one of the most important offices in her household, and clear evidence of influence in Catherine's household earlier in the reign. Dr Murphy, the biographer of Bessie's son, for example, suggested that 'such a prestigious position can only be the fruit of an already successful relationship with Catherine of Aragon'.[36] Darell was so respected that he received a visit from the king during his summer progress in 1520, further evidence of royal favour.[37] He had also been a knight of the body to the king. Darell was married to Bessie's great-aunt, Alice Croft, the sister of her grandmother, Anne Croft. Although Bessie's great-grandfather, Sir Richard Croft, had died on 29 July 1509, it is clear from the Blount family's continuing links to the Guildford and, later, the Dudley families (to whom they were related through Dame Eleanor Croft) that they retained strong links with the family. Darrell also served with Bessie's father as a Spear, something that may have brought John's promising eldest daughter to his attention.

In 1512 Bessie had no surviving brothers. Given that her parents had been married for some years, it must have seemed possible that they would not produce a male heir. As a result of this, Bessie and her sisters stood to inherit the family estates as co-heirs. Although the estates of a landowner who died leaving no sons were divided amongst his daughters, this division was not necessarily equal and Bessie, as the eldest, would have had a strong claim to the principal lands of the family, something that may have encouraged her better-connected kin to promote her to a prominent court position, in the hope of finding her a higher-status husband. It is not impossible that Lord Mountjoy and Sir Edward Darell worked together in securing a place for Bessie. Certainly, their duties with the queen often brought them together and, when the officers who were to attend the queen on the court's visit to France (known as the Field of the Cloth of Gold) in 1520 were listed, Mountjoy was named as the first of the barons, whilst Darell was the first of the knights.[38]

Two other connections of the Blounts were also prominent in their attendance at the Field of the Cloth of Gold: the half-brothers Sir Henry and Sir Edward Guildford.[39] The Guildfords, to whom Bessie was connected through her great-grandmother, Eleanor Croft (whose granddaughter by her first marriage, Eleanor West, married Sir Edward Guildford), were very prominent at court and in high favour. In the sixth year of his reign, for example, Henry made a very generous grant of clothing from the Great Wardrobe to Lady Guildford 'the younger' of:

First sixteen yards of green velvet for a gown price any yard fifteen shillings. Item seven yards of cloth of gold damask. Item half a

pound of Venice gold for the embroidering of the same gown.
Item five yards of green sarcenet for the same gown price any
yard five shillings. And also this we will and command you that
ye content and pay for the workmanship and making of all the
foresaid stuff.[40]

The recipient of this was John Blount's cousin, Eleanor West, Lady
Guildford. Sir Henry Guildford was also a trusted member of the
king's household, eventually becoming comptroller of the household.
His mother, Jane Vaux, Lady Guildford, was an established member of
the royal household, having served Henry's mother, Queen Elizabeth
of York, as one of her ladies.[41] She was the governess to Henry VIII's
sister, Mary Tudor. As master of the revels, Sir Henry Guildford
was responsible for choosing the participants in court masques and
entertainments and his patronage of Bessie can be seen in her early
involvement in court revels. Although it was Sir Edward, rather than
Sir Henry, who had the direct family connection to Bessie, the two half-
brothers were close, both appearing in court entertainments during the
early years of the reign. For example, in the first year of Henry's reign
Sir Edward Guildford was one of only eight men chosen to take part in
jousts before the court, declaring to the queen that they did so 'for the
love of Ladies'.[42] It is certainly not impossible that the two men helped
to secure a place for Bessie, especially given the continuing links that
the two families enjoyed, with the Blount family's connection to the
Dudley family (which came through the marriage of Edward Guildford's
daughter, Jane, to John Dudley, the future Duke of Northumberland)
demonstrating that the two families remained close. It may be that
Bessie's parents used a number of different connections to act as patrons
for Bessie in the hope of obtaining a coveted court placement for her.

There is some uncertainty over when Bessie first joined the court. In a
list of payments made by the king, preserved in the National Archives,
it is noted on 8 May 1513 that Elizabeth Blount received 100 shillings
as payment for the previous year's wages ending 'at the annunciation
of our Lady last past' (i.e. 25 March 1513). This payment was half
of the amount that would usually be paid to a maid of honour and
was an irregular payment, not included with those of the other maids
and members of Catherine's household. Bessie's position had become
formalised by Michaelmas (29 September) 1513 when Bessie was
included in a list of 'years wages due at Michaelmas' for the maids
of Catherine of Aragon's household, receiving the same sum of 200
shillings as six other girls.[43] Wages in the royal households tended to
be paid in arrears, with the second payment therefore suggesting that
Bessie came to court by at least 29 September 1512. The first payment
is something of an anomaly. It has been suggested that it means that
Bessie came to court on 25 March 1512, but that she received only

a half salary as she did not, at that stage, have a post in the queen's household.[44] However, given that 100 shillings was half of the figure for a year's wages for a maid of honour, it would appear more likely that it refers only to a period of six months, rather than an entire year.

Although the September 1513 payment was for a full year's wages, in general the maids were paid half yearly in arrears in March and September, receiving 100 shillings each. This was the case for Bessie and her fellow maids in March 1514 and September 1514, for example.[45] The March 1513 payment to Bessie, although not made at exactly the same time as the other maids, is therefore not that anomalous and should be seen as Bessie's half year's salary as a full maid of honour, indicating that she arrived at court in September 1512. Given that this was the first time that Bessie became entitled to any payment, it is entirely possible that she could have been initially overlooked and only received her wages after a reminder. The September 1513 payment of a whole year's wages still requires an explanation but even this would only suggest an arrival date of September 1512, not March 1512. It seems very implausible that Bessie's payment in March 1513 related to the period between March and September 1512 as Bessie, as a new maid, would have relied on her salary to support herself. Perhaps the maids received a bonus payment in September 1513 or, more likely, the figure entered was a mistake and should, in fact, have referred to half-year wages at 100 shillings rather than full-year wages at 200. In any event, the evidence of Bessie's payments makes it almost certain that she arrived at court in September 1512 as a full maid of honour to Catherine of Aragon.

In September 1512 Bessie was around fourteen years old – a similar age to that of her father when she was born. Although young, she would not have been considered a child by her contemporaries. It was common for children of both sexes from the gentry or nobility to be boarded out with a more prestigious family and the royal household was, of course, the most prestigious household of all. This practice caused particular comment on the continent, with one foreign visitor recording, in around 1500, that Englishmen did not know how to love:

> This want of affection in the English is strongly manifested towards their children; for after having kept them at home till they arrive at the age of 7 or 9 years at the utmost, they put them out, both males and females, to hard service in the houses of other people, binding them generally for another 7 or 9 years. And these are called apprentices, and during that time they perform all the most menial offices; and few are born who are exempted from this fate, for every one, however rich he may be, sends away his children into the houses of others, whilst he, in return, receives those of strangers into his own.[46]

The reason behind this was, the visitor was told, in order to ensure that 'their children might learn better manners'. Whilst Bessie was considerably older than seven or nine in 1512, it is likely that this was, in part, the reason behind her family seeking the position. The main reason, however, was for her to have better access to a pool of potential husbands.

It would have been expected that Bessie would arrive at court well dressed, with a selection of new clothes suitable for court life. When Anne Basset came to court in 1537, for example, she immediately required a number of new items, including a new kirtle, a velvet bonnet and frontlet (to cover her hair).[47] To Anne's mother's dismay, the queen then ordered that the remaining clothes that Anne had brought to court would not do, requiring that 'she must have provided a bonnet or ij, with frontlets and an edge of pearl, and a gown of black satin, and another of velvet, and this must be done before the Queen's grace's churching. And further, she must have cloth for smocks and sleeves, for there is fault founden that their smocks are too coarse; and also they must have chests.'[48] Further gowns were required to ensure that Anne met the queen's exacting standards. The queen's household was, in this respect, similar to that of any other great lady of the period where 'clothing indicated status and, naturally, shabby or unfashionable attendants reflected badly on the lady of the house'.[49] It may, perhaps, reflect something of the expense of keeping his daughter at court that caused John Blount to seek nearly a whole year's advance of his wages as a Spear in May 1513.[50] Whilst it was not unheard of for Spears to receive a year's wages in advance, it was rare.[51] This payment suggests that Bessie had already made an impression on the king and was reasonably generous: normally, the Spears received their wages monthly in arrears.[52] Given the cost of court dress, and the requirement that everyone at court arrive sufficiently well attired, it is perhaps no surprise that the king took a personal interest in the business of dress. In a warrant dating to 20 November 1514, for example, signed personally by the king, Henry ordered that four 'chamberers with our dearest wife the Queen' receive gifts of russet damask for gowns, to be furred 'with good mink'.[53] That Elizabeth, Lady Boleyn, the daughter of the Duke of Norfolk and the wife of the prominent courtier Sir Thomas Boleyn, received one of these gowns, is evidence that such gifts of clothing were welcomed by even the most prominent members of the court given the expense of court dress. Two years earlier Margaret Pennington, a chamberer to the queen, had also received a gown of russet satin edged with fur, as well as a kirtle of yellow satin bordered with crimson velvet.[54] She was evidently in high favour and had received the gift of a damask gown edged with fur the previous year, along with three of her colleagues in the queen's household.[55] Henry personally authorised the materials to be delivered from his Great Wardrobe to members of the court, demonstrating the importance of dress to his prestige. For example, he signed warrants to deliver seven yards of broad cloth for a gown and coat, in addition to 'as much lining of yellow cotton as shall suffice for the same gown and coat' to one of the grooms of his privy chamber in August 1515.[56] Only the previous month he made a gift of ten yards of fine black cloth for clothing for another gentleman of his chamber.[57] That same month Henry ordered enough green cloth as was necessary to make coats for 132 of his guards.[58] In earlier years Henry had provided black velvet and damask for his chaplain's coats, to be lined with sarcenet and for black satin to be made into doublets.[59]

Fashions for women changed little during the mid-Tudor period.[60] Fashionable women wore tight-fitting clothes on their upper body and arms, often with a low square neckline. A woman of Bessie's status would have worn an undergarment of bleached white linen, designed to be washable and to prevent the non-washable outer clothes from becoming soiled. Over her shift, Bessie would have worn a pair of bodies, which flattened her stomach and chest and pushed up her breasts. Over these, a gown and a kirtle were worn. The skirt would be full and, until at least 1530, it is probable that Bessie's clothes had a train. Sleeves were sometimes attached to the gown and sometimes separate, in which case they were laced or pinned to the dress. In addition to this, a pair of trailing over-sleeves might be worn. Finally, a hood or cap would complete Bessie's clothing. When she first arrived at court, as her portrait on the side of her parents' tomb shows, this would have been an English gable hood, which kept her hair modestly hidden. Bessie's dress in this image shows her wearing a fashionable square-necked gown, with large over-sleeves. She would have worn such dresses daily during her time at court. Her court dress would have been on a more lavish scale than the clothes that she wore at home. Anne Basset, for example, on being sworn as one of the queen's maids, obtained a new gown of Rysell worsted, which was a material with a satiny surface, turned up with black velvet. Her sister, who had arrived at court at the same time but had failed to find an appointment in the queen's household, had to make do with her old gowns being recycled as kirtles and had to have her black satin gown repaired, rather than receiving the extensive new wardrobe that her sister did.[61]

Bessie joined an established and well-organised household in September 1512 and immediately found herself as just one of a number of young women at court, with her arrival causing no contemporary mention. In the payments for the Michaelmas wages in 1513, for example, Bessie was just one of seven girls named Elizabeth on the list of women in the household. She received the same sum as six other girls. The girls were expected to be 'sober, sad, wise and discreet and lowly above all things'.[62] They were governed by the mother of the maids, who, at the time of Bessie's arrival, was a Mrs Stoner. She played something of the role of a boarding school matron, taking the young maids under her control on their arrival at court.

For a young girl away from familiar surroundings for the first time, the court could be a bewildering place. The royal court was a highly organised and vast establishment. Ordinances for the household, made at Eltham Palace in 1526, give some idea of the wide range of offices and roles that were filled.[63] The head offices of the household were those of Lord Steward, the Treasurer, and the Comptroller. Various areas of household life were then divided into different departments – for example, the counting house, bake house, pantry, cellar, buttery, clerks of the spicery, ewery, confectionery, clerks of the kitchen, master cooks and the larder. Each of these departments contained their own complement of staff, with rules and regulations in relation to that office. For example, for the master cooks, the ordinances declared that:

> It is ordained that every of the master cooks give their daily attendance in serving the king, the queen, and his household, and that their meats be good and sweet, and to see the same well dressed; and to cause the cooks under them to see all such victuals as shall come to their hands be well and seasonably dressed, and the same to serve out at the dressers by the oversight of the said clerk of the kitchen, without embezzling or taking away any part of the same; according to the old custom of the king's house.[64]

The court was crammed with officers, servants and other visitors and hygiene was a major issue, with one of the Eltham Ordinances declaring that scullions should henceforth refrain from working naked in the kitchens; this would avoid infections and ensure that the food they prepared was cleaner. The galleries and courts at the palace in which the king was staying were also to be cleaned twice a day due to the 'filth and uncleanness'. Dogs were banned for similar reasons of hygiene, although lapdogs for the ladies were excepted from the prohibition. Given that floors were covered with rushes, with a new layer put down after every eight or ten days, it is easy to see how buildings could quickly become unsanitary.[65] Particular care was taken in relation to the appointments made for the officers of the king's and queen's households, with the chief officers of those households being given a commission to 'make view, search, and report, of the sufficiency, ability, demeanour, and qualities, of all such persons as be officers, minsters, and servants in the said household and chambers'.[66] As a maid of honour, Bessie's day would have revolved around service to the queen. The role of the queen's ladies, like that of the gentlemen of the king's privy chamber, was to ensure the quiet, rest and comfort of their mistress, and the preservation of her health.[67] The king rose at 7 a.m., or earlier, and would be immediately dressed by his attendants. Days followed a similar pattern in the queen's household, and the comment in the Eltham Ordinances that 'the king's pleasure is, that the said six gentlemen shall have a vigilant and reverent respect and eye to his Grace, so that by his look or countenance, they may know what lacketh, or is his pleasure to be had or done'[68] would also have held true for the queen. Bessie's role, like that of the other maids, was to anticipate the needs of the queen and to ensure that she was kept comfortable and content. Such close proximity to the sovereign's wife could be beneficial to the maid in question and real friendships could develop between the queen and her ladies. Henry's mother, Elizabeth of York, for example, had paid for the board of one of her maids, Anne Say, when she became ill at Woodstock and was forced to leave the court for eight weeks.[69]

By the time of Catherine of Aragon, there were four grades of lady in waiting at court.[70] These were the great ladies, the ladies of the privy chamber, maids of honour and the chamberers. Bessie, as a young unmarried girl from a gentry family, occupied the third tier: that of maid of honour. She was far removed in rank from the queen's great ladies, which included ladies from the highest families in the land, such as Margaret Pole, Countess of Salisbury, who was a niece of Edward IV, and Elizabeth and Anne Stafford, sisters of the princely Duke of Buckingham. The Countesses of Oxford, Surrey and Derby were also prominent in the queen's household. These ladies had their own households and extensive estates to run and, in spite of their court appointments, were rarely in attendance on the queen, providing a more ceremonial role. It was, instead, the second tier of ladies, the ladies of the privy chamber, who served as the queen's main companions and these were usually drawn from the wives of barons. The maids of honour, of which Bessie was one, were unmarried girls, again from good families and Bessie, as a member of a minor gentry family, was lucky to find herself placed in an office that was often reserved for the daughters of the nobility. The duties of the maids and ladies have been described as very menial and the ladies would often actually serve the queen, for example holding a basin to allow her to wash before eating. Such tasks were sought after and provided close proximity to the queen. Bessie, who was given free board and expected to keep her own servant, as well as receiving licence along with the other ladies to keep a spaniel if she so desired, [71] would have considered it an honour to be approached by the queen to carry out a task for her.

In addition to her duties to the queen, Bessie, along with the other maids, was expected to continue her education whilst in the queen's household, something that included both domestic crafts and music.[72] It is not impossible, given the evidence of her later acquaintance with him, that Bessie received some French tuition from John Palsgrave, the schoolmaster for the king's sister, Mary Tudor, a girl of a similar age to Bessie.[73] Religious observance in the household of the pious Catherine of Aragon was also important. Meals, even on ordinary days, could take up a great deal of time and were particularly elaborate. The Eltham Ordinances confirm that, in the royal household, dinner was served at 10 a.m. or earlier, with supper at 4 p.m. Different fare was served to individuals depending on their rank, with the king and queen enjoying a daily menu that could include bread, beer, ale, wine, pottage, beef, stew, venison, mutton, carps, veal, swan, goose, storks, capons, custard and fritters, amongst other fare.[74] Surviving menus for the queen's lord chamberlain, her ladies and gentlewomen, who all ate together, are only slightly less elaborate.[75] On Sundays, Mondays, Tuesdays, Wednesdays and Thursdays, for example, Bessie and her colleagues could expect a dinner that included ale, wine, beef, mutton, veal, capons, hens, pig, goose, lamb and pigeons. For supper there was ale and wine again, as well as sliced beef, boiled mutton, capons, hens, lamb and pigeons. Fridays added some variety when, for religious reasons, fish was served in place of meat. For dinner, there would be herring, ling, salted salmon, salted eels, whiting, gurnet, plaice, smelts and flounders, all washed down once again with wine or ale.

These menus were just for ordinary days; banquets could be considerably more elaborate, playing an important part in court ceremonial. A banquet in 1504, for example, to celebrate the appointment of William Warham as Archbishop of Canterbury, had included a first course of fourteen dishes (including delicacies like eels, pike, salmon and carp).[76] In addition to this, the second course had sixteen dishes, equally fine. It was almost certainly during a court entertainment that Bessie first came to the attention of the king, not long after she first joined the court. Alice Perrers, the infamous mistress of Edward III, had started a pattern of English kings drawing their mistresses from their wives' attendants[77] and, with her beauty and accomplishments, Bessie soon found herself as the object of desire of the king of England himself.

# 6

# COURT LIFE

Bessie entered a glittering world when she arrived at court in September 1512 at the age of around fourteen. With her beauty and accomplishments, along with the assistance of her kinsman by marriage, the master of the revels Sir Henry Guildford, it was not long before she made an impact on the court, attracting the attention of some of the highest-ranking gentlemen there, including the king himself.

One of the main reasons behind John and Katherine Blount's decision to place Bessie at court would have been to secure a prestigious husband for her. Bessie's prospects dipped significantly in 1513 with the birth of her brother, George, and any chance that she had of inheriting a share of her family's estates was entirely extinguished over the next few years with the births of two further brothers: William and Henry. In spite of this, Bessie was both beautiful and accomplished. When Henry VIII's second wife, Anne Boleyn, first came to the English court, she was able to use her wit and appearance to ensnare the heart of Henry Percy, the heir to the Earl of Northumberland, in spite of the fact that the young gentleman was considerably above her socially.[1] It is very likely that, if Anne and Percy had been able to keep their secret for a few more months, Anne Boleyn would have been remembered as a countess of Northumberland rather than queen of England. It was only the intervention of Cardinal Wolsey and Percy's father which kept the match from going ahead. Given that, to contemporaries at least, Bessie was more beautiful than Anne, it must have seemed entirely possible that she would be able to charm a higher-status husband than she would otherwise hope to obtain.

No firm evidence survives of any suitors for Bessie before the king. The antiquary Hubert Burke, in his *Historical Portraits of the Tudor Dynasty*, wrote that, in relation to Bessie, 'Henry had recourse to the vilest of stratagems to decoy this gifted and beautiful woman. Her knightly suitor, Anthony Penrose, suddenly disappeared, and was never heard of more.'[2] Burke unfortunately does not give any source for this and Dr Murphy, the biographer of Bessie's eldest son, was forced to dismiss this, finding no evidence for any such person. Given the very specific description of Bessie's suitor (i.e. his name and that he was of a knightly rank), it would seem odd that Burke would actually falsify this person, although it is clear that the implication that Henry ordered Penrose's 'disappearance' is intended to show the king in an unfavourable light. It does seem possible that Burke may have had access to a document that hinted at a marriage between Bessie and an Anthony Penrose, or a man of a similar name, which is unfortunately now lost.

Penrose is a Cornish name. The manor of Penrose in that county was held by a family of the same name from the time of the Norman Conquest until 1744.[3] Given that Cornwall was very far removed from Kinlet and other Blount centres of interest, it would seem unlikely that Bessie was destined to spend her life at Penrose, a manor that was prettily situated beside a small creek in a wooded valley. In a visitation made to Cornwall in 1620, it was recorded that a Richard Penrose of Penrose died in the thirty-first year of Henry VIII's reign (1540–41), leaving a son aged over twenty-one.[4] This would imply that Richard would have been around the same age as Bessie or, perhaps, a little older. No siblings are given for Richard in the visitation but it is certainly not impossible that the family included a now entirely forgotten Anthony. Richard Penrose also served as sheriff of Cornwall in 1526,[5] suggesting a family of a similar rank to Bessie's own. Finally, a connection between Bessie and the Penrose family can be identified. In December 1525, her kinsmen William Blount, Lord Mountjoy, and Sir Edward Darrell, alongside Sir Robert Dymock (who was a kinsman of her then husband, Gilbert Tailboys) agreed to act as three of the seventeen trustees named in a marriage settlement between John Arundel, son and heir of Sir John Arundel, and his bride, Elizabeth, daughter of Gerard Danet.[6] Interestingly, one of the other trustees was Richard Penrose. This was some years after any marriage could have been proposed between Bessie and a member of the Cornish Penrose family but it does suggest that such a match was not entirely impossible.

An alternative to the Cornish Penrose family is in the Welsh place name Penrhos, which is similar enough to Penrose to be confused with it. There are a number of places with the name both in Wales and on the Welsh borders, for example Penrhos in Anglesey or Penrhos near Abergavenny, which was connected to the earldom of Pembroke.[7] Perhaps the most likely place of origin for Bessie's apparent suitor is this Penrhos in Pembrokeshire, which was very close to the important Raglan Castle, where Henry VII spent much of his youth. The lords of the manor of Penrhos in Bessie's time were the Williams family, a family that, like the Blounts, numbered both Welsh and English gentry amongst its ancestors.[8] Sir Roger Williams of Penrhos, who was born in around 1540, was a noted soldier during the reign of Elizabeth I. His father, Thomas, would probably have been somewhat younger than Bessie. Unfortunately, once again, there is no Anthony listed as a member of the Williams family. Any attempt to identify Bessie's alleged suitor must be speculation only. However, what is clear from a consideration of both the Penrose family of Cornwall and the Williams family of Penrhos is that they are the most likely candidates for the families to have produced 'Anthony Penrose'. Both were gentry families of equivalent status to the Blounts and with significant local interests and some court connections. If any conclusion can be drawn from Burke's vague allusion to 'Anthony Penrose', it is that Bessie's family aspired to, and intended, a marriage for her to a family very much like her own, and that they expected her to marry a knight, or an esquire, with a good local power base but of little national significance.

That Bessie was probably originally intended for marriage to a local figure is also suggested by the marriage made by her sister, Anne, to Richard Lacon, esquire, of Willey. The Lacons were an ancient family, with an impressive brass surviving in the church at Harley in Shropshire depicting a member of the family and his wife in the second half of the fifteenth century.[9] The brass, which is on a large scale and depicts the couple's eight sons and five daughters below, as well as the family's arms, demonstrates the reasonable level of wealth that the family had acquired. In addition to this, there was space, below each of the principal figures, to include Latin verses on a fashionable theme of the recognition of the realities of death, which have been translated as:

Rotting and wasting away is my flesh like dung in the furrow.
That fliest upon heaven's bright way may God's Breath impraise on the morrow;
Set it at His right hand, and from all pollution deliver,
Where is the glory attained, and the tear is banished forever.

Who so thou art that passeth this part, stay and read with contrition:
I am what thou shalt be and I once was like thee: bid for me thy petition.
Though my life by death's hand be slain, yet my soul may Christ quicken again:
Though my dust in the dust may lie, let my spirit be waited on high.[10]

This was a familiar theme and one which Rowland Lacon, Bessie's own nephew and a descendant of the couple depicted on the brass, would return to when he commissioned a tomb for his uncle, George Blount, at Kinlet, depicting a rotting cadaver beneath the effigies of his uncle and his family. The Lacon family's principal seat was at Willey in Shropshire. However, in the mid-fifteenth century they had also acquired Harley, only a few miles from Kinlet, upon the marriage of the heiress Elizabeth de Peshall to Sir Richard Lacon of Willey.[11] This was a lucky acquisition by Sir Richard and, after his wife's death, he was able to take control of the manor even before the death of his stepson, John Grendon, who was described as 'an idiot', and the property passed into his stepfather's somewhat self-interested custody.[12] After Sir Richard Lacon's death, the manor passed through the Lacon family to Anne Blount's husband. The first Sir Richard Lacon of Willey (the husband of Elizabeth de Peshall) served as sheriff of Shropshire in 1415 and all six of his descendants who held the manor also served in the same office.[13]

Richard Lacon was a prosperous local landowner, but he had no reputation outside of Shropshire. The fact that Bessie's sister, when widowed, entered into a court case regarding 'a cup of byrrall set in silver' and other possessions of her husband's, such as a mirror, suggests that these possessions had been well regarded by her husband and were amongst the most valuable that he possessed.[14] During her second marriage, to a husband somewhat below Richard Lacon in rank, Anne also possessed a silver plate which she lent to the dignitaries of Much Wenlock when they received a visit from the Bishop of Worcester, something that formed the centrepiece of the display made by the town for the illustrious visitor.[15] Although the cup and plate were evidently of reasonable value, they pale into insignificance when compared with the plate that Bessie is known to have owned during her own marriage to Gilbert Tailboys. There is no evidence that Richard Lacon was ever intended as her husband but, given that Bessie was older than Anne, it is not impossible that this was the case. Certainly, from as early as 1513 John Blount had his eye upon Richard Lacon, appointing him as his petty captain in the French wars.[16] Anne was, in 1513, still very young, being at most around nine years old and possibly a year or so younger. In all probability, marriage negotiations had already begun between the Lacon and Blount families in 1513. If this is the case, Bessie, who was closer to Richard Lacon in age, would have been their original subject. Even if she was not originally intended for Richard Lacon, a similar husband could have been expected to be found for her.

As it turned out, Bessie was not, at least at first, destined for marriage. On her arrival at court she, like everyone else, found themselves drawn to the figure at the centre of it. Henry VIII, who had acceded to the throne in 1509 shortly before he turned eighteen, was a true Renaissance Prince. Even as a child, he had shown great promise. Bessie's kinsman Lord Mountjoy was particularly learned and had an interest in humanism. In 1499 he invited his friend, the scholar Erasmus to England. During his visit, Erasmus went with his fellow scholar Thomas More to visit the younger children of Henry VII, recording that on his arrival he found the royal family assembled as a group. 'In the midst stood Prince Henry, then nine years old, and having already something of royalty in his demeanour, in which there was a certain dignity combined with singular courtesy.'[17] The young Henry received a present of some writing from More, embarrassing Erasmus, who had brought nothing. He then showed his precocity by sending a message to his visitor at dinner to challenge something from his pen. A few years later, as heir to the throne, Henry showed even more promise, with the Spanish ambassador recording in 1504:

> It is quite wonderful how much the king likes the Prince of Wales. He has good reason to do so, for the Prince deserves all love. But it is not only from love that the king takes the Prince with him; he wishes to improve him. Certainly there could be no better school in the world than the society of such a father as Henry VII.[18]

By 1507 Henry was corresponding with Erasmus himself.[19] The scholar continued to take an active interest in him, and Lord Mountjoy wrote to Erasmus with his hopes for the future on Henry VIII's accession:

> I have no fear, my Erasmus, but when you heard that our Prince, now Henry the Eighth, whom we may call our Octavius, had succeeded to his father's throne, all your melancholy left you at once. For what may you not promise yourself from a Prince, with whose extraordinary and almost divine character you are well acquainted, and to whom you are not only known but intimate, having received from him (as few others have) a letter traced with his own fingers? But when you know what a hero he now shows himself, how wisely he behaves, what a lover he is of justice and goodness, what affection he bears to the learned, I will venture to swear that you will need no wings to make you fly to behold this new and auspicious star.[20]

Henry's reign was hailed as a new era for England.

A number of descriptions of Henry have survived, including the extremely useful pen-portraits created by Sebastian Giustinian, the Venetian ambassador to England, and his colleagues. Giustinian, a very experienced diplomat who was then aged around fifty, was resident in England during Bessie's time at court and recorded the king as he would have appeared during his relationship with her. Giustinian arrived in England in April 1515 and made his way to Richmond, where the king was staying. He was given his first audience with the king on St George's Day, 26 April.[21] Giustinian and his colleagues found the whole court assembled for the St George's Day festivities, a date that was particularly important for the prestigious Order of the Garter. After being escorted into the great hall by a large number of lords, prelates and knights, he found the king standing near a fine gilt chair, under a canopy, with the floor covered in a golden carpet. Henry was dressed splendidly in his garter robes and received his guests regally before going to mass. Giustinian's secretary Nicolo Sagudino was certainly impressed, writing a few days later of the king's guard which consisted 'of three hundred English, all very handsome men, and in excellent array, with their halberds, and, by my faith, I never saw finer fellows'.[22] Henry had dressed to impress and he 'wore a very costly doublet, over which was a mantle of violet-coloured velvet, with an extremely long train, lined with white satin, on his head was a richly jewelled cap of crimson velvet, of immense value, and round his neck he wore a collar, studded with many precious stones, of which I never saw the like'.[23] At dinner, the king's gold plate and silver was displayed for the visitors to see, causing wonder. Afterwards, the king again summoned the ambassadors and addressed them in a mixture of French, Latin and Italian, showing himself to his visitors to be 'affable'. A few days later, Giustinian was invited to see the king joust, at which he excelled. Another Venetian, at the same meeting, noted that:

> His Majesty is the handsomest potentate I ever set eyes on; above the usual height, with an extremely fine calf to his leg, his complexion very fair and bright, with auburn hair combed straight and short, in the French fashion, and a round face so very beautiful, that it would become a pretty woman, his throat being rather long and thick.[24]

Henry was well aware of his good looks and not above boasting about them, as the Venetian ambassador extraordinary, Piero Pasqualigo, discovered:

> His Majesty came into our arbour, and, addressing me in French, said: 'Talk with me awhile! The king of France, is he as tall as I am?' I told him there was but little difference. He continued, 'Is he as stout?' I said he was not; and then he inquired, 'What sort of leg has he?' I replied, 'Spare'. Whereupon he opened the front of his doublet, and placing his hand on his thigh, said, 'Look here! and I have also a good calf to my leg.'[25]

In his youth, Henry was reputed to be one of the handsomest men in Europe. Bessie and the other maids must have delighted in any attention that he gave them. When she first met him, Henry was clean-shaven, although later on in their relationship, on hearing that the king of France wore a beard, he allowed his own to grow, with his natural reddish colour ensuring that 'he has now got a beard which looks like gold'.[26] The king was always richly dressed, often wearing bright colours in rich fabrics.[27] He particularly delighted in exotic foreign fashions, with his wardrobe including clothes in French, Italian, Spanish and Turkish styles. Henry also owned a considerable number of shoes, purchasing so many comfortable pairs with velvet uppers that he must have worn them out at a rate of approximately one pair a week.[28] On quiet days at court, he was known to wear slippers. The king was at the centre of fashion at court, in spite of the fact that his second wife, Anne Boleyn, and her brother were later charged with having laughed at his clothes.[29] When, in 1527, the king hurt his foot whilst playing tennis and was forced to wear slippers to the court entertainments that evening, many of the other gentlemen copied him.[30] Bessie had ample opportunity to meet the splendid king and, as well as less formal visits, he is known to have visited the queen's chamber to hear the offices of vespers and compline every morning.[31]

Henry VIII was not an ogre or a monster, as often depicted. He could be very charming and, in his youth at least, he was jovial and good humoured more often than not. In the 1970s, the historian Professor G.R. Elton noted two specific examples to demonstrate that the king was less autocratic than commonly portrayed and that his position was, to some extent, open to challenge by those around him. The first incident Elton quoted was in relation to Sir George Throckmorton, who challenged the king's marriage to Anne Boleyn in public and to the king's face, without any censure. The second indication that Elton found to suggest that Henry was not necessarily 'the Henry VIII of our imaginings' was in relation to a visit to court in April 1536 by the imperial ambassador, Eustace Chapuys.[32] Chapuys had been negotiating with the king's then chief minister, Thomas Cromwell, for some time to secure an Anglo-Imperial alliance. On his arrival, he found the king unfavourable to the proposals. Henry then withdrew a little way with Cromwell and another member of his council. Chapuys was too far away to hear, but could see what was going on. He apparently witnessed a furious quarrel between the king and his chief minister. Cromwell then moved away, complaining that he was thirsty and went to sit out of Henry's sight. Soon after, Henry himself went to look for Cromwell. Elton mused 'should we really have expected that Cromwell would so publicly argue with the king, would so unceremoniously leave the royal presence (making his fury plain to all), would sit down for a drink (even if out of sight), and that Henry's only reaction would be to come looking for his minster?'[33] Elton felt that this demonstrated that Henry was far more relaxed and bewildered in his public behaviour than is commonly recognised. These observations are interesting for what they demonstrate of Henry's character, although it should be pointed out that Cromwell was, eventually, executed on the king's orders and Throckmorton badly frightened with an enforced stay in the Tower (although for an offence unrelated to his challenge of the king's marriage). However, certainly, it must be remembered that the king was a man and, during Bessie's time at court, a young one. He had friends and loves and was a popular and generous man, at least until ill health and other circumstances took their toll on his character in later life.

As well as his good looks and charm, the king was also a more than proficient musician, with Giustinian commenting that he 'plays almost on every instrument, sings and composes fairly'.[34] He was reputed to practice his music daily.[35] He certainly owned a wide array of musical instruments. In one inventory, it was recorded that the king owned six pairs of double regalls, as well as single regalls, virginals, and other 'instruments of sundry kinds'.[36] These included a pair of clavichords containing gilt leather, lutes, shalmes and even 'a bagpipe'. In addition to this, the king owned cases, allowing the instruments to be transported safely, and 'sundry books and scrolls of songs and ballads'. Henry was a composer of some repute. One composition by him, the song 'Pastance with Good Company' sums up the mood of the early years of Henry's court:

Pastance with good company
I love and shall until I die
Grudge who will, but none may deny,
So God be pleased this life will I
      For my pastance,
      Hunt, sing, and dance,
      My heart is set,
      All goodly sport
      To my comfort
      Who shall me let?

Youth will needs have dalliance,
Of good or ill some pastance;
Company me thinketh best
All thought and fancies to digest.
      For idleness
      Is chief mistress
      Of vices all;
      Then who can say
      But pass the day
      Is best of all?

Company with honesty
Is virtue – and vice to flee;
Company is good or ill
But every man hath his free will.
      The best I sue,
      The worst eschew;
      My mind shall be
      Virtue to use;
      Vice to refuse
      I shall use me.[37]

The young king was very far removed from the tyrant he would become in his later years and Bessie, like everyone else in his cultured court, was in thrall to the personality at its centre.

Music was highly regarded at court and most leading members of the royal family and the nobility employed their own troupes of minstrels.[38]

Henry's own accounts show numerous payments for musicians, including, in May 1511, payment for two women who came especially from Flanders to dance and play music before the king.[39] Ladies were expected to be accomplished musicians, with Princess Mary known to have received instruction on the virginals and the lute.[40] Bessie's early biographer, Childe-Pemberton, claimed that she was likely to have had lessons on the virginals whilst she was at court.[41] There is no actual evidence for this, but some music tuition, both before she went to court and after she arrived, is likely. She was also apparently proficient on the clavichord and lute and was an excellent singer, with one suggestion being that she accompanied Henry and Master Dionysius Memo, a Venetian organist whom Henry had appointed as his chaplain due to his excellent musical ability.[42] Memo was a particular favourite of the king's, with the entire court assembling to listen to his instrumental music in a recital that lasted four hours in July 1517 'to the so great admiration of all the audience, and with such marks of delight from his Majesty aforesaid, as to defy exaggeration'.[43] Memo arrived at court in September 1516,[44] which suggests that if Bessie did indeed accompany him, it would have been during her time as the king's mistress. There is no doubt that Bessie was, indeed, particularly musically gifted, with her contemporary Edward Hall, who had court connections, recording that she was so skilled in singing that it was one of the accomplishments that helped her win the king's heart.

One recent writer has claimed that Bessie wrote a song whilst at court.[45] This song was discovered in a manuscript volume of songs, ballads and instrumental music which is known to have belonged to Henry VIII.[46] The song in question is addressed to Henry by an unknown lady. It is clear that there was some romantic involvement between the two as the lady refers to Henry tilting at the ring for her sake, along with other suggestions of a relationship between the two. Given that it has been suggested that Bessie was the composer of the song, it is worth quoting it in full:

> Whilst life or breath is in my breast
> My sovereign lord I shall love best.
> My sovereign lord, for my poor sake,
> Six courses at the ring did make,
> Of which four times he did it take:
> Wherefore my heart I him bequest,
> And, of all other, for to love best
>     My sovereign lord.
>
> My sovereign lord of puissance pure
> As the chieftain of a warrior,
> With spear & sword at the barrier –
> As hardy with the hardiest

He proveth himself, that I say, best
    My sovereign lord.

My Sovereign lord, in every thing
Above all other – as a king –
In that he doth no comparing:
But, of a truth, he worthiest is
To have the praise of all the best,
    My sovereign lord.

My sovereign lord when that I meet
His cheerful countenance doth replete
My heart with joy; that I behete,
Next God, but he: and ever pressed
With heart & body to love best
    My sovereign lord.

So many virtues, given of grace,
There is none one live that hace –
Behold his favour and his face,
His personage most godliest!
A vengeance on them that loveth not best
    My sovereign lord.

The sovereign lord that is of all
My sovereign lord save, principal!
He hath my heart & ever shall.
Of God I ask – for him request –
Of all good fortunes to send him best
    My sovereign lord.[47]

The song is contained within a book prepared within the first three or four years of his reign, making it just possible for Bessie, who arrived in the third year of Henry's reign, to have been its composer. Certainly, one song, which references 'Katherine' and an 'infant prince', must have been composed in the early months of 1511 during the brief life of Catherine of Aragon and Henry VIII's eldest son. The song itself is anonymous, bearing only the name 'W. Cornyshe', who, as a gentleman, certainly did not compose the lyrics. William Cornish, who was a priest, was also a noted composer and a gentleman of the chapel of Henry VII and Henry VIII.[48] He was appointed as the master of the king's chapel in the sixteenth year of Henry's reign (1524–25), apparently dying shortly afterwards. He had a somewhat turbulent career, being first noticed by Henry VII in 1493 when he received a payment by the king for a 'prophecy'. He composed a Christmas carol nine years later which further drew Henry VII's attention. In 1504, for some unrecorded offence, the musician was imprisoned in the Fleet prison, and it was not until December 1508 that he was restored to favour, with a position in the king's chapel. Henry VIII inherited his services on his accession. It appears that Cornish was employed by the song's writer to set her words to music. It is not impossible by any means that the song was written by Bessie. It is clear from the lyrics that the lady had an intimate and affectionate relationship with the king which, of course, Bessie had. However, the only actual evidence to identify the lady in question relates to the fact that the king tilted at the ring for her, winning four out of the six times. Sadly, this provides no assistance in the identification due to both the poor survival of jousting scores and the regularity with which the king tilted at the ring during the early years of his reign. The only other clue relates to William Cornish. Cornish is known to have been a friend of the poet John Skelton and set a number of his compositions to music.[49] John Skelton was associated with the Howard family, writing one of his most famous poems, the *Garland of Laurel*, about the ladies in the household of Elizabeth Tylney, Countess of Surrey.[50] Elizabeth Tylney's first marriage had produced a daughter, Margaret Bourchier, who was the mother of Sir Francis Bryan and his sister, Elizabeth Carew, who is described in more detail later. It is therefore arguable that Elizabeth Carew, who appears to have won the king's affections before Bessie, may be a more plausible candidate for the song's author. A less likely alternative, given the early date of the manuscript, would be Mary Boleyn, who was also the granddaughter of Elizabeth Tylney. This is only speculation. It is possible that Bessie was the song's author, but this is the most that can be said about it. The song does, at least, demonstrate something of the way in which the king's affairs developed, with him seeking to demonstrate his prowess in the tiltyard as a means of showing his adoration.

Bessie's mistress, Catherine of Aragon, had been married to the king for only three years at the time that Bessie came to court. Catherine was the daughter of Isabella, Queen of Castile, and Ferdinand, King of Aragon, the monarchs who united Spain.[51] Catherine, who was born in December 1485, had been betrothed to Henry's elder brother, Prince Arthur, in 1489. The marriage between Catherine and Arthur was a very prestigious one for the newly established Tudor dynasty, with one of Catherine's recent biographers commenting that her 'presence in England said that the Tudors were more than good enough for the powerful monarchs of Spain'.[52] At the time of their marriage Henry and Catherine were in love, with Henry writing in a song composed in the early years of his reign that 'I love true where I did marry'.[53] Catherine wrote to her father soon after the marriage, expressing her love for her husband (albeit coached in the language of daughterly duty): 'as to the king, my lord, amongst the reasons that oblige me to love him much more than myself, the one most strong, although he is my husband, is his being so true son of your Highness'.[54] In 1513, whilst Bessie was at court, Henry paid Catherine the compliment of appointing her as regent of England when he went to fight in France. Catherine had, in any event, already played something of an honorary role in Henry's French wars, with a ship named the *Katherine Pomegranate* appearing alongside the *Rose Henry* in the list of Henry's navy in 1512.[55]

Both Bessie's father and grandfather served in France with the king, with Thomas Blount recorded as having been present when Henry won his greatest military victory, taking the city of Tournay on 24 September 1513.[56] Bessie's grandfather evidently distinguished himself as he was made a knight banneret during the campaign, a rank above that of simple knight, although still below the nobility.[57] Given that Thomas had previously been knighted at the Battle of Stoke by Henry VIII's father, it is evident that he was a solider of some repute and had lost none of his skills in the intervening years. He attended the king in 1513 with a troop of twelve men that he had mustered from his Shropshire lands.[58] It is perhaps indicative of the already poor relationship between Bessie's father and grandfather that they attended the king separately, with Thomas employing his favourite son, Edward, as his petty captain, and John appointing his future son-in-law, Richard Lacon, as his.[59] John Blount served with the king as one of his Spears, mustering with Henry in June 1513.[60] He continued to reside close to the court until at least late 1515 in accordance with his duty as a Spear; for example, he featured in the procession at Blackheath that went to meet an emissary from the pope who brought the king a cap and sword on 21 May 1514.[61] For John, there was then a gap in his court employment, with the disbanding of the Spears, which had proved to be a rather costly exercise. He was forced to wait until the relationship developed between the king and Bessie before he received further employment in London, which suggests that, from late 1515 until around 1517, Bessie's parents spent much of their time at home at Knightley.

Bessie remained behind in England with her mistress during the campaign of 1513. With much of the nobility and gentry in France, the court must have seemed deserted, with only a skeleton staff of advisors remaining with the queen. During Henry's absence, his brother-in-law, James IV of Scotland, took the opportunity to invade. The English army annihilated the Scots at Flodden Field, killing the Scottish king and much of his nobility. Catherine of Aragon, although not physically present with her army, maintained an active interest in the campaign and proved herself to be truly the daughter of the martial Isabella of Castile, sending her husband the bloodied gauntlets of the Scottish king, which he was wearing at the time of his death.[62] Catherine did not stop with James IV's gauntlets, writing in triumph (and a little boastfully):

My husband, for hastiness, with Rouge Cross, I could not send your Grace the piece of the king of Scots' coat which John Glyn now bringeth. In this your Grace shall see how I can keep my promise, sending you for your banners a king's coat. I thought to send himself unto you, but our Englishmen's hearts would not suffer it. It should have been better for him to have been in peace than have this reward.[63]

Henry, whose campaign in France had been less conspicuously successful, may have had mixed feelings about his wife's triumph. The wider Blount family also profited from the war with France, with William Blount, Lord Mountjoy, being appointed as governor of Tournay in January 1515, with the financially valuable power of granting safe conducts there.[64]

Although Henry VIII, as an absolute monarch, was outwardly in control of England, within a few years of coming to the throne he had allowed Thomas Wolsey, a cleric and the lowly son of an Ipswich butcher, to rise to great prominence at court. In 1507 Wolsey had been appointed as a royal chaplain to Henry VII and he was sent on several diplomatic missions by the old king.[65] His first promotion under Henry VIII was to the position of almoner in November 1509 and he joined the royal council in June 1510. Wolsey's ascent has been described as meteoric after he helped to organise the French campaign in 1513. In February 1514 the cleric was appointed as Bishop of Lincoln. In July of the same year he was made Archbishop of York, becoming a cardinal in September 1515. In December 1515 Wolsey became Lord Chancellor and gained authority over the English church in 1518 when he was appointed as a papal legate. He was an extremely clever man and quickly came to dominate the young king, with the Venetian ambassador commenting at the end of his four-year stay in England that:

> The Cardinal is the person who rules both the king and the entire kingdom. On the ambassador's first arrival in England, he used to say to him, – 'His Majesty will do so and so'. Subsequently, by degrees, he went forgetting himself, and commenced saying, 'We shall do so and so': at this present he has reached such a pitch that he says, 'I shall do so and so'.[66]

Wolsey became very wealthy in the king's service, although his reputation was not entirely negative and he was noted by contemporaries for being just and favoured the poor. He was, however, also popularly renowned for his arrogance, with one contemporary ballad, sung after his death, speaking of his 'great pride' and that he 'oppressed the people'.[67] A satire written in the 1520s was on a similar theme, noting that:

> First, as I said, there is a Cardinal,
> Which is the ruler principal
> Through the realm in every part.[68]

To confirm this point, the author further stated of Henry that 'by the Cardinal ruled he is, to the de-staining of his honour'. The poet John

Skelton, who unflatteringly referred to Wolsey as a 'mastiff cur' and a 'butcher's dog',[69] satirised Wolsey's usurpation of the king's authority, writing:

> Why come ye not to court?
> To which court?
> To the king's court,
> Or to Hampton Court?
> Nay, to the king's court!
> The king's court
> Should have the excellence,
> But Hampton Court[70]
> Hath the pre-eminence,
> And York's Place,[71]
> With my Lord's Grace!
> To whose magnificence
> Is all the confluence,
> Suits and supplications,
> Embassades of all nations.[72]

Henry later very sternly showed Wolsey just who the master was, bringing about his ruin in 1529, with the cardinal dying on his way to face trial for treason in 1530. However, there is no doubt that, in his youth, the king relied heavily upon the cardinal and that it was Wolsey who directed much of royal policy. He also ordered many other elements of Henry's life and Bessie would later find her own life very much directed by the king's chief minister.

In her first few years at court, Bessie attracted little notice. However, by the autumn of 1514, at the latest, when she was aged around sixteen years old, she had established herself as a member of the highest social circle in the land, being well known to the king himself, a feat that she achieved through her success in the court entertainments that dominated so much of court life during the early years of Henry VIII's reign.

# 7

# COURT PAGEANTRY

Bessie, with her good looks, musical ability and skill in dancing, was one of the most accomplished ladies at Henry VIII's court. She excelled in the pageantry of the court and, with a little help from her family connections, soon found herself as one of the stars within the queen's household.

It has been commented by one twentieth-century historian that 'a seemingly interminable round of pageants, feasts and tournaments formed the principal occupations of the court at the beginning of Henry's reign'.[1] This is largely true and both Henry VIII and Catherine of Aragon delighted in court entertainments, with tournaments a regular feature of court life during the day, and banquets and masques in the evenings. Bessie, as a woman, was obviously only ever a spectator in the grand tournaments of Henry's reign but would presumably have delighted in the principles of chivalry and courtly love with which the tournaments were concerned.[2] Henry loved jousting, and took great care over his appearance; on May Day 1515, for example, he appeared on a war horse decked out in cloth of gold and was so finely dressed that 'in truth he looked like St George in person on its back'.[3] Henry impressed everyone during that particular tournament when he 'exerted himself to the utmost', particularly working hard to impress the assembled French ambassadors with his prowess.

The king had good reason to feel frustrated and anxious to prove himself when he first inherited the throne in 1509. His father, Henry VII, who had already lost three sons, had no intention of placing his last surviving son in danger, refusing to allow the prince to take part in tournaments.[4] It is clear that the young Henry was unhappy with this, with a contemporary poem entitled 'The Justes of the moneths of May and June', which was printed in around 1507, recording a description of Henry as he watched the gentlemen of the court take part in the tournament:

For to say true I esteem verily
Every man of them was the more ready
Perceiving that our young prince Henry
Should it behold

Which was to them more comfort manifold
Than of the world all the treasure of gold
His presence gave them courage to be bold
And to endure

Since our prince most comely of stature
Is desirous to the most knightly ure
Of arms to which marvel adventure
Is his courage

Notwithstanding his young and tender age
He is most comely of his personage
And as desirous to his courage
As prince may be.[5]

The poet marvelled at the prince's willingness to allow gentlemen of low degree in his presence 'to speak of arms and of other defence'. Clearly tournaments had already become the young prince's favourite enthusiasm and those who took part were both a source of jealousy and great interest. Charles Brandon, who would later become the king's greatest friend, took part in the jousts described by the poet and, as a star of the tournaments, Henry was drawn to him.

Henry's first recorded tournament was on 12 January 1510, when he took part incognito with his friend Sir William Compton.[6] Henry's debut was a roaring success as he broke many staves, winning the praise of the assembled crowd. The day was marred, however, when Compton was injured, with it being feared that he would die. Clearly Henry's disguise was not entirely successful and one person in the crowd, who was aware that the king was taking part and apparently feared that it was he that was hurt, cried out 'God save the king'. Henry was forced to reveal himself to the crowd to reassure them that he was unhurt, 'to the great comfort of all the people'. This first sally into the lists did, at least, set a precedent and the king was able, from thenceforth, to compete with some regularity.

As can be expected, Henry tended to win the tournaments in which he took part. In the 1980s, the historian Neil Samman, undertook an interesting study of surviving jousting scores as part of his doctorate, commenting that 'the king's true ability is perhaps better illustrated by his performance at the Field of the Cloth of Gold against French courtiers, where nothing was to be gained politically in allowing Henry to win'.[7]

Using these results, from 1520, it was possible to show that Henry won rather less commonly than he did in England, although the contests with English courtiers did help to improve his scores. 'Otherwise, Henry's jousting was below standard. His scores were very erratic, varying from six broken lances obtained in six courses (a very good score indeed), to as low as only one out of six. Although it was difficult to be consistently good in the tilt yard, even for the best of jousters, unco-operative opponents could sharply reduce the king's score.'[8] Samman concluded that, given the strong winds at the tournament, which troubled the other participants as well, Henry 'acquitted himself relatively well'. Tournaments in which Henry took part were probably not entirely fixed, but he certainly often received a helping hand towards victory from his opponents. Whatever the true nature of Henry's jousting ability, he was certainly an enthusiastic participant throughout the early years of his reign. Within a year of his accession it was reported that he spent two days a week at such sports.[9] Bessie would often have seen the king joust when the court assembled for the regular tournaments. The queen and her ladies were central to the sport and the knights would joust in the queen's honour or for her favour.

When he was not jousting, Henry's favourite form of exercise was hunting, at which he excelled, sometimes tiring out eight or ten horses in one session.[10] In his wardrobe accounts for 1516, Henry ordered a number of garments to wear for his favourite pastime, purchasing a riding gown of black velvet and lined with black satin, for example.[11] More specifically, in the same year he ordered green velvet for riding and stalking coats.[12] The principal method of hunting during Henry's reign for a member of his class was pursuing a deer on horseback with hounds.[13] Henry kept his own dogs and it is evident that he grew attached to his favourites, with five shillings paid from his privy purse in May 1530 'in reward for bringing home Ball the kings dog that was lost in the forest of Waltham'.[14] The king also enjoyed shooting deer with arrows. There is evidence that he might need to make repairs to his equipment whilst out in the field, with another expense in 1530 'paid to a woman in reward that gave the king forked heads for his Crossbow'.[15] Shooting, in particular, was a form of hunting that Henry could participate in with female companions. He purchased bows for Anne Boleyn before their marriage, presumably intending that they would shoot together.[16] The king was less involved in hawking during his youth, although there is some evidence of his participation.[17] Bessie's kinsman Sir Edward Guildford provided the king with a falcon as a gift, which suggests it was considered that it would be welcome.[18] At the time of his death, Henry possessed an angling rod, suggesting a wide-ranging interest in blood sports. Whilst hunting was a sport, it also had romantic overtones, as will be shown later. It could provide a useful setting for Henry to meet with women, and Anne Boleyn, for example, is known to have accompanied Henry on hunting expeditions unchaperoned by female companions.[19] The king's daughter, Princess Mary, also enjoyed hunting.[20] Catherine of Aragon was a competent huntswoman, with it being recorded in 1504 that Henry VII had taken Catherine to Windsor, where 'they stayed twelve or thirteen days, going almost every day into the park and the forest to hunt deer and other game'.[21] There is good evidence from Bessie's later life that she enjoyed hunting, and it is plausible to imagine her taking part with the king in his pursuits during their relationship. Her enjoyment of hunting also shows another side to Bessie's character. Hunting could be dangerous, with Francis I of France, for example, being injured in September 1519 when he collided with a branch whilst galloping in the chase.[22] Henry himself was not immune from danger and Bessie's enjoyment of the hunt demonstrates physical bravery.

In addition to this, Henry played tennis and was known to enjoy gambling at cards and dice, sometimes losing heavily.[23] He was apparently not entirely expert in either game, with it being recorded that he played for some time with a group of foreigners 'till the king, finding them to be cheats, at length chas'd 'em away'.[24] His father employed a tennis coach to improve his game, something that Henry may have benefitted from in his youth.[25] As a child, Henry had been precocious at cards, with the sum of 6 shillings 8 pence being entered into Henry VII's account book when his son, then Duke of York, was only seven years old, for 'the king's loss to my lord of York'.[26] Gambling was a popular entertainment at court for both gentlemen and ladies. For example, in December 1536 Princess Mary's privy purse expenses record that she received 65 shillings to use as her stake in card games.[27] She obviously enjoyed the games, losing a further 49 shillings at cards the following month. Henry gave Anne Boleyn playing money for cards, for example the large sum of £5 in December 1530.[28] Henry's fourth wife, Anne of Cleves, would later ask to be taught a card game that she might play with the king in advance of their first meeting, with Bessie's second son, George Tailboys, being one of the young men who undertook to instruct her. It is reasonable to assume that the ladies of the queen's household played together and with the king and gentlemen of the court in Bessie's time. Certainly only a few years later the peculiar tripartite relationship between Henry VIII, Catherine of Aragon and Anne Boleyn would see the three all sitting down to play together, with Catherine making a pointed dig at her rival when she remarked on seeing that Anne had drawn a king that 'My Lady Anne, you have good hap to stop at a king, but you are not like others, you will have all or none.'[29] Catherine also apparently often insisted on Anne joining her at cards, so that the king would have a better opportunity to see a small deformity to Anne's hand in the form of a second nail on one finger.[30] Bowls was another game in which the ladies of the court could take part alongside the king as Anne Boleyn is known to have played.[31]

In a letter written to her father only a few months after her marriage, Catherine of Aragon commented that her time passed in continual feasting and festivities.[32] Court masques were introduced into England from Italy during the early years of the Tudor dynasty.[33] Masques, which were often on a lavish scale, involved the participation of both gentlemen and ladies of the court, who appeared, disguised, to dance a well-rehearsed pageant.[34] The whole court would then dance, with the participants being unmasked to reveal who had taken part. Masque costumes could be lavish. For example, at the time of his death, Henry had retained in his possession a number of masque costumes, such as eight coats in the Turkish fashion made of cloth of gold and decorated with purple, black and green.[35] The coats included large sleeves, made of cloth of gold and blue satin. The under-sleeves were made of red and white sarcenet. The outfits were completed by headpieces also in a Turkish fashion, made of blue, red and yellow sarcenet. Many of the costumes were taken from the royal stores and Henry also owned a number of costumes for women, including:

Viij Italian gowns for women with Ruffs Sleeves iiij of flat cloth of gold striped with silver Chevroned with Crimson Satin upon the Labels or pendants of yellow sarcenet hanging of great Tassels at the skirts the nether basses or skirts of purple velvet upon silver the under sleeves of Crimson Tilsent cut upon white sarcenet thither iiij of flat cloth of Silver striped with gold with Ruff sleeves nether sleeves Labels and Chevrons as thither First iiij the nether skirts of cloth of gold Tissue blue viij Coifs of Venice gold with their peeks of hair hanging to them and long Labels of coloured Lawn.[36]

Obviously, a masquer's outfit was incomplete without some means of covering their face and, essentially, Henry also possessed 'xij dozen Visors and Masks for men and women new and serviceable with beards and without beards'.[37]

In the first few years of his reign, Henry took particular pleasure in delighting the queen, often appearing in disguise in her chambers. In 1510, for example, whilst the court was at Westminster, the king and eleven other noblemen suddenly burst into the queen's chambers in the morning, disguised as Robin Hood and his men, and masked as well.[38] Catherine and her ladies were 'abashed, as well for the strange sight, as also for their sudden coming'. However, they composed themselves enough to dance with the intruders before the outlaws departed as suddenly as they had come. In the same year the king held a banquet, again at Westminster, before slipping away with a number of the noblemen of his court.[39] Henry and the Earl of Essex then reappeared dressed in the Turkish style, with long robes powdered with gold and wearing Turkish swords, once again to the delight of the company. They were followed by other noblemen in Russian and Prussian costumes, as well as torchbearers with blackened faces. Afterwards, the company danced, before the king appeared in yet another disguise. A number of ladies also entered, with their skin blackened with make-up, with the king's sister, Mary, the chief of them. Unlike Henry's fourth wife, Anne of Cleves, who failed spectacularly to recognise the king when he appeared to her disguised as a rather large and overfamiliar messenger before their marriage, Catherine of Aragon was undoubtedly aware of who the chief of the 'strangers' was on every occasion that Henry burst into her chamber to delight her. However, she always played along, feigning shock and surprise when it was finally 'revealed' who her visitor was.

In the early years of Henry's reign, Catherine of Aragon took part in some court masques.[40] She does not appear to have entirely relished the role as, by the time of Bessie's arrival at court, her active participation had almost entirely ceased, with the queen making one final appearance on 6 January 1513.[41] She still played a prominent part as an observer. The ladies who featured in the masques were drawn from the queen's household. It has been noted that to be related to Sir Henry Guildford, the master of the revels, was an important factor in a lady being given the chance to perform.[42] Regular performers included Guildford's nieces, Anne Brown and Anne Wotton. Elizabeth Carew, an apparent associate of Bessie's, was Guildford's relative, as was Bessie herself through her connection to his half-brother and his wife. For the great majority of court masques, the lists of participants do not survive. However, Bessie is known, with certainty, to have danced in masques on 31 December 1514 and on 5 October 1518.[43] This is certainly the tip of the iceberg.

Although she is not named, Bessie would presumably have been amongst the ladies who attended Catherine of Aragon and her sister-in-law, Mary Tudor, at the latter's proxy marriage to Louis XII of France at Greenwich on 13 August 1514.[44] Henry summoned the court to witness the marriage which had been arranged between the beautiful young princess and the aged king of France as a symbol of the new peace between the two nations. The court turned out in their finery, with the lords in attendance dressed in cloth of gold and silk and wearing gold chains. Henry himself wore a gown of cloth of gold and ash-coloured satin, together with 'a most costly collar round his neck'. Catherine, who was midway through a pregnancy, wore ash-coloured satin to match her husband's, as well as chains and other jewels and a cap in the Venetian style. Her sister-in-law was dressed in a similar costume, and it is reasonable to assume that Bessie and the other ladies also dressed to compliment their mistress. The assembled crowd heard mass before going to dinner. After they had eaten, the marriage ceremony was performed, with the Duke of Longueville representing King Louis. The assembled company then danced to the sound of a flute, a harp, a violetta and a fife, with a ball that lasted nearly two hours. Bessie can be expected to have attended the queen at most state occasions during her time at court. In October 1515, for example, she may well have been one of the ladies who attended the queen as she and the king dined aboard his new ship, the *Henri Grace de Dieu*, for its official launch.[45] Once again the queen was pregnant, but there was much merriment and the king threw himself into his naval role, appearing dressed in 'galley fashion'.

The first masque in which Bessie is known with certainty to have taken part took place on New Year's Eve 1514. According to Edward Hall, Henry, the Duke of Suffolk and two others appeared wearing mantles of cloth of silver slashed so that the lining of blue velvet could be seen. They had long capes in the Portuguese style, with their coats and other clothing matching the mantles in colour and design:

> With them were four ladies in gowns, after the fashion of Savoy, of blue Velvet, lined with cloth, the Velvet all to cut, and mantels like tippets knit together all of silver and on their heads bonnets of burned gold, the four torchbearers were in Satin white and blue. This strange apparel pleased much every person, and in especial the Queen, and thus these four lords and four ladies came into the Queen's chamber with great light of torches, and danced a great season, and then put off their visors, and then they were well known, and the Queen heartily thanked the king's grace for her goodly pastime, and kissed him.[46]

The festivities were spectacular. Yellow sarcenet was used 'for covering the necks and faces of mummers'.[47] Venice ribbons and caps of white velvet were also provided for the dancers. No expense was spared, particularly in the ladies' apparel, with the female dancers appearing in coifs of damask gold, white satin dresses and mantles of blue velvet which matched their bonnets. As well as the king and Suffolk, it is clear that the usual people, who were in the king's most intimate circle at court, took part in the dance, with Sir Nicholas Carew (a close friend of the king) and Sir Henry Guildford prominent. Carew's 'young wife', Elizabeth, also took part, as did Bessie, who was named as the third lady on the list. Only eighteen people were permitted to take part in the masque, including the musicians. It was therefore a privilege for Bessie and demonstrates how quickly she had been adopted into the king's closest circles at court. When the dancers took their masks off at the end of the night, it was discovered that Bessie had been dancing with the king. Given Henry's unusually tall and athletic build, it is implausible that Bessie, or the assembled audience, can have failed to have been aware of whom she was dancing with. This masque must certainly be a statement of the king's emerging interest in Bessie, although it is unlikely that she was then his mistress.

She was not selected to take part in the next court masque on Twelfth Night.

The court itself was a glittering place so it is no surprise that masque costumes were equally elaborate. No inventory of Catherine of Aragon's jewels survives but, from inventories for other royal women, it is clear that the queen would have been richly furnished. In particular, many of the jewels possessed by Anne of Denmark, who was the queen of James I in the early seventeenth century, had previously passed through inventories made of Henry VIII's, Mary I's and Elizabeth I's possessions, suggesting that they were family heirlooms.[48] For example, there was 'a jewel of gold in form of a Roman H having vij fair Diamonds, v table & two pointed; with iij fair Pear pearls pendant, having iiij knots of carnation ribbon'.[49] Another jewel that may also have belonged to Henry VIII was described in Anne's inventory as 'a jewel in form of a Ship of gold under sail with this word *Amor et gratin cum verbo*, & a woman at the helm'.[50] Was this, perhaps, the jewel depicting a maiden in a storm-tossed ship which was commissioned for Henry by Anne Boleyn in order to signify her turmoil when she finally agreed to become his wife?[51]

The queen would have a large quantity of jewels, which were often broken up and remade as fashions changed. Not all jewels were made into jewellery and the queen would also have jewelled accessories as a mark of her wealth and status. Anne of Denmark, for example, possessed a jewelled purse and whistle. Anne's jewels were numerous and included many strings of pearls, pearl bracelets and pearl pendants. Other jewels were set with diamonds and various different precious stones. A more contemporary inventory – that of the jewels given by Henry VIII to his fifth wife, Catherine Howard, at the time of their marriage – demonstrates the finery that would routinely decorate a Tudor queen.[52] Catherine Howard, who does not enjoy the most scholarly of reputations, was evidently interested in books more as fashion accessories than for reading, and owned a number of small jewelled books to be hung from her gown, including 'one book of gold, enamelled with black, garnished with xxvii rubies, having also a chain of gold and pearl to hang at by, containing xlii pearls'. Henry's daughter, Princess Mary, loved to dress in fine clothes and jewels as an adult, with her privy purse expenses recording payments for such fine cloths as yellow satin, black velvet and white satin.[53] An inventory for her jewels survives from the last years of her father's life, demonstrating that the princess would have appeared lavishly adorned at court, wearing such jewels as a brooch of gold depicting the history of Moses and set with diamonds, and jewelled tablets, chains, bracelets and rich crosses.[54] Henry's younger daughter, Elizabeth I, is well known for her love of fine clothes and jewels. An inventory of her goods from during her reign shows she owned a great deal of finery, including fine plate and golden clocks.[55] She even possessed a silver bed pan.[56] There is, unfortunately, little direct evidence for Catherine of Aragon's clothes and jewellery, although her surviving portraits show that she would always appear richly dressed. Henry occasionally ordered clothes for her himself, for example presenting her with a gown of purple velvet decorated with gold and ermine in November 1509.[57] A few months later he presented Catherine with a further gown of crimson cloth of gold, again furred with ermine. Catherine continued to dress well even as her piety increased, although, in the later years of her marriage, she always wore the habit of St Francis under her clothes as a sign of her personal religious devotion and humility.

Few details survive of Bessie's own attire (save where her costume was described in a masque) and there are few records of her personal possessions. The two surviving representations of her do not show her wearing any jewellery, although her mother in her tomb effigy wears rich jewels, suggesting that Bessie might also have appeared similarly adorned. Her contemporary Jane Parker, Viscountess Rochford, who joined the court not long after Bessie left, owned a good deal of rich property. Her situation is somewhat different in that she was the wife of George Boleyn, brother of Anne Boleyn and, as such, moved in slightly higher circles than Bessie. However, it is likely that her possessions can be considered approximately comparable. Lady Rochford's wardrobe demonstrates the rich clothes that one of the queen's ladies could obtain, with records revealing that she owned a pair of sleeves of crimson velvet set with goldsmith's work, for example.[58] She also owned sleeves of white damask, amongst other rich garments. At the time of her death, she possessed a nightgown of black taffeta, a kirtle of black velvet and other fine black gowns.[59] She had a number of jewels, including pearls, and an enamel and diamond brooch. Her possessions included jewelled books, as well as a bedstead of wood painted and gilded with burnished gold.[60] Bessie would have been equally accustomed to such finery, probably receiving gifts of jewellery and other personal items from the king once their relationship began. At the very least, on her funeral effigy she was depicted with lace cuffs and a lace collar, adornments that were luxury items.

Henry VIII also loved his finery; the royal crown, which was decorated with *fleur de lys* and the emblems of St George, glistened with gem stones.[61] On special occasions both Henry and his queen would appear dressed in their royal regalia, with both having a crown and sceptre.[62] The king possessed many gold chains and golden collars, as well as a quantity of fine gold plate. One cup listed in an inventory of Henry's plate was evidently a gift from Catherine of Aragon, and depicted an image of St Catherine and was enamelled with a wreath of the queen's badge, the pomegranate.[63] Another item in the king's collection, a candlestick of gold, had also been commissioned to display the love between the king and his first wife, with the initials 'H' and 'K' engraved into one side alongside the couple's respective emblems of a rose and a pomegranate.[64] A full inventory of the king's possessions at the time of his death in 1547 survives and again shows the rich objects that he was surrounded with. One entry recorded 'the king's crown of gold the border garnished with vj Ballaces v Sapphires five pointed Diamonds Twenty Rubies Nineteen pearls and one of the crosses of the same Crown garnished with a great Sapphire an Emerald crazed iiij pearls not all of one sort and three sapphires'.[65] The king also possessed more exotic items, such as a piece of 'unicorn' horn.[66] His jewels were kept in a number of coffers in the Tower of London and brought out when he required items. In addition to this, the court itself would have been expensively furnished and decorated, with rich hangings decorating the walls, such as the two pieces of crimson cloth of gold embroidered with Henry's arms and the portcullis badge of the Beaufort family (through which Henry's father had claimed the throne).[67] At the time of his death, Henry possessed a set of arrases showing the seven deadly sins, as well as others detailing the history of King David, and the Emperor Constantine the Great. He owned cushions and carpets, including a silk carpet that had been imported from Turkey.[68] Bessie would have quickly become accustomed to opulence after her arrival at court and it was well established that conspicuous display was one of the requirements of kingship.

As well as dancing in court masques, Bessie was also able to shine in daytime ceremony at the court. On May Day 1515 at Greenwich, for example, she took part in a very public ritual carried out by the queen. According to the report of Nicolo Sagudino, the secretary to the Venetian ambassador, he and the other members of the embassy were invited to come to court early on May Day, joining on horseback a number of the chief noblemen of the kingdom.[69] Once they were assembled, Catherine of Aragon appeared, 'excellently attired' and accompanied by a number of her maids, all mounted on white horses trapped with embroidered gold. Bessie took her place amongst the other excited young maids of the court, each wearing a costly dress slashed with gold and decorated with an expensive trim. The women were escorted by footmen in their own fine uniforms and, once everyone was in position, Catherine, followed by Bessie and her other attendants, rode out for a distance of two miles from the palace, entering a wood where they professed their surprise to find Henry surrounded by his guard dressed in their green livery and armed with bows. Over one hundred members of the nobility and gentry were present, richly dressed. Henry himself appeared all in green velvet, from his hat to his shoes.[70] The ladies delighted at the sight and, as they entered, found that the wood had purposely been filled with singing birds, filling the air with their music. To add to the effect, the king had ordered a number of wagons to attend, trapped out for the occasion and carrying musicians playing the organ, lutes and flutes. The gentlemen and ladies then all sat down in a clearing in the wood for a picnic breakfast before once again forming into a procession. One further delight for Bessie and the other ladies was when giants made of pasteboard and mounted onto carts were escorted back through the wood surrounded by the king's guards. The whole court rode back happily as musicians sang and played, with Nicolo Sagudino declaring 'by my faith, it was an extremely fine triumph'. Once back at Greenwich, everyone went to mass before dinner was held and then jousts to celebrate the season. It seems likely that Catherine and her ladies had set out that morning ostensibly to collect May Dew with which to wash their faces, something that was a Spanish custom imported to England by the queen. The custom was an important one and, in 1623, when Charles, Prince of Wales, visited the Spanish Infanta in Madrid, he used the princess's custom of collecting May Dew at a summer house near the city as a means of meeting her.[71] There were practical considerations behind the need to gather May Dew and it was believed to ensure the continuing beauty of its user, with the seventeenth-century diarist Samuel Pepys, for example, commenting of his wife's hunt for May Dew that it 'is the only thing in the world to wash her face with'.[72]

By the seventeenth century, when his earliest biographer, Lord Herbert of Cherbury, was writing, Henry had developed a reputation for lasciviousness. Herbert was able to confidently declare, after listing the king's accomplishments, that:

> One of the liberties which our king took at his spare time, was to love. For, as all recommendable parts concurr'd in his person, and they, again, were exalted in his high dignity and valour, so it must seem less strange, if amid the fair ladies, which liv'd in his court, he both gave and receiv'd temptation.[73]

By 1661, Henry's reputation as a lothario was so established that a visitor to the Tower of London was shown 'a peculiar relic, King Henry VIII's swansdown coverlet, which he used to wear over his codpiece, into which the English girls and women as an obeisance stick a pin and remove it, and take it with them as a titillating keepsake'.[74] This reputation is based on Henry's six wives and it must be remembered that, in Bessie's time at court, Henry had been married for some years to only one wife. Any suggestion that he might take a further five wives later in his life would have seemed preposterous to those around him.

Henry VIII, in spite of his six wives, has been described as 'a model of husbandly temperance'.[75] His affairs during his marriage to Catherine of Aragon tended to be fairly casual, with the mistress in question gaining little from the liaison. By 1515, only six years after their marriage, Catherine, who was five years older than her husband, appears to have been rapidly losing her looks. The secretary to the

Venetian ambassador, Nicolo Sagudino, for example, declared that Catherine 'is rather ugly than otherwise, and supposed to be pregnant; but the damsels of her court are handsome, and make a sumptuous appearance'.[76] This appears to have been a rather harsh criticism, although the Venetian ambassador himself did later describe the queen as 'not handsome, but [she] has a very beautiful complexion. She is religious, and as virtuous as words can express.'[77] In 1519 Francis I of France commented that 'He [King Henry] has an old deformed wife, while he himself is young and handsome'.[78] During his marriage to Anne Boleyn, Henry took the opportunities presented by all three of his wife's pregnancies to take a mistress. Sexual intercourse during pregnancy was generally considered harmful to the child and it appears that Henry tended to seek solace elsewhere during the months that his wife was effectively out of bounds. There is less direct evidence for this during Catherine of Aragon's marriage to the king, although the earliest evidence of Henry being unfaithful to his wife occurred during her first pregnancy.[79]

In early 1510 the Spanish ambassador claimed that Henry had become attracted to one of the married sisters of the Duke of Buckingham and had sent his friend, Sir William Compton, to woo her on his behalf.[80] This caused something of a stir in the Buckingham family and another sister, Lady Elizabeth Ratcliffe, who was a favourite of the queen's, informed her brother of all that was happening, causing the duke to verbally attack both Compton and the king and leave the court. The object of Henry's affection, Lady Anne Hastings, was removed from court by her husband and taken sixty miles away to a convent. This occasioned the first quarrel between Catherine and Henry and the king ordered that she dismiss Lady Elizabeth from court, to his wife's fury. 'Afterwards, almost all the court knew that the Queen had been vexed with the King, and the King with her, and thus this storm went on between them.' Even after the couple had reconciled, Catherine continued to show her ill will towards Compton, which displeased Henry. Given the queen's reaction, it seems probable that Anne Hastings was indeed the king's mistress. At New Year 1513 he gave her the third most expensive New Year's present, a gift that implies an intimate relationship. Alternatively, it is possible that this was merely part of the game of courtly love.[81] If that was the case, however, it is difficult to see how the Duke of Buckingham, Anne's husband, her sister and the queen would have failed to understand the rules of courtly love, which, after all, focused on the chaste adoration of an unobtainable lady. In any event, any affair with Anne Hastings was rapidly over and she instead turned her attentions to Sir William Compton, with Cardinal Wolsey accusing the pair of adultery in 1527. Compton, who had denied the cardinal's charge, later left sums for prayers for Anne's soul and a life interest in some of his lands after his death, suggesting that there was truth in the rumours: presumably once the king's interest had waned.

By the time of Bessie's arrival at court in 1512, Catherine of Aragon had already undergone a number of pregnancies, but had failed to produce a child that had lived longer than a few weeks. In the sixteenth century, royal pregnancies were not publicly announced. It is therefore necessary to pick through the documents to determine the number of pregnancies endured by the queen.[82] Catherine conceived very soon after her marriage to Henry in 1509, with the king writing proudly to his father-in-law, Ferdinand of Aragon, in November 1509 that 'the queen, our dearest consort, with the favour of heaven has conceived in her womb a living child, and is right heavy therewith, which we signify to your majesty for the great joy thereof that we take, and the exultation of our whole realm'.[83] In late December 1509, word of this reached Venice and the Doge and Senate there wrote to ask their ambassador to congratulate the king.[84] By late April 1510 the Venetian ambassador was reporting that the queen had not yet been delivered, suggesting that the birth was believed to be imminent.[85] Unfortunately, in May the queen wrote to her father to inform him of the birth of a stillborn daughter.[86] Some uncertainty exists over the date of birth of this child, and it appears that, in spite of Catherine's assertion that the birth had happened recently, she had in fact borne her daughter on 31 January, keeping the news secret in the mistaken belief that she was still carrying a surviving twin.[87] This was a misfortune, but Catherine conceived again almost immediately, which suggests that she and Henry had ceased to believe in the possibility of a second baby within a few weeks of the first birth, allowing them to resume sexual relations.[88] On New Year's Day 1511, only an hour and a half after midnight and to the great rejoicing of everyone in England, she bore a son, who was named Henry, after his father, and declared Prince of Wales.[89] According to a contemporary, Edward Hall, there was much rejoicing at the birth of the child 'for the honour of whom, fires were made, and diverse vessels with wine, set for such as would take thereof in certain streets in London, and general processions thereupon to laud God'.[90] Henry, who was still aged only nineteen, was thrilled and, on 12 February 1511, he took part in a tournament before the queen, jousting under the name of 'Sir Loyal Heart'.[91] A song included in a manuscript book that belonged to the king may also have been composed by him, demonstrating his joy in his son:

Adieu; adieu le company!
I trust we shall meet oftener,
Vive le Katerine et vive le prince
Le infant Rosary.[92]

Preparations were made to appoint the young prince's household, with Henry Knight, for example, receiving an appointment to be clerk of

the signet to the Prince of Wales on 21 February 1511.[93] One William
Lambert was appointed as the prince's keeper of the wardrobe.[94]
Sadly, the prince lived for less than two months, dying suddenly on
23 February to the grief of both his parents.[95] Henry's sorrow can be
seen in the grand funeral that he appointed for his son at Westminster
Abbey and in the annuity of £20 a year that he began to pay from
Easter 1511 to Elizabeth Pointes, 'late nurse unto our dearest son the
Prince'.[96] In September 1511 Wolsey, who was in a position to know,
believed Catherine to be pregnant, which suggests that she may have
had a miscarriage soon afterwards.[97] On 8 October 1513 Catherine
once again fulfilled her dynastic purpose and bore the king a son,
who, it was confidently declared, 'will inherit the crown, the other son
having died'.[98] This second son died within hours or perhaps days of his
birth. In September 1514 the first rumours arose that the king intended
to divorce 'his brother's widow' due to her inability to bear healthy
children.[99] This is rather implausible, however, given that, by that time,
Catherine must have been advanced in pregnancy. She bore a third son,
who was either stillborn or died soon after birth, in late December or
early January 1515 in her eighth month of pregnancy.[100] Although Bessie
was first recorded to have danced with the king in December 1514, she
was not the main object of the king's affections during this pregnancy.
Henry instead turned to a French lady to fill the role of royal mistress,
Jane Poppincourt, who left England in 1516 with an extravagant gift
of £100 from the king.[101]

The loss of Catherine's third son was popularly believed to be due
to 'the misunderstanding between her father and her husband', with
Henry apparently reproaching the queen for her father's ill faith when he
abandoned his alliance with England.[102] Given Catherine's difficult record
of pregnancies, it is no surprise that Henry grew increasingly solicitous of
her, for example concealing the death of her father, Ferdinand of Aragon,
in early 1516, until after Catherine had been delivered to ensure that she
was not upset in the final, dangerous weeks of pregnancy.[103] The winter
of 1515/16 was a fortuitous time for royal births and, in October, one
Venetian correspondent mused that there were 'then in England three
pregnant queens'.[104] Henry's two sisters, Queen Margaret of Scotland and
Queen Mary of France, each delivered a healthy child. On 20 February
1516, Catherine finally gave birth to a child who survived to adulthood.
Unfortunately, for both her and Henry, this was a daughter, Mary, which
caused some disappointment in the country and in Europe, with the
Venetian ambassador commenting in his dispatch that 'I shall go to pay the
due congratulations in the name of your Highness; and had it been a son, I
should have already done so, as in that case, it would not have been fit to
delay the compliment.' Henry was, however, philosophical about the birth of
a girl, commenting when the Venetian ambassador both congratulated and
commiserated with him in equal measure that 'We [Henry and Catherine]

are both young: if it was a daughter this time, by the grace of God the sons will follow.'[105] Catherine's second and third son appear to have been at least a month premature and, given that there was only an eight-month space between the claimed birth of a stillborn girl in May 1510 and the birth of Catherine's eldest son, it is certain that he was also early (even allowing for a perhaps slightly earlier realisation by Catherine that she was not, in fact, pregnant in spring 1510, which would have allowed the resumption of marital relations). Mary, by arriving on time, must have seemed like a break in the pattern of premature and sickly infants, justifying Henry's hope for the future. The princess was a precocious child, much loved by both her parents. When, shortly after her second birthday, she was brought in by the king to see the Venetian ambassador, she received 'the greatest marks of honour being paid to her universally, more than the queen herself'. When the infant spotted the king's Venetian chaplain, the renowned organised Dionysius Memo, she called out forcefully and repeatedly 'Priest! Priest!' until he was forced to play for her.[106] In August 1517 there were rumours that the queen was again pregnant, but these came to nothing.[107] Catherine finally conceived again early in 1518, with the news being reported by the Venetian ambassador in June, who described it as 'an event most earnestly desired by the whole kingdom'.[108] In July 1518 it was reported that she already had 'a belly something great' and *te deums* were sung in church in celebration.[109] Even the pope took an interest in what would prove to be the queen's last chance at childbearing, with the pontiff commenting that he hoped it would be a prince 'who will be the prop of the universal peace of Christendom'.[110] Henry was on tenterhooks, writing in the summer of 1518 to Cardinal Wolsey to confess that:

> Two things there be, which be so secret that they cause me at this time to write to you myself;[111] the one is, that I trust the Queen my wife be with child, the other is, the chief cause why I am so loath to repair to Londonward, because about this time is partly of her dangerous times, and because of that I would remove her as little as I may now. My Lord I write this unto not as a ensured thing, but as a thing wherein I have great hope and likelihoods, and because I do well know that this thing will be comfortable to you to understand, therefore I do write it unto you at this time.[112]

Henry's words about Catherine's 'dangerous times' suggest that there were other miscarriages that have not been recorded in between the pregnancies that produced live or stillborn children, something that can only have added to the royal couple's misery.[113]

The birth of Catherine's last child was expected in late November or December.[114] As her mistress prepared for the delivery towards the end of 1518, Bessie came to realise that she had her own happy news to tell the king.

# 8

# BESSIE'S LITERARY INTERESTS

Whilst court entertainments and her duties as a member of the queen's household took up a great deal of Bessie's time, she also found time to indulge in her other interests. Bessie's surviving reputation, as a mistress of the king and an active participant in court masques and entertainments, does not do her justice: she is associated with a number of weighty texts and it is clear that she had wide-ranging literary interests during her time at court and afterwards.

A number of books can be associated with Bessie either firmly or tentatively and they give some idea of her leisure interests and her obvious intelligence. The book that is most firmly associated with her is a manuscript of John Gower's *Confessio Amantis*, which is now held by the British Library. Bessie's signature as Elizabeth Taylbys (her first married name) appears in a number of scribbled entries to the margins of the work.[1] In addition to this, the annotations to the book include references to her second husband, Edward, Lord Clinton, and contains his signature and that of his third wife, Elizabeth Fitzgerald.[2] Very strong proof that the book was Bessie's can be found in an inscription added to a margin at the beginning of the work which relates that:

> This book the right honourable and my most honoured Aunt the Lady Catherine Burghe gave me at Scarborough Castle the 5th day of April A Domini 1609. And the Book was the right honourable Lady's, the Lady Elizabeth Taylbys wife to the Lord Taylbys of Kyme and after his decease was the first wife to the right honourable Lord Clinton who was after created Earle of Lincoln Lord high Admiral of England and had by her this lady Catherine Burghe the lady Margaret Willoughby and the Lady Bridget Dymoke my mother.
> E. Dymoke[3]

Since the book belonged to Bessie's own daughter and was passed to her grandson, it is very likely that the facts are indeed as Sir Edward Dymoke described. The book became something of a family heirloom and on folio 2 the birth of Bessie's second husband's eldest son, who was born to his second wife, was proudly recorded as having occurred on 6 June 1542 'between one and two of the clock at after noon'.[4] This child, who later became the second Earl of Lincoln, was later involved in a long and bitter dispute with his kinsman, Sir Edward Dymoke, and his nephew's possession of the book in which his own birth was noted cannot have improved relations between Bessie's grandson and her husband's son.[5] The name 'Willoughby' also appears on folio 212v, presumably referring to Bessie's youngest child, Margaret Willoughby. There are also other signatures and annotations relating to Bessie's relatives and associates which link the manuscript firmly to her.

The manuscript is a fine object and would have of been of considerable value in the early sixteenth century. It was produced in the early fifteenth century by a scribe then active in London who also prepared fine editions of the more famous medieval works the *Canterbury Tales* and *Piers Plowman*.[6] The manuscript is richly decorated, with the text written in black and red in a fine, clear hand. It is also a beautiful work: folio 142v, for example, is particularly ornate with coloured borders and a decorated initial letter picked out in gold, blue, red, green and purple.[7] Another page, earlier in the work, had fine scrollwork in blue, gold, red and purple entwined with the text.[8] The manuscript also boasts one fine picture[9] although it must be pointed out that this was one fewer than the standard production for an early fifteenth-century manuscript of Gower's work. The manuscript has been described as an 'economy de luxe' manuscript by a recent commentator.[10] Whilst this may be the case, by the early sixteenth century when printing was beginning to become established, a fine manuscript was of particular value.[11]

The question must be asked as to how Bessie came to acquire such a fine object. Manuscripts were often passed down through families, even at the highest levels of society. One surviving early fourteenth-century illuminated copy of *The Romance of the Holy Grail* bears the signatures of both Henry VIII's mother, Elizabeth of York, and her sister Cecily, added during the reign of their father, the book-loving Edward IV.[12] This book had previously belonged to the Haute family, who were related to the princesses through their mother, Elizabeth Woodville. Elizabeth of York later possessed the famous *Bohum Psalter*, produced for Humphrey de Bohun, Earl of Hereford, the maternal grandfather of Henry V. This book had evidently been passed through the royal family. Elizabeth of York passed it on to her daughter-in-law, Catherine of Aragon. The *Confessio Amantis* itself had a particular association with the Lancastrian royal family. The first edition of the work (of which Bessie's copy is a version) was favourable to King Richard II but a second edition turned overtly hostile as Gower moved to support Richard's successor, Henry IV, who usurped the throne to become the first Lancastrian king. Henry IV's own copy of the work survives, as do versions belonging to his sons and his daughter-in-law Jacquetta de St Pol, the mother of Henry VIII's maternal grandmother, Elizabeth Woodville.[13] Whilst there is evidence that old books were not seen as a suitable gift for royalty in the sixteenth century,[14] it is entirely possible that Bessie could have received her fine manuscript as a gift from the king. In at least two places a reader drew the faint outline of a crowned Tudor rose in the margins of the manuscript.[15] In addition to this, folio 214v, which contains a Latin inscription added by a reader and Bessie's name as Elizabeth Taylboys, also includes the initial 'HR'. Whilst this is not in Henry VIII's own hand, it does, perhaps, suggest that the book's owner was reminded of the king when she viewed the manuscript. Henry loved books and the inventory of his possessions produced at his death listed a great number of fine editions, including a manuscript of the *Confessio Amantis* decorated with gold engraver's work.[16] Alternatively, Bessie may have purchased the book herself with her wages or funds received from the king. Gower's *Confessio Amantis* was a popular work amongst the courtiers at Henry VIII's court. Bessie's friend the Duke of Suffolk also owned a surviving manuscript, as did the king's kinsmen, the St John family, and his great-niece Margaret Clifford.[17] Bessie's ownership of a copy demonstrates that she was at the forefront of literary fashion at the Tudor court.

Whilst Bessie's ownership of a manuscript of John Gower's *Confessio Amantis* is clear, it is less easy to prove that she actually read the book. One recent commentator has noted that 'owners are not necessarily readers, but there is a good deal of evidence that the *Confessio* was attentively read in the fifteenth and sixteenth centuries'.[18] Whilst it is evident that families in the sixteenth century began to inscribe their names as a sort of autograph album in manuscripts in their possession, as indeed happened in Bessie's own manuscript, the fact that her own annotations appear in various places throughout the book[19] does suggest that she also read and was familiar with its content. It is therefore very likely that this book, which was evidently one of Bessie's most treasured possessions, was also something that appealed to her as a work of literature.

In the fifteenth and sixteenth centuries, the poet John Gower was commonly held to rank amongst the greats of English literature, with a reputation comparable to that of his contemporary and friend Geoffrey Chaucer.[20] The *Confessio Amantis*, one of Gower's most popular works, was first printed by William Caxton in 1483, with a second printed edition made by the royal printer in 1532 and a third edition in 1554.[21] In addition to this, it is the first English work known to have been translated out of the vernacular; a Spanish translation existed from the early fifteenth century and there are references to an early Portuguese version.[22] The work itself contains both Latin and English verse, although the bulk of the text is in English. For Bessie, the main interest of the book is likely to have been its theme which, as Gower himself elaborated in the preface, was 'somewhat of lust, somewhat of love'.[23] The book, which used the theme of a confession by a lover to Genius, the priest of the goddess Venus, was designed to elaborate on ideas of exploring the self.[24] The work begins with the observation that love rules the world:

> And that is love, of which I mean,
> To treat, as after shall be seen.
> In which there can no man him rule,
> For love's law is out of rule,
> That of too much or of too little
> Well nigh is ever man to wyte,
> And natheless there is no man
> In all this world so wise, that can
> Of love temper the measure,
> But as it falleth in adventure.[25]

Gower further contended that there was 'no medicine to salve of such a sore [as love]' before calling love the master of all.

After making a number of observations about love, Gower introduced the narrator, a man separated from his beloved. For the narrator, love was a 'malady' and he called out to Cupid and Venus for pity. It was then that he began his confession to Genius, the priest of love, with all the religious fervour of a true penitent:

> And with that word I gan down fall
> On knees, and with devotion
> And with full great contrition
> I send thane: 'Dominus, Mine holy father Genius'.[26]

For the remainder of the work, Gower set out a series of historical and mythological tales on various themes, designed to demonstrate love. These included such classical tales as Medusa the gorgon, as well as the sirens. The seven deadly sins were included, as well as a warning to any female readers that men might woo 'with words feigned to deceive'.[27] The stories themselves, many of which would already have been familiar to Bessie and her contemporaries were rather daring, with one recent commentator noting that the women described, for example, 'introduce us to a range of different types of femininity, from silent modesty and submissiveness to monstrous promiscuity, murder and witchcraft'.[28] Unlike the cautionary tales in *The Book of the Knight of the Tower*, Gower made it clear that his sympathies were not always with his most virtuous subjects. For example, in the tale of Canace and Machaire, the poet chose to emphasise the isolation and youth of the two siblings who committed the sin of incest.[29] Instead of censuring the couple, Gower focussed on their father's anger and the inequality of the punishment that they received – Canace and her child suffered death, whilst Machaire escaped all blame. Bessie's own response to what she read in Gower's work is not recorded but, as a woman who bore at least one child out of wedlock, she may well have sympathised with some of the more morally questionable characters in the work. The theme of love and classical allusions fits well with the second book known to have been owned by Bessie.

A copy of Chaucer's *Troilus and Criseyde* now in the possession of the University of Manchester bears the signature 'Elesabeth Blount'.[30] A link between this book and Bessie's Gower manuscript was first raised recently by a commentator who suggested that both may have belonged to Henry VIII's mistress.[31] Very little of Bessie's writing survives and it is therefore very difficult to compare the signature in the University of Manchester's *Troilus* with the most certain examples of Bessie's writing in the British Library's Gower manuscript. Signatures were also potentially variable. For example, the 'Elizabeth Clynton' who signed two folios of the Gower manuscript drew a very different initial 'E' in both cases, although the other letters are similar enough for it to be certain that they were signed by the same person.[32] There are enough similarities between the Manchester signature and the examples of Bessie's hand in the Gower manuscript to suggest a strong probability that she was the owner of the University of Manchester's early printed edition of Chaucer's work.[33] A further analysis of the book also makes it certain that it belonged to her. As well as a further addition of the name 'Elysabethe' to the first page of the book, a very smudged note on another page appears to bear the signature 'Lady Talboys'.[34] A note referring to 'London' on another page also includes the signature of someone with the Tailboys surname. Although the Christian name is not legible, it appears to end with 'yt', suggesting that it could have been Gilbert Tailboys, Bessie's husband (given the eccentric spelling of the period).[35] The identification of Bessie as the Elizabeth Blount of the Chaucer book is supported by three lines written in the same handwriting as the signature 'Elesabeth Blount' at the top of the same page in the edition of *Troilus and Criseyde*. The handwriting, with its looping letters is similar to handwriting which appears to have been Bessie's in the Gower manuscript. The lines in the edition of Chaucer are odd, reading:

here endeth the prologue
And here begynnethe
Hyere indith the prologe

They are clearly copies of the headings in the text which they are written next to, which suggests that Bessie was practising her letters idly in her book and supports the view that she was relatively young when she acquired this work. There is also clear evidence from the margin notes added to the book that someone read the book very closely. For example, on one page, a note was added stating 'Troilus naming his love' next to that section of the text.[36] The book's owner evidently used the text as a source of inspiration for their own musical compositions, in a number of places marking out verses to be used as songs. Troilus's song, which was made up of four verses, was identified in this way, with the final verse being marked with the word 'finis'.[37] A further song about love was demarcated by a note in the margin and a line firmly drawn with ink and marked with 'finis' to demonstrate where it ended.[38] Given Bessie's musical ability and the fact that she was one of the book's owners, it does not seem impossible that she used the text to select lyrics for songs of her own composition: the image of the doomed love affair between Troilus and Criseyde would have been a very appropriate one in relation to the theme of courtly love.

Unlike the Gower manuscript, Bessie's copy of *Troilus and Criseyde* was a copy of the edition printed by William Caxton in 1483. Such a book would have had considerably less value than the Gower manuscript and may even more firmly reflect Bessie's own reading tastes. Only four copies of Caxton's edition of *Troilus* survive and, interestingly, three of these appear to have circulated among gentlewomen of the early sixteenth century, as well as members of the London merchant class.[39] This was exactly the sort of circle that Bessie's grandmother, Isabel Stanley, and her second husband, John Russhe, moved in and perhaps reflects Bessie's own connections when she first came to London. The work itself, like Gower's *Confessio Amantis*, was a popular one, with a second edition, printed by Wynkyn de Worde, appearing in 1517.

Bessie's ownership of an edition of Chaucer's *Troilus and Criseyde* supports the view that her literary interests were focused on romance and English verse, themes popular amongst her sex and class. *Troilus and Criseyde* was written in the 1380s, shortly before Gower produced his *Confessio Amantis*.[40] The theme of the work has been described as 'meditating the nature of love, and mainly human love, as it enraptures and afflicts us in this sublunary world, which is under the government of Fortune'.[41] The story centred on the dying days of Troy when Troilus, the son of the king of Troy, fell in love with Criseyde, a widow living in the city whose father had defected to the Greeks. The work deals with Troilus's despair at Criseyde's initial rejection of his love, then her acceptance, before the couple were separated when Criseyde was exchanged with the Greeks for a Trojan prisoner of war. Although Criseyde promised to remain faithful to her lover, she soon proved faithless and entered into a flirtation with another man. When Troilus discovered this, his grief led to his death in battle.

The themes in *Troilus* are very similar to those of the *Confessio Amantis*, as can be seen from one early passage that proclaims:

> And also pray for those that have despaired
> In love and look for no recovery;
> Also for those maliciously ensnared
> By wicked tell-tales, whether he or she;
> Pray this to God in His benignity
> To grant them soon their passing from earth's face
> That have despaired of love and of his grace.[42]

The work then described Criseyde's great beauty, commenting that:

> Criseyde this lady's name; and, as for me,
> If I may judge of her, in all that place
> There was not one so beautiful as she,
> So like an angel in her native grace;
> She seemed a thing immortal, out of space,
> As if a heavenly, perfected creature
> Had been sent down to earth in scorn of nature.[43]

Bessie signed her copy of *Troilus* in her maiden name and must have acquired it at around the time of her affair with Henry. It may therefore have had particular resonance for her as she read of the Trojan prince's custom of watching the ladies of the town to identify the most beautiful. Once he had seen Criseyde, he thought only of her, making himself ill until he was finally able to bring her to love him. Although no details of Henry's courtship of Bessie survive, his love letters to Anne Boleyn, when he was hoping to make her his mistress show a similar longing to that of Troilus for Criseyde.[44] Chaucer, like Gower, depicted love as a sickness or a fever, something that can also be seen in Henry VIII's own approach to courtship. It is certainly interesting that the two books most firmly associated with Bessie should also be on the theme of love, something on which, of course, her reputation rests.

Although the editions of Gower and Chaucer are the only known books to have a direct association with Bessie, there are other works with which she is potentially connected and which also merit comment. A manuscript now held by the British Library and known as the 'Devonshire Manuscript' is bound in its original sixteenth century binding dating to around 1525–29.[45] A later addition to this binding are the initials 'MF' and 'SE' stamped in gold. The manuscript contains approximately 184 poems, with many written by members of Henry VIII's court, including Thomas Wyatt, Thomas Howard, the king's niece Lady Margaret Douglas, Mary Shelton, Henry VIII's great-nephew Henry, Lord Darnley and even, perhaps, Anne Boleyn. The book was circulated and used to record verses of interest and the number of different hands evident in the book has been estimated at twenty-three. Of these, only three were major contributors: Mary Shelton, Lady Margaret Douglas and Bessie's own daughter-in-law, Mary Howard (i.e. Mary Fitzroy, the 'MF' of the binding). It has been suggested that the book was originally in the possession of Mary's brother, Henry Howard, Earl of Surrey, and his friend, Bessie's son Henry Fitzroy, before the pair visited France in 1532. Given Bessie's known connection with her son during his childhood, this certainly suggests a possible link to her and it would be tempting to see her hand at work in some of the poems – perhaps in relation to the extracts from *Troilus and Criseyde* which appear in a number of folios in the book.[46] However, unfortunately given the paucity of the evidence for Bessie's handwriting, it is impossible to identify whether or not she played any part in the compilation. The medieval poems have also been identified to be in the handwriting of Mary Shelton.[47] In all probability, the book has no association with Bessie other than its links to her son. But this, coupled with evidence that she moved in similar circles to the manuscript's compilers, may at least suggest an interest in its themes. Other works with a familial, rather than direct, association to Bessie include her step-grandfather John Russhe's editions of the *Canterbury Tales* and Aesop's Fables. The feud between her grandmother and the printer Richard Pynson, who by the time of Bessie's arrival at court had become the king's printer, may perhaps explain why she chose to obtain a copy of Caxton's edition of *Troilus and Criseyde* rather than Pynson's later publication.

The surviving evidence demonstrates that Bessie had an interest in English romance. However, there is also a suggestion that she read more weighty texts. As previously discussed, it is tempting to suggest that she had access to her long-dead step-grandfather's store of books which, as well as the popular *Canterbury Tales*, included considerably more worthy books such as Boccaccio's *Fall of Princes* and an edition of a book of chronicles (perhaps the *Chronicles of England* first printed by Wynkyn de Worde in 1497).[48] This edition of the *Fall of Princes* was a particularly fine one, printed on large paper and decorated with nine woodcut illustrations to mark the start of each chapter.[49] Pynson also supplied John Russhe with a number of religious works, including mass books and religious primers. There is direct evidence for Bessie owning at least one religious book, which was depicted open before her on her funeral brass. Whilst it is not possible to confirm which book was depicted, it is likely to have been a prayer book or a mass book, and it is probable that Bessie, by having herself depicted as a kneeling figure before an open prayer book, deliberately intended to reference her famous, and considered near-saintly, kinswoman, Lady Margaret Beaufort. The similarity between Bessie's kneeling pose and that of Henry VIII's grandmother in one of her most famous portraits is striking and, once again, is evidence that Bessie also had sincerely held conservative religious beliefs. A reference to Margaret Beaufort in Bessie's funeral brass also provides a further suggestion that she was aware of her step-grandfather's literary stock. Henry VIII's grandmother was a great patron of printing, even translating works for publication herself. Following the death of William Caxton in 1492, she first turned her attentions to the printing company of Richard Pynson, and it has recently been suggested that his edition of the *Officium* for the Feast of the Name of Jesus was printed in 1494 at Margaret Beaufort's request.[50] It has further been suggested that Pynson's edition of a *Life of St Margaret* prepared at around the same time would have been intended to flatter this important new patron. Whilst Margaret soon turned her attentions towards a third printer, Wynkyn de Worde, it was around that time that John Russhe first began to have dealings with Pynson. It is probable that Pynson came to his attention through his wife's kinswoman, Margaret Beaufort, and Bessie's referencing of her royal kinswoman in her funeral effigy suggests an awareness of her link to the king's grandmother and her family's literary links to her.

If Bessie was able to obtain any of her step-grandfather's books, then she would have acquired a copy of *Dives and Paupers*, the jewel of his stock of books. This was a didactic treatise, written in English and based on the Ten Commandments.[51] The work was written in the early fifteenth century and is made up of a prologue and ten books, each detailing a commandment. The work is written in the form of a conversation between a rich man and a pauper, although it is the pauper who is the main focus of the book. It was apparently written by a Franciscan friar and has been described as a work intent on helping people to know 'righteous from unrighteous conduct in relation to God, self, and their neighbours'.[52] This includes a disapproval of gambling, ecclesiastics taking part in hunting and the practice of holding fairs in the church itself. The author had a contempt for fashion, complaining of 'the foul stinking pomp & pride of array that is now used in this land'.[53] As was common in the fifteenth century, the work included a number of stories to illustrate its conclusions, such as the tale of a prince who married beneath him, forcing him to serve as a knight-errant. On his death in battle he ordered that his bloody shirt be sent to his wife together with a request for her to remain faithful to his memory, pointing out that he had died for her sake. Such tales were popular and would have been read by people of Bessie's class. There is no direct evidence that Bessie either read or possessed a copy of

*Dives and Paupers* but it is probable that one would, at least, have been available to her given its family connection.

Bessie also has potential connections with other religious works which are worthy of further consideration. Amongst the papers of the Earl of Ashburnham towards the end of the nineteenth century was a fourteenth-century religious manuscript, the *Officia Liturgica, Septem Psalmi Poenitenciales, et alia; Calendario Praemisso*.[54] The book, which is bound in crimson velvet, contains the signature of Henry VIII's mother, Elizabeth of York. A considerably later certificate was attached to the book, saying, 'This book was given me by my mother, who told me that it belonged to Mary, Queen of Scots, and was given by her, the night before she was beheaded, to one of her attendants who was of my mother's family. – Dorothy Osborne'.[55] A second note confirmed that this was 'Written at Cheriton, and at my request, by Mrs Osborne in 1787. Edmund Ferrers, Rector of Cheriton, Hants'. The lady who apparently received the book from Mary, Queen of Scots, was Dorothy, the daughter of Sir Christopher Willoughby and Elizabeth Tailboys, a sister of Bessie's first husband, Gilbert Tailboys. Although, at first glance, this book does not appear to have a connection to Bessie, the connection to her family is an interesting one. Following the death of Bessie's two sons by Gilbert and of her daughter, Elizabeth Tailboys, the Tailboys estates were divided amongst the families of Gilbert's sisters.[56] It is therefore not inconceivable that a family book, in the possession of Bessie's daughter, the childless Elizabeth Tailboys, could have passed to the Willoughbys. Another possibility rests on the fact that Bessie's youngest daughter, Margaret Clinton, married into the Willoughby family. Given that Bessie's daughter Katherine inherited her Gower manuscript, it seems not improbable that Bessie could have passed a second valuable book to another daughter. This can only be speculation, but there is no evidence that Dorothy Willoughby did indeed receive a book from Mary, Queen of Scots or that the Scottish queen ever owned it.[57] If she did not, it raises the question of how she came by such a valuable and royally-connected book. It is just possible that this could have been a gift to Bessie from the king, who was already aware of her interest in books. Alternatively, could the book in question be the 'Book of Psalms covered with crimson velvet and garnished with gold' listed in Henry VIII's inventory at his death?[58] If so, it could not have passed into Bessie's hands. However, as will be discussed later, it is not entirely improbable that Bessie's daughter, Elizabeth Tailboys, could have acquired this book through her own important connection to the king. If the book was indeed still in Henry VIII's possession at the end of his life then there is no question of it being passed to his great-niece, Mary, Queen of Scots, with whom he was on far from friendly terms.

The final book with which Bessie has a connection is also a religious one. In the late nineteenth century, the great Ashburnham Library was broken up and sold at auction. A number of the books passed into private hands and are now untraceable, including a particularly fine edition of the *Horae Beate Virginis Maria*, a religious work, printed in 1520.[59] The book was printed upon vellum and has been described as 'a volume of extraordinary rarity and beauty'.[60] Its importance lies in the signatures and messages added to its pages. These make it clear that the book belonged to Elizabeth Cheney, the wife of the poet Thomas, Lord Vaux, both of whom were first cousins of Henry VIII's sixth wife, Catherine Parr. Traditionally the book had first belonged to Maude, Lady Parr, Catherine's mother. Annotations to the book contain a number of fond messages to Lady Vaux which will be discussed later, including inscriptions by Catherine Parr and her brother. Bessie and her first husband, Gilbert, also added their signatures to the select group, with Bessie declaring, 'Madame I am yours wt all my hart Elizabeth Taylboys'. In this present chapter the interest lies in the book itself and it is clear that Bessie had this book in her hands, even if it is less clear that she would actually have read it. Whether she read it or not, it is good evidence that she was acquainted with the poet Thomas, Lord Vaux, who was said by his contemporaries to rank alongside the famous Sir Thomas Wyatt and Henry Howard, Earl of Surrey.[61] Vaux, whose themes often touched on love, as well as more weighty matters, was a complicated character, renowned for his staunchly traditional religious beliefs and stubborn character.[62] He was also rather melancholy: towards the end of his life, he wrote such lines as 'so, to and from, this loathsome life I draw' and 'that to the last of this my fainting breath, / I wish exchange of life, for happy death'.[63] Perhaps rather more appealing to Bessie's literary tastes, his verses often turned to unrequited love, in a similar vein to Gower's lover in the *Confessio Amantis*:

If ever man had love too dearly bought,
Lo I am he that planes within her maze:
And finds no way, to get the same I sought,
But as the Deer are driven unto the gaze.
And to augment the grief of my desire,
Myself to burn, I blow the fire:
But shall I come nigh you,
Of force I must fly you.

What death, alas, may be compared to this?
I play within the maze of my sweet foe:
And when I would of her but crave a kiss,
Disdain enforceth her away to go.
Myself I check: yet do I twist the twine:
The pleasure hers, the pain is mine:

But shall I come nigh you,
Of force I must fly you.

You courtly wights, that wants your pleasant choice,
Lend me a flood of tears to wait my chance:
Happy are they in love that can rejoice,
To their great pains, where fortune doth advance.
But sith my suit, alas, cannot prevail!
Full fraught with care in grief still will I wail:
Sith you will needs fly me,
I may not come nigh you.[64]

Vaux was some years younger than Bessie, being born in 1510. However, there is good evidence that, during her first marriage at least, she was on friendly terms with the poet and his family. His poems are a good indication of the sort of verses members of Bessie's circle liked and read.

There is no doubt that Bessie was interested in literature and that she moved in literary circles. This interest began before her marriage and apparently had its roots in her family background. One other point not directly connected with Bessie is worth noting as evidence of her family's continuing interest in the written word. Bessie's first cousin, Joyce Blount of Astley, settled in Stratford-upon-Avon. Long after her death and Bessie's, her eldest son named his child William, in honour of the family's close friend and neighbour, the playwright William Shakespeare.[65] In his will of 1616, Shakespeare left young William Reynolds 26 shillings and 8 pence to buy a ring to remember him by, testifying to the continuing interest that he took in his godson. Whilst the connection between William Shakespeare and the Blounts is a remote one and of little direct relevance to Bessie's own life, it does show something of the circles that the family continued to move in and their interest in literature as a whole. For Bessie, an interest in literature may well have helped to endear her to the well-educated Henry VIII and was, perhaps, an added attraction. However, it is clear that it was her physical charms that initially drew him towards her.

# 9

# THE KING'S MISTRESS

It was at one of the court revels, in which she excelled, that Bessie first came to the attention of Henry VIII. In a letter written by the king's closest friend, Charles Brandon, Duke of Suffolk, from France on 25 October 1514, after giving the king news of his sister, Mary Tudor, who had been sent to France to marry Louis XII, the duke concluded by saying, 'I beseech your Grace to [tell] Mistress Blount and Mistress Carew the next time that I write unto them or send them tokens they shall either write to me or send me tokens again.'[1] This is the first evidence that Bessie had been noticed by the king.

Suffolk's letter implies that he was well used to both Bessie and her fellow maid, Elizabeth Carew, sending him tokens or messages and that, in addition to this, both he and the king were familiar with the pair. By the late sixteenth century, England was particularly noted for the freedom which it gave to its women, with one visitor to the country commenting that 'the women have much more liberty than perhaps in any other place'.[2] Charles Brandon, Duke of Suffolk, was one of the highest ranking subjects in England.[3] Only just over five years previously he had served as an esquire of the body at the funeral of Henry VII alongside Bessie's father. He also served with John Blount as a member of the king's Spears. It is with these two appointments that any similarities in the careers of John Blount and Charles Brandon ended, however. Following Henry VIII's accession, Brandon's rise was meteoric, helped in no small part by the fact that he had served in the royal household since childhood and was well known to the king, who was only a few years younger than him.

At first, after his accession, Henry had a small circle of favourites made up of his childhood friends, including Edward Howard, Thomas Knyvet and the half-brothers (and Bessie's kinsmen) Edward and Henry Guildford. Brandon was also in this circle. The deaths of Knyvet and Howard during Henry's French wars helped to clear the field somewhat for Brandon. He soon became the king's greatest friend, taking part in court masques and jousts at the king's side. Physically, the two men were similar in both build and appearance and the two would sometimes wear the same clothes. By the end of 1513 Brandon had become the king's leading courtier, being appointed as a knight of the garter and a viscount, in right of his betrothed bride, Elizabeth, Viscountess Lisle. On 1 February 1514 Henry took the highly unusual step of creating his favourite Duke of Suffolk, something which, as it proved, was not the pinnacle of the favourite's ambition.

Even compared to Henry VIII, Suffolk had a complicated marital history. In 1503 he had fallen in love with Anne Browne, who was a gentlewoman of the queen. The couple were secretly betrothed before consummating their relationship, causing Anne to fall pregnant. Before the birth, however, Brandon met Anne's aunt, the wealthy Margaret Mortimer and decided to marry her instead. This relationship lasted until 1507 when Brandon returned to Anne, who had borne him a daughter, marrying her the following year. Anne Browne died in childbirth in 1510, leaving Brandon once again a bachelor (if the still very much alive Margaret Mortimer is discounted). He soon became engaged to the child heiress Elizabeth Lisle, although no formal marriage ceremony ever occurred between the couple. In the autumn of 1513, his flirtatious conduct with Margaret of Austria, Regent of the Netherlands, who was the daughter of the Emperor Maximilian and the former sister-in-law of Catherine of Aragon, gave rise to rumours that he meant to marry her. Henry even spoke to Margaret about the possibility of the match, with Margaret attempting politely to refuse. Brandon joined in, swearing to Margaret, as she herself reminisced, that he 'would continue all his life my right humble servant'.[4] He then took a ring from the startled regent's finger, refusing all requests to return it. It is unclear whether Suffolk was in earnest with Margaret, but it is certain that he desired a royal bride. Love was in the air during Henry and Suffolk's visit to Margaret's court and, at the same time, Henry promised a 10,000-crown dowry to one of Margaret's ladies in waiting,[5] a sum that suggests a little more than a mere flirtation. The rumours of the relationship between Margaret and Suffolk were so widespread that the regent was forced to write to her father denying the match. Less than two years later, in the early months of 1515, Suffolk was again involved in a scandal when word reached England that he had finally acquired a royal bride.

Suffolk's letter makes it clear that both Elizabeth Carew and Bessie Blount had caught the eye of the king and his friend. Elizabeth Carew, who served as a maid of Catherine of Aragon at the same time as Bessie, was the sister of Sir Francis Bryan, a favourite of the king's.[6] The family were far from pious and Sir Francis, who would later lose an eye jousting in one of the king's tournaments, was particularly lax in his morals, earning the nickname of 'the vicar of Hell' from his sovereign. In 1514, whilst she was still very young, his sister Elizabeth married another royal favourite, Nicholas Carew. Elizabeth was well known to Bessie, and the pair often appeared together in court entertainments. Suffolk's reference to them together suggests that they were friends. It is easy to imagine the two young girls flirting with the king and his handsome friend in the autumn of 1514. Surprisingly, given Bessie and Henry's later relationship, it appears that it was Elizabeth who first caught the king's eye. As set out in an earlier chapter, it was not unusual for the king to give gifts of clothing to the queen's maids and other members of the court. However, in the king's wardrobe accounts, which survive for 1516, it is clear that Elizabeth and her husband were particularly favoured.

Elizabeth Carew is often not considered to have been one of the king's mistresses.[7] Certainly, there is no direct evidence for her enjoying a love affair with the king. However, it should be pointed out that, without the birth of Henry Fitzroy, Bessie's own affair would probably have gone unrecorded. Equally, the more famous Mary Boleyn is only recalled as a mistress of the king due to the unusual pattern of grants that her husband received and rumours that were recorded after the king turned his attentions to her sister. It would certainly appear from Suffolk's letter that both he and Henry had an interest in Elizabeth and Bessie. In the 1516 wardrobe account, Nicholas Carew was particularly well provided for, receiving gifts of a purple mantle with black fur on one occasion.[8] He also received a crimson velvet gown with a stylish high collar, again furred, along with a great number of other gifts. Later, he received 'a doublet & hose of crimson cloth of gold the ground of damask gold'.[9] Carew was one of the king's friends, but the gifts to him do appear to have been particularly rich when compared to others made in the same period. Elizabeth Carew was similarly honoured with numerous presents during the period. For example, she received crimson tilsent for a stomacher.[10] A stomacher, which was designed to be worn close to the body was a somewhat intimate item of clothing which Henry is also known to have supplied for Catherine of Aragon on at least one occasion,[11] which suggests that he may have considered it a suitable gift for a lover. In addition to this, Elizabeth received other gifts, such as tawny velvet for a gown, which was to be lined with crimson velvet.[12] Henry gave Elizabeth two yards of cloth of silver of damask for other items of clothing.[13] She appears to have been particularly fond of cloth of silver, receiving further gifts of cloth of silver damask, and of white cloth of silver.[14] The king thought of Elizabeth when his wardrobe was found to contain a remnant of white cloth of silver checked damask, which he gave to her.[15] Clearly, Elizabeth Carew received good quality and expensive gifts from the king. Certainly, it was good enough for the queen herself and the same accounts show that Catherine received a gift of silver damask, presumably similar to that received by Elizabeth

Carew, for the lining of a gown.[16] Henry later paid for fine clothes for Anne Boleyn, a lady with whom he was certainly romantically involved, which suggests that fine clothes were considered to be a suitable gift for a mistress.[17] The gifts to Elizabeth Carew in 1516 go far beyond anything received by the other ladies of the queen's household during that period in both quantity and quality. Bessie received nothing, which strongly suggests that she was not yet the king's mistress. Of the two women named in Suffolk's letter, therefore, it is more likely that Elizabeth Carew first caught the king's attention.

Elizabeth Carew continued to move in royal circles long after she had ceased to be favoured by the king. She later became friends with Henry's eldest daughter, who had been raised in early infancy by Elizabeth's mother. The pair are known to have played cards together.[18] In addition to this, they exchanged New Year's Gifts, with Princess Mary paying a reward to a servant of Lady Carew's in January 1537 and noting the arrival of Lady Carew's gift the following year.[19] Mary stood as godmother to one of Elizabeth Carew's daughters.[20] Elizabeth's husband, Nicholas Carew, was executed in March 1539 for his role in the Exeter Conspiracy against Henry which also involved Henry VIII's Yorkist cousins, the Pole family. This led to the confiscation of the family's property and Elizabeth was forced to plead with the king's chief minister, Thomas Cromwell, for the return of at least some part of her property. She wrote:

> In the most humblest wise I beseech your lordship to be good lord to me and my poor children, to be a mediator unto the king's grace for me, for my living and my children's; and that your lordship would speak to his grace, that I may enjoy that which his grace gave me, which is Bletchingley and Wallington, trusting that his grace will not give it from me. And I humbly desire your good lordship to speak a good word to his grace for me, that I may enjoy it according to his grace's grant. And, to advertise your lordship, I have but twenty pounds more of my husband's lands, which is a small jointure; and if he had not offended the king's grace and his laws, I should have had an honest living, which should have been the third part of his lands; but now I cannot claim that, by reason that he is attainted. I trust his grace will be good to me and my poor children, to reward me with some part of it.[21]

For good measure, Elizabeth Carew ended by pointedly noting that 'all that I have had in my life hath been of his grace, and I trust that his grace will not see me lack; but whatsoever his grace or your lordship shall appoint me, I both must and will be content'. The estate mentioned by Elizabeth in her letter had, along with other lands, been settled by Nicholas Carew's father on the couple at the time of their marriage.[22]

This seems very similar to the way in which Bessie's own future in-laws, the Tailboys family, provided for her and her husband Gilbert on their marriage, something that is usually seen to have been carried out under pressure from the king as his reward to Bessie as his former mistress. Given Elizabeth Carew's own comments on owing the grants to the king and the similarity to the pattern of grants later made to Bessie, this can be considered to be further evidence that she was also the king's mistress for a time. Henry evidently still thought well of her and in 1539, after her appeal was made, she was allowed to retain some property, although she lived in retirement for the rest of her life.[23]

If it was indeed Elizabeth Carew who was the object of the king's affections in late 1514, is it possible that Bessie was involved in an affair with the Duke of Suffolk? This can be inferred from Suffolk's letter.[24] Interestingly, Bessie's own daughter, who, as will be seen, may well have been an illegitimate child of the king, was on friendly terms with Suffolk's illegitimate son, Sir Charles Brandon, suggesting a friendship between the two families.[25] Another connection can be seen in the fact that Sir Edward Grey, Lord Powys, who was the husband of Suffolk's eldest daughter, Anne, stood as godfather for Bessie's nephew, Edward Lacon, in 1541.[26] Given that the child was also named after his sponsor, it would appear that the two families were close. Some historians think this is unlikely given the fact that Bessie never acquired a bad reputation (as the king's later mistress Mary Boleyn did after enjoying affairs with both the king of France and England).[27] This is not entirely the case, however, and John Palsgrave, the ex-tutor of Bessie's own son, later complained that the well-marrying of 'Besse Blount' had encouraged other women to concubinage. Palsgrave had his own agenda behind this comment, using it as an attack on Cardinal Wolsey. However, it does suggest that Bessie's reputation was not, in fact, spotless. Mary Boleyn found that her reputation was no bar to her attending court, although this may have been helped by her sister's position. In fact, the only time that Mary was actively banned from court was when she made a marriage far beneath her in rank – something that, to modern eyes at least, would appear more socially acceptable than an illicit affair, regardless of who her partner was. It is therefore not impossible that Bessie was, indeed, Suffolk's mistress before she became involved with the king.

It appears more likely that the king had already expressed an interest in both ladies by autumn 1514, although it was apparently Elizabeth Carew who was central to his affections. Bessie had a family connection to Suffolk through his betrothed (and later discarded) bride, Elizabeth, Lady Lisle. By May 1513 her grandfather Thomas had been appointed as bailiff and parker of her manor of Chaddesley Corbett[28] and this connection may have been the first thing to bring her to Suffolk's attention. In any event, although they were friends, it is unlikely that

Suffolk was later able to share the details of any romantic entanglements with the king. On 25 October 1514 he had written from France to inform the king of the exemplary way in which his sister, Mary Tudor, had adapted to her new role as queen of France, assuring Henry that she was behaving both wisely and honourably and that her elderly husband 'reckoned he had of him the greatest jewel ever one prince had of another'.[29] The exertions of marriage proved all too much for Louis, who was as anxious to beget a son as his English brother-in-law. On 1 January 1515 the French king died suddenly, leaving his lovely young bride a widow. Suffolk was once again sent to France, this time to negotiate with the new king, Francis I, for Mary's return. He found the queen secluded with a reduced household in enforced mourning, in terror that she would be forced to make a second arranged marriage. Mary was renowned as the most beautiful princess in Europe and she looked upon Suffolk as her saviour, begging him to marry her, which he duly did, in secret. Although Henry later came to accept Suffolk as his brother-in-law and welcomed the couple back to England, it appears very unlikely that he would have tolerated public infidelity on the part of his brother-in-law. It was well accepted that Suffolk, who was described in a couplet on his wedding portrait as 'cloth of frieze', had married significantly above him to 'cloth of gold' and it was Mary who was, socially at least, the dominant partner. It therefore does seem very unlikely that Bessie was ever Suffolk's mistress. At most, there may have been a flirtation between her and the duke at the same time that a more serious relationship developed between Elizabeth Carew and the king.

There was ample opportunity for Bessie to mix with the men of the court. For example, on 7 July 1517, the Venetian ambassador recorded that, at a banquet to follow the day's jousting, the ladies of the queen's household sat alternately with the gentlemen of the court, something that facilitated a good deal of flirting and high spirits.[30] After the meal, the tables were removed to allow for dancing which lasted until two in the morning. Henry has been described as a 'one-woman man',[31] tending to remain faithful to his mistresses. The assumption would therefore be that Bessie became the king's mistress as his affair with Elizabeth Carew came to an end at some point after 1516.

The evidence for Bessie's affair with the king is scant. This is in common with most of Henry's other love affairs as, for obvious reasons, the king had no desire to make them public. At New Year 1515 Bessie was noted to have danced with the king during the revels, something that is suggestive of the fact that she had already caught his eye. Suffolk's letter also implies this. On 23 July 1515 the king made an order in favour of Bessie's father, granting 'to John Blount one of the King's Spears of honour open a warrant for his wages at iij s. iiii d. the day for two whole years which the King hath advanced unto him beforehand that is to say from the first day of this present month of July unto the end of ij years next & immediately ensuing'.[32] Given that the king was already beginning to grow tired of his Spears and that they would soon be disbanded,[33] this payment is a considerable mark of favour and points to Henry's growing interest in Bessie. Given the gifts of clothes made to Elizabeth Carew in 1516, it would appear that she was still firmly ensconced as the king's principal interest until at least early 1517. However, it is certainly not impossible that the king had begun to look favourably on Bessie before that time, subtly favouring her family in a way that, given the payment was an advance rather than a gift, did not actually require much of a financial outlay. He was also not feeling so generous towards Bessie's father that he was prepared to overlook the fact that John had been paid his salary for March 1515 twice, ensuring that it was deducted from the wage advance in July 1515.

One recent historian has commented that it is unlikely that Bessie's affair with Henry began before 1518, asking 'could a relationship of some four years' standing really escape all gossip and censure?'[34] The argument is that the birth of Princess Mary in February 1516 gave Henry the incentive to remain faithful to his wife due to his renewed hopes of an heir. However, there is, of course, no reason why Henry could not have remained hopeful of conceiving another child with Catherine whilst carrying out an affair with one or more of her ladies. There were obviously times when the queen would not be in a position to fulfil her marital duties and when, in any event, conception was unlikely. Dr Murphy considers that Catherine's pregnancy in 1518 triggered the beginning of Bessie's affair, which she described as a short-term liaison. The surviving evidence, such as it is, does point, however, to an affair of considerably longer duration.

Bessie does not appear to have received any substantial gifts or other rewards during her time as the king's mistress. Her family fared a little better. John Blount was appointed as one of the king's esquires of the body in 1517, an appointment that was probably largely due to the king's interest in his daughter. This was a considerably more prestigious office than any he had previously held. It required personal service to the king, with one ordinance, setting out the role during the reign of Henry's father, confirming that:

> All knights and esquires for his body, at such time as they be in his court present, give their due attendance upon his Highness; and that one of the said esquires be nightly at his cup-board marking, and serve him for all night; and he, with others, upon the pallet to lie; upon pain for the first time to be punished by the Lord Chamberlain.[35]

John also received the grant, for his lifetime, of the keepership of Cleobury Park in February 1519, a local honour.[36] At the same time he received the joint stewardship with his father of the manor of Bewdley.[37] The timing of these grants, which occurred midway through Bessie's pregnancy, may also have been significant. Quickening, when the mother first felt the child move, was a significant event in any Tudor pregnancy as it both proved conclusively (in an era with only rudimentary medical care) that the woman was actually pregnant and also signified that the child was likely to live. In a mother's first pregnancy, the first realisation that the baby is moving can come relatively late in the pregnancy and these grants may well tie in with this event for Bessie, indicating that Henry remained interested and involved in her pregnancy.

Although the grants were generous, John received little else from his daughter's relationship with the king and did not receive a knighthood until 1529. His appointment as master of the game in Wyre Forest, which occurred around this time, may also have been due to Bessie's affair.[38] The grants potentially increased the friction between Bessie's father and grandfather. The Bewdley grant, which was a joint one to John and Thomas, was made only after Thomas had been required to surrender his patent, which he had obtained from Henry VII, granting him the stewardship in the sole name. Equally, it would appear that John lost some autonomy in the grant as, at the same time, father and son were appointed as parkers of the parks in the forest of Wyre, something that would have given Thomas an interest in an area that had previously been under John's authority alone. Thomas Blount was appointed as sheriff of Shropshire in 1518, although this office, for which he was more than qualified, need not necessarily have been due to Bessie's influence.

John was unable to retain Bewdley for long, losing it to Sir William Compton on Thomas' death in 1524.[39] It was only returned to him after Compton's death. As will be demonstrated later, there was considerable hostility between John Blount and Sir William Compton. Does this, alongside the fact that John benefitted very little from Bessie's relationship with the king, suggest that he did not approve of the relationship? Given Compton's role in procuring Lady Anne Hastings for the king, it is not impossible that he was employed to play a similar intermediary role with Bessie. Certainly, when Henry sought a Mistress Amadas as his mistress, who was the wife of a former master of the jewel house, it was at Compton's house that the meeting was planned, again suggesting Compton's unofficial role in the king's love affairs.[40] Perhaps John, aware of this and angered by his daughter's lost honour, came to resent this, thus dividing the family, with his father and brother Edward retaining friendly links with the king's favourite. John Blount did, however, benefit from his daughter's involvement with the king, particularly in later years following the birth of Henry Fitzroy, suggesting a tacit complicity or, at least, acceptance. The king's privy purse expenses for 7 January 1530, for example, record a sum 'the same day paid to a servant of John Blont's in reward for bringing a horse to the kings grace'.[41] This suggests that the horse had been Bessie's father's New Year's gift to the king, demonstrating his increased status that only the king's affair with his daughter and the birth of Henry Fitzroy can have brought. Both John and Thomas were included in the gentlemen permitted to attend the Field of the Cloth of Gold in 1520, which was the king's lavish meeting with the king of France.[42] Tellingly, father and son were once again separated, with Thomas representing Shropshire and John Staffordshire.

The recent biographer of Bessie's son claimed that 'Elizabeth [Bessie] herself might well have received personal gifts of jewels or money, but none of this demonstrates the sort of marked generosity one would expect from the king if the relationship had been of any duration'.[43] Dr Murphy considers that the affair may only have lasted a few months. It is certainly true that there are few records of the relationship, aside from the very obvious presence of the couple's son. The only near contemporary reference can be found in Edward Hall's writings, in his entry for the year 1525, in which he stated that:

> You shall understand, the king in his fresh youth, was in the chains of love, with a fair damsel called Elizabeth Blunt, daughter to sir John Blunt knight, which damsel in singing, dancing, and in all goodly pastimes, she won the king's heart: and she again showed him such favour, that by him she bare a goodly man child, of beauty like to the father and mother.[44]

John Blunt was not knighted until 1529, which suggests that Hall's entry must have been written, at its earliest, over a decade after Henry Fitzroy's birth. The lack of contemporary notice of the affair is not particularly surprising. Given the lack of evidence about all of Henry's affairs (with the exception of his relationship with Anne Boleyn which, of course, eventually led to marriage), it is entirely plausible that the affair with Bessie may have been of considerably longer duration. There is not a great deal of evidence for Henry's relationship with Mary Boleyn, one of his best-documented affairs. In the nineteenth century it was even common for rumours of the affair to be viewed as slander. The evidence for the Mary Boleyn's affair is somewhat scattered and includes details of grants made to her husband. There is also the evidence of a letter from Sir George Throckmorton to the king, describing a meeting that he had had with Henry during Anne Boleyn's time as queen, stating that he had warned the king against marrying Anne 'for it is thought you have meddled both with the mother and the sister'.[45] On hearing this, the king apparently blushed, muttering 'never with the mother', a response to which the king's chief minister, Thomas Cromwell, was forced to add 'nor never with the sister either, and therefore put that out of your mind'. Clearly the affair with Mary Boleyn was common knowledge, as was the implausible rumour that Henry had been romantically involved with Elizabeth Boleyn, the Boleyn sisters' mother.[46] The king certainly never made any formal declaration of his interest in Mary. Mary Boleyn personally received no recorded grants. Jane Seymour, whom the king later married, received small tokens during the king's attempts to make her his mistress: the gift of his portrait set into a pendant and a bag of gold coins (which she rejected).[47] Her family received little before her marriage to the king, with her brother only receiving the gift of a fine new apartment at court as a means for the king to be better able to visit Jane in private there.[48] Anne Boleyn also received a picture of the king early in the relationship, an attempt by Henry to ensure that he remained in her thoughts; however, few other gifts are recorded before she had agreed to become his wife.[49] The assumption must be that Bessie received small tokens, such as jewellery, money and clothing, but nothing substantial until her marriage was arranged. That no record of these gifts survives is entirely plausible given their trifling nature. None of Henry's mistresses (with the exception of Anne Boleyn before her marriage, if she can be considered to have been the king's mistress) attained any overt political role and their influence over the king leaves very little trace in the records. It is therefore necessary with all Henry's mistresses to reconstruct details of their affairs with the often limited evidence. This is the same for Bessie.

The absence of any known grants to Bessie during the time of the affair may also have another meaning. During her time at court, Henry was the handsomest prince in Europe. Perhaps the simplest explanation for Bessie's lack of ambition is that she loved him. Certainly, Lord Herbert of Cherbury, writing in the following century using sources that are no longer available, declared, specifically in relation to Bessie, that the king 'both gave and receiv'd temptation'.[50] Bessie may simply have been attracted to the handsome and powerful king and fell in love. In return, she also appears to have been one of Henry's favourite mistresses, with Herbert commenting that she was thought 'for her rare ornaments of nature, and education, to be the beauty and mistress-piece of her time', causing 'entire affection' to pass between them.

There is also another piece of evidence that suggests that the king's interest in Bessie may have begun earlier than commonly allowed. In the inventory of Henry VIII's goods, prepared after his death, it was noted that Henry possessed two flagons 'hereafter mentioned by the right honourable Edward Lord Clinton high Admiral of England as a present from the king's Majesty to the French queen at the christening of her son'.[51] Edward, Lord Clinton, would later become Bessie's second husband in the 1530s. He was not born until 1512 and there is therefore no possibility that he would have been at court, or remembered the christening of Mary Tudor's first son by her second husband, Charles Brandon, Duke of Suffolk, which occurred in March 1516. It is not impossible that it was Bessie who remembered the christening, and the nature of the king's fine gift, and had mentioned this to her second husband in later life. Bessie was long since dead by the time that the inventory was prepared but such an interpretation is not unlikely. It seems otherwise odd that Lord Clinton was so definite in his identification of the flagons as having been the king's christening gift to his nephew.

It is obviously not possible to confirm when the relationship between Henry and Bessie was first consummated, and it appears that, at least at first, Bessie was not the king's primary interest, merely being an object of admiration and someone with whom he could flirt. However, it does seem likely that Bessie had fully supplanted Elizabeth Carew in the king's affections by at least the end of 1517, at the latest. It has been suggested that Sir Francis Bryan, the brother of Elizabeth Carew, may have acted, at first, as the go-between for Henry and Bessie.[52] This is possible. Bryan was known to Bessie, and she and Bryan danced together in a court masque in October 1518. Bryan is also known to have actively supported his cousin, Anne Boleyn, in her rise to prominence before, after quarrelling with her, bringing another cousin, Jane Seymour, to court, apparently with the intention of her becoming the king's mistress.[53] However, it seems implausible that Bryan would have worked to supplant his own sister with Bessie, a woman with whom he shared only a distant connection through the Guildford family. Instead, if Henry required a go-between at all to arrange meetings with Bessie, Sir William Compton, who is known to have performed that particular office before, must be the most likely candidate. On becoming the king's mistress, Bessie would have regularly found herself alone with the king in his most intimate room: his bedchamber. There were ways for the king to meet secretly with a lady, away from the prying eyes of the court. In the months before his marriage with Jane Seymour, for example, Henry moved her brother and sister-in-law into a chamber connected to his own by means of a secret staircase, something that facilitated regular meetings with his beloved. Henry fiercely guarded his privacy and he ensured that his innermost apartments were as opulently furnished as the rest of the court. The inventory taken at the time of Henry's death shows that he owned a fine bed which had originally belonged to the Duke of Buckingham, who was executed in 1521. Such beds would have been very comfortable, with down and fustian used for comfort and quilts for warmth, such as the two old Turkish silk quilts that the king owned at his death, paned with the Tudor colours of white and green.[54] He made a present of 'one of the most magnificent and gorgeous beds that could be thought of' to Anne Boleyn following their marriage, which suggests that he liked to be comfortable.[55] At the Palace of Westminster, Henry had a study off his bedchamber, allowing him to work in the comfort of private surroundings.[56]

Henry did not really have a 'type' in the women that he selected as his wives and mistresses, with his tastes often veering between very different kinds of women. For example, the dark, elegant and outspoken Anne Boleyn was supplanted by Jane Seymour, a lady who cultivated a meek and unassuming nature and was described as 'so fair that one would call her rather pale than otherwise'.[57] It was considered positive in 1538 when Christina of Denmark, a lady that the king was considering marrying without having met her, was described as resembling Margaret Shelton, one of Henry's former mistresses. However, it does appear that Henry had rather eclectic tastes and Bessie, in spite of her widely regarded beauty and accomplishments, cannot have expected the king's attentions. It is also clear from the evidence of Henry's other relationships that he liked to pursue a woman rather than simply being offered her favours without any show of honour. When Jane Seymour married the king in 1536 when she was in her late twenties, the imperial ambassador, Eustace Chapuys, archly commented that he had doubts that she could still be a virgin, having spent so long at Henry's court.[58] The king's fifth wife, Catherine Howard, in spite of her young age at the time of her marriage, had also already lost her virginity. Regardless of any doubts over the purity of the object of his affections that the king might have, he liked to pursue them, bombarding Anne Boleyn with love letters when she withdrew from court during the early months of his interest in her. Henry's courtship of Bessie would, presumably, have involved a similar pursuit, with the king acting as a gallant suitor.

For Bessie, agreeing to become the king's mistress was a major step. It has been recently observed that all sixteenth-century texts on the role of women contain the basic themes of chastity, silence and obedience and this 'can be briefly summarised as the requirements that women should be celibate if unmarried and faithful if married, should recognise the superiority of their menfolk, and should neither gossip nor put their own ideas forward'.[59] Truly chaste young gentlewomen stayed in the home and were chaperoned by their female relations. This was a theme drawn upon in the works of the Spanish educationalist Luis Vives, who was commissioned by Catherine of Aragon to write a treatise on female education for the benefit of her daughter, Princess Mary. Vives was particularly concerned about girls socialising outside the home, with all the perils to their virginity that this entailed. He considered dancing to be particularly abhorrent, with its 'shaking and bragging and uncleanly handlings gropyings and kissings and a very kindling of lechery'.[60] This paints a rather lurid picture of the dancing and court entertainments at which Bessie excelled and may help to explain how she so quickly became intimate with the king. There was, of course, a certain stigma in being an unmarried girl engaged in a sexual relationship with anyone in the sixteenth century. Mary Boleyn, for example, was described unkindly both as 'a very great whore and infamous above others' and as an

'English mare' by Francis I of France, with whom she had been involved in a brief liaison before she returned to England. However, in spite of her sullied reputation, she remained included in her family and even secured a court appointment, which suggests that an illicit relationship need not necessarily be a bar to some level of respectability. Catherine Parr, aware of what had happened to the king's five previous wives, is also reputed to have declared that she would rather be his mistress, again suggesting that a relationship with someone of a significantly higher rank, such as the king, need not destroy a woman's reputation. For Bessie, therefore, there must have been a great deal of gossip, which is likely to have been uncomfortable. However, even without the king's assistance, the relationship would have been no bar to her finding a husband and her character was very far from ruined. Discounting her first marriage, which was arranged by Cardinal Wolsey, Bessie's later suitors (such as the king's cousin, Lord Leonard Grey) are likely to have been attracted to her connection to the king, and thus her probable influence with him, rather than repelled by it.

Bessie therefore seems to have attracted the king as early as New Year 1515. However, given his prior interest in Elizabeth Carew, it is likely that there was, at most, a flirtation between the pair, with Bessie also enjoying a flirtation with the Duke of Suffolk. At some point in 1517, when Henry's affair with Elizabeth Carew came to an end, the king turned his attentions to Bessie in earnest. Given the grants and appointments to her family, however modest, it appears that Bessie was ensconced as the king's mistress by the middle of 1517, with the affair having far more serious implications in the autumn of 1518.

## IO

# MOTHER OF THE KING'S SON

Although the origin of her affair with Henry VIII is shrouded in mystery, what is certain is that, by the last few months of 1518, Bessie was aware that she was carrying the king's child. Methods of contraception were known in the sixteenth century and Bessie's successor as the king's love, Catherine Howard, who became his fifth wife, later commented that she knew ways to avoid conceiving a child. However, accidents could happen and, for Bessie, who was already the king's mistress, there was little further stigma in bearing the king's child. In fact, given Catherine of Aragon's poor childbearing record, Bessie would have known that she would be richly rewarded if she bore the king his first surviving son, even if that son was illegitimate. Her overriding emotion, on realising that she had conceived, would therefore have been pleasure, as would the king's.

The Tudor royal court, like its medieval predecessor, was highly mobile. It has been noted that Henry rarely stayed in one place for more than a month, something that was largely due to hygiene and the need for a palace to be deep-cleaned.[1] Moving the entire royal court could be a major undertaking, as a visitor to the court of Henry's daughter, Elizabeth I, noted:

> When the queen breaks up her court, with the intention of visiting another place, there commonly follow more than 300 carts laden with bags and baggage; for you must known that in England, besides coaches, they use no wagons for the goods, but have only two-wheeled carts, which however are so large that they carry quite as much as wagons, and as many as five or six strong horses draw them.[2]

Whilst in the winter months the court tended to remain in the vicinity of London, in the summer the king and his court would go on progress.

The king's comfort was, of course, assured, but the progress may have been less welcomed by other members of the court. Often the residence chosen for the king's stay would be too small for the entire court. Lucky courtiers would find lodging in a local inn, but tents would also be pitched to ensure that the king and queen travelled with a suitably magnificent household.[3] Even Greenwich Palace was not large enough to accommodate Henry's entire court, with the king renting properties close to the palace.[4] Details of the great efforts that were made to secure lodgings for everyone can be seen in the records of the preparations made for the Emperor Charles V's visit to England in 1522. Detailed notes were made of the number of people a host could lodge; for example, one Dr Smith was noted to have ten beds, with a hall, parlour, four chambers, two garrets, a chapel and ten feather beds.[5] Another host, one Master Lylly, a schoolmaster, provided four beds. Provisions would be issued to the hosts for their charges, with the king's officers noting, in preparation for the emperor's visit, that clerks were to 'see every lodging furnished with bread, beef, mutton, wild fowl, wax, and spices, and all other things necessary, and beer, ale, and wine, to be couched in their lodgings by the King's officers'.[6] The king often stayed in the homes of favoured courtiers, with Bessie's great-uncle, Sir Edward Darrell, receiving a visit in the summer of 1520.[7] This could be something of a poisoned chalice, with the king often being forced to pay reparations to householders after they found that members of the court helped themselves to their belongings. It was lamented in a set of the king's household ordinances that:

> It is often and in manner daily seen, that as well in the king's own houses, as in the places of other noblemen and gentlemen, where the king's grace doth fortune to lie or come unto, not only locks of doors, tables, forms, cupboards, trestles, and other implements of household, be carried, purloined, and taken away, by such servants and others as be lodged in the same houses and places, but also such pleasures and commodities as they have about their houses, that is to say, deer, fish, orchards, hay, corn, grass, pasture, and other stores belonging to the same noblemen and gentlemen, or to others dwelling near about, is by … taken, despoiled, wasted and spent, without licence or consent of the owner, or any money paid for the same, to the king's great dishonour.[8]

The court was a rowdy, noisy, dirty place, but it was also exciting and the centre of society in England.

In order to carry out her duties in the queen's household, Bessie moved with the court. Apart from brief visits to religious sites, Catherine tended to stay with the king.[9] It is possible to construct something of the itinerary of the court during Bessie's time there, demonstrating the ever-changing environment in which she would have found herself. For example, between May and June 1513, the court was at Greenwich, a favourite palace of the king's.[10] In late October of that year, the king could be found at Windsor, remaining there until December.[11] In early 1514 the court was at Richmond, moving to Lambeth by 30 January 1514.[12] Henry was at Greenwich in March 1514, remaining there into April.[13] At the end of the month he moved to Eltham Palace, where he had spent much of his childhood, staying into June.[14] That autumn the court slowly made its way down towards Dover in order to bid farewell to Henry's sister, Mary Tudor, who travelled to France to marry the elderly French king.[15] They then returned to Eltham before moving to Greenwich in November 1514.[16] This pattern of constant movement continued throughout Bessie's time at court and she must have been constantly used to packing and unpacking her possessions, as well as helping to ensure that the queen's belongings and furniture were safely stowed away for their journeys. By far, the king's favourite palace during Bessie's time at court was Greenwich, where, in 1515, for example, he spent 64 per cent of the year, compared to only 12 per cent at Richmond and 7 per cent at Windsor.[17] In 1519, a year that Bessie spent away from the court, the king spent 45 per cent of the year at Greenwich. Of considerable interest is, of course, Henry's itinerary during the later months of 1518. Given that Bessie would not have been allowed to appear at court visibly pregnant during her last appearance in October 1518 and that her son received advancement and his own household in June 1525, implying that he had recently turned six, it has been very plausibly suggested that Henry Fitzroy was born in June 1519.[18] This would mean that he was conceived in the autumn of 1518, perhaps at some point in September or October. In early August 1518, the king was staying at Greenwich Palace.[19] He moved to Eltham on 15 August, remaining there until the middle of September. His next visit was to Greenwich, where he remained until the early days of October, before moving on to Durham Place. Catherine of Aragon was, by that stage, heavily pregnant, and the king kept her, and her household, close to him. He would also not have risked having sexual relations with Catherine at that late stage of pregnancy, ensuring that Bessie, as his mistress, had the king's attentions entirely to herself. Based on the surviving details of the king's itinerary, it would appear very likely that Greenwich Palace can be considered the place that Bessie conceived the king's child. Alternatively, Eltham or Durham Place are plausible.

Bessie made her final appearance at court early in October 1518. Earlier that year Francis I of France sent ambassadors to Henry to discuss the return of Tournay, a city that the English king had taken during his campaign in 1513.[20] An agreement was soon reached, with Francis agreeing to pay for the city's redemption, as well as sums as payment for the improvements that Henry had made to the town. As an added incentive for peace, Francis offered his eldest son, the Dauphin, as a husband for Princess Mary. On 3 October a general peace between England and France was proclaimed in London.[21] Henry, Cardinal Wolsey and the French ambassadors went to St Paul's Cathedral, where they ceremonially swore to uphold the peace, before going to the palace of the Bishop of London to dine. The entire company then moved to Wolsey's own palace for an even more sumptuous supper. Bessie, although present in the palace, did not attend the supper, instead spending the time dressing and making last-minute rehearsals for the masque in which she had been selected to play a prominent part. According to the Venetian, Sebastian Giustinian:

> After supper, a mummery, consisting of twelve male and twelve female maskers, made their appearance in the richest and most sumptuous array possible, being all dressed alike. After performing certain dances in their own fashion, they took off their visors; the two leaders were the king and the queen dowager of France, and all the others were lords and ladies, who seated themselves apart from the tables, and were served with countless dishes and confections and other delicacies. Having gratified their palates, they then regaled their eyes and hands, large bowls, filled with ducats and dice, being placed on the table for such as liked to gamble; shortly after which, the supper tables being removed, dancing commenced, and lasted until after midnight.[22]

Whilst Henry danced with his sister, Mary Tudor, Bessie was partnered by the king's friend, Sir Francis Bryan. Edward Hall gives a more detailed account of the festivities:

> Persons disguised were in one suite of fine green satin all over-covered with cloth of gold, under tied together with laces of gold, and masking hoods on their heads: the ladies had attires made of braids of damask gold, with long hairs of white gold. All these maskers danced at one time, and after they had danced, they put off their visors, and then they were all known.[23]

This must have been one of the most sumptuous masques in which Bessie danced and it was her parting triumph.

Two days later the court assembled once again to witness the betrothal of the infant Princess Mary to the French Dauphin. Catherine of Aragon, heavily pregnant with her last child, stood richly dressed with her daughter, alongside both her husband and his sister whilst the ceremony took place. Bessie, as one of the queen's attendants, was present in the room and, as she watched Henry and Catherine give their consent to the marriage whilst a ring was placed by Wolsey on the little princess's finger to symbolise her marriage, Bessie's thoughts must have been drawn to the child that she knew she was carrying and the future that they could expect themselves as a child of the king.

During the early months of her pregnancy, Bessie probably continued much as before, remaining in the queen's household. However, once her pregnancy became obvious she could not decently expect to stay with the queen, particularly after Catherine's own pregnancy ended in disappointment. Around a month early, on 10 November 1518, Catherine was 'delivered of a daughter, to the vexation of everybody'.[24] This daughter did not even provide her mother with the consolation of surviving as she was either stillborn[25] or died within hours of her birth. She was the last child that Catherine conceived, with the queen, who was then only just approaching her thirty-third birthday, suffering from an early menopause. There was added heartbreak for the queen when she learned of her maid's pregnancy following her own disappointment, particularly when, as the months advanced, it became increasingly clear that Bessie would carry the king's child to term, unlike Catherine, whose children tended to be some weeks premature.

Bessie cannot have remained at court for very long into her pregnancy given the fashion for tight-fitting bodices which left little to the imagination. There is little evidence for maternity clothes in the Tudor period, although it does appear from portraits depicting pregnant women that they continued to wear their usual clothes, merely leaving their outer dresses open at the front as they became impossible to close.[26] Often the lady in question would hold the dress in place with a belt or decorative chain, which may also have been used to emphasise her fertility. The imperial ambassador, Eustace Chapuys, commented that Anne Boleyn had added a panel to the front of her gown due to her advancing pregnancy 'as ladies in the family-way are wont to do in this country, when they find their robes get too tight'.[27] Henry's third wife, Jane Seymour, appeared in public with her gown open-laced as a sign of her own approaching confinement.[28] Bessie would presumably have modified her own clothes in a similar manner to accommodate her growing bulk. It is likely that she spent her pregnancy at the Priory of St Lawrence at Blackmore in Essex, where her child was born. She stayed in the prior's house on the site, rather than in the priory itself. The arrangements for her stay were made by Cardinal Wolsey, who took an active interest in Henry's illegitimate child from the outset. The king tended to take an interest in his wives' pregnancies, ensuring that the women were comfortable and that their wishes were granted and there is no reason why Bessie could not have expected similar treatment. Jane Seymour, for example, received regular deliveries of plump quails from France as soon as she made her craving for them known to her husband.[29]

Blackmore, which is in the heart of Essex and only a few miles from Chelmsford, was dominated by its priory and it is likely that Wolsey chose the location as one that was sufficiently quiet not to rouse unwelcome gossip, but close enough to London, and to other royal residences, to ensure that Bessie and her child could be quickly reached if required. The priory had been founded during the reign of King John in the early thirteenth century.[30] It was occupied by canons of the Order of St Augustine, enduring until 1527 when it was dissolved by the king, and granted to Cardinal Wolsey to form part of the endowment of his college at Oxford. Following the cardinal's fall, the former priory was returned to crown ownership. The king then granted it to Waltham Abbey, only for it to once more fall into royal hands with the general dissolution of the monasteries in England. The priory stood close to the church but nothing now survives of the fabric of the building, which was pulled down later in Henry VIII's reign.[31] The priory church, with its fine wooden tower, survives today and would be the only building in the area recognisable to Bessie.

It has been suggested that the king dissolved the house originally due to his concerns over the moral standards of the canons. If this was the case, it was a rather circular argument. The priory appears to have had something of a poor reputation due to Henry's own conduct, with one eighteenth century author noting that it 'is reported to have been one of King Henry the Eighth's Houses of Pleasure; and disguised by the name of Jericho. So that when this lascivious Prince had a mind to be lost in the embraces of his courtesans, the cant word among the courtiers, was, that He was gone to Jericho.'[32] Blackmore does indeed seem to have had something of a bawdy reputation. It is clear that it was known as Jericho in Bessie's time as a lease from 1529 of the manor, lordship and rectory of Blackmore also made provision for a tenement 'called Jericho' to be included in the grant.[33] There is no record of any other mistress of the king being housed there other than Bessie and its reputation may be somewhat exaggerated. It is certainly an exaggeration to assert, as one nineteenth-century writer did, that the 'specimens of levity' witnessed at the house when Henry was visiting 'for the purposes of lascivious dissipation' caused him to turn against all monastic houses, bringing about the dissolution of the monasteries.[34] Bessie did not arrive at the priory until some months into her first pregnancy and the rumours do suggest that the king visited her there, and that their affair continued after her arrival there. As will be argued in a later chapter, it is likely that the affair endured for some months or even years whilst Bessie remained at Blackmore. There are no records that the king ever stayed the night at Blackmore[35] and his visits to Bessie, who may have felt very isolated from affairs, must have been fleeting. Bessie Blount, regardless of her personal influence over the king, can certainly not be credited with bringing about the dissolution of the monasteries!

One hint that the occupants of the priory cannot indeed be described as models of sobriety, quiet contemplation and service to God can be seen in the records of the dissolution of the priory. At the time that it was dissolved, the prior was found to owe over £35, a sum that was over a third of the house's total annual income.[36] These sums were not all borrowed to promote the works of the house, with the records showing that the prior owed eleven pounds to one Anne Clowdon for services and 'certain stuff' that she had lent him, as well as a number of vague references to 'works', and over eight pounds for three pairs of hose and cloth (a vast sum for clothing). There were also sums he owed to individuals for loans. From the records of the house, it does appear that the prior was somewhat more worldly than he should have been. The year 1527 was an early date for dissolution, which suggests that there were ecclesiastical and royal concerns over the house.

Whatever its reputation, Blackmore had the advantage of being close to the royal residence of Newhall, which was renamed Beaulieu in 1523.[37] Although there is no record that Bessie ever visited the palace, she remains associated with it to the present day, with rumours, enduring into the twentieth century, that the king built the house for her.[38] There is simply no evidence for this and, given the fact that Bessie never took up residence in the manor, with it instead remaining in royal hands, it is clear that it is a false assumption. It does again, however, suggest that Bessie's presence in Essex was widely known and that, although Newhall was never Bessie's base, it was the king's when he set out to visit her. This is once again evidence that Bessie's departure from court was not the end of the affair between her and the king.

Although it was not built for Bessie, Newhall was a fine residence and one that the king fitted out to the highest standards for his own comfort, making it one of his favourite residences for a time. Henry purchased the manor from his future father-in-law, Sir Thomas Boleyn, in 1516, having taken a fancy to it on a visit during his summer progress in the previous year.[39] He spent considerable sums of money in renovating the palace between March 1517 and June 1521 and was a frequent visitor throughout that period and later. Surviving accounts relating to the palace demonstrate that it was sumptuously furnished, with one of the king's agents making two trips to London from the palace specifically to survey the king's wardrobe for hangings that would fit the palace.[40] Fine Holland cloth was purchased for the soft furnishings, as well as carpets of tapestry work and hangings for the windows. Newhall became such a favourite of Henry's that, in 1522, he spent more time there than at Richmond and Windsor combined.[41] He remained fond of the residence, spending time in the gardens there during his visits.[42] A major advantage to Newhall, as far as the king was concerned, was that it was spacious enough for his entire household to be lodged there and was also close to London. In addition to this, it was situated in an area in which the king liked to hunt. As will be shown later, it is very likely that the close proximity of Blackmore to Newhall was no accident. It would have been entirely possible for the king, out on a day's hunting, to slip away with only a few attendants to ride the short distance to Blackmore if he so chose. Given the romantic associations of hunting, this would also have appealed to Henry's own sense of chivalry and it is perhaps no accident that Bessie found herself situated close to one of the king's favourite hunting grounds. Hunting was not just a sport and it has been pointed out that, in the Middle Ages at least, it was commonly associated in literature with ideas of chivalric love: 'traditionally, hunting had a clear erotic meaning, but not only was the pursuit of the quarry a metaphor for love, but the hunting field could provide a suitable venue for amorous dalliance'.[43] Hunting would be used as a metaphor in the later romance of the king with Anne Boleyn, with the king's friend (and Anne's own former suitor) Sir Thomas Wyatt composing a poem that compared the future queen to a deer in the hunt, pursued by a number of suitors, of which the king was, unsurprisingly enough, the most successful:

> Whoso list to hunt? I know where is an hind!
> But as for me, alas! I may no more,
> The vain travail hath wearied me so sore;
> I am of them the furthest come behind.
> Yet may I by no means my wearied mind,
> Draw from the deer; but as she fleeth afore
> Fainting I follow; I leave off therefore,
> Since in a net I seek to hold the wind.
> Who list her hunt, I put him out of doubt
> As well as I, may spend his time in vain!
> And graven with diamonds in letters plain,
> There is written her fair neck round about;
> 'Noli me tangere;[44] for Caesar's I am,
> And wild for to hold, though I seem tame.[45]

It is not hard to imagine the king, whilst undertaking his favourite pastime of hunting, also casting himself in the role of a gallant lover as he made his way from Newhall to Blackmore on a visit to his mistress.

Bessie spent the final months of her pregnancy at Blackmore, awaiting the birth of her child. Childbirth in the sixteenth century was dangerous. Henry's own mother, Elizabeth of York, as well as two of his wives, Jane Seymour and Catherine Parr, died of complications relating to childbirth, in spite of the highest level medical care that they could expect to receive. When Bessie went into labour, she would have been attended by a midwife, who played a key part in all births.[46] In England in Bessie's time, midwives did not require any formal training, with the only qualification necessary to practise being a licence obtained from a bishop (something that was associated with the need to baptise newborns who were not expected to live rather than for any medical purpose). However, Bessie, as the king's mistress can at least have expected that her midwife and other medical attendants would have had good reputations. Such matters were almost certainly left to Cardinal Wolsey, who oversaw so much of Bessie and her son's lives, to arrange. It is likely that some of Bessie's female relatives would have been in attendance, including, perhaps, her mother, who had finally completed her own family a year or so before. Her sisters were still young, but it is not impossible that they were there, although it may have been considered that attendance on their unmarried sister as she gave birth would have had a detrimental effect on their own characters.[47] Bessie had a number of aunts who could have been called upon to provide assistance, including Katherine Smyth, who, as a resident of Thames Ditton near Hampton Court, was well placed to have been called upon to attend her niece in the final months of her pregnancy. The presence of family must have been some comfort as childbirth then, as now, was excruciatingly painful. Given the religious view that women must endure such pain, nothing effective was done to counter this and Bessie, along with all her female contemporaries, was merely required to endure. No details of Bessie's labour survive. Often, with first children, the trial could be long. Henry's third wife, Jane Seymour, for example, suffered for over two days before finally bearing the king a son. For Bessie, the final result would have been just as satisfactory: illegitimate or not, a son was always preferable to a daughter in the sixteenth century.

A royal child could expect their nursery to be presided over by a lady mistress, with rockers and other servants in attendance. There is no evidence of what was provided for Bessie's son, Henry Fitzroy, by way of servants, although it is improbable that Bessie would have been expected to care for him herself. Almost immediately after birth, Fitzroy would have been tightly wrapped, in order to keep his limbs straight – the usual practice for babies at the time.[48] As a gentlewoman, Bessie would not have suckled her own child; a wet nurse would have been engaged before the birth. The wet nurse would have been very carefully selected, perhaps with Bessie playing a role, with it commonly believed that the nurse would pass her temperament on to the child with her milk.[49] More practically, it was also necessary to engage a healthy woman.

No details of Henry Fitzroy's christening survive, although it is known that Cardinal Wolsey was his godfather. The other godparents are not recorded. His future close associate, the third Duke of Norfolk , who has been suggested as a possible candidate, is unlikely given the fact that in 1519 his father was still alive, making him a more obvious choice. It is not, however, improbable that the second godfather would have been Henry VIII himself. It was not at all uncommon for close relatives to act as godparents, with Henry taking the role at the christening of his nephew, Henry Brandon, in March 1516[50] and his daughter, Princess

Mary, standing as godmother for her half-brother, the future Edward VI, in 1537. Often the child was named after one of their godparents, although, in the case of Henry Fitzroy, it is probable that Henry would have required his son to bear his name regardless of who stood as his sponsor at the font. The godmother's name also does not survive, although it would seem probable that it was a member of Bessie's family – perhaps her mother?[51] Wolsey may have attended the baptism in person although Henry was certainly not there. On 18 June 1519, Wolsey was with Henry and the court at Windsor. The next day, although expected at Hampton Court, he vanishes from the records, only reappearing on 29 June at Westminster.[52] One recent historian makes the valid point that, given that 18 June 1525 was the date chosen by Henry to elevate his son to the peerage (with the same date in a previous year being chosen for a royal grant to Bessie and her husband), that may also have been his birthday. If that was the case, the king and Wolsey were together when news of the birth reached them and Wolsey went immediately to Blackmore with the king's blessing. More significantly for Bessie, he came with something much more precious: confirmation that the king recognised the baby as his son and would allow him to use both his own Christian name, and the surname 'Fitzroy', meaning literally 'son of the king'.[53] With Wolsey as the godfather and the king's acknowledgement, Bessie must have been satisfied as she gave her son her own blessing before he was carried to the chapel at Blackmore for his baptism a few days after the birth.

Henry Fitzroy's birth otherwise caused no stir and was kept entirely secret at court. Although it has been suggested by a biographer of Catherine of Aragon that Henry made a public show of celebration following the birth of his illegitimate child, there is no evidence for this.[54] It appears more likely that the king, whilst privately overjoyed to father an apparently healthy son, was also anxious to ensure that this child was likely to survive before he made the world aware of his presence. Henry Fitzroy was also, after all, a child begotten in adultery, something that it was not necessarily desirable to crow about in public, although the innermost circles of the court must soon have been aware of Bessie's son's existence. He was probably an open secret and, as has been suggested, it is not at all impossible that the king made loud private comments and celebrations about the birth of his son during a banquet that he held that summer whilst visiting Newhall, something that would further account for Bessie's rumoured association with the manor.[55]

Once Henry Fitzroy had been christened and his care passed into the control of his nurses and other attendants, life resumed pretty much as before for Bessie in the quiet of Blackmore. Given the king's desire for secrecy, she must have been aware that any return to court in the near future was unlikely, although it is probable that Cardinal Wolsey, during his brief visit to Blackmore, informed her that she could shortly expect a visit from the king himself.

# MOTHER OF THE KING'S DAUGHTER?

As with so much of her life, Bessie's whereabouts following the birth of Henry Fitzroy are far from clear. Although generally historians have assumed that her affair with Henry ended before the birth of Henry Fitzroy, it is highly likely that the relationship was considerably longer-lasting than previously supposed.

The first reference to Bessie's marriage to Gilbert Tailboys, a young man of Cardinal Wolsey's household, is on 18 June 1522 when the king granted the couple the Warwickshire manor of Rugby. The year 1522 has generally been accepted to have been when the couple married. Interestingly, 1522 was also the year that Henry VIII first spoke of obtaining a divorce from Catherine of Aragon, apparently speaking to the Bishop of Lincoln on the subject. One recent writer has suggested that there was a chance that Henry was considering a marriage to Bessie herself, although they do point out that this is pure speculation.[1] Henry was, in any event, apparently informed that a divorce was impossible and no further action in relation to his marriage was taken until five years later. There were certainly later commentators who thought that a marriage to Bessie did make good sense for the king.

Bessie's second child was a daughter, Elizabeth Tailboys. In a document dated to 26 June 1542, Elizabeth was described as then twenty-two years old.[2] The document was an *Inquisition Post Mortem* relating to Elizabeth's younger brother, Bessie's second surviving son by Gilbert. Such documents, which involved an enquiry into the estates and family of a deceased landowner, were usually very carefully compiled and thus accurate. This would mean that Elizabeth Tailboys must have been born at some point between July 1519 and June 1520. Clearly, she cannot have been born within nine months of her elder brother's birth in June 1519, meaning that April 1520 must be the earliest possible birth date. Even a birthdate of June 1520, the latest possible birthdate, would mean a conception in early September 1519. Dr Murphy, Henry

Fitzroy's recent biographer, has dismissed the possibility that Elizabeth could have been a daughter of Henry VIII as 'given Henry's desperate lack of useful issue, it seems untenable that any offspring of his, even if she were only a daughter, would have remained unacknowledged'.[3] Given that Henry failed to make effective diplomatic use of either of his daughters, Princesses Mary and Elizabeth, after they were declared illegitimate, this is perhaps not actually the case. For example, when, in the 1540s, he required a bride to cement an alliance with the Scottish Earl of Lennox, it was his niece, Lady Margaret Douglas, who was selected, rather than either of his daughters. Additionally, the position of an illegitimate daughter who was older than the legally illegitimate Princess Elizabeth was problematic. When, towards the end of his life, Henry re-established Mary and Elizabeth in the succession, he did so without legitimising them. To the end of his life Henry maintained that his first two marriages had been invalid and, effectively, had never happened. To include two 'illegitimate' daughters in the succession but not a third would suggest that some of his illegitimate daughters were perhaps less illegitimate than others – a political point that the king in no wise wished to make. That Henry did in all probability see Mary and Elizabeth as more legitimate than a child who was born to a mother that he never married would be a very good reason for him to stop short of recognising any other daughters who were born completely out of wedlock, particularly a daughter who was older than Princess Elizabeth and could, arguably, expect to take a place in the succession before her if it became established that illegitimate children could succeed.

Gilbert Tailboy's father, Sir George Tailboys, contracted an illness in around 1499 which caused him to be considered insane.[4] He had undergone an at least partial recovery by 1509, when he was appointed to act as a knight of the body for the king. Four years later he served in France. Gilbert was named as one of Cardinal Wolsey's servants in 1517, around the time that his father was recognised to be permanently incapacitated.[5] In spite of his service with Wolsey, there is no evidence that Gilbert was actually made his ward, something that suggests that he was over the age of twenty-one in 1517.[6] Sir George Tailboys' father had died in 1494 and Sir George served as sheriff of Lincolnshire two years later, which suggests he was a mature man by the time of his father's death.[7] Gilbert was one of at least three sons and five sisters.[8] As the eldest surviving son, he is likely to have been one of the eldest children of his parents' marriage. In his will of 16 November 1494, Gilbert's grandfather, Sir Robert Tailboys, noted that 'a marriage is intended between my son George, and Elizabeth, sister to Sir William Gascoigne, Knight'.[9] This marriage, which was George Tailboys' second, did indeed take place and so, based on this evidence, Gilbert seems likely to have been born between 1495 and 1496, making him a little older than Bessie. It is therefore entirely possible that Gilbert could have been the father of Elizabeth Tailboys, based on his age, and it is therefore necessary to look to other surviving evidence to consider her paternity.

One piece of evidence to consider is that, as for Elizabeth Tailboys, there is evidence of the birth date of Bessie's third child, a boy named George who, since he was named after Gilbert's father, was clearly Gilbert's son and born after their marriage. On 25 March 1539, George was stated to have been sixteen years old.[10] This would mean that he was born between April 1522 and March 1523 and that there was at least a two-year age gap between Elizabeth Tailboys and George Tailboys, whilst there was only a one-year gap between Bessie's daughter and Henry Fitzroy. This in itself must support the greater probability that Bessie's first two children had the same father, rather than her second and third. Another point is that the king began to be conspicuously generous to Gilbert Tailboys in April 1522, with Bessie first recorded as his wife in June 1522. This suggests that the couple married in spring 1522, something that, assuming Bessie fell pregnant immediately (which appears very plausible given her rapid second pregnancy), could mean that George was born towards the end of 1522 or in the first months of 1523. Additionally, it would seem likely that George Tailboys was a young sixteen in March 1539, rather than nearly seventeen. This is because he was still considered a minor at that time in relation to the lands that he inherited from his grandfather. Whilst, in the sixteenth century, the age of majority was twenty-one, eighteen also had a special significance and a seventeen-year-old would commonly be treated as though they were almost an adult. For example, Henry VIII came to the throne a few months before his seventeenth birthday and was not considered to require a regent.[11] The evidence of George Tailboys' birth strongly suggests that the early 1522 marriage date for his parents is correct. At the very least, it demonstrates that Elizabeth Tailboys must have been born before 1522 and that there was no error in the statement that she gave about her age in 1542. With the evidence of George Tailboys' birth, the only possibility that Elizabeth Tailboys could have been legitimate is if Bessie and Gilbert married a considerable time before they began to receive any grants from the king – something which seems improbable when it is considered that Gilbert was required to take the king's abandoned mistress off his hands.

Henry VIII took a great deal of interest in Elizabeth Tailboys during her lifetime. During his northern progress of 1541, for example, he spent the night of 13 October at Nocton in Lincolnshire, the home of Elizabeth and her husband, Thomas Wymbish.[12] In addition to this, he appeared peculiarly interested in protecting her rights. Elizabeth's first husband had become a royal ward after the execution of his guardian, John, Lord Hussey, in June 1537.[13] Wardship gave the crown the right to bestow the ward in marriage and, in 1539, Henry VIII granted the wardship and marriage of Thomas Wymbish to Bessie's husband at the time, Edward, Lord Clinton, an arrangement that preceded the marriage.[14] Wymbish had been betrothed to Dorothy, a daughter of Lord Hussey, a match that was broken off to ensure that he was free to marry Elizabeth.[15]

The marriage of Elizabeth Tailboys and Thomas Wymbish was a turbulent one, with little love lost between the couple. Following the death of Bessie's two sons by Gilbert, Elizabeth succeeded to the family estates and titles. As such, she was entitled to call herself Baroness Tailboys and her husband, a member of a local gentry family, petitioned for the right to describe himself as Lord Tailboys. By the late middle ages it had become established in law that a married woman could not own personal property (a position that was not overturned until the nineteenth century).[16] On marriage, all of a woman's property passed to her husband's control, allowing her husband to even bequeath the property on his death. There were some exceptions to this, and custom had emerged by the late medieval period whereby a widow could expect a life interest in a certain portion of the marital property on her husband's death. In addition to this, some items were so personal to the woman that, for all intents and purposes, they were considered to be hers although, as some reports of early cases make clear, this was often limited just to clothes. Thomas Wymbish had good grounds in law for petitioning for the use of his wife's title.

Unusually, the king heard the case personally at court, taking a detailed interest in the proceedings, which were opposed by Elizabeth, apparently intent on retaining the title for her personal use. According to reports, when all the parties assembled,

> [Henry demanded] of the two chief justices, whether by law Mr Wymbish ought to have the name of Lord Taylboys, in the right of his wife or not? They answered, that the common law dealeth little with the titles and customs of chivalry. But such questions have always been decided before the constables and marshals of England.[17]

The king then asked Stephen Gardiner, Bishop of Winchester, whether Thomas Wymbish ought to succeed in his suit. To this Gardiner replied 'that by the law which he professeth, dignity was denied both to women and to Jews'. Henry shook his head at this, declaring, 'I like not that law, which putteth Christian women and Jews in one predicament.' He questioned those assembled on what the custom in England was and was informed:

> That it hath been always used so in England as in France, that the husband of a baroness by birth should use the style of her barony

so long as she liveth, and if he be but tenant by courtesy, then that he might use it for the term of his life. The chief justice confesseth that custom by courtesy be consonant to the common law, for the common law admitteth him to all his wives inheritances, of which she was seized during the coverture, and that might descend to their issue, and the dignity is a parcel of the inheritance.

Henry agreed in principle with the judge's decision, stating 'as it standeth by law, that tenants by courtesy should have the dignity, so it standeth with reason; but I like not that a man should this day be a lord, and to-morrow none, without crime committed, and it must so fall out in the husband of a baroness, if she die having never had by him any children'. The judges agreed with the king's reasoning and confirmed that, without a child being born to the couple, Thomas Wymbish could not use the title of Lord Tailboys.

The proceedings caused Henry to consider the question of the succession in more detail and he asked 'if the crown of England should descend to his daughters, whether her husband would use the style of England? The Chief Justice answered, not by right, but by grace, because the crown of England is out of the law of courtesy, but if it were subject thereto, then it was clear.'[18] Is it just possible that Henry was concerned that the next title Thomas Wymbish might aspire to would be somewhat higher than mere Lord Tailboys? In any event, the outcome of the case cannot have helped marital relations. The judgment was also somewhat unfair given that, many years earlier, Henry had allowed his friend Charles Brandon to use the title of Viscount Lisle after merely becoming betrothed to the Lisle heiress.

Elizabeth Tailboys and Thomas Wymbish continued to be associated together throughout the last years of Henry VIII's reign, for example jointly petitioning Henry's chancellor, Thomas Wriothesley, concerning the detention of deeds relating to their property in Croydon and Barrington.[19] It is apparent that the king had no great opinion of Thomas Wymbish's capabilities and when in May 1546 he was informed that Wymbish's castle of Harbottle, which played a key role in England's defences against Scotland, was in disrepair, moves were immediately made to acquire it for the crown from its owner.

In addition to safeguarding Elizabeth's title and inheritance, Henry VIII made sure that she was financially secure. A document of 2 December 1546 made only weeks before the king died contains the details of an exchange of lands between Henry and Wymbish and Elizabeth in the north of England.[20] The couple desired this exchange, signing the document personally. The document also confirms that the couple 'do fully and clearly bargain and sell unto the same our sovereign lord the King', something that suggests that the bargain was welcome to them. In exchange for their lands in Northumberland, the king gave two manors, one of which had been confiscated from the recently dissolved religious house of Little Malvern in Worcestershire. Such religious land was highly coveted and, although the transaction involved an exchange rather than a grant, Elizabeth and her husband achieved an advantageous deal. In addition to this, it was made very clear that Elizabeth was expected to benefit from the exchange, with the parties being named in the deed as Henry VIII and 'Thomas Wymbysh esquire and Lady Elizabeth Taylbois wife unto the said Thomas'. The couple had already arranged to sell some of their acquisitions and, just over three weeks later, Wymbish sold the lands that he had received from the king in Hanley in Worcestershire to a local man, William Pynnock.[21] Tellingly, in the charter recording the sale, Thomas Wymbish declared that he had obtained the lands, amongst other property, by 'the gift and grant of the king'. Further lands acquired by the couple from the king in Warwickshire and Worcestershire, which were to be held by Wymbish and Elizabeth and then for Elizabeth's heirs alone, were sold by the couple in the first year of Edward VI's reign.[22]

There is further evidence that Henry VIII took an interest in Elizabeth Tailboys above that which would be expected of a child of a former mistress. At a meeting of the royal council on 6 February 1547 at the Tower of London to discuss the minority of the young king, Edward VI, following Henry VIII's death, it was contended by Sir William Paget, the old king's secretary:

> Considering that the nobility of this realm was greatly decayed, some by attainders, some by their own misgovernance and riotous wasting, and some by sickness and sundry other means, [Henry] entered also devise with me for the advancement of divers to higher places of honour, wherein when I had said to him whom I thought mete, he willed me to make unto him a book of such as he did chose to advance.[23]

Amongst the members of the nobility and gentry named by the king were Edward Seymour, the uncle of the new king, who was suggested to become a duke; the old king's brother-in-law, William Parr, Earl of Essex, was to become a marquis; and the king's kinsman Lord St John was to become an earl. Surprisingly, at the end of a long list one 'Sir __ Wymbisshe' was suggested to become a baron. The only 'Wymbish' known to have had any sort of association with Henry VIII was Elizabeth Tailboys' husband. Whilst the gentleman named above was called a knight, a title that Elizabeth's husband never obtained, it does seem entirely possible that he was the 'Wymbisshe' that the king meant. If this was the case, his inclusion in a list that included both the grandees of the late Henrician court and family members of the king would seem surprising. It is, however, less surprising if there was indeed a family connection between the king and Elizabeth Tailboys' husband.

Mr Wymbish was never, in the event, to attain his barony. This did not mark the end of the Privy Council's interest in Elizabeth and her husband and, at a meeting at Greenwich on 13 June 1550, the council were called upon to consider 'a domestic quarrel', discussing 'the controversy between the Lady Tailbois and her husband, Mr Winbushe'.[24] The details of the quarrel between Elizabeth and her husband are not recorded. However, it was distinctly unusual for the Privy Council to be called upon to consider a domestic quarrel. Even more unusually, the Lord Great Chamberlain, the Lord Admiral and the king's Master of Horse, all prominent officials, were deputed to consider the matter in further detail. The three officials duly made their enquiries and the matter was raised again the following month before being discharged.[25] Although, as a baroness in her own right, Elizabeth had a certain standing in society, the interest taken by the Privy Council in her affairs appears surprising. It would be less surprising, however, if the lady that they considered was commonly, if privately, known to be the king's half-sister, rather than merely the daughter of a long-deceased former royal mistress. Relations remained frosty between the couple in spite of the Privy Council's involvement and, in his will written just over two years later, Thomas Wymbish left Elizabeth only a life interest in some of his lands agreed at the time of their marriage, his household stuff and all his 'fat beasts and wild beasts within the lordship of Kyme and all my hay in Kyme except my hay in the middle field'.[26] Elizabeth was granted the first option to purchase her husband's chattels from his executors, as well as receiving a bequest of his bay gelding and the corn growing at South Kyme. The remainder of his estate was divided amongst other members of his family and household, including his mother and sister and a number of servants, with his mother, brother-in-law and a friend acting as executors. The bequests to Elizabeth were small and this is evidence that the marriage was not altogether a close one.

Further evidence of royal interest in Elizabeth Tailboys can be seen from her second marriage to Ambrose Dudley, the son of John Dudley, Duke of Northumberland, who attempted to place the Protestant Lady Jane Grey on the throne in place of the Catholic Princess Mary in 1553. Ambrose, along with his father and brothers, found themselves prisoners in the Tower following Mary's jubilant accession. In late 1554 Elizabeth Tailboys commissioned the noted scholar Roger Ascham to write a Latin petition on her behalf to Queen Mary's new husband, Philip of Spain, begging for the release of her husband.[27] The king evidently listened to this petition and only four months later Elizabeth sent a further petition, thanking the king for restoring her husband to liberty, and requesting that he now also restore her lands to her.[28] That King Philip took a personal interest in Elizabeth Tailboys is clear from this correspondence

– something which once again demonstrates the unusual level of royal access possessed by Bessie's daughter, who was, after all, at that stage the wife of an accused traitor.

If Elizabeth Tailboys is to be identified as Henry VIII's daughter, born just under two years before the marriage of Gilbert and Bessie, the question must be asked as to how she came to take Gilbert's name and be accepted in society as his daughter. It can perhaps be reasoned that Gilbert, who benefited both financially and in gaining his independence through his marriage to Bessie, was unconcerned about 'adopting' his stepdaughter as his own. Bessie had already proved herself capable of bearing a healthy son and Gilbert would have had reason to believe that his own sons would soon follow.[29] It is likely that he considered Elizabeth's chances of inheriting his estates to be remote. There is also some evidence that Elizabeth Tailboys was not entirely accepted by the Tailboys family and this again can be taken as evidence of her paternity. Bessie's mother-in-law, Elizabeth, Lady Tailboys (née Gascoigne), was a thorn in her side during her marriage and proved to be equally troublesome to her daughter in later years. During Edward VI's reign a legal case was brought by the younger Elizabeth Tailboys and Thomas Wymbish against the elderly Lady Tailboys, alleging that Gilbert's mother:

> Wherefore with force and arms the close of them the said Thomas and Elizabeth she broke, and their grass to the value of 4ol. there lately growing with certain cattle eat up, tread down, and destroyed, and other wrongs to them did, to the great damage of the said Thomas and Elizabeth, and against the peace of the lord Henry the eight late King of England.[30]

The old lady's incursions into her 'granddaughter's' lands continued from August 1544 until April 1547 and involved a widespread destruction of their crops with cattle, horses, hogs and sheep. At the end of their tethers, Elizabeth and Thomas obtained a writ against the elder Lady Tailboys in 1547 before bringing an action for damages in the sum of one hundred marks. Throughout the proceedings Elizabeth Tailboys was referred to as the granddaughter of Sir George Tailboys, Gilbert's father. However, it is possible that the elder Lady Tailboys' defence contained a statement of the family's own beliefs about her true paternity. In her defence, the elder Lady Tailboys claimed that she had committed no trespass on the land which was included in the Tailboys manor of Goltho. This was because, in a document signed in the fourth year of Henry VIII's reign, George Tailboys had settled the manor on himself and his wife and then to the 'heirs of their bodies between them lawfully begotten'. It is arguable that the elder Lady Tailboys, who appears to have had a deeply antagonistic relationship with Elizabeth Tailboys and her husband, meant to imply that Bessie's eldest daughter could not be included in the category of one of the heirs of the body of her and her husband lawfully begotten. This was not made explicit in the case but it is perhaps telling that the court, which gave credence to the document produced by the defendant, did consider that Elizabeth Tailboys and her husband had a right to enter the land at Goltho, although they could not recover all the damages that they claimed. Clearly, the court felt that the document gave Elizabeth, as the granddaughter of George Tailboys, a right to enter and make use of the lands, notwithstanding the interest of George's widow which was apparently something less than a full life interest given the judgment of the court. The elder Lady Tailboys would surely have read and understood the terms of this document, something which does suggest very strongly that her objection was based on Elizabeth Tailboys having no rights to the land due to her failure to satisfy the requirement of being one of the heirs of her and her husband's body lawfully begotten.

A second case brought over the land at Goltho in the final year of Edward VI's reign also suggests hostility towards Elizabeth by the wider Tailboys family. At the Lincoln assizes in 1552 or 1553, Elizabeth and Thomas complained that Sir William Willoughby, Lord Willoughby of Parham, Sir Edward Dymock, the elder Lady Tailboys and her son William Tailboys had disseized them of their freehold of Goltho, denying their rights to the manor.[31] Lord Willoughby of Parham was the grandson of the elder Lady Tailboys and Sir Edward Dymock was her son-in-law. Gilbert's younger brother, William Tailboys, was a priest and Lord Willoughby and Sir Edward Dymock were therefore amongst the co-heirs looking to inherit the Tailboys lands if Elizabeth Tailboys died without issue. The facts of this case once again hint at the truth of Elizabeth Tailboys' birth being known in the family and her position as heiress to the titles and estates therefore being challenged by those that saw themselves as the true heirs. Once again, the elder Lady Tailboys proved intractable in court, declaring that the writ that had previously been obtained by Elizabeth and her husband to allow them access to the manor was 'insufficient in law to compel her'. She further stated that 'she hath no necessity, nor is by the law of the land bound to answer the said writ in manner and form aforesaid obtained: and this she is ready to verify'. The hostility of the Tailboys family towards Elizabeth and her husband is evident and it appears that the family grouped together in an attempt to limit Bessie's daughter's rights to the Tailboys estates. Clearly, the family had no objection to a woman inheriting the family titles and lands, as the inclusion of the Willoughbys of Parham and the Dymocks in the case shows. The hostility instead appears to have been personal towards Elizabeth Tailboys and, whilst not conclusive proof, does again tantalisingly hint that she was the king's daughter rather than Gilbert's. Elizabeth even moved in quasi-royal circles, receiving a bequest in the will of Sir Charles Brandon, an illegitimate son of the king's brother-in-law, the Duke of Suffolk, for a ring to the value of five marks.[32]

It has long been argued that, whilst Henry Fitzroy was the only illegitimate child of Henry VIII's to be recognised by the sovereign, the king was in fact the father of others. A number of potential children have been named, although the most plausible are Henry and Catherine Carey, the children of Mary Boleyn. Mary Boleyn married her first husband, William Carey, on 4 February 1520.[33] The marriage was attended by the king and the bridegroom was a member of his household. Mary took part in a court masque in March 1522 and, around that time, William Carey began to receive a series of royal grants, with the king's generosity lasting until 1526.[34] Mary's father, Sir Thomas Boleyn, was made treasurer of the household on 24 April 1522 and, the following year, he became a knight of the garter. On 18 June 1525 he was created Viscount Rochford, something very likely to have been associated with his daughter's role as royal mistress. Mary Boleyn's recent biographer has pointed out that the king's relationship with Mary is unique in that she became pregnant twice during their relationship and the king did not abandon her (at least during her first pregnancy).[35] As seems likely, this was not in fact unique and Bessie's relationship with the king also endured beyond her first pregnancy and, perhaps, even after her second. The paternity of Mary Boleyn's two children has long been debated. Her eldest child, Catherine, was probably born in 1524 and her younger, Henry, on 4 March 1526. Henry never acknowledged either of these children although it has been recently claimed that the circumstantial evidence suggests that he fathered them both.[36]

A strong case can be made for Mary Boleyn's children being the children of the king, particularly in the case of Catherine Carey. Given that they are now widely accepted to have been Henry's, it is interesting to compare the evidence for their paternity to that surviving for Elizabeth Tailboys. Given all the evidence above for Elizabeth Tailboys, it is arguable that an even stronger case can be made for her than for the two Carey children. One argument that has often been made in favour of the Carey children being the children of Henry VIII is that Henry's daughter, Elizabeth I, made much of them during her reign, providing Catherine with a grand funeral after her death, for example. However, as one historian has pointed out in a recent study of the Carey family, there may well have been reasons for this closeness far removed from any potential relationship as half-siblings. Family was very important in the Tudor period, particularly for Elizabeth I, who, by the mid-sixteenth century, had very few relatives left. Elizabeth I and the Careys were undoubtedly cousins (notwithstanding any relationship through Henry VIII) as their mothers were sisters. It has been pointed out that their usefulness may well have been in the fact that they were maternal rather than paternal kin: 'Elizabeth, confident that their non-royal status presented no threat to her throne, used them to staff her government, which placed them at the political centre of the kingdom'.[37] Another argument against Catherine and Henry Carey being the children of Henry VIII is that, unlike Henry, they were remarkably fertile, with Catherine bearing thirteen children and Henry fathering twelve, many of whom survived to adulthood. This is not a problem for Elizabeth Tailboys, who does not appear to have borne a child during either of her two marriages. In a letter written by Henry VIII after Fitzroy's death, and also in a set of instructions given to his ambassadors at the same time, Henry referred to Fitzroy as his only bastard son, something which also counts against Henry Carey.[38] Again, however, this does not say anything about Elizabeth Tailboys' paternity. If anything, the fact that Henry specified that he had only one bastard 'son' may suggest that there were also daughters.

In spite of the difficulties in attributing the paternity of the Carey children to Henry VIII, there is reasonable evidence to assume that they were indeed fathered by him. There were contemporary comments on Henry Carey's likeness to Henry VIII and there was clearly gossip surrounding him.[39] In addition to this, it has been pointed out that both Carey children 'attracted Henry VIII's benevolent if distant attention'.[40] Catherine Carey was appointed as a maid of honour to Anne of Cleves in 1539.[41] In addition to this, when she married in 1540, her husband, Francis Knollys, was appointed as a Gentleman Pensioner. At the same time, parliament confirmed their rights to the Knollys' family manor of Rotherfield Grey, with further action taken on the king's part over the next few years to ensure that it would eventually pass to the couple. For Henry Carey, the evidence of the king's direct involvement is less clear, although the choice by Queen Elizabeth of the title 'Baron Hunsdon' for him may suggest that he spent some time in his childhood with her at the royal manor of Hunsdon. What seems particularly striking is that Henry's interest in Catherine and Henry Carey has been considered evidence that he was taking a paternal interest in them. However, this interest pales into insignificance beside the very clear interaction that Henry VIII had with Elizabeth Tailboys to ensure her well-being. If Catherine and Henry Carey can be considered to be Henry VIII's children on the basis of this evidence, then Elizabeth Tailboys surely must be as well.

A final suggestion of Elizabeth Tailboys' royal background can be seen in her second marriage. Following Thomas Wymbish's death, Elizabeth married Ambrose Dudley, future Earl of Warwick. Although Elizabeth Tailboys and Ambrose were related through their mothers, it is unlikely that this was sufficient in itself to recommend Elizabeth to such a prestigious husband: although reasonably wealthy, she was no match for her powerful and prominent cousin. There is instead some evidence that there may have been a political motive behind the match. Ambrose's brother, Robert, who was the chief favourite of Elizabeth I, appears to have had information about the paternity of Mary Boleyn's children. According to one early account of Robert Dudley:

Moreover Thomas Earl of Sussex, then Lord Chamberlain, was his [Dudley's] professed antagonist to his dying day, and for my Lord Hunsdon [Henry Carey], and Sir Thomas Sackville, after Lord Treasurer, who were all contemporaries, he was wont to say of them that they were of the tribe of Dan, and were noli me tangere, implying that they were not to be contested with, for they were indeed of the queen's nigh kindred.[42]

The reference to the tribe of Dan is from the Old Testament. This is particularly revealing, especially due to the fact that the Bible was widely read and understood in Elizabethan England.[43] In the Old Testament, Dan was the son of Jacob by his mistress Bilhah, who was his wife's handmaid – a situation that echoed the relationship of Henry VIII with Mary Boleyn, his wife's maid. Additionally, in Deuteronomy, Moses called Dan a 'lion's whelp'.[44] Caution should be given to this interpretation as, based on other biblical references to Dan, it is possible that Dudley meant to suggest that the Careys were treacherous rather than allude to any royal descent. References to Dan in the Bible include Genesis 49:17 in which Jacob referred to his son as a serpent that bites a horse's heels to make its rider fall backwards. Equally, there is no suggestion that Sir Thomas Sackville, who was included within the remark, was a child of Henry VIII's. It does seem possible that Dudley meant the allusion to work on both levels. Dudley's brother Ambrose was married to Elizabeth Tailboys. Is it possible that Dudley's antagonism towards the Careys was in part a recognition that, with regard to the illegitimate children of Henry VIII he and his brother, in selecting the childless Elizabeth Tailboys, had effectively backed the wrong horse? Robert Dudley later married into the Carey family, taking Catherine Carey's daughter, Lettice Knollys, as his second wife. Dudley's use of the Latin phrase *noli me tangere* (touch me not) is striking and may reference the paternity of the Careys again. In the well-known poem by Sir Thomas Wyatt the Elder quoted in a previous chapter and clearly written about Anne Boleyn, the poet included the line '*Noli me tangere*, for Caesar's I am'.[45] Wyatt was a popular poet in the Tudor period and his works were widely read. The connection with Anne Boleyn in the poem would have seemed particularly pertinent to the Carey family and it is highly probable that, in the case of the Careys, Dudley intended to imply that they too belonged to Caesar.

In order for Elizabeth Tailboys to have been the daughter of Henry VIII, it would have been necessary for him to have visited Bessie at Blackmore during the summer of 1519, in the months following Henry Fitzroy's birth. Henry VIII's itinerary was extensively reconstructed by Dr Samman in the 1980s. According to Samman's research, Henry was at Windsor in June 1519 before moving to Richmond on 20 June.[46] He spent much of the summer in Sussex before briefly returning to Greenwich. The court then moved to Enfield before reaching Essex on 20 August. The king was at Havering-at-Bower between 20 and 23 August before arriving at Newhall later that day, remaining there until 12 September. Between 12 and 14 September the king was at Heron Hall in Essex. He then spent two nights at Barwick before spending the rest of the month at Wanstead. On 30 September the king finally returned to London. Bessie is known during that summer to have been at Blackmore, which is only thirteen miles from Newhall. Havering-atte-Bower is a similar distance away. Heron Hall is even nearer at only just over six miles away. Given that the court, which was encumbered with baggage and household goods, was able to travel an average of nine miles a day, thirteen miles was an easy ride for a small party on horseback.[47] It is inconceivable that Henry, who was so desperate for a son, would not have taken the opportunity to see Henry Fitzroy for himself.

Given that Bessie had been pregnant on her arrival at Blackmore, it seems more likely that it was the period after Henry Fitzroy's birth that saw the king's visits which gave rise to Blackmore's reputation as the scene of Henry's 'lascivious dissipation'.[48] Traditionally, a garter of the Order of the Garter which was kept in a house at Blackmore was said to have been left with Bessie by the king on one of his visits to her.[49] Seeing Bessie again may have reawakened his feelings for her and, given the endurance of his affair with Mary Boleyn through at least one of her pregnancies, it is entirely probable that neither Henry nor Bessie had seen her pregnancy as the end of their affair. It may even have been expected that she would return to court, as Mary Boleyn would later do after the birth of her first child, although a rapid second pregnancy ended Bessie's hopes in that regard. The king was evidently in good spirits when he arrived at Newhall, a place chosen as the 'climax' of his summer progress that year, and he spent over £200 on a masque to be held there.[50] Is it possible that the king's jovial good mood was linked to both the birth of his son, and to the reawakening of his affair with Bessie?

Based on the evidence of Henry's interest in Elizabeth Tailboys, the likely time that she was conceived and Henry's presence in the area at that time, it seems highly probable that she was the king's child. Her gender simply meant that she was of little significance to the king and he had no reason to acknowledge her as he did her elder brother, particularly following the bastardising of the daughters of his first and second marriages. The later sixteenth-century antiquary John Leland recorded that it was well known that Henry Fitzroy was born at Blackmore to Bessie when she was 'then Lady Talboys'.[51] Perhaps this misapprehension was due to an extended stay at the religious house due to the birth of a second child, who did indeed take the Tailboys name. It is very unlikely that Bessie and Gilbert were married until 1522, when they began to receive grants of property, as Gilbert's consent to a marriage with the king's cast-off mistress would almost certainly have had to have been bought. One further piece of evidence is perhaps the most compelling of all. In the seventeenth century Lord Herbert of Cherbury wrote an early biography of Henry VIII, having the benefit of sources that are now no longer extant. In his work he mentioned the love affair between Bessie and Henry, commenting of their son that 'the child, proving so equally like to both his parents, that he became the first emblem of their mutual affection'.[52] The word 'first' in this context could be taken to mean 'foremost', suggesting that Henry Fitzroy was the principal emblem of Henry and Bessie's love. However, it is possible that 'first' should be given its more literal meaning and that Lord Herbert was aware of evidence that Henry Fitzroy was only the first child of his parents, implying that there were at least rumours of another.

It is likely that Bessie remained at Blackmore following the birth of her son and, after private visits there by the king, she soon became pregnant with a second child. Although there is no direct proof of this, it seems probable that she would have retained the custody of her son for the time being, perhaps playing a part in raising both Henry Fitzroy and Elizabeth Tailboys until her marriage early in 1522. Alternatively, as Fitzroy's recent biographer has pointed out, Princess Mary's household was reorganised in 1519 when the Countess of Salisbury was appointed to replace Margaret, Lady Bryan, as the Lady Mistress of her household.[53] Two of the princess's rockers also left her household at the same time. In her biography of Henry Fitzroy, Dr Murphy raised the interesting, and highly probable, suggestion that Lady Bryan had a role in Bessie's son's upbringing. In 1536 Lady Bryan wrote that 'when my Lady Mary was born it pleased the king's grace [to make] me Lady Mistress, and made me a baroness, and so I have been a m[other to the] children his grace have had since'.[54] As Murphy points out, the wording of this letter suggests at least one other child in between Princess Mary and Henry's younger daughter, Princess Elizabeth, who was born in 1533. It does indeed seem probable that this was Henry Fitzroy. This does not, in itself, exclude Bessie from her son's early upbringing as it is clear that she did later play some role in his childhood. It is not impossible that Mary's household could have been reorganised some time before her former servants found posts with Henry Fitzroy. Alternatively, if Fitzroy was placed in Lady Bryan's care at an earlier age, Bessie could still expect to be consulted on important matters relating to his upbringing. For example, Anne Boleyn, the mother of Lady Bryan's later charge, Princess Elizabeth, was called upon to consider when her daughter should be weaned, with one of the king's officers writing that 'the King's Highness; well considering the letter directed to you, from my lady Brian, and other my lady Princess' officers; His Grace, with the assent of the Queen's Grace, hath fully determined the weaning of my Lady Princess, to be done with all diligence'.[55] There were some decisions that that a mother had to be involved in. Regardless of this, the date of Bessie's marriage in 1522 must be considered the cut-off and, by then, if not before, she had certainly resigned custody of her son to his father, whilst retaining her daughter in her own care.

Henry began a casual affair with Arabella Parker, the wife of a London merchant, at some point soon after Henry Fitzroy's birth. The date of Bessie's marriage coincides with the beginning of Henry's relationship with Mary Boleyn, suggesting that some affection between Bessie and Henry had continued to exist until that point, when Henry finally brought the relationship to an end after a period of around five years. Mary Boleyn was around the same age as Bessie, apparently being born in 1499. She was more conventionally beautiful than her younger sister Anne, with fair hair and a round face. Anne was the more intellectually promising of the sisters and it was she who was selected by their father to serve in the household of Margaret of Austria, Regent of the Netherlands, in Brussels in 1513. This was a highly sought-after post that their father, Sir Thomas Boleyn, was able to secure through his personal friendship with the regent. In October 1514 Mary received an appointment of her own, sailing to France in the household of Henry VIII's sister, Mary Tudor, when she went to marry Louis XII of France. Mary Boleyn, who was joined by her sister in France, passed into the household of Queen Claude, the wife of Francis I of France, following Mary Tudor's widowhood and return to England. Francis I, who was only nineteen when he came to the throne and was tall and handsome, apparently excited the elder sister's interest and she became his mistress.

Mary Boleyn's reputation was decidedly damaged when she was hurried home to England by her family, but she was able to secure a court appointment with Catherine of Aragon. It is possible that she was there at the same time as Bessie and, certainly, she was a member of the court by the time of her marriage. Bessie, absent in Essex and busy in childbearing, was unable to compete with Mary and, by 1522 at the latest, she had become the king's established mistress. On 5 February 1522 Mary's husband, William Carey, was appointed keeper of the manor and estate of Newhall by the king.[56] Following Bessie's arrival at Blackmore at the end of 1518 nearby Newhall must have become associated in the king's mind with her and he used it as his base from which to visit her. Even Henry VIII had tact and it seems unlikely that he would have passed the manor into the control of the husband of his new mistress whilst continuing to stay there whilst meeting with his old mistress, particularly since William Carey and Mary Boleyn were given permission to occupy the manor as though they owned it.[57] Almost certainly, therefore, this grant can be considered to mark the end of Bessie's affair with the king. Henry was not a man to have more than one serious mistress at any time and Bessie knew that she had lost her hold on him and could expect no further visits. She apparently accepted the decision with good grace. Around the time that his affair with Mary Boleyn began, Henry decided to pension Bessie off, ordering Cardinal Wolsey to provide a suitable husband for her.

# PART 3
# LADY TAILBOYS OF SOUTH KYME,
## 1522–1530

## 12

# FIRST MARRIAGE

The husband chosen for Bessie, Gilbert Tailboys, was three or four years older than her. He was the eldest child of Sir George Tailboys of South Kyme and his second wife, Elizabeth Gascoigne. The Tailboys family originally had northern roots, with extensive lands in County Durham and Northumberland.[1] They moved to Lincolnshire in the fourteenth century.

South Kyme, the principal manor of the Tailboys family, had originally belonged to the de Kyme family, who lived there from the early Norman period.[2] The de Kyme family were a prominent one, originally hailing from Bullington.[3] They were one of the oldest families in Lincolnshire, with branches of the family still in existence in the area in Bessie's time.[4] The second member of the family to hold South Kyme, Simon de Kyme, for example, married the daughter of the steward of the powerful Earl of Lincoln. Their son, Philip de Kyme, became steward to the earl in his turn, as well as serving as sheriff of Lincolnshire in 1168 and 1169. He was summoned to attend the king's great council in London in 1177, which demonstrates that he had a national reputation. His son, Simon de Kyme, also served as sheriff, as well as being amongst the barons who forced King John to sign the Magna Carta.[5] Some generations later, another Philip de Kyme served with Edward I during his campaigns in Wales and Scotland. He was a somewhat troublesome figure who was accused in 1316 of failing to repair the river banks that ran through his manor, causing South Kyme priory to be flooded. The second Philip de Kyme also added acquisitiveness to his sins when he appropriated land on the public highways as pasture for his animals, as well as cutting hay on lands to which he had no claim. His son William inherited the manor in 1322 and apparently lived more quietly. Upon his death in 1337, the manor passed to his sister, Lucy, and her husband, Gilbert de Umfraville, Earl of Angus.

The de Umfravilles, like the de Kymes, were an ancient family, reputedly descended from a relative of William I.[6] It was the son of

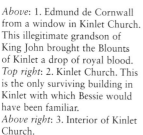

*Above*: 1. Edmund de Cornwall from a window in Kinlet Church. This illegitimate grandson of King John brought the Blounts of Kinlet a drop of royal blood.
*Top right*: 2. Kinlet Church. This is the only surviving building in Kinlet with which Bessie would have been familiar.
*Above right*: 3. Interior of Kinlet Church.
*Right*: 4. Kinlet Hall. This eighteenth-century building replaced the earlier hall that Bessie's family knew.
*Below right*: 5. Bewdley in Worcestershire, a town with which the Blount family had a long association. It may have been one of Bessie's childhood homes.

*Above left*: 6. Elizabeth de Cornwall from her tomb in Kinlet Church. Elizabeth's early death led to Kinlet passing into the hands of the Blount family in the mid-fifteenth century.

*Above right*: 7. The tomb of Bessie's great-grandparents, Sir Humphrey and Dame Elizabeth Blount, in Kinlet Church.

*Above left*: 8. Sir Humphrey Blount from his tomb in Kinlet Church. Bessie's great-grandfather was a prominent local figure.

*Above right*: 9. Elizabeth Blount (*née* Winnington) from her tomb in Kinlet Church. Bessie was named after her great-grandmother.

10. Croft Castle, the home of Bessie's prominent great-grandfather, Sir Richard Croft.

*Top left*: 11. Sir Richard Croft from his tomb at Croft Castle. Bessie's great-grandfather acted as guardian to the young Edward IV. He was also one of the leading officers in the household of Prince Arthur.

*Top right*: 12. The tomb of Bessie's great-grandparents, Sir Richard and Dame Eleanor Croft.

*Centre left*: 13. Eleanor Croft from her tomb at Croft Castle. At the time of her death she was claimed to have more than 340 descendants living, including her great-great-grandson, Henry Fitzroy.

*Centre right*: 14. John Russhe's memorial brass at All Hallows Church, Barking. Bessie's step-grandfather was a merchant and patron of early printing.

*Right*: 15. The tomb of Bessie's parents from Kinlet Church.

*Top left*: 16. Sir John Blount from his tomb in Kinlet Church. Bessie's father received little benefit from his daughter's relationship with the king and struggled to obtain his inheritance from his father.

*Top right*: 17. Katherine Pershall from her tomb in Kinlet Church. Bessie's mother was an heiress and often found herself in court defending her claims to her inheritance.

*Above left & right*: 18. & 19. Pages from the fifteenth-century Beauchamp Pageant showing the birth and baptism of Richard Beauchamp, Earl of Warwick. The images provide useful information on childbirth and baptism in the late medieval period.

*Left*: 20. Bessie Blount from the side of her parents' tomb.

*Above left*: 21. Bessie was depicted with a demure expression on the side of her parents' tomb.

*Centre left*: 22. Anne Blount from the side of her parents' tomb.

*Centre right*: 23. The third sister depicted on the side of John Blount and Katherine Pershall's tomb. This is likely to be Rose, the sister to whom Bessie was closest.

*Above right*: 24. Bessie's younger sister, Anne married twice and was prominent in Shropshire.

*Below left*: 25. The fourth sister depicted on the side of John Blount and Katherine Pershall's tomb. This is likely to be Isabel, who married a gentleman of Surrey and died young.

*Below right*: 26. Albora Blount from the side of her parents' tomb. Bessie's youngest surviving sister never married but was popular within the family, with her sister Anne naming one of her daughters after her.

*Above left*: 27. The three eldest sons of John Blount and Katherine Pershall depicted on the side of their tomb. The eldest two, who were the siblings closest in age to Bessie died young. The third was her brother, George Blount.

*Above right*: 28. Bessie's brothers, William and Henry, depicted on the side of their parents' tomb. Bessie had already left for court by the time that her brothers were born, although she took an interest in their early lives and advancement.

*Above left*: 29. Sir George Blount. Bessie's eldest surviving brother was a prominent Shropshire gentleman during the mid-Tudor period.

*Left*: 30. The sixth sister depicted on the side of John Blount and Katherine Pershall's tomb. Claims that this sister was named Margaret and married into the Pigott family are false and it appears she died in infancy.

*Above*: 31. The tomb of Sir George Blount at Kinlet Church. George chose to bequeath his estates to his nephew, Rowland Lacon, who paid for his elaborate tomb.

*Above left*: 32. Bessie's brother, George, from his tomb in Kinlet Church. George enjoyed a turbulent reputation, with local legends claiming that he haunted Kinlet after his death.

*Above right*: 33. Constance Talbot, wife of Sir George Blount. Bessie's sister-in-law was a kinswoman of the Earl of Shrewsbury and Katherine Pershall took great pains to secure the match for her son.

*Above left*: 34. Bessie's nephew, John Blount, from his father's tomb at Kinlet. John was George Blount's only son but died in childhood, reputedly dying after choking on an apple.

*Above centre*: 35. Bessie's niece, Dorothy Blount, from her father's tomb at Kinlet. George Blount's only surviving child married beneath her. She was disinherited by her father but retained good relations with her cousins, the Lacons, who took the Blount estates in her place.

*Above right*: 36. A memorial brass to a member of the Lacon family at Harley Church in Shropshire. Bessie's sister, Anne, married Richard Lacon, a man who had almost certainly been previously intended for Bessie herself.

*Above left:* 37. Bessie's uncle, Walter Blount, from his tomb in Astley Church.

*Above right:* 38. Joyce Blount of Astley from the side of her father, Walter Blount's, tomb. Joyce's family moved to Stratford upon Avon and were close friends of William Shakespeare.

*Left:* 39. Bessie's cousin, Robert Blount, from his tomb in Astley Church.

*Below left:* 40. The tomb of Bessie's cousin, Sir Thomas Blount, in Kidderminster Church. Thomas' father, Edward, was a favourite of his father, who attempted to disinherit his eldest son in his favour.

*Above left*: 41. The tomb of Sir Edward Blount with his two wives, in Kidderminster Church. Edward was the grandson of Bessie's uncle, Edward Blount. The Kidderminster Blounts became the most prominent branch of the Blount family in the seventeenth century.

*Above right & below left*: 42. and 43. Two views of London by Anthony von Wyngaerde in *c.*1550. Bessie's family had connections to London and she would have arrived in the capital shortly before her appointment to the queen's household.

*Above right*: 44. Henry VIII shown in a later copy of the parliament roll of 1512. This was the year that Bessie first met Henry. He had only turned twenty the year before.

45. Great Tournament Roll of Westminster depicting the king taking part in a joust to celebrate the birth of his eldest son by Catherine of Aragon. Sadly, the prince lived only a few short weeks.

*Above left*: 46. King Henry VIII from King's College, Cambridge. Henry VIII quickly took an interest in Bessie following her arrival at court.

*Above*: 47. 'Pastyme with good companye', a song composed by Henry VIII in his youth. During his relationship with Bessie, the king was in his prime. He was reputed to be the most handsome prince in Europe.

*Below left*: 48. Catherine of Aragon. Bessie's appointment to serve Henry VIII's first wife was a prestigious one, and brought her to the attention of the king.

*Bottom*: 49. Richmond Palace, another palace that Bessie visited with the king.

*Below*: 50. Henry VIII's lock for his private apartments. The Tudor royal court was highly mobile, with courtiers constantly being forced to pack and unpack their belongings. Henry took his own lock with him on his travels, keeping the master key himself.

KATHERINA VXOR HENRICI · VIII.

RICHMOND

*Above left*: 51. Greenwich Palace, one of Henry VIII's favourite palaces and one of the residences in which he conducted his love affair with Bessie.
*Above right*: 52. Henry Fitzroy. Bessie's eldest son bore a strong resemblance to his royal father, who delighted in him.

*Above left*: 53. Princess Mary in childhood. Catherine of Aragon's daughter was a rival to Bessie's son, with the Imperial ambassador commenting after his death that it was no bad thing for the princess.
*Below*: 54. An allegorical representation of the betrothal of Princess Mary to the Duke of Orleans in 1527. In spite of the king's elevation of Henry Fitzroy, Princess Mary remained the king's heir presumptive until the divorce of her parents.
*Above right*: 55. Mary Boleyn, the woman who supplanted Bessie as the king's mistress.

*Above left*: 56. The tomb of Catherine Carey in Rotherford Greys Church. Catherine was the daughter of Mary Boleyn and it has been suggested that she was also the daughter of the king. Even stronger evidence suggests that Bessie's own daughter, Elizabeth Tailboys, was the daughter of Henry VIII.
*Above right*: 57. The tower at South Kyme. These are the only surviving remains of Bessie's marital home.

*Above left*: 58. South Kyme Church. The church was remodelled during the early nineteenth century and is now considerably smaller than it would have been in Bessie's time.
*Above right*: 59. Interior of South Kyme Church. Bessie's husband, Gilbert, was buried inside the church following his death in 1530.

60. Bessie's replica memorial brass in South Kyme Church.

*Above*: 61. The remains of the memorial brass commissioned by Bessie for Gilbert at South Kyme Church. The brass depicting Bessie is a replica of the original which is now in the British Museum.

*Right*: 62. The early twentieth-century memorial marking the site of Gilbert Tailboys' grave in South Kyme Church.

*Above left*: 63. Lincoln Cathedral. The Tailboys family were prominent in Lincolnshire, with Bessie's parents-in-law founding a chapel in the cathedral.

*Above right*: 64. The tomb of Bessie's parents-in-law, Sir George Tailboys and Elizabeth Gascoigne in Lincoln Cathedral.

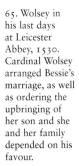

65. Wolsey in his last days at Leicester Abbey, 1530. Cardinal Wolsey arranged Bessie's marriage, as well as ordering the upbringing of her son and she and her family depended on his favour.

*Above left*: 66. The tomb of William Tailboys, Gilbert's brother, which lies beside his parents' tomb in Lincoln Cathedral.
*Above centre*: 67. Anne Boleyn. At one time Bessie was considered a potential rival to Anne for the king's affections.
*Above right*: 68. Bessie's second husband, Edward, Lord Clinton. After Bessie's death he went on to become Earl of Lincoln.

*Above left*: 69. Katherine Willoughby, Duchess of Suffolk. Katherine was the heiress to the great Lincolnshire Willoughby family into which both Bessie's sister-in-law, Elizabeth Tailboys, and her daughter, Margaret Clinton, married.
*Above right*: 70. Catherine Parr from her tomb at Sudeley Castle. Bessie was friendly with the Parr family and they moved in the same Lincolnshire circles.

*Above*: 71. The 3rd Duke of Norfolk from his tomb in Framlingham Church. After Wolsey's fall, Norfolk began to take an interest in Henry Fitzroy, eventually securing him as his son-in-law.
*Above right*: 72. Framlingham Church. Henry Fitzroy, who was originally buried in Thetford Priory, now lies buried in the church at Framlingham with members of the Howard family.
*Right*: 73. The tomb of Henry Fitzroy in Framlingham Church.
*Below right*: 74. Louth Church. The Pilgrimage of Grace began in the church in October 1536, spreading throughout Lincolnshire and Yorkshire.

*Above*: 75. The tomb of Henry Howard, Earl of Surrey in Framlingham Church. Surrey was Henry Fitzroy's brother-in-law and best friend.

The Lady of Richmond.

*Above left:* 76. Bessie's son-in-law, Ambrose Dudley, Earl of Warwick, from his tomb in Warwick Church.
*Above right:* 77. Mary Howard, Duchess of Richmond and Somerset. Henry Fitzroy's marriage remained unconsummated and, after his death, his widow found that the king disputed the validity of a union arranged by Anne Boleyn. Hans Holbein portrait.

Lucy de Kyme, a second Gilbert de Umfraville, who built the tower at South Kyme which still survives. He also fought for the king at the Battle of Neville's Cross against the Scots. As a very prominent ancestor, it is likely that it was for him that Bessie's husband, Gilbert, was named. The manor remained in the Umfraville family for two further generations until the death of Robert de Umfraville in 1436. His heir was his aunt, Elizabeth, the wife of Gilbert Burdon who herself had only one surviving daughter, Elizabeth Burdon, the wife of Henry Tailboys. It was through this marriage that the Tailboys family acquired the manor, with Elizabeth Burdon's son, Walter Tailboys, taking possession of the estate. He was Gilbert Tailboy's great-great-great-grandfather.

The Tailboys family was another ancient family, reputedly descended from the Norman lord Ivo de Taillebois, who received generous grants of land in Lincolnshire from William I.[7] Ivo was a semi-legendary figure by the fifteenth and sixteenth centuries and much that has been written about him may well be inaccurate. He was claimed to be the brother of Fulk, Earl of Anjou, who later became King of Jerusalem, although there is little evidence for this.[8] It has been claimed that he married twice: first to a daughter of King Aethelred II (a lady who would have been significantly advanced in years by the time of the conquest)[9] and secondly to Lucia, a sister of Harold II's second wife, Ealdgyth of Mercia (again, an improbable lineage for this lady). This second marriage was claimed for Ivo by the Crowland Chronicle, which claimed to have been a contemporary record of events.[10] However, the early part of the Crowland Chronicle is now considered to be highly dubious, with its date of composition perhaps being the fourteenth or fifteenth century. The information it contains about Ivo's marriage, and his troublesome character, is fascinating and may well have been family legend by Bessie's time, with tales of Ivo's tyranny towards the people of Hoyland, of which he was lord:

Although they bestowed upon him all the honours they possibly could, and all the services they were bound, still he did not, repaying that confidence, show any love for them; but tortured and harassed, worried and annoyed, incarcerated and tormented them, every day loaded with fresh burdens, and, by his cruelty, compelled most of them to sell all their property, and seek other countries. But against our monastery and all the people of Croyland, he was, by the instigation of the devil, aroused to such an extreme pitch of fury, that he would follow the various animals of the people of Croyland in the marshes with his dogs, give them a great distance, drown them in the lakes, mutilate some in the tails, others in the ears; while often, by the breaking the backs and legs of the beasts of burden, he would render them utterly useless.[11]

The rivalry apparently culminated with Ivo bringing about the deposition of the abbot, as well as bringing in his own, more compliant, monks from Anjou. This account must be taken with a very large pinch of salt, and there are even some doubts that Ivo, who is only known with certainty to have produced one legitimate daughter, was even the progenitor of the Tailboys family. However, what is important, to Bessie, is that this was what was believed in her time, something that gave Gilbert's branch of the family kinship with all those others claiming descent from the quarrelsome Ivo de Taillebois. Equally, given that Gilbert's family emerged in one of the areas of influence of Ivo de Tailboys, they may at least have been descended from a kinsman of his, even if they could not claim descent directly through him. What is certain is that Ivo was appointed as Baron of Kendal by William I. The senior branch of the family eventually married into the Parr family, who were lords of Kendal during the fifteenth and sixteenth centuries and from whom Catherine Parr, Henry VIII's sixth wife, was descended. Another branch of the Tailboys family which claimed descent from Ivo lived in Raithby in Lincolnshire, a village close to South Kyme.[12] Their only claim to kinship with Gilbert's branch of the family was through Ivo (with the Raithby branch apparently being descended from his elder son and the South Kyme branch from his younger). Such a distant kinship link must be treated with suspicion. However, it would seem probable that the two branches of the family were related in some way or, at least, believed to be related, something that would be enough to establish a connection between them. The Raithby Tailboys family had originally been a prominent one. Their manor had its own chapel: a mark of significant honour. However, by Bessie and Gilbert's time, the family had fallen on hard times. From being lords of the manor, they had become little more than free tenants.[13] They still had claims to be of gentry status, and surviving inventories of their possessions show that the family still had some means. One member of the family, Robert Tailboys of Raithby, was also repeatedly fined in the late fifteenth century for his failure to attend a local great court, something that was expected of the local gentry.[14] However, they must have been considered to be poor relations by Gilbert's family. The family were just one of many in Lincolnshire with which the South Kyme Tailboys family could claim kinship.

Although their earliest origins are not entirely clear, it is certain that the South Kyme Tailboys family originally came from the north of England, holding lands in Northumberland, as well as the manor of Hurworth in County Durham.[15] By the reign of Edward I, the head of the family was a Luke Tailboys, who was employed by the king as a collector of subsidies. He also served as sheriff of Northumberland in 1303–04. It was Luke's grandson who acquired South Kyme through his marriage to the Umfraville heiress.

After inheriting South Kyme, members of the Tailboys family served regularly as sheriffs of Lincolnshire, with the first Sir Walter Tailboys of South Kyme being appointed in 1390.[16] His son, a second Sir Walter, served in 1423. The second Sir Walter's grandson, Sir Robert Tailboys, served as sheriff in 1481, whilst his son, Bessie's father-in-law, served in 1496. Gilbert himself served as sheriff during his marriage to Bessie.

By the fifteenth century, the Tailboys family of South Kyme moved in royal circles, with William Tailboys (Gilbert's great-grandfather) playing a prominent role in the Wars of the Roses as a partisan of the controversial William de la Pole, Duke of Suffolk, a leading advisor to the Lancastrian king, Henry VI. As a mark of his ambition he styled himself 'Earl of Kyme'.[17] William Tailboys was a particularly turbulent individual who – in spite of his loyalty to the Lancastrian royal family, which saw him flee into exile in Scotland with Henry VI's queen, Margaret of Anjou, following the accession of the Yorkist King Edward IV[18] – fell out with most of his Lincolnshire neighbours at one point or another. A surviving letter written by him at some point before 1450, illustrates this rather well:

> Please it your good Lordship to be remembered how afore this time Hugh Wythom hath said he would be in rest and peace with me, and not to malign against me otherwise than law and right would; that notwithstanding, upon Monday last past, he and iij. men with him come unto a servant's house of mine in Boston, called William Shirref, and there, as he set at his work, stroke him upon the head and in the body with a dagger, and wounded him sore, and pulled him out of his house, and set him in prison without any cause reasonable, or without writ, or any other process showed unto him.[19]

The letter continued in the same vein, complaining that Lord Welles – who, as the stepfather of the future Henry VII's mother, Lady Margaret Beaufort, was also a good Lancastrian – had come to Boston and taken Shirref away, declaring that he was a thief who would be hanged, before taking him to Tattershall Castle. That this was a local feud rather than anything connected to the Wars of the Roses is clear from the fact that Tailboys' neighbours, Lord Willoughby and Lord Cromwell, were also involved. His bad reputation was such that he was one of twenty men from throughout England named in a petition to parliament in 1459, which described them as 'universally throughout all this realm famed and noised, known and reputed severely for open robbers, ravishers, extortioners, and oppressors' of the king's people.[20] Tailboys – who was later accused in the Star Chamber of trying to murder the powerful Ralph, Lord Cromwell, of Tattershall Castle – came to a bad end, being attainted for treason by Edward IV in 1461 whilst he was still at large in Scotland. He was captured in 1464, reputedly hiding in a coal pit at Newcastle, and beheaded, with his head being placed over the gate at the city of York.[21] Gilbert's grandfather was, eventually, restored to the family's estates, taking a conscious decision to eschew overt political involvement during his lifetime.

Gilbert's parents were a somewhat ill-assorted couple. As has already been seen in relation to her dispute with her 'granddaughter', the younger Elizabeth Tailboys, Gilbert's mother, the senior Lady Tailboys, was a forceful and dominant personality. Elizabeth, or Isabella as she was occasionally known,[22] came from a noble background and, as well as being the granddaughter of the third Earl of Northumberland, also had kinship links to the dukes of Buckingham and Norfolk. She was a descendant of Joan Beaufort, the only daughter of John of Gaunt, third son of Edward III, and Katherine Swynford.[23] Although none of the Beauforts were born in wedlock, John of Gaunt later caused consternation in Europe by marrying their mother and securing the legitimisation of their children. It was through the Beauforts that Henry VII had claimed the crown, something that made Gilbert's mother, and Gilbert himself, distant kin to the king. The elder Lady Tailboys was the daughter of Sir William Gascoigne of Gawthorpe in Yorkshire. She was Sir George's second wife, whom he married after the death of his childless first wife, Margaret, the daughter of Sir Thomas Burgh of Gainsborough.[24] Elizabeth would later sue her own brother for £222 4s 5d, which remained unpaid from her marriage portion; she claimed, inaccurately, that the sum had been left to her and her husband by her father-in-law, Sir Robert Tailboys, in order to provide for the marriage of her daughters.[25] This court case, which apparently dragged on for some time, must be seen in the light of Elizabeth's evident financial problems, which are detailed below. However, it is very clear from the surviving documents that it was a spurious case.[26] Elizabeth took the action after her husband's death in 1538. She had dominated her weaker-willed husband, ultimately taking over the governorship of his person.

George Tailboys was a good servant of the crown in his early years, serving both as sheriff of Lincolnshire and Northumberland in the years before 1499. He was knighted in 1497.[27] However, during that year, whilst serving as lieutenant of the east and middle marches at Berwick, he contracted a sickness referred to in contemporary documents as 'the land evil'. The nature of this illness is not recorded, but it addled Gilbert's father's wits. He was thought to be a lunatic and only narrowly avoided having his lands taken into wardship by the crown when he made a bargain with Henry VII, paying him the sum of 800 marks to effectively 'buy his freedom'.[28] This was a large sum and indicates the danger that George's illness had placed him in. It was the king's prerogative to take over the estates of madmen, ostensibly for their own good:

Also the king shall provide, when any, that beforetime hath had his Wit and Memory, happen to fail of his Wit, as there are many per lucida intervalla [i.e. with lucid intervals], that their Lands and Tenements shall be safely kept without Waste and Destruction, and that they and their Household shall live and be maintained competently with the Profits of the same, and the Residue besides be kept to their use, to be delivered unto them when they come to right Mind; so that such Lands and Tenements shall in no wise be aliened; and the king shall take nothing to his own Use. And if the Party die in such Estate, then the Residue shall be distributed for his Soul by the Advice of the Ordinary.[29]

Whilst this elucidation of the king's prerogative had lofty ideals, in reality, as George Tailboys himself was to find, such royal wards were usually exploited.

George Tailboys had made a sufficient recovery by December 1509 to be appointed as a knight of the body by the king, as well as being licensed to appoint justices in Redesdale.[30] He was involved in a dispute with Lord Dacre which went to the privy council in July 1509, concerning a bond for 2,000 crowns made by Lord Dacre to Sir George concerning the keeping of Harbottle Castle.[31] In addition to this, George, in common with most of the English nobility and gentry, crossed the channel in 1513 to serve with Henry VIII in his French campaign. During this period, there was nothing overt to suggest that there were still concerns over George's sanity. He was also found to be of sound mind at an inquisition into his mental state held at Lincoln in 1516, although the fact that it was felt that there was a need for such an inquisition does strongly suggest that he was not entirely recovered from his illness.[32] Given subsequent events, he may only nominally have been in control of his estates and offices, instead relying heavily on his wife and other kin. Certainly, by March 1517, concerns over his mental state were such that he and his lands had been placed in the custody of Cardinal Wolsey, who had links to Lincoln as a former Dean of Lincoln, and eight of George's relations and neighbours, on account of 'the said Sir George being a lunatic'.[33] Gilbert, who had by then reached his majority, but had no position in society given his father's continued survival, also passed into Wolsey's custody at the same time. However, this was as a member of his household rather than through any wardship.[34]

As well as Gilbert, the marriage of his parents produced a son, William, who became a priest, and five daughters.[35] Anne married a neighbour, Sir Edward Dymoke, before taking another local man, Robert Carre of Sleaford, as her second husband. Elizabeth married another Lincolnshire gentleman, Sir Christopher Willoughby. Margaret married George Vernon. Cecily married William Ingleby of Ripley in Yorkshire before also taking a second husband. A fifth daughter,

Dorothy, remained unmarried – presumably living with her parents at Goltho during Bessie's time. A third son, Robert, was also reportedly still living in 1541, but it would appear that he died soon afterwards, leaving no issue.[36] Three further children have also been suggested for the couple: Matilda, John and Walter.[37] It is possible that they died in infancy. Certainly, they left no issue. Gilbert's younger brother, William, was a favourite of his parents, remaining close to them throughout his life. In 1528, for example, he was named as executor in the will of Sir Robert Sparke, who was then the priest at Goltho.[38] Sparke trusted William enough to leave funds in his hands for the payment of a secular priest to daily say mass for the good of his soul.

It is highly likely that Gilbert and Bessie had the opportunity to meet during Bessie's last few years at court. Although Cardinal Wolsey did not reside at the court, in order to ensure his continuing influence over his sovereign he made it his business to remain close to the king wherever he went. Between 1519 and 1523, for example, it has been noted that the king and the cardinal were less than ten miles away from each other for over 60 per cent of the year.[39] In addition to this, for nearly 80 per cent of the year they were less than twenty-five miles apart. In 1519 they remained within fifty miles of each other throughout the year, a distance which would have allowed messages to pass between the two men rapidly. There was ample opportunity for the young men of the cardinal's household to meet with the ladies of court. Although the cardinal had a large household, which was assessed at 429 men in 1527, Gilbert, as a gentleman, had free access to the court when his master was there.[40] Indeed, Henry Percy, who was a contemporary of Gilbert's in the cardinal's household, used the opportunity afforded by his master's frequent visits to court to fall in love with the young Anne Boleyn, who had newly returned from France. According to Wolsey's servant, George Cavendish, the cardinal's servants were accorded regular access to the queen's ladies:

> When it chanced the Lord Cardinal at any time to repair to the court, the Lord Percy would then resort for his pastime unto the queen's chamber, and there would fall in dalliance among the queen's maidens, being at the last more conversant with Mistress Anne Boleyn than with any other; so that there grew such a secret love between them that, at length, they were insured together, intending to marry.[41]

It would have been a simple matter for Gilbert to get to know Bessie whilst she was still at court or, at least, to have been aware of her by sight.

One opportunity for Gilbert and Bessie to meet would have been at a banquet that was held at Greenwich on 7 July 1517.[42] Gilbert, who was listed as one of the cardinal's servants, sat at the eighth table to dine, along with a number of his fellows and some of the queen's own servants and attendants. Bessie's table is not recorded, but it is not impossible that she found herself sitting close to her future husband. In any event, the banquet was, for the court, a fairly intimate affair, with only ten tables of guests. Bessie was, by that time, established as the king's mistress and is very unlikely to have paid much attention to a lowly young servant of Wolsey's. However, there would have been rumours circulating concerning her relationship to the king which, coupled with her beauty and accomplishments, may well have been enough to draw Gilbert's attentions to her. Bessie's undoubted charms, of which Gilbert was well aware, must have been additional incentive to him when a marriage with her was first proposed, even if it had been some years since he had last seen her. Bessie's early biographer, Childe-Pemberton, speculated that Bessie would have had some choice over her marriage, considering that suitors, who had presumably been carefully vetted by Wolsey, would have been allowed to visit her during the years after Henry Fitzroy's birth.[43] It is probable that Bessie would have met Gilbert before she was fully committed to the marriage. She was in an anomalous position as her family would have played no role in arranging the marriage. However, it does seem most likely that the king instructed the cardinal to find a suitable husband for his discarded mistress and it is therefore very unlikely that Bessie would have been permitted to object to the future decided for her. It has been suggested that, by choosing Gilbert as Bessie's husband and 'thereby banishing her to an unheard of village, which was inaccessible for much of the year because of floods',[44] Henry intended to rid himself of Bessie. However, as will be shown, she was certainly not banished to South Kyme and, whilst Bessie chose to make it her home, she was free to visit court when she wished. There was certainly no intention of banishing her when her marriage was arranged.

Bessie had no reason to object to the marriage arranged for her in any event and, whilst few details of Gilbert's character and none of his appearance survive, he was, at least, very close to her in age, something that counted in his favour. Gilbert's funeral brass, which once faced Bessie's on their memorial, has long been lost, although it apparently originally showed Bessie's first husband kneeling in armour and wearing a tabard that displayed the arms of the Tailboys family.[45] Like Bessie's, which was found to bear the traces of black pigment,[46] the brass would have been painted to give it a more lifelike effect. No other images of Gilbert are known to have been produced. Given that he chose to write an inscription in a book belonging to a friend, Lady Vaux, in French, it is clear that he was educated, something that gave him a common interest with the literary Bessie.[47] The Tailboys family were more than a step up from the Blount family socially, as well as being considerably wealthier. At the time of his death in 1495, Gilbert's grandfather, Sir Robert Tailboys, had more than enough manors to leave to his heir, George, as well as settling lands on his daughters and younger sons for life.[48] His daughter Elizabeth, the widow of Sir John Vavasour, who died in 1509, also had a number of fine possessions to distribute, recording in her will that she left 'to the Priory and Convent of St Elyns my basin and ewer of silver, my brother Robert Taylboys; to my sister Maud Tirwhit, my chain and cross of gold, and to my cousin Agnes, her daughter, my collar of gold and xx marks'.[49] It has been suggested that Bessie, with her birth and personal attributes, might have achieved as good a marriage by herself.[50] This is not impossible and marriages were often arranged between people of different social statuses: for example, Charles Brandon and Mary Tudor or, later, Brandon's widow, Katherine Willoughby and the lowly Richard Bertie. However, such matches tended to be clandestine in nature and they were still few and far between. The plain truth is that Bessie, whilst the daughter of a good local gentry family, was no match for the ancient Tailboys family.

Gilbert Tailboys flourished in Wolsey's household, being appointed to a commission of the peace in Lincolnshire even before his marriage.[51] In June 1521 he was also appointed to a commission of sewers in the county.[52] It is certain that his marriage to Bessie offered him freedom and, within a few months of the wedding, he was able to act largely free of the cardinal's influence in Lincolnshire, building his own power base. Gilbert was regularly appointed to commissions of the peace in his home county, for example.[53] He was also often appointed as one of the gentlemen commissioned to collect the king's subsidies in Lincolnshire, a role that may, perhaps, have made him less than popular in the local area.[54] In 1523, the year after his marriage, he received the first of three nominations as sheriff of Lincolnshire.[55] He may have sat in parliament that year. He was certainly a member of parliament by 1529, the year that he was created Baron Tailboys of Kyme.[56] This is in stark contrast to many of the cardinal's other servants, who found it particularly difficult to break free of his control, even after attaining their inheritances and their majorities. A surviving letter by Henry Percy, a fellow of Gilbert's in Wolsey's household, after he had succeeded as Earl of Northumberland, makes this clear, with Percy lamenting to his kinsman that:

> I received by my servant, Letters from you bearing date the xxth day of July, delivered unto him the same day at the king's town of Newcastle; wherein I do perceive my lord Cardinal's pleasure is to have such books as was in the Chapel of my late lord and father (whose soul Jesus pardon). To the accomplishment of which at your desire I am conformable, notwithstanding I trust to be able one day to set up a chapel of mine own.[57]

Both Gilbert and Bessie were determined to have autonomy over their own affairs following their marriage.

The 1523 session of parliament had particular relevance for both Bessie and Gilbert. It is probable that both were in London when an Act of Parliament was passed in Bessie's favour, ostensibly following a petition by Gilbert and his father, the incapacitated Sir George:

> Humbly showith unto your most excellent Highness your true and faithful subjects and servant Sir George Tailboys Knight and Gilbert Taylboys son and heir apparent to the said Sir George, That where the said Gilbert hath married and taken to wife Elizabeth daughter of John Blount Esquire, by which marriage as well the said Sir George Taylboys Knight as the said Gilbert Taylboys have received not only great sums of money, but also many benefits to their right much comfort. In consideration whereof and for the great love favour and affection that as well the said Sir George Taylboys as the said Gilbert Taylboys his son have and toward the said Elizabeth, your said Orators most humbly beseecheth your Highness that by the assent of the Lords Spiritual and Temporal and the Commons in this present parliament assembled and by authority of the same, to ordain establish and enact that the said Elizabeth may have hold and enjoy for terms of her life natural without impeachment of any waste the Lordships Manors Lands Tenements and Hereditaments hereafter ensuing which be of the inheritance of the said Sir George Taylboys, that is to say; All the Houses Lands and Hereditaments that the said Sir George Taylboys or Gilbert Taylboys his son or any of them or any other person or persons to their use or the use of any of them have or hath in possession or reversion or otherwise in the City of Lincoln; and the Manors of Skeldingthorpe, Bamburgh, Freskeney, Sotby and Faldingworth in the County of Lincoln.[58]

In addition to this, Bessie received a life interest in manors in Yorkshire and Somerset belonging to her father-in-law. Finally, the Act declared that this alteration to the usual principals of hereditary succession was only for the duration of Bessie's life, with the statement that 'the remainder of all the said Messuages Manors Landes Tenements and Hereditaments and other premises and after the decease of the said Elizabeth to such person and persons as they should have done if this present Act had never been had nor made'.

It has been suggested that this Act was due either to Henry's wish to make further provision for Bessie or, alternatively, for Gilbert's benefit in removing property from the control of his father's guardians.[59] Both motives are probable. Certainly, Gilbert, for whom little evidence of his character survives, was entirely happy to increase his own wealth and prestige through his marriage, regardless of the effect that it had on his family. The grant enriched Gilbert and Bessie at his parents' expense, with the value of Gilbert's lands rising rapidly during the 1520s from £66 13s 4d to £343 – a vast increase given that his father was still very much alive.[60] In addition to this, the claim that Gilbert and his father 'have received not only great sums of money, but also many benefits to their right much comfort' from the marriage hints at the negotiations that must have gone on behind the scenes between Wolsey, the king and Gilbert in order to secure the young man's consent to his marriage. He was knighted at around the time that the Act was passed, raising him to a status equivalent to that of his father and, significantly, ensuring that Bessie bore the same rank as her formidable mother-in-law. The Act gave Bessie an unusual degree of power in her marriage, since she held the life interest in the Tailboys estates, not Gilbert. Naturally, as a sixteenth-century married woman, at law, what belonged to Bessie actually belonged to Gilbert. However, the fact that Gilbert gained immediate title to his family's lands through her in some ways placed Bessie in the position of an heiress. As the case of Bessie's own mother and daughter shows, an heiress, even though she could not own property independently of her husband, could have a great deal of independence and influence.

The first grant made by the king to Gilbert and Bessie was on 18 June 1522, with the grant of the manor and the town of Rugby in Warwickshire, which had previously belonged to the executed Duke of Buckingham.[61] The date of 18 June, which was later chosen as the day of Henry Fitzroy's ennoblement in 1525, was evidently significant for Bessie and Henry and it may well have been Henry Fitzroy's birthday. Perhaps Henry VIII liked the coincidence of the date and the fact that, for economy's sake, the grant could then be taken both as a wedding gift to the couple and as a mark of the end of Henry Fitzroy's early infancy. The grant was made to Gilbert and Bessie jointly (referring to her as already Gilbert's wife).[62] The Duke of Buckingham, who was a distant kinsman of Gilbert's through his mother, had been executed by the king in 1521, but it was not until July 1523 that the king took the trouble to attaint him in parliament for treason. As was usual in an attainder, Buckingham's possessions were declared forfeit to the crown, although the king, remembering Bessie and Gilbert, took steps to ensure that there were no difficulties in them claiming title to Rugby, in spite of the attainder. The Act contained a provision, noting that the manor of Rugby, which had belonged to the Duke of Buckingham, had been granted to Gilbert and Bessie and that:

> This Act of Attainder, or any other Act or Acts in this present Parliament made or to be made, be not in any way prejudicial or hurtful to Gilbert Tailboys and Elizabeth his wife, nor to the

heirs of their bodies lawfully begotten, nor to the heirs of the said Gilbert, of, for, or concerning the Manor of Rugby and Town of Rugby, within the County of Warwick, given and granted to the said Gilbert and Elizabeth, and to the heirs of their bodies lawfully begotten, and for default of such issue, to the right heirs of the said Gilbert, by our sovereign Lord Henry the Eighth.[63]

The Act went into further detail, declaring that nothing should be done that was hurtful or prejudicial to the couple concerning their right to the knight's fees, benefices of churches, rents, waters, mills, fisheries and any other benefits of the manor and town. The Act was so comprehensive in its defence of Bessie's rights that one commentator has declared that 'Elizabeth Lady Talboys had been, and was probably then, the king's mistress'.[64] As has been seen, it is unlikely that Bessie and the king were still romantically involved, although, certainly, the grant was part of her reward for past services rendered. It may also have been significant that Gilbert and Bessie's joint issue were to inherit first, presumably intending that a daughter of them both would receive the manor in precedence to a son by Gilbert's second marriage (if he had one). Arguably, Henry was also therefore providing for Elizabeth Tailboys, who did eventually inherit the manor, selling it in 1560.[65]

An earlier grant, on 28 April 1522, of the wardship of George Vernon, a minor heir, was probably the Tailboys family's immediate reward for Gilbert's consent to the marriage as it was made jointly to Wolsey, Sir William Tyrwhitt, Gilbert's mother and Gilbert himself.[66] George Vernon was a wealthy young man and the grant, which gave his guardians custody and use of his lands during his minority, also effectively purchased a rich marriage for the Tailboys family, with the young man shortly afterwards marrying Gilbert's sister, Margaret.

With her marriage to Gilbert, Bessie was, for the very first time, mistress of her own household. She immediately took steps to ensure that it was she, rather than her mother-in-law, who was able to play the role of most prominent lady in the Tailboys family.

# MARRIED LIFE

Marriage to Gilbert Tailboys gave Bessie a social status that had been denied her due to the illicit nature of her relationship with the king. For the first time she took on the role for which her mother had prepared her in childhood: that of mistress of her own household and estates.

In November 1523, Gilbert was appointed as sheriff of Lincolnshire for the first time and, if the couple had not already travelled to his home county by that time, they certainly would have spent the majority of their time there during his year of service.[1] Gilbert and Bessie acquired the Tailboys' family's principle residence at South Kyme, whilst Gilbert's parents remained at a lesser manor at Goltho in Lincolnshire which they had used as their home since at least 1517.[2] It is certainly not the case, as one recent historian has stated, that Bessie moved her mother-in-law out of South Kyme to the smaller manor of Goltho,[3] although Gilbert's parents may have found it rather harder to visit South Kyme after their son and daughter-in-law's arrival. They were clearly denied access to its resources, with Gilbert's mother later complaining that she was no longer able to use the cattle from the estate to furnish her table cheaply with meat.

All that remains of Bessie's home is a tower that stands very close to the church on the outskirts of the small, pretty village of South Kyme, which is close to Sleaford in southern Lincolnshire. The tower, which now stands towards the edge of a field and close to a track, has four sides of equal length and four floors, rising to a height of 77 feet.[4] It has one room on each floor, which are linked to each other by means of a spiral staircase in a turret on the south-east corner of the building. With the exception of some of the palaces in which she stayed whilst a member of the court (such as Windsor Castle) and the manor at Bewdley, the tower of South Kyme is of particular interest as a surviving building that Bessie actually occupied. The tower was built by Gilbert's ancestor, the second Sir Gilbert de Umfraville of Kyme, in the fourteenth century, and his arms are displayed prominently in the building. Whilst the style of the window heads suggest a mid-fourteenth-century date, it would appear that the building work took some time to be completed, with the panelled work at the top of the staircase suggesting a date somewhat later in the century. The tower was intended to form part of the manorial residence, rather than serve any defensive purpose, as indicated by its large windows on each face of the building on the upper three floors, as well as a door on the ground floor, allowing easy access to the building. The tower was a grand undertaking, with quality ashlar stonework, as well as a wide staircase and window heads filled with glass. It has been suggested that the staircase led between what was a suite of elegant rooms. There are no fireplaces or garderobes in the building, implying that it was not a self-contained structure. This is also indicated by the beam holes above the first-floor entrance, which demonstrate that the tower was attached to a two-storey building on one side, which has now entirely vanished. This would have been the main part of the manor, which was demolished between 1720 and 1725, with some of its fittings, such as a fine chimney piece of carved stone, being carried to other houses in the area.[5] A visitor to the tower in 1791, which even then had become a tourist attraction, commented that 'the tower is, below, well-vaulted, well-stair'd, and the upper floors well plank'd; from the battlements is an extensive prospect'.[6]

Few other details of the manor survive, and there is no known drawing. Bessie's contemporary, John Leland, who evidently visited the house, recorded only that the manor was a 'goodly house and park'.[7] The remains of a moat have been noted and, in 1825, one writer claimed that 'a few years ago there were some inhabitants who remembered the remains of a draw-bridge, and the ruins of a building like an observatory, on the top of which, according to tradition, ladies were placed to be spectators of the bull-baiting, a pretty general diversion in former times'.[8] Bull baiting was indeed a popular pursuit, with Henry VIII's fourth wife, Anne of Cleves, recorded as having been gazing out of the window at the sport when the king arrived to visit her for the first time. Certainly, Bessie's home would have been comfortable and an observatory is a likely addition to a comfortable late medieval manor house. Another account, written in 1837, just over a century after the manor house was pulled down, claimed that 'old people were living a few years ago who remembered the remains of the castle; and they state generally, that the walls were adorned with carvings representing equestrian figures in armour and other enrichments'.[9] The manor apparently resembled a castle, with a moat, drawbridge and towers, although it is unlikely to have had any real defensive purpose when it was built, with the claim that the first room of the tower 'was unquestionably a dungeon' seeming particularly fanciful, especially given that it sat above ground level.[10] In 1592, the hall at the manor is recorded to have had two large windows which were decorated with stained glass bearing eighteen coats of arms depicting the families from which the Tailboys family claimed descent.[11] It is certain that the hall must have been a light and airy structure: very far from a true castle. The manor also had a deer park, as evidenced by the names of nearby fields, and details of Bessie's own hunting parties at South Kyme, as well as Leland's description.

Although the South Kyme tower had a domestic purpose, a large part of its function in the medieval period and later was display. Even in Bessie's time, there would have been few buildings to rival it. The tower stands only eight miles from a similar structure at Tattershall and the parallels between the two towers have been described as striking.[12] Tattershall Castle stands higher than its counterpart at South Kyme, at 110 feet. It also has an extra storey and a basement and appears to have been more comfortable, including fireplaces and garderobes. However, one modern commentator has pointed out that the two towers fulfilled a similar function:

> Both of these neighbouring towers reflect the dignity and standing of their owners through their towering height and the richness of their apartments. The first-floor chamber at Tattershall, for instance, was an independent hall with a canopy over the high table at the upper end. The first-floor chamber at South Kyme has windows reaching almost to the floor which was covered by patterned tiles.[13]

It has been suggested that the two towers may have been considerably more linked. In 1437 Walter Tailboys, Gilbert's great-great-grandfather, inherited South Kyme. He was a close friend of Ralph, Lord Cromwell, who owned Tattershall and the two men were often associated together. On Walter's death in 1444, however, relations soured with the accession of his turbulent son, William, who has been discussed earlier, to the Tailboys lands. He has been described as Lord Cromwell's arch-enemy and this would seem an accurate description. Cromwell, who was born into a minor Lincolnshire family, became one of the most powerful men in England.[14] He served as treasurer of England in the mid-fifteenth century and his marriage to an heiress brought him great wealth. Cromwell constantly built and rebuilt his principal seats, including Tattershall. The tower was a late addition to the site, which was potentially not planned from the start. In 1449, William Tailboys' animosity towards Cromwell had grown so intense that he sent spies to Tattershall in an attempt to determine whether it would be possible to kidnap his rival. When this proved to be impossible, he sent men to try to murder Cromwell whilst he was walking with his chaplain. This plan also failed, with Cromwell being well protected by his retainers. Tailboys, who obviously bore an almighty grudge, was still not deterred, instead making an attempt to blow up the house adjacent to his rival's London residence. In the obsessive way in which Gilbert's great-grandfather pursued his enemy, it is perhaps possible to see the origin of the madness that later afflicted Gilbert's father. Once again the plan failed, with Tailboys being imprisoned. It has been suggested by Matthew Johnson, in his work on English castles, that it may have been the Tattershall tower that finally pushed William Tailboys over the edge. Work began on Tattershall's tower soon after Walter Tailboys' death, perhaps being delayed until then by Cromwell out of respect for his friend. William Tailboys was already aware that the manor that he had inherited was considerably smaller than his neighbour's but, as Johnson points out, at least he had a tower: 'he can therefore hardly have viewed the almost immediate start of construction of a tower that dwarfed his with equanimity – particularly in an age when a 'honour' was a central component of elite male identity'.[15] Certainly, it was a grave provocation and Tattershall Castle, which still overshadowed South Kyme in Bessie's time (and even today is considerably more impressive), must have been a constant source of irritation to the family. The importance to Bessie of the rivalry between the two towers is that, even in her time, the Tattershall tower served as a reminder to her new family that, whilst they were of ancient and noble lineage, they were very much part of a network of local lords and families, each of whom vied with the others for prestige in the local area: the fact that his tower was not the most impressive would have brought home to Gilbert, as it did his ancestors, that he was very far from the only power in southern Lincolnshire. This would have been mitigated somewhat by the grant in April 1525 to Gilbert of the position of bailiff of the manor of Tattershall and keeper of the castle, which had previously been held by Sir William Compton, the enemy of Bessie's father.[16] Three months later, Gilbert also obtained the lease of Tattershall park, which had previously belonged to the king's grandmother, for a period of twenty-one years.[17]

South Kyme was dominated by the manor and the church in Bessie's time, and the two stood close together. In the late eighteenth century it was commented that the roads to the village were good in summer but very bad in winter, something which must have made South Kyme feel isolated for much of the year.[18] Churches in Lincolnshire are commonly large and impressive structures due to the wealth of the county in the medieval period thanks to the wool trade. Even very small settlements have sizeable churches. South Kyme church, as it now stands, is a noticeable departure from this. The small church with no tower that survives today was extensively 'restored' in the early nineteenth century. By 1791, it is known that the church in which Bessie would have worshipped had fallen into great disrepair. Writing at that time, Viscount Torrington recorded that the church was 'of such beautiful antiquity. However, within, the filth and ruin would beggar all description! The roof falling in! – A dirt floor! – An altar table that a pauper would not feed from!!'[19] As far as Torrington could see, only the fine monument commissioned by Bessie for Gilbert following his death survived untouched, with the visitor commenting that 'I look'd around me; but dared not plunder'. Within a few years of Torrington's visit someone else was bolder, with only the rivet holes and inscribed plaque of the monument surviving in situ.

Apart from the tower, little of the surrounding countryside would now be familiar to Bessie. South and North Kyme, which were neighbouring manors and belonged to the Tailboys family, lie within the Lincolnshire fens. North Kyme, which is the smaller settlement, was built on the site of a Roman encampment and road.[20] The fens around Kyme are recorded to have been drained in 1635, although the manors of North and South Kyme, which contained nearly 9,000 acres of land, were still being described in the early nineteenth century as only 'tolerably well drained'.[21] In Bessie's time, the land around South Kyme would have been considerably wetter, with frequent floods making agriculture on much of the land a challenge. Perhaps as a result of this, the village at South Kyme has never supported a great population, with one observer writing in the early nineteenth century that 'the population of South Kyme has not increased so much as its hamlet since the time of Queen Elizabeth, for we find there were then in South Kyme sixty-three families, and in North Kyme twenty-five. The return in the year 1821 states the former place to contain eighty-nine families, constituting a population of five hundred and sixteen, and the latter to have fifty-three families, making a population of two hundred and eighty-three.'[22] It can be posited that the population between the reigns of Henry VIII and his daughter Elizabeth I would not have seen any great decrease and that, therefore, society for Bessie must have been fairly limited.

After the manor house, the most prominent building in South Kyme was the priory, which housed canons of the order of St Augustine.[23] The canons, who followed a less strict rule than monks, would have been a familiar sight to Bessie in the early years of her marriage, in their long black and white cassocks with black cloaks and hoods. Canons also had beards and wore caps on their heads. The priory had been founded by Gilbert's ancestor, Philip de Kyme, in around 1170 and it had been substantially enlarged by his son, Simon de Kyme. The Tailboys family took a strong interest in the priory, with Gilbert's grandfather, Sir Robert Tailboys, for example, requesting burial in the priory church. It may be that he was the member of the Tailboys family recorded to have enlarged the building once again. By the time of the dissolution of the monasteries, the priory possessed lands and rents worth more than one hundred pounds a year and there must have been considerable turmoil in the local areas when, on 6 July 1539, Ralph Fairfax – the last prior, who had been in his office since 1511 and with whom Bessie must have been familiar – surrendered the priory with his remaining nine canons to the crown, in return for a pension of £30 per year. Nothing now survives to show where the priory stood, although until at least the nineteenth century there was a field called the 'Abbey Yard', which suggests that it lay on the site of the former religious house.

For Bessie, the move to South Kyme must have been a difficult one at times, something which may account for her eagerness to have her sister, Rose, close by (something which is discussed in a later chapter). By the early sixteenth century, Lincolnshire, unlike many other counties in England, was dominated by a series of noble and gentry families, rather than with one aristocratic influence.[24] No one family was able to dominate the local area, with a number of great estates, such as that of the Willoughby family, passing into the hands of an heiress, with the corresponding loss of estates and influence that this often entailed. As one historian has commented, through a study of the Lincolnshire gentry's involvement in the 1536 rebellion against the king, 'one result of the extinction of great families, and the lapse of great inheritances to the crown was that a mass of lands and offices came into the latter's disposal. Who was to benefit? The question stimulated ambitions and generated tensions.'[25] By this interpretation, Bessie has been seen as a court incomer who helped to perpetuate the troubles in the area.

It is certainly true that Bessie was not a native of Lincolnshire and it is not impossible that tensions were caused in the wider Tailboys family by her association, and apparent friendship, with the Duke of Suffolk. Suffolk had had an interest in Lincolnshire since at least 1513 when he received a number of lands that had previously belonged to the rebellious de la Pole family in the county. In 1525 this interest was cemented by the choice of the title, Earl of Lincoln, for his eldest surviving son, who was ennobled at the same time as Bessie's own eldest child. The Willoughby family was a major one in the county, holding over thirty manors, as well as lands in Norfolk and Suffolk. The ninth Lord Willoughby had, after a childless first marriage, married Maria de Salinas, a Spanish maid of the queen's. This match produced in 1519 a daughter, Katherine, who was named as heir to her father on his death in 1526.[26] As part of his interest in the area, Suffolk secured Katherine's wardship, originally intending for her to marry his son. Following the death of his wife, the elder Mary Tudor, he took the opportunity to marry her himself, bringing her extensive estates under his control. Katherine Willoughby's succession to her father's estates was by no means a certainty and an element of the hostility felt by Bessie's mother-in-law towards her may have had its origins in the dispute over the Willoughby inheritance. In 1512, the ninth Lord Willoughby's brother, Sir Christopher Willoughby, had married Gilbert's sister, another Elizabeth Tailboys.[27] The bride's father was still, at that stage, in control of enough of his own affairs to promise 1,000 marks to Lord Willoughby in exchange for the peer making over lands in Lincolnshire and Suffolk worth 600 marks to his brother and his wife, as well as a promise that, should he die without heirs, he would will his barony and lands (which were worth 400 marks a year) to his brother. In 1512, this must have seemed a good deal to Gilbert's family. It soon became apparent that Lord Willoughby had little intention of honouring his side of the bargain, refusing to make the conveyance of the lands. To add insult to injury, when he married in 1516, he settled a number of the manors in question on his bride. In his will Lord Willoughby confirmed this position, leaving all his property to his daughter (save that which had already been settled on his wife). No mention was made of his brother's claims.

The dispute over the Willoughby inheritance was a bitter one, with Sir Christopher complaining plaintively to the king that Maria had not informed him of his brother's sickness or death and had barred him from the funeral.[28] It was also a dispute in which Gilbert's family had a major interest. Soon after his brother's death, Sir Christopher took steps to occupy some of his brother's lands, including the family's principal seat of Eresby.[29] Gilbert's sister supported her husband, arriving at Eresby shortly afterwards to keep Lent there with her household.[30] In retaliation, Maria de Salinas occupied another house at Parham in Suffolk before helping herself to Sir Christopher's belongings there. She must have been a formidable opponent as she later defied the king himself, forcing her way into the home of Catherine of Aragon as she lay dying in order to comfort her. The dispute dragged on for some years, with most local sympathy given to Sir Christopher. Matters were finally resolved legally in February 1536 when Suffolk persuaded parliament to enact in his favour, ordering Sir Christopher to leave two manors, and confirming his right to only another eight, in exchange for him abandoning his claims. This settlement was by no means satisfactory to the Willoughbys and even in April 1536 Suffolk and Sir Christopher were disputing openly before the king. It is perhaps no surprise that Gilbert's nephew, William Willoughby, was one of the leaders of the Lincolnshire rebellion in late 1536 which formed part of the Pilgrimage of Grace. It is to be expected that the Tailboys family would have thrown their weight behind Sir Christopher and his wife and, to a large extent, this is probably true. Bessie was, however, in a very difficult position as Sir Christopher's sister-in-law and as Suffolk's friend. Suffolk would also later become her near-neighbour at South Kyme when, in 1537, he took up residence in Tattershall Castle. Given the known hostility that existed between Bessie, her husband and her mother-in-law, it would appear likely that the couple took Suffolk's side in the argument or, at least, refused to be drawn to either side. For Bessie, there may also have been an element of solidarity with Suffolk due to his position, like hers, of being a newcomer to the area. One historian has commented, after discussing Suffolk's involvement in the dispute over the Willoughby inheritance, that 'the theme of the intrusion of an alien and predatory courtier into the Lincolnshire scene cannot be left without a glance at the troubles of a second great family'.[31] This was a reference to Bessie herself.

Gilbert and Bessie were living at South Kyme when the grievance that the elder Lady Tailboys had been nursing since their marriage finally burst out into the open. The elder Lady Tailboys had remained living at Goltho with her incapacitated husband following Bessie's marriage. She was unable to develop a good relationship with her daughter-in-law, in spite of the fact that the couple paid tribute to her husband in naming their eldest son after him. Gilbert's mother complained to her son and daughter-in-law about her financial situation, with them responding that she mismanaged the parts of the estates still under her control.[32] Perhaps in revenge, Gilbert and Bessie then attempted to acquire these lands, using their powerful court connections. Gilbert was evidently at court at this time and, given the accusations of his mother that Bessie was involved in the dispute, it would be reasonable to assume that she was with her husband. Cardinal Wolsey threw his considerable weight behind the couple, declaring to Gilbert in person that he ought to return to Lincolnshire to ensure that order was kept, also promising custody of his father and his remaining lands. Matters did not go as the elder Lady Tailboys hoped and, on 15 May, Wolsey wrote to her, ordering her to deliver lands to a yearly value of £100 to Gilbert, which was the remainder of the £200 sum appointed to him and Bessie by the Act of Parliament, along with an annuity of £40. Gilbert's mother was furious, and responded desperately trying to change the cardinal's mind, stating that, although she could deliver the lands worth £100, the annuity of £40 was impossible, declaring that she hoped the cardinal would 'admit my reasonable excuse and lack of ability for non-doing thereof in that behalf':

First, I your said beadwoman trusteth, that since the time of my husband's visitation, and that he was by the king's highness committed to your grace, the revenues of his lands have been well employed, and converted to the pleasure of God in necessary causes, as keeping of the household, servants' wages, and marrying of my husband's children and mine, and not in prodigal and wasteful expenses.

Item, at this hour there is behind of the marriage-money of one of my husband's children and mine the sum of 150 marks; for the contention whereof the most nearest friends that I have stand bound, who must needs be discharged.

Item, my husband and I have one son, brother to my said son Sir Gilbert, who yet hath none assignment for his living, and needs must be provided for.

Item, an old servant of my husband's, named William Bengham, accustomed to make provisions for wheat, malt, and other grain for my husband's household, is gone away with as much money of my husband's as should have made provision for such grain for this whole year, to the loss of my husband of 100 marks, whereby I was constrained to make new provision for grain, and for the same not only to take rents of such lordships as my son Sir Gilbert would have, but also the revenues and profits of other my husband's lands, as my son knoweth very well.

Item, in the lordship of Kyme there was wild beasts to the number of ten score, out of the which my husband and were wont to have our beefs for household; which cattle now we have no profit of, which is a great hindrance unto us.[33]

Gilbert's mother was obviously having difficulty, not least with the need to marry her many daughters and the theft of her household funds by her husband's servant. The fact that Gilbert and Bessie would no longer permit her to take cattle from South Kyme is also indicative of the poor state of their relationship: gifts of meat were common as a mark of respect in Tudor England. Gilbert's mother sought to put the worst possible sheen on her situation in order to win the cardinal's sympathy, although there is no doubt that she did find herself in a difficult position, being forced to act as though she were a widow and run her own household, but without the comfort of a widow's dower. She was later forced to borrow over one hundred pounds from a gentleman, Richard St Paul, apparently later having difficulty in repaying the fifty pounds of his 'money goods and chattels' that still remained with her after his death.[34] Lady Tailboys continued:

My lord, since the first visitation of my husband, I have lived, as God knoweth, with little comfort, and for the pleasure of God I have yielded me thereunto, and now, my husband being aged, if he and I should live in penury, and lack that thing that he and I should discharge our friends with that be bound for us, and have not that that should be necessary, and be compelled to break up house and spargle [i.e. scatter] our children and servants – as surely, of necessity, my husband and I must do in [case] my said son should obtain this his said demand – I might think mine fortune hard. Wherefore most humbly I beseech your good grace, by the way of pity and compassion, graciously considering the state of my husband and me your said beadwoman, our small comfort and great charges, and, on the other side, the great pieces of land that my son Sir Gilbert hath in his hands already.

The elder Lady Tailboys had evidently been informed that it was Gilbert who had been soliciting the cardinal for further funds and she complained that he already held lands worth the very specific sum of £342 17s 11¾d, which was 'as much or more' than that still held for the benefit of herself and her husband. Clearly, the loss of a further £40 a year was a great one for Gilbert's parents. Lady Tailboys finished her letter lamenting that 'My lord, I have none to make suit nor complain me unto, but only to your good grace; as our Lord knoweth, who ever preserve your noble grace in good, long, and most prosperous life.' If Lady Tailboys was correct in her figures, Gilbert and Bessie's wealth had very substantially increased since March of the previous year when Gilbert had been assessed for a subsidy as having lands worth £66 13s 4d.[35] Whilst it was obviously in Gilbert's interest to return as low a figure as possible for his income where the calculation of tax was concerned, it is clear that he and Bessie had been very successful both in obtaining royal grants and in taking custody of Sir George Tailboys' property in the months before Gilbert's mother set her complaint in writing to Wolsey.

Unfortunately, Wolsey's response does not survive, but it is very unlikely that the elder Lady Tailboys succeeded in persuading him to support her. Bessie and Gilbert knew that they could rely on Wolsey's support. Gilbert's parents were not left entirely destitute: they were able to commission a fine tomb in Lincoln Cathedral in a chapel that they had themselves founded.[36] Also, regardless of what the order giving Wolsey and others the governance of Sir George Tailboys said, it is clear that it was his wife who exercised authority over the Tailboys estates, with one legal case declaring that 'the said Elizabeth took upon her the rule administration of the goods and chattels that of the said Sir George Tailboys in his lifetime'.[37] Lady Tailboys' hostility towards her son and daughter-in-law may have had its roots in their interference in the position that she had established for herself as governor of the Tailboys estates and of her husband. However, they were evidently in some financial difficulty, for example owing arrears of rent for a farm to Queen Anne Boleyn at the time of her death.[38]

Evidently still hoping to influence the cardinal, the elder Lady Tailboys made use of her own contacts, writing to her cousin, Thomas Heneage, who was Wolsey's secretary. In addition to this, she attempted to bribe the cardinal with six fat oxen which were delivered at Easter 1529.[39] By early 1529, Gilbert and his mother were barely speaking, with both Bessie and Gilbert again travelling up to court early that year in order to deal more directly with Wolsey.[40] According to the elder Lady Tailboys' letter to Heneage, Bessie was very much involved in the dispute:

> Cousin, I marvel that my son and my daughter [Bessie] do think
> or say that you take a part with me against them, considering that

you at all times are and have been good to them, and indifferent [impartial] betwixt me and them; and so I pray you to be. My son of late sent me word by old Blesby that I am the cause of his going up to the court, and that I shall pay for his costs ere he come home.

Lady Tailboys claimed that Gilbert had offered to leave his parents with 400 marks and the manor of Goltho in exchange for him paying their debts to Sir Robert Dymoke – which related to the sums promised on the marriage of Anne Tailboys to Sir Robert's eldest son – as well as dropping his claim to his £40 pension. However, it appears that Gilbert was not disposed to be so generous once he reached the court, perhaps realising that he could achieve more from his parents after speaking to the cardinal or the king. He then denied that the offer had been made, instead stating that he wanted half of his father's lands and, as a concession, would then be prepared to pay half of the sums owing to Sir Robert Dymoke. Lady Tailboys responded to this by declaring that she was sure that another kinsman, George Heneage, Dean of Lincoln, who was the father of Thomas Heneage, would vouch that the first offer had been made. This suggests that Gilbert, and perhaps Bessie, had visited his mother between Lady Tailboys' letter to Wolsey and her letter to Heneage in an attempt to broker some settlement, with the negotiations being formal enough to require the Dean of Lincoln to attend.

Bessie was not prepared to remain silent during the dispute and, whilst she was at court with Gilbert, she summoned the Tailboys servant 'old Blesby' to deliver a message for him to take to her mother-in-law. According to the account of Lady Tailboys:

My daughter [Bessie] reported to Blesby, as he saith, that my son nor she did never make any request to the king's highness, or to my lord's grace [Wolsey], for any more of his father's lands; but she saith that my lord's grace of his own mind called my son to him, and said he should go home and see good order kept in the country and that he should have the custody of his father and his lands.

It is hardly surprising that Gilbert's mother believed Bessie to have sufficient influence with the king and the cardinal to persuade them to provide her and Gilbert with a larger living (at the expense of his parents). Her presence at court is a strong indication that she was still in high favour and had an excellent relationship with her former lover and his chief minister. In some respects, Bessie tried to take on the role of peacemaker between her husband and his mother, trying to avoid any misunderstandings between them, although her major interest was clearly her own financial well-being and that of her husband and

family. Bessie and Gilbert do not come out of the business in an entirely
good light and they appear predatory in their attempts to take Gilbert's
inheritance during his father's lifetime. Bessie's assurances that she had
not solicited the king or Wolsey do not ring entirely true and it would
be surprising if she had not used her very great influence at court to
the advantage of her husband and herself, particularly given her poor
relationship with her mother-in-law. Lady Tailboys certainly did not
believe that the orders had come unsolicited from the cardinal, declaring
that she would continue to put her trust in him and commenting, in her
letter to her cousin:

> I marvel my son would presume to make any motion touching
> his father's lands without knowledge of the pleasure and
> commandment of my lord's grace. It is folly for him or her so to
> do; for they shall never order me at any time without knowledge
> of my lord's pleasure, and his gracious commandment, whereunto
> I shall ever be obedient.

Once again, Bessie's active involvement can be seen in the comment by
the elder Lady Tailboys that 'if they cease not of their unfitting words, I
shall surely put up my bill of complaint to my lord's grace [i.e. Wolsey]
for remedy'. Clearly the people speaking 'unfitting words' were Gilbert
and Bessie. Bessie could evidently be as dominant a personality as her
mother-in-law when she wanted to, and she intended to get what she
had been promised. Bessie's mother-in-law's claim that she and Gilbert
were soliciting support without the cardinal's knowledge suggests that
the couple turned to the only power in England higher than Wolsey:
the king himself.

In spite of Bessie and Gilbert's support at court, it was in the
power of Gilbert's mother to make life very difficult for the couple
in Lincolnshire. In her letter to her kinsman she rather tellingly
commented that the couple's attempts to win more lands from her
and her husband, as well as to take custody of Sir George, alarmed
her, stating that 'I cannot be in quietness for them; whereupon all our
friends, both in these parts and in the north, doth wonder'. These
friends almost certainly included Sir Christopher Willoughby, who had
his own axe to grind with the court, and in all probability he would
have been happy to link his grievance with his mother-in-law's. A
second son-in-law of Lady Tailboys', Edward Dymoke, is also likely
to have supported her. It was his wife's marriage money that Lady
Tailboys claimed was at risk and it is clear that she had difficulty
in paying for the very expensive marriage that had been made for
her daughter Anne.[41] The Dymoke family, although only of gentry
status, were based at Scrivelsby Court near Horncastle.[42] They had
acquired the manor in the fourteenth century. One curious fact that

vastly increased the status of the family and hints at why the Tailboys family were so eager to secure the match for Anne is that the owner of Scrivelsby also had the right to act as the king's champion. A Sir John Dymoke acted as champion at the coronation of Richard II, whilst his son, Sir Thomas, took the role at the coronations of Henry IV and Henry V. Thomas's son, Sir Philip, acted in the same role for Henry VI whilst his son, another Sir Thomas, was champion to Edward IV. Anne Tailboys' father-in-law, Sir Robert, was a formidable local figure and had the distinction of acting as champion for three monarchs: Richard III, Henry VII and Henry VIII. The role involved the champion riding into the great hall during the coronation banquet and laying down a challenge to anyone who disputed the sovereign's title to the throne. Sir Robert perhaps waited with baited breath when he laid down his challenge on behalf of Richard III and Henry VII, although Henry VIII's own accession was entirely popular and undisputed. Like Bessie's own family, the Dymokes had a connection through marriage to Lady Margaret Beaufort via the marriage of the second Sir Thomas Dymoke to Margaret's stepsister, Margaret Welles. Interestingly, as well as the distant connection with Margaret Beaufort, Sir Robert Dymoke also had stronger links to Bessie through the queen's household. He served as Catherine of Aragon's chancellor from 1527, a position that was lower in rank only to the positions of Bessie's two kinsmen: Lord Mountjoy and Sir Edward Darrell. The Dymoke family's support for Gilbert's mother is suggested by the fact that, in February 1531, after the fall of Wolsey, a new commission for the custody of George Tailboys was issued, this time excluding Sir Robert Dymoke from his previous position as one of George's governors.[43]

Given the local support that the elder Lady Tailboys could undoubtedly rely upon, it is no surprise that Gilbert and Bessie chose to spend time at court. However, they also spent time at South Kyme and the marriages of two of Bessie's daughters (by her second marriage) to the sons of Sir Christopher Willoughby and Sir Edward Dymoke does not suggest any great attempt to exclude her from local society. Gilbert's younger brother William, who had a very good relationship with his parents, apparently remained on good terms with his sister-in-law, leaving a generous bequest to her daughter from her second marriage, Bridget Clinton, in his will.[44] Whilst Bessie was indeed an incomer to Lincolnshire, she can hardly be considered urbanised or a creature of the court: rather, her background as the daughter of a country gentry family, was sufficient to ensure that she was able to fit in as the mistress of her own household in an equally rural setting.

Gilbert and Bessie were never successful in winning custody of Sir George Tailboys and the dispute was allowed to drop with the fall from power of Cardinal Wolsey in late 1529. In any event, Gilbert may already have been in ill health by 1529 and, certainly, within a few months, Bessie had more important things to worry about than her poor relationship with her mother-in-law.

When Bessie was not at court, she spent her time running her household and assisting in the organisation of the family estates. The manor at South Kyme was the first home in which Bessie had been able to establish her own independent household and, as can be seen from the fact that she later chose to remain at the manor after Gilbert's death, she was fond of it. As has already been noted, the Tailboys family was a wealthy one. Surviving inventories of the possessions of members of the very distantly related Raithby Tailboys family are helpful in a consideration of the sort of life that Bessie would have led. One John Tailboys of Raithby, who was a gentleman, owned a wide range of possessions in 1579.[45] These included money in his purse of £4, as well as items of pewter and brass. He possessed a great deal of agricultural equipment, such as a wagon, a cart and a plough, as well as three horses, three mares, two fillies and some foals. Four calves were also listed, as were crops growing in the field such as rye, beans, barley and malt. Wheat, barley and rye were stored in the barn. In addition to this, John Tailboys' house had a hall, in which two tables, a chair and a cupboard were situated. His parlour, which would have been the most comfortable room of the house, contained two feather beds and mattresses. It is evident from the inventory that John Tailboys of Raithby was able to live in some comfort, in spite of the fact that his branch of the family had fallen on hard times. This can also be seen in the inventory of one Robert Tailboys of Raithby, which was taken three years earlier. Robert, like his kinsman, owned agricultural equipment and animals, such as two mares and a foal. Clearly Bessie, as the wife of the son of the head of the Tailboys family (who later became a peer in his own right), would have expected a higher standard of living than these poor relations, and it is likely that her own house was furnished on a considerably grander scale. Gilbert's own brother, William, was able to leave 'one standing cup of silver and double gilt' in his will, which suggests a reasonable level of wealth.[46]

Although Bessie and Gilbert lived in the finest house in South Kyme, it has often been noted that manor houses in the medieval and Tudor periods tended to be smaller than their successors in the seventeenth and eighteenth centuries, and with relatively simple furnishings. In the late nineteenth century, for example, a survey was carried out by studying the extant sixteenth-and seventeenth-century wills in Lincolnshire.[47] In the will of John Asfordby, who was the lord of the manor of Asfordby in Bilsby in Lincolnshire, he listed the number of rooms in his house. 'What do we find? Why that there were only eight rooms altogether for the Lord of the Manor, his wife, children, and servants to live in. These were the Hall, the Parlour, the little Parlour, the low Parlour, the chamber over the Parlour, the Gallery Chamber, the Buttery, and the

Kitchen.'[48] In addition to this, to modern eyes at least, the rooms were sparsely furnished. The hall had a folding table, a long carved settle, a fine chair and a painted hanging of canvas over the high dais. While the hall, buttery and kitchen lacked beds, the sitting rooms all had them, with one in the parlour, two in the little parlour and two in the chamber over the parlour. There were two in the gallery chamber and three in the low parlour, including a four-poster bed. In spite of this sparseness, the Asfordbys had a fine collection of plate for display, as well as an alabaster head of St John the Baptist, which was the only ornament. Obviously Gilbert was a somewhat more prestigious and important lord than the squire of Asfordby. However, a more analogous household can be seen in the inventory of the house of Sir Peter Carew, the second husband of Bessie and Gilbert's daughter-in-law, Margaret, Lady Tailboys, which was prepared in the 1550s. According to the inventory, which was produced for his wife's benefit, Carew's house included only six rooms that contained furniture.[49] These rooms were sparsely furnished, with chattels such as a long table board and trestles and three old bedsteads. Amongst the fairly meagre possessions listed were chamber pot and a birral pot. The manor at South Kyme, which would have been crowded with Bessie and Gilbert and their family and servants, would not have been as glamorous, or as comfortable, as life at court and it is clear that they often sought to return to London when they were able to.

The evidence suggests that Bessie's marriage to Gilbert was a contented one. As well as Elizabeth Tailboys, who was probably not Gilbert's daughter, Bessie bore her husband two sons named George for Gilbert's father and Robert for his grandfather.[50] Given that he was sixteen in March 1539, George must have been conceived very soon after Bessie's marriage, which suggests the couple had a liking for each other. Gilbert died eight years after their marriage, in April 1530, but there is evidence to suggest that Bessie bore a total of at least four and possibly five children (discounting the disputed Elizabeth Tailboys), which demonstrates that the couple spent a considerable amount of time together and that they were close. This rate of children suggests that when Gilbert attended court, for example, Bessie invariably accompanied him. When the church at South Kyme was substantially rebuilt in 1805, the vault containing Gilbert's tomb was opened whilst the foundations were laid for a new north wall.[51] Four lead coffins were found inside, below the monument erected to Gilbert's memory by Bessie. These contained a fully grown adult and three children. Unfortunately few details of the discovery survive, although it was noted that one of the children's coffins had been opened at some point in the past and the body was very decayed. Another coffin was opened by the workmen and found to contain a child aged around five or six years old. This child had been immersed in 'some kind of spirituous liquid' and was very well preserved, appearing to observers to be only a recent burial.⁵² It was believed, at the time, that these were the children of Gilbert Tailboys. This would seem probable given that his remains were certainly contained in the adult-sized coffin. Also, given that none of his children or brothers had children, and that his parents were based at Goltho and so are unlikely to have buried their own infants at South Kyme, there are really no other candidates for the children's parents than Bessie and Gilbert. The fact that one of the coffins had been opened accidentally suggests that they were not all interred there at the same time, with the coffins being moved around to make room for others. Bessie's youngest recorded son, Robert, died in childhood and it may be that his coffin is one of those buried in the vault although, as a Baron Tailboys in his own right, it would seem strange that no memorial was added for him if he was indeed interred there. Also, he died in March 1542, nearly twelve years after his father. Assuming that he was born a year or so before Gilbert's death, he would already have been approaching his teenage years at his youngest and may have therefore been too big to be one of the children buried in the vault, particularly given the very great disparity apparently noted in the sizes of the children's coffins compared to the adult's coffin. Bessie's eldest son by Gilbert, George, died aged seventeen or eighteen and it is improbable that his coffin could be included in the vault. This suggests that Bessie bore at least two, and possibly three, further children, who are not recorded, including one that survived to the age of five or six. The efforts taken to preserve this child hint at the grief of its parents: the loss of a child who had already survived infancy must have been particularly hard to bear. Given the fact that Bessie's marriage only lasted eight years and that her first child by Gilbert, George, was probably born in late 1522 or early 1523, it seems highly likely that a child who survived to five or six may have outlived its father, leading to further grief for Bessie after she was widowed. It has been suggested that Bessie's son, Robert, may have died due to the unhealthy fen climate.⁵³ This is possible, although the loss of children was something that most Tudor parents endured. It is odd that Bessie was not included in the vault, which also bore her funeral brass alongside Gilbert's. However, given that the workmen in the nineteenth century were adamant that the three coffins were those of children, it is unlikely that any of them would have been confused with the burial of an adult woman. Bessie's own burial will, of course, be considered in more detail later. It must be noted, however, that no report of the opening of the vault survives from 1805 and, within a few years of the discovery, rumours were already circulating in the local area, with one visitor in the 1830s being assured by a local woman that she possessed a 'well-glazed brown earthen jar' which had been found in the vault and had contained Gilbert's bowels. The writer was rightly sceptical, commenting that the jar appeared 'of too modern a structure to have been appropriated to any such purpose'.⁵⁴

Although she lived mostly in Lincolnshire, Bessie was not cut off from court. She and the king had parted on good terms and the common interest of Henry Fitzroy and Elizabeth Tailboys provided a continuing link. The former couple participated in gift exchanges at New Year, something that was a very public display of whom the king favoured.[55] In 1529, for example, Bessie is known to have given a New Year's gift to Henry, and to have received one in return.[56] Although there are no details of what the gifts given actually were, Henry was evidently pleased with Bessie's gift as the reward he gave to her servant for delivering it, 13s 4d, was somewhat greater than that received by the servants of most ladies employed in the same office. In 1532 the king gave Bessie a gilt goblet with a cover, which was the heaviest present of any lady below royal rank – a mark of singular honour.[57] Her gift was significantly more expensive than that given to Mary Boleyn, who was listed in the ranks of ladies two below Bessie. Whilst the king chose not to give his estranged wife, Catherine of Aragon, a gift that year, he provided presents for his sister, Mary Tudor, the French Queen, and his daughter, Mary.[58] Other great ladies also received gifts, such as the royal Countess of Salisbury and the two duchesses of Norfolk, as well as Anne and Mary Boleyn's mother, the Countess of Wiltshire, who received a gilt cup. The king did not forget the servants of his fiancée, with a number of presents listed for ladies then 'with the Lady Anne'. Henry Fitzroy, of course, received extravagant presents from his father, the preparation of which would have brought Bessie to the king's mind. Bessie gave the king her own present that year, although the details of what she supplied do not survive. Many ladies, such as Mary Boleyn, chose to make the king a gift of clothes and Bessie may have followed this. Only Bessie, Lady Darrell and Lady Carew of the ladies who gave presents to the king were not then at court, indicating that they, perhaps, had a special status that set them apart from the more conventional methods of giving gifts to the king which, for ladies, tended to require their actual presence 'with the king'. Lady Carew, as previously discussed, had, like Bessie, been the king's mistress. The king's New Year's gift lists are extremely fragmentary, with only four years in any way extant. The evidence of the two years in which Bessie features suggests that she was regularly high up the king's present-giving list. Gilbert also continued to prosper under Henry VIII, receiving the wardship of a minor, William Ingleby, in February 1529.

Further evidence of the king's continuing affection for Bessie can be seen in an agreement made in March 1535.[59] This impressive document, which survives in the National Archives with its wax seals still intact, documented that, in the last few months of Gilbert's life, he and Bessie were at court and engaged in detailed negotiations with Sir Edward Seymour, the king's future brother-in-law. In two agreements made on 16 November 1529 and 30 November 1529, Gilbert and Bessie together bargained with Seymour to sell some of their lands. Gilbert died less than six months later, before the couple could honour their side of the bargain, although Seymour had already paid over a substantial sum. The agreement had apparently been Gilbert's idea and Bessie only agreed to please her husband, something that provides some indication of their close relationship during their marriage. After Gilbert's death, she had second thoughts and, finally, in 1535, 'at the request and desire of the said Dame Elizabeth [Bessie] and of other of the friends of the said Dame Elizabeth', Seymour was persuaded to abandon his claims, in return for the repayment of the £600 that he had already paid to her. The names of Bessie's 'friends' are not recorded but, given the further content of the deed, it was almost certainly the king himself and, perhaps, his chief minister, Thomas Cromwell, who was friendly with her parents. It is evident that Seymour was not entirely happy to abandon his bargain, particularly as he received no additional sums to compensate him for the several years that Bessie had been in possession of his money. Bessie did not intend to repay this sum, with the agreement of March 1535 further relating that Seymour was in debt to the king for a sum of over £400 in relation to some lands in Hertfordshire. Henry, by his own 'express commandment' ordered that these lands should be transferred, free of debt to Seymour and his wife for them and their heirs to enjoy. In exchange, Seymour transferred to Henry the benefit of the agreements made with Gilbert and Bessie and their subsequent amendment: i.e. the right to claim £600 from Bessie. There is no record of whether or not Henry did indeed reclaim this sum from his former mistress, but it would seem unlikely. Almost certainly Bessie, pressed by the ambitious Seymour and unwilling to part with the lands bargained, as well as being unable to find the sum of £600 to repay him, went to the king to request his assistance. That Thomas Cromwell was also a party to the agreement is telling and the king's acceptance of the debt of £600 should probably be looked upon as a gift to the mother of his son.

By 1527 Gilbert had also been appointed to the king's chamber,[60] an appointment which required a regular attendance at court. It is very likely that Bessie often accompanied him. In spite of her evident contentment in her marriage, Bessie and Henry VIII always shared a connection, which was embodied in their children but, most particularly, in their precocious son, Henry Fitzroy.

# 14

# HENRY FITZROY, DUKE OF RICHMOND & SOMERSET

Henry VIII, as Bessie would have expected, retained custody of their son following her marriage, but Bessie's relationship with Henry Fitzroy was never denied and she and her family were regularly associated with him during his childhood.

Fitzroy lived in obscurity during the first six years of his life, emerging suddenly onto the international stage in June 1525 when his father decided to promote him to the highest rank of the nobility. This should not be seen as the start of royal interest in the boy. One indication that Henry Fitzroy was already in receipt of royal favour even before his ennoblement can be seen in a surviving list of 'Wardrobe stuff appointed for my lord Henry'.[1] The 'lord Henry' in question is not identified but, given that the subject was not considered to require a title and that the list has survived with further documents relating to the household established for Fitzroy after his ennoblement, it would seem reasonable to assume that it is Henry Fitzroy. The fact that Fitzroy was not given his title of Duke of Richmond is evident that the goods, which included hangings for his house and chapel, as well as his closet, great chamber, dining chamber, bed chamber and other rooms, were originally designated for him before his ennoblement (although when it was already planned given the large suite of rooms that he was expected to furnish). The familiar way in which he is described as 'my lord Henry' is also interesting and suggests that, amongst the officers close to the king, at least, his existence was hardly a secret.

Another indication that Henry Fitzroy had some prominence before his ennoblement has been suggested in relation to Cardinal Wolsey's accounts, with the claim that the cardinal gave Henry Fitzroy a New Year's gift in 1525, some six months before he was promoted to the peerage. This interpretation is based on an entry in a list of items delivered to Wolsey by Robert Amadas, a goldsmith of London.[2] One of the entries relates to a 'karkenyt' and a hanging pearl, which are recorded to have been 'for my lord of Richmond'. This entry is directly below the account of a fine gold cup and cover given 'to the king for his New Year's gift'. It would therefore seem plausible to assume that this was indeed Henry Fitzroy's New Year's gift for 1525. However, this interpretation should be treated cautiously since there is no mention that it was definitely a New Year's gift. Bessie's son was also referred to as 'lord of Richmond', a title that he had not attained by New Year 1525. Equally, Robert Amadas's entries continue on the next folio of the manuscript, with the items following Fitzroy's gift bearing the date of 10 July 1525. The final entry recorded by Amadas was dated 20 September. Evidently, Amadas recorded the deliveries to Wolsey towards the end of the year, something that could account for him referring to Henry Fitzroy as the Duke of Richmond, even in relation to a delivery that predated this. However, it seems just as likely that the gift was made in the summer of 1525, perhaps in honour of Henry Fitzroy's ennoblement. In the sixteenth century, gifts were not exclusively made at New Year, with other occasions, such as christenings, meriting presents.[3] The gift certainly cannot be definitely considered to have been a New Year's gift in 1525, although the fact that the cardinal honoured Fitzroy with the gift, at the latest, shortly after his ennoblement, does demonstrate that Wolsey showed an interest in him that, coupled with the cardinal's role as the boy's godfather, is likely to have been apparent in the years before the child was publicly recognised. Another gift in a set of Wolsey's accounts, which was delivered sometime after 1518, may with more certainty be dated to the period before Fitzroy's ennoblement. Wolsey purchased 'one garter of Crown gold for my Lord of Richmond'.[4] Given the subject matter of this gift, it may have been commissioned to mark Fitzroy's appointment as a knight of the garter. Wolsey is also known to have given Fitzroy New Year's gifts in the years after his ennoblement, such as a spoon of gold recorded in an inventory of Fitzroy's goods after his death.[5]

In spite of the uncertainty over when Wolsey's gift was commissioned and given, it is highly likely that Wolsey had already shown considerable interest in his politically important, and highly promising, young godson. After his elevation, Fitzroy's council believed that the cardinal required detailed knowledge of their young charge's health, reporting in one letter, for example, that 'your honourable young and tender godson my lord of Richmond is at this present time (laud be God) in good and prosperous health, and as towardly a young prince as ever hath been seen in our time'.[6] Whilst it was, of course, only natural for Wolsey to take an interest in the boy after his elevation, the letters of Fitzroy's council do suggest that a more personal relationship had already been established. In the same letter, the council assured Wolsey that the boy, on hearing that a letter to his godfather was being prepared, 'beseecheth your grace of your daily blessing, and of the continuance of your gracious favour towards him, in like manner as evermore your grace (without any his desert) hath always been in times passed'. A further indication of Fitzroy's fondness for his godfather can be seen in a letter to Wolsey by Dr Magnus, written nearly a year later, when he declared that, 'immediately upon the making of this my letter, my lord of Richmond's grace, hearing that I sent unto your grace at this time, instantly required me to recommend him unto your said grace, beseeching you of your blessing'.[7] Fitzroy also wrote to the cardinal, expressing his close relationship to him, for example in March 1529 stating that he was more bound than any creature living to Wolsey's favour and goodness 'and like it hath pleased Almighty God and the King's Highness much part by the means and good favour of your Grace to prefer and advance me in honour'.[8] Fitzroy saw in Wolsey something of a father figure, a role that fully supports the view that the cardinal had remained in close contact with him during his infancy and early childhood. This is further supported both by Wolsey's continuing contact with Bessie and Gilbert, as well as the fact that, on the morning of his elevation it was from Durham Place, Wolsey's London residence, that Henry Fitzroy set out by water to travel to Bridewell Palace to meet his father. One account of his elevation recorded that Durham Place was 'where at he kept his household', suggesting a stay of some duration and that it may, perhaps, have become well known as his principal residence.[9]

There is some evidence that Henry Fitzroy's existence was already reasonably well known publicly before his elevation. In the late nineteenth century two verses were found written on the blank leaves of an early printed book in Ripon Minster Library.[10] One of the verses, although heavily damaged, contained 'A little ballad made of the young duke's grace'. Whilst the title to the ballad refers to Fitzroy as a duke, suggesting that the ballad was written down after his elevation, the fact that he is everywhere in the song referred to as 'Henry Fitzroy', with no mention of his title in the actual substance of the verses, suggests strongly that it may have been composed, and sung popularly, before June 1525. Although fragmentary, the verse speaks of the hopes vested in Fitzroy, for example beginning:

> I[n] grace honour and prosperity
> I[n] health in wealth & tranquillity
> Fro' damage and captivity
> To our comfort & only Joy
> Good lord preserve Henry Fitzroy.

The second verse has been largely lost, but the third continues in the same vein, declaring:

Good lord grant us this our petition
That Henry it is king of this region
Both he & his unto thy tuition
May come to be in eternal Joy
And long to preserve him and Henry Fitzroy.

If this ballad can indeed be dated to the period before Fitzroy's elevation, as seems likely, it is good evidence that the king's only son was even then being looked upon as something special and, perhaps, even an eventual successor. This is strongly suggested by the pairing of Henry Fitzroy with his father in the ballad. The recognition of this is a great departure from the generally accepted view that Fitzroy was a largely unknown quantity until June 1525. The composer's hopes for Fitzroy also echo those expressed by his first tutor, John Palsgrave, in a letter to Bessie, when he alluded to her son as a potential future ruler, something that suggests that even by the mid-1520s Fitzroy's eventual accession to the throne was in no way impossible. Whether this would have been desirable or not is another matter and a young page in Fitzroy's household, Nicholas Throckmorton, later recalled that, whilst he served Bessie's son 'and waited, still at hand', he lived in 'fear of blows, which happened in his rage'.[11] A quick temper may have been a side-effect in a boy raised to be almost a prince but with the stain of illegitimacy hanging over him – another royal bastard, the tenth-century boy king Edward the Martyr was also noted for his quick temper and ability to alienate supporters. Equally, a certain coldness can be seen as the result of an upbringing in which the child was entirely aware of his own importance: Fitzroy's half-brother, Edward VI, was able to dispassionately order the executions of two of his maternal uncles, but he was still well liked and praised. Fitzroy too formed lasting friendships with the boys in his household and was evidently well liked, in spite of his quick temper. How much credence can be given to Throckmorton's words is debatable. Throckmorton and Fitzroy were evidently friendly enough for Bessie's son to give him some of his outgrown clothes, including a riding coat in November 1531.[12] The following month Fitzroy personally handed a doublet of cloth of silver to the page, although, it should be noted that this garment was described in an inventory of Fitzroy's possessions as 'sore worn'.[13] A second doublet, of black satin lined with black sarcenet, was obviously in better condition and was also given to Throckmorton by Fitzroy himself in December 1531.[14] Fitzroy even gave the boy his cast-off pairs of hose.[15]

The decision to elevate Fitzroy can only have come from the king himself. In March 1524 he had received a compelling reminder of his own mortality when he was nearly killed by the Duke of Suffolk in a joust, something that helped focus his mind on his lack of legitimate sons.[16] Cardinal Wolsey was deeply involved in Henry's decision to promote his only surviving son. A letter from the cardinal, written in the weeks before the boy's advancement, states that 'your Grace, also, shall receive, by this present bearer, such arms as Your Highness hath devised, by Page, for your entirely beloved son, the Lord Henry Fitzroy'.[17] The coat of arms that Henry Fitzroy was granted quartered the royal arms of France and England, with only a 'baton sinister' across them to indicate his illegitimacy.[18] Another indication that Fitzroy's elevation had been long planned and was not a made on the spur of the moment by the king was Henry's intention to ennoble other members of his court at the same time. This was not always a welcome honour as a letter from John Arundel to Wolsey dated 9 June 1525 shows. Arundel declined the offer to create him a baron, on the same day that Fitzroy was to be ennobled, due to his unworthiness. He also mentioned what was likely to be his real motive for refusing the honour: lack of funds to support the greater financial demands placed on a baron.[19]

Preparations for Henry Fitzroy's ennoblement moved feverishly during the weeks and days before it occurred, with rumours reaching the Venetian ambassador in early June that 'the king will be in London tomorrow because he intends to confer a dukedom on a natural son of his, who is seven years old, and also to give him considerable territory. He has legitimised him, and loves him like his own soul.'[20] Henry's affection for his son was well known at court and suggests that the boy might, on occasion, have visited court, as his sister Princess Mary often did. Alternatively, Henry tended to place his children in manor houses not far from London, with Hatfield and Hunsdon being particular favourites. This was common in the royal family. Henry himself, as a younger son, had been raised with his sisters at Eltham Palace, not far from London. If Henry Fitzroy was lodged in one of these palaces there would have been nothing to stop the king making regular visits, as he later did to his daughter, Princess Elizabeth, during her infancy. Henry's intentions towards Bessie's son stopped far short of legitimisation, but the fact that this was even rumoured speaks volumes about the king's relationship with him. The Venetian ambassador was not so well informed that he was able to accurately report the titles that Henry Fitzroy received, later referring to him as Duke of Buckingham and Earl of Richmond.[21] He later corrected himself to report, more accurately, that the king had conferred on his son 'the highest grade in the kingdom, so that now he is next in rank to his Majesty'.[22]

It has been suggested by a number of historians that Henry's decision to advance Henry Fitzroy was intended as a slight to the Emperor Charles V, the nephew of Catherine of Aragon and the head of her family, for breaking his long-standing betrothal to Princess Mary on 7 June 1525. Cardinal Wolsey's earliest biographer, for example, claimed that Henry considered the broken betrothal 'to reflect some Disgrace on his Daughter'.[23] Alternatively, there have been arguments advanced that the elevation was a reaction to the peace terms agreed between Charles V and Francis I after the French king's capture in battle: Henry VIII had been hoping to use the opportunity to conquer France. However, neither argument seems entirely persuasive, particularly given the clear evidence that plans for Fitzroy's elevation had been afoot long before Mary's betrothal was broken. There is no doubt that Catherine of Aragon and her family were offended by Fitzroy's elevation, which was highly unusual in England at that time. Edward IV's illegitimate son, Arthur Plantagenet, who was then still alive, had not even received a peerage from his father, whilst there had not really been any prominent royal bastards since the twelfth century – the illegitimate sons of Henry I and Henry II. The crucial difference, however, is that Edward IV, for example, had fathered legitimate sons as well as illegitimate. By 1525 Henry was married to a woman long since past childbearing and had no sons to show for his marriage. The age of six was recognised in the sixteenth century to be the end of infancy[24] and, given the fact that Fitzroy almost certainly turned six in June 1525, it would have been expected that Henry VIII would make some provision for him. The extent of the provision should be considered both a reflection of paternal pride and the fact that Fitzroy represented proof of Henry VIII's rather doubtful virility to the world. In addition to that, Henry had very few male relatives on whom he could rely. Given that he had already ennobled his best friend to the highest rank of the English peerage, it is perhaps not surprising that he also elevated his son in a similar way. Arguably, the new prominence given to Henry Fitzroy was more about demonstrating to the world that the royal fertility problem was the queen's and not the king's, something that seems probable given Henry's later touchiness on the subject of his virility. When the imperial ambassador later asked the king directly why he thought he would achieve a legitimate son, the king demanded, 'Am I not a man like other men?' Henry Fitzroy, who appears from his surviving portrait to have borne a marked resemblance to his father, was his proof that he was indeed a man, just like any other. No other explanation is necessarily needed for the king's generosity to the child, nor his continuing generosity to Bessie herself. It seems unlikely that he had at that stage decided to make Fitzroy his heir, particularly as, at the same time, Princess Mary was sent to Ludlow to govern Wales and the Marches: a position traditionally associated with the heir to the throne.

The first honour to be bestowed upon Fitzroy was that of a knight of the Order of the Garter, an honour which, in order to have been bestowed, would have required him to be previously knighted. The Order of the Garter had, since the reign of Edward III in the fourteenth century, been the premier chivalrous order in England. Knights were elected only rarely when a position fell vacant, with Henry Fitzroy the twenty-third knight to be elected to the order during his father's reign.[25] The twenty-fifth, who was elected not long afterwards, was the boy's kinsman, William Blount, Lord Mountjoy. Fitzroy's election possibly occurred as early as 23 April 1525. He had certainly been elected by 7 June 1525. He was first installed in the order at Windsor on 25 June, taking possession of the second stall on the sovereign's side of the chapel. As a mark of his existing status as an illegitimate son of the king, Fitzroy was referred to at his election as a baron, rather than as a prince or a knight (the three categories of persons eligible for the order). Clearly his father's rank had already conferred a certain status on him which was recognised by his contemporaries. At the time of his investiture, he was provided with a mantle of purple velvet, which again emphasised his royal blood. It was lined with white sarcenet and decorated with a great cross of St George embroidered with a garter.[26] A further mantle of crimson velvet with a hood was provided at the same time.

Henry was not content with merely including his son in the Order of the Garter and he had great plans for his future. For his son's elevation, he chose one of his favourite and newest palaces, that of Bridewell, which sat close to the Thames in London. According to the sixteenth-century antiquary John Stow, Bridewell was 'a stately and beautiful house', which had been built in honour of the Emperor Charles V's visit to England in 1522.[27] The honours conferred upon Bessie's son were unparalleled, with no person in England, save the sovereign himself, ever before him holding two dukedoms and an earldom at the same time.

On the morning of 18 June 1525, Bessie's six-year-old son set out from Durham Place by water, accompanied by a company of gentlemen. He arrived at Bridewell at around nine o'clock in the morning and made his way to the great hall.[28] Fitzroy was dressed in the robes of an earl in a side room before being led into the hall flanked by the earls of Arundel and Oxford.[29] In front of him walked the Earl of Northumberland carrying a girdle and a sword in its scabbard by the point. Garter Kings of Arms walked before them all carrying Fitzroy's patent of nobility. The party walked through the crowded long gallery into the chamber, where the king sat under a canopy of estate, flanked by both bishops and temporal lords, including Fitzroy's godfather, Cardinal Wolsey. What would have been a bewildering occasion for a boy who was only six years old must have been made somewhat easier by the fact that he had evidently been coached on how to behave. On approaching his father, Fitzroy knelt, before the king commanded him to stand. Henry VIII took the patent and passed it to Sir Thomas More, who read it aloud. At the appropriate moment Fitzroy kneeled again and the king put the girdle around his neck, with the sword hanging over his chest. Henry then passed the patent, which created Fitzroy Earl of Nottingham, to the boy, who was led back out to the gallery. Once outside, Fitzroy was quickly helped to change, reappearing dressed in the habit of a duke and flanked by the dukes of

Suffolk and Norfolk, with the Earl of Arundel walking in front of them carrying a cape of estate with a circlet on it. The Earl of Oxford walked before them carrying a rod of gold, whilst the king's cousin, the Marquis of Dorset, carried a sword by its point and the Earl of Northumberland carried a duke's robes of estate, which were made of crimson velvet and furred.[30] Once again, a patent was carried before them all. As before, Fitzroy knelt before his father to be created Duke of Richmond and Somerset before the assembled company. There is no evidence that Bessie was present to witness her son's triumph, but she may well have been. Fitzroy's biographer, Dr Murphy, has suggested that Gilbert was almost certainly present in his capacity as a member of the cardinal's household.[31] Given that there is evidence that Bessie later accompanied her husband to court it would seem probable that she would have made a point of being in London on such an important occasion.

In the same ceremony that Fitzroy was elevated, other members of the royal family were similarly honoured, with the king's young nephew Henry Brandon, the son of the Duke of Suffolk and Mary Tudor, Queen Dowager of France, honoured as Earl of Lincoln, a title that had previously belonged to the nephew and heir apparent of Richard III. The king's cousin Henry Courtenay, who was the grandson of Edward IV, was given the title of Marquis of Exeter, whilst Lord Roos, who was the great-nephew of Edward IV, was created Earl of Rutland. Other peers were created at the same time, but what can most plainly be seen in the ceremony at Bridewell was an attempt by Henry to shore up and define the greatly depleted English royal family. Effectively, Henry demonstrated just whom he considered to be his kin and a member of the blood royal: Henry Fitzroy was recognised as the first of them, ranking only behind the king, the queen and their legitimate offspring in England.[32] The boy also received administrative appointments and, as well as being appointed as Lord High Admiral,[33] he was made Lieutenant-General North of the Trent and Warden of all the Marches towards Scotland,[34] a post which necessitated the immediate removal northwards of both Bessie's son and his council and household. At the same time that he was elevated to the peerage he was made keeper of the city and castle of Carlisle.[35] Other appointments followed later. In 1529, for example, Fitzroy was made governor and captain of Berwick-upon-Tweed.[36] Fitzroy also received a liberal grant of lands and other revenues in order to allow him to support a lifestyle as befitted his rank. In August 1525 the king granted him the honours, castles, rents and other hereditaments which had belonged to the king's paternal grandparents, Edmund Tudor, Earl of Richmond, and Margaret Beaufort, as well as those that had previously belonged to Margaret Beaufort's father, John Beaufort, Duke of Somerset.[37] In addition to this, the boy received a number of fine properties, including his great-grandmother's favourite residence of Collyweston.[38]

Henry Fitzroy set out for Sheriff Hutton Castle in Yorkshire soon after his elevation, on a journey that took a month. Something of the boy's already strong-willed character can be seen in the fact that, apart from a short stage of only three or four miles, he resolutely refused to ride in the fine horse-litter that Wolsey had provided for him, which was decorated with the boy's arms on crimson velvet. Fitzroy instead rode the entire distance on his little pony, something which must have exasperated his attendants.[39] He conceived a long-lasting dislike of the litter during the short time that he spent in it, with it being recorded in an inventory made of his possession in 1531, after his return to the south, that it was left behind by Fitzroy at Sheriff Hutton when he came out of Yorkshire.[40] Fitzroy evidently saw himself as a man and had no intention of riding in a litter like a woman or child, regardless of his age. Sheriff Hutton was to remain as his principal residence for some years.

It was intended that Henry Fitzroy's household should be magnificent, as befitted both the son of a king and a major peer in his own right. Although, at the time of his arrival at Sheriff Hutton, Fitzroy was a child of only six, few allowances were made for his age. A set of sample menus survive for his household which demonstrate that, even on ordinary days, the boy was expected to be hospitable on a lavish scale.[41] For example, an 'ordinary diet for my lord and his board from Michaelmas until Christmas upon all flesh days' included two courses, with such fare as pottage, beef, mutton, capons, pigeons, pheasant and wildfowl. On Fridays and Saturdays in the period after Christmas and up to Lent, Bessie's son could expect to receive a wide variety of fish at any one sitting, including ling, cod, salted and fresh salmon, pike and turbot. Such fare would be washed down with wine, something that even young children were expected to drink since the water was not considered to be healthy. Henry Fitzroy and his immediate attendants were given the most lavish fare, as befitted his rank. Other members of his household, who ate in a strictly hierarchical order, were also well provided for. His chamberlain and the controller of his household received two courses at meals, with foods including boiled beef or mutton, capons, pigeons and pottage. Below them were the gentlemen waiters, who received pottage, beef and other rich foodstuffs. The yeomen had a similar, if slightly less elaborate, menu. Surviving kitchen accounts for Fitzroy's household from March 1527 to September 1528 and from October 1535 to August 1536 show that staple provisions were also regularly purchased to feed the household, such as butter, eggs, milk and cream.[42] Purchases of yeast demonstrate that his kitchens baked bread on a daily basis.

Fitzroy had an impressive household of officers and servants to maintain. According to a list of his officers and councillors, as well as more prominent members of his company, such as the Dean of York, he was also attended by four chaplains, two gentlemen ushers, two cupbearers, two carvers, two sewerers of the chamber, eight gentlemen waiters, two yeomen ushers of the chamber, twenty yeomen of the chamber, two grooms of the privy chamber, two grooms of the outer chamber, a page of the privy chamber, two pages of the outer chamber, two footmen, staff for the pantry, cellar, buttery, ewery, hall almoner, kitchen and boiling house, pantry and scalding house, scullery, slaughter-house, laundry and stable, as well as porters and apothecaries.[43] Fitzroy was considered to require thirty-four gentlemen, forty-six yeomen, three pages, sixty-three grooms and seventy-nine gentlemen's servants, as well as more menial servants to attend him. The most important appointment for the six-year-old, however, was surely his nurse, Anne Partridge, who remained with him until 1530. She evidently had her work cut out in caring for such an active little boy, something that required the purchase of a bay ambling horse for both her and her maid.[44]

At the time of its establishment, it was estimated that one year's household charges for Henry Fitzroy would amount to over £3,100, with more than £50 alone set aside for rewards and presents to those that served him. As set out above, food for the household was elaborate and feeding everyone present must have been a major undertaking, with nearly £350 per year spent on provisions. In the first six months of the household's existence, it was necessary for Fitzroy's leading officers to find £440 15s 5d in wages for his officers, on top of the £91 that the boy's master of horse, Sir Edward Seymour, was able to spend in ensuring that the contents of Fitzroy's stables reflected his high rank.[45] In addition to this, within nine months of his promotion, Fitzroy had received nearly £90 worth of new clothes, as well as lavish new hangings purchased for his chambers. In contrast, the fifth Earl of Northumberland, who was then one of the greatest noblemen in England, spent only £933 6s 8d in 1512 for his entire household for one year, including all food purchased and the wages for his staff.[46]

As a great lord, Henry Fitzroy was expected to be generous and further expenses were quickly incurred in New Year's gifts and rewards for servants. The provision of New Year's gifts was evidently a major headache for Fitzroy's council during their first winter at Sheriff Hutton, with the council writing anxiously, as a whole, to Wolsey to ask whether:

> It may stand with your grace's pleasure, to provide for the king's highness a New Year's gift to be sent unto his highness at the beginning of this next New Year from my lord of Richmond. And for that purpose we have sent this bearer William Amyas to London for making and for provision of the same. And how we shall use ourselves therein, for the devise and value thereof, we beseech your grace that this said bearer may know your grace's pleasure. And if it may stand with the same your pleasure that we shall in like manner provide any other New Year's gifts, for the queen's grace, the French queen, the dukes of Norfolk and of Suffolk, and for the marquises

of Exeter and of Dorset, we do most humbly beseech your grace
that this bearer may also know your pleasure concerning the same,
which we have commanded him to observe in every behalf.[47]

Just what Catherine of Aragon would have thought of a lavish gift from
her husband's illegitimate son, and a potential rival to her daughter, is
not recorded, but it is unlikely that the boy was included on the queen's
own gift-giving list. As well as lavish New Year's gifts, Fitzroy gave lavish
alms, as well as spending sums on enjoyment, such as purchasing saddles,
greyhounds and other dogs, and on rewarding players and minstrels who
entertained him.[48]

That Bessie was not recorded as a potential recipient on the list is not
significant as any gift to her was uncontroversial and would not have
required the cardinal's sanction. Bessie was able to freely make gifts to her
son, as an inventory of his goods made in 1531 shows, in which she was
recorded to have given him two bay horses and a doublet of white satin.[49]
Fitzroy had a love of sports and it is perhaps not surprising that Bessie
chose to make him a present of horses, demonstrating a level of awareness
in his interests. They were not an altogether successful gift, however, with
the boy exchanging one of the horses with his chamberlain for a gelding,
whilst the second horse died in the park at Sheriff Hutton. The doublet
was evidently a more appreciated present and there is evidence that Bessie
retained an interest in her son's clothes. In the 1531 inventory, a number
of later notes were added to the records of clothing to explain what had
happened to the items once they had been outgrown or worn out. Whilst
the Duke of Norfolk and Fitzroy appear to have been involved in deciding
whom such items should be distributed to, a third person, described as
'my Lady's Grace', was also involved in the distribution. This lady made
recorded gifts on 7 January 1532 and 28 March 1532. Whilst Bessie was
already referred to in the text of the inventory as Lady Tailboys, this does
not preclude her from being the 'Lady's Grace' mentioned in the notes,
which were added by different hands some months, and sometimes some
years, later. Henry Fitzroy did not marry until 1533, to a wife who was
also still a minor, and it is therefore very unlikely that the references to
this lady refer to her. There is really no other candidate for this unnamed
lady other than Bessie herself, something that suggests that she visited
her son with some regularity, actively going through his clothing after he
had outgrown it and deciding to whom it should be distributed. Bessie
made gifts of hose to Nicholas Throckmorton and Henry Partridge (who
was presumably a young kinsman of Fitzroy's nurse).[50] A further gift of a
gown of black velvet was given to George Cotton, a member of Fitzroy's
household.[51]

Further evidence of the continuing connection between Bessie and her
son can be seen in the fact that two of her brothers, George and Henry,
who were born in 1513 and c.1515–16 respectively, found positions in

their nephew's household.[52] Although they were a few years older than their sister's son, they may have shared their nephew's lessons. Henry VIII's sixth wife, Catherine Parr, for example, who was four years older than Princess Mary, has traditionally been supposed to have shared her lessons with her during her childhood. Although this suggestion has often been dismissed due to the girls' age difference, the evidence of a book belonging to Catherine's cousin, Elizabeth Vaux, who was raised with her, does suggest that it may in fact have been true. Amongst a number of signatures and comments made by members of the Parr and Vaux families, including Catherine Parr herself (and, as will be discussed, Bessie and Gilbert), there was written a prayer in a sixteenth-century hand, which was headed: 'This prayer following which beginneth in Latin; *concede michi misere cors Deus*, was first made by Saint Thomas of Aquinas translated into English by the most excellent [Princess] Mary the year of Our Lord M CCCCC XXVII [1527]'.[53] Catherine Parr would later enlist her stepdaughter in a translation project during her time as queen. It appears, from the evidence of this book that she had first become aware of the younger girl's language skills during shared lessons during their childhood. Given that Mary did not publish this translation, it otherwise raises the question of how it came to be inserted in a book so personal to the Parr and Vaux families and their friends.

Based on this evidence, it is not unlikely that Mary's half-brother, Fitzroy, would have similarly shared his lessons with a number of boys with a wide range of ages (he is already known to have been educated with contemporaries). The appointments for her brothers, which were almost certainly procured by Bessie, were beneficial to both boys. In his epitaph, provided by his nephew, Rowland Lacon, it was recorded of George Blount:

> But the palace of his King delighted his youth,
> In manhood Scotland and the realms of France
> Felt his generosity in war; in both he was a terror.[54]

The king's palace where he spent his youth refers to his time with his nephew, with his participation in the king's military campaigns during the last years of his reign a mark of the esteem in which George Blount was held. In addition to this, Bessie's second son, George Tailboys, was appointed as one of the noblemen to meet the king's fourth wife, Anne of Cleves, when she arrived in Calais on her marriage journey to England in late 1539.[55] Another man listed to attend the new queen at Calais was one named 'Blunte', who may well have been one of Bessie's brothers – perhaps the eldest, George.[56] What Anne of Cleves can have thought of Henry's tactless reminders of mistresses past is not recorded. Another man chosen to attend her at Calais was 'Young Stafford, that married the Lady Carey [Mary Boleyn]'. George Blount was prominent enough to play a role in the funeral procession of Henry VIII in 1547, carrying one of the twelve banners showing the king's descent.[57] He remained in his nephew's service until Fitzroy's premature death.[58] The third brother, Henry, profited from the court connections that his relationship with his nephew provided. By 1538 he was one of the gentlemen in the household of the king's chief minister, Thomas Cromwell.[59] Bessie's second brother, William Blount, also benefitted from his sister's royal connections and is known to have served with Henry VIII in France during his Boulogne campaign of 1544.[60] He found a place with his nephew after his return from Sheriff Hutton, being listed as one of Fitzroy's gentlemen at the time of the latter's death in July 1536.[61] He had court connections, with his sister, Anne Lacon, using him as a means of procuring her son's wardship from the king following the death of her first husband.

Henry Fitzroy also built a relationship with his half-brother, George Tailboys, which suggests that the pair met with some regularity, perhaps when Bessie and George visited Sheriff Hutton or Fitzroy's other residences. The two boys, who were three and a half years apart in age, enjoyed a brotherly relationship, with George receiving Fitzroy's outgrown clothes as hand-me-downs, something which suggests their mother's direct attention and an excellent relationship with her children, particularly since, as set out above, Bessie is likely to have played some role in distributing Fitzroy's outgrown clothes. In the 1531 inventory, the very richest clothes that belonged to Fitzroy were later distributed to his half-brother. For example, a gown of purple taffeta, edged with purple velvet and with buttons of gold decorated with roses, was passed to George on the order of the Duke of Norfolk on 3 August 1533.[62] On the same day he also received a gown of blue tinsel, lined with black satin and edged with black velvet. Other garments included a doublet of cloth of gold.

During the late 1520s, Fitzroy spent most of his time at Sheriff Hutton Castle in Yorkshire, although he also moved to other residences in the north. He was not entirely exiled from London and visited the capital on occasion, for example in May 1526 witnessing a charter at Westminster.[63] An inventory taken after his death demonstrates just how richly furnished Henry Fitzroy's residence would have been.[64] As well as fine tapestries and hangings, he possessed three great carpets and twelve small carpets, which would have travelled with him when his household changed residence. He owned a chair covered in cloth of gold and fringed with red silk and gold, as well as having four panels of silver and gilt. He also possessed a chair of crimson velvet, which was embroidered with his arms and fine cushions of cloth of gold, purple and russet velvet. The boy had twelve great beds at the time of his death, ensuring that he must always have been comfortable. In addition to this, he possessed his own kitchen stuff, chapel material and stable equipment.

The duke always appeared richly dressed, with 'a gown of crimson damask embroidered all over with gold and furred' noted in the inventory taken after his death.[65] The gown was decorated with buttons of gold, whilst another was made of black velvet, embroidered with a border of Venice gold and lined with black velvet and satin. At the time of his death, the boy possessed a princely gown of purple velvet which was embroidered with Venice gold and lined with yellow satin and decorated with seventeen gold buttons. Such garments were evidently regularly part of the duke's daily wardrobe, with the inventory diligently recording that Fitzroy had lost one of the buttons for his purple gown. He also possessed a mantle of the garter for more formal occasions, which was made of purple velvet and velvet gold. There was a crimson velvet kirtle and also a green satin riding coat with a silver fringe which, given Fitzroy's love of sports, must have received regular use. Bessie's son possessed a coat of white cloth and white velvet which was lined with rich sarcenet. There was a doublet of black velvet embroidered with a fringe of velvet gold and a crimson satin doublet trimmed with a fringe of Venice gold and lined with yellow sarcenet. When he was cold, the boy had furs to keep him warm. He possessed two swords and a gilt wood knife. According to the earlier inventory, from 1531, he had also owned a dagger. Fitzroy appeared heavily bejewelled when the occasion demanded, possessing a jewelled collar, a whistle of gold, rings, bracelets and garters, amongst other items. One rich item of jewellery, which was to be worn at Fitzroy's throat and was made of gold and set with seventeen white roses, was sent as a gift from the king. The white roses, as the badge of the royal house of York, made a significant reference to Fitzroy's royal descent and it is no surprise that members of his household, emboldened by his high status and the finery of his dress and household referred to him as a prince. Fitzroy possessed a large quantity of fine plate, which was used for display in noble households. Many items were gifts from his father, including a particularly fine golden salt which was supposedly made of unicorn horn and was set with pearls. Interestingly, a spoon bearing Catherine of Aragon's pomegranate badge found its way into Fitzroy's plate collection, although it seems unlikely that it was a direct gift from the queen to her husband's illegitimate son.

Henry Fitzroy was too young to be aware at the time of his elevation that he had a rival in the form of his elder half-sister, Princess Mary. Understandably, Catherine of Aragon, who must have resented Henry Fitzroy's very existence, was distinctly displeased at the prominence that the king gave him. Within days of Fitzroy's elevation, the Venetian ambassador, who had good access to gossip at court, recorded that 'it seems that the queen resents the earldom and dukedom conferred on the king's natural son and remains dissatisfied, at the instigation, it is said, of three of her Spanish ladies, her chief counsellors; so the king has dismissed them the Court, – a strong measure, but the queen was obliged to submit and to have patience'.[66] Only the king's previous romantic interest in Anne Hastings had caused such a stir between the royal couple and Catherine's reaction must suggest something of the queen's ongoing relationship with Bessie herself when she visited court. It is perhaps no surprise that Bessie was never welcomed back into the queen's household and that, when she visited court, she did so merely as a private noblewoman. She must have encountered a distinctly frosty welcome from the king's wife and her friends, something that would only have increased after June 1525. There is no actual evidence that the king intended to name Henry Fitzroy as his heir in the 1520s. Before he had begun his relationship with Anne Boleyn and instigated his divorce with Catherine of Aragon, Henry may well have considered the eventual succession of his illegitimate son a possibility, albeit a remote one given the great legal difficulties in a bastard inheriting the throne. Catherine's daughter, Princess Mary was by 1525 showing all the signs of fulfilling her early promise. In an account written in 1531, when she was fifteen years old, it was recorded that she was small, but pretty and well proportioned, with a beautiful complexion. She was well educated and spoke Spanish, French and Latin, as well as her native English, with a thorough grounding in Greek and conversational Italian.[67] In an account written only a few months after Fitzroy acquired his dukedoms, an observer stated that Mary was 'of her age as goodly a child, as ever I have seen'.[68] That year Mary left court for Ludlow 'not only well accompanied with a goodly number, but also with divers persons of gravity'. Although she was never formally created Princess of Wales, the choice of Ludlow for Mary's residence was clearly significant. In the late 1520s Princess Mary must always have been considered to be a more probable successor to the crown, providing that she could be backed by a powerful enough husband. However, the Wars of the Roses had shown that the man in possession of the crown was not always the person with the strongest title, and, in a disputed succession, a son of a king would always have been a powerful contender. John Palsgrave, Fitzroy's tutor, who alluded to his hopes for the boy's future in a letter to Bessie, was probably not alone in looking upon his charge as a potential future king and, even with Henry's renewed hopes of a legitimate son given the beginnings of his relationship with Anne Boleyn, Fitzroy's eventual succession was not beyond the realms of possibility, particularly with the doubts cast by Henry VIII himself on the legitimacy of Princess Mary. The king himself, however, never lost sight of Fitzroy's great defect, referring to him pointedly in one letter as his only 'bastard' son.[69]

As Henry Fitzroy rode slowly northwards on his pony in the summer of 1525 in order to take up his position as ruler of the north, he must have seemed to observers as a fully accepted member of the royal family. He was well received everywhere that he stopped on the route, even drawing one northern gentleman, Sir John Husee, out to greet him, even though Husee was so ill that he could hardly ride.[70] Bessie, whether in Lincolnshire or in London at the time, must have followed reports of her son's success eagerly. She is known to have kept a watchful eye over his household once he reached Sheriff Hutton.

# 15

# HENRY FITZROY IN THE NORTH

Although she lived some distance away from Sheriff Hutton, Bessie was able to keep a watchful eye on her eldest son's household during his time at the castle.

Bessie had connections with a number of members of Fitzroy's household, including the most prominent. In her copy of John Gower's *Confessio Amantis*, for example, the names 'Wylyam Parre, Lord, Wylyam Parre' were added, amongst a list of names, by one hand in the margins of one of the pages.[1] The names are not signatures but their presence in a book that belonged to Bessie is telling. The Parr family and their close kin, the Vauxs, were prominent courtiers. Sir Nicholas Vaux – who was the stepfather of the senior Sir William Parr, as well as being the brother-in-law by his second marriage of Sir William's elder brother, Sir Thomas Parr, and father-in-law to Sir William's niece, Elizabeth Cheney – was appointed as one of the overseers of the building works on the king's lodging at Guisnes in preparation for the Field of the Cloth of Gold in 1520.[2] The extensive correspondence, in which Vaux assured Cardinal Wolsey that 'we trust the buildings will please the king's highness and you', brought Vaux to the attention of the cardinal, as well as the assurance that the buildings would 'be esteemed to be more than Bridewell, Greenwich, or Eltham'. Vaux took great pains to ensure that the works were ready in time for what would be the greatest spectacle of Henry's reign and his reward was to be the first named of the knights listed to accompany the king to France.[3] Maud, Lady Parr, the mother of Catherine Parr and the younger William Parr (and also Vaux's step-daughter-in-law by his first marriage and the sister of his second wife), was Bessie's contemporary in the queen's household. She was favoured by the king, making him a gift of coat of cloth from her manor of Kendal in May 1530, for example.[4]

Further evidence of the connection between Bessie and Gilbert and the Parr and Vaux families can be seen in the signatures contained in a manuscript of a religious work, the *Horae Beate Virginis Mariae*, which was contained within the Ashburnham Library in the nineteenth century. The book, as previously discussed, belonged to Elizabeth Cheney, the cousin of Catherine Parr and the wife of another cousin of the future queen, Thomas, Lord Vaux. It is clear that the inscriptions in the book were collected over a number of years as the last inscription to be added, 'Margarett Nevill', is likely to have been made by the stepdaughter of Catherine Parr, the daughter of the future queen's second husband, Lord Latimer, whom she married in 1534. Gilbert, who also gave his autograph, died in 1530, which indicates that the two were never likely to have been in each other's presence. However, in spite of this and the lack of dates for the signatures, they do provide good evidence for Bessie and Gilbert's friends and associates during their marriage. Nicholas Carew, the husband of Bessie's predecessor as the king's mistress, was one of the first signatories, declaring, 'Madame, I require you to pray for me, your loving brother and poor Villen Nicholas Carew'. The younger William Parr, who was the brother of Catherine, declared, 'I pray you, Madam, pray for your loving godson and Cousin William Parr', whilst Henry VIII's sixth wife declared, 'Madame when you your time best do find, I pray you remember and have in mind, your loving Cousin to her little power Katherine Parr'. An inscription which read 'Time tryeth truth Tyrwhyt' was presumably written by a member of the Tyrwhitt family, a Lincolnshire family which were neighbours to the Tailboys family and to whom Gilbert was related. The Parrs were also related to the Tyrwhitts, with one member of the family, Lady Tyrwhitt, attending Catherine Parr's deathbed in 1548, for example.[5] This Lady Tyrwhitt, who may well have written the inscription, was the wife of Sir Robert Tyrwhitt.[6] Her husband was the son of Maud Tailboys, Gilbert's great-aunt, making him the cousin of Gilbert's father, Sir George. He was also a cousin of Catherine Parr's first husband, Edward Burgh, who was the son of his aunt, Agnes Tyrwhitt. The close relationship between the Tyrwhitts and the Parrs is attested by the fact that Catherine Parr chose Sir Robert as her master of horse when she became queen. Lady Tyrwhitt was later linked by the future Edward VI to Catherine Parr's sister, Lady Herbert, and her cousin, Lady Lane, when he sent greetings to the three in 1546 in a letter to his half-sister, Princess Mary.[7] Thomas, Lord Vaux, also added his inscription, stating, 'Remember me your loving Husband Thomas Vaux', whilst his nephew, Sir Nicholas Throckmorton, who, as the son of his half-sister (who was also a half-sister to the elder Sir William Parr and his siblings), was also his wife's first cousin, noted that 'I pray you madam pray for me your loving now and ever will be Nicholas Throckmorton your Valentine'.[8] Bessie's own inscription, 'Madame I am yours with all my heart Elizabeth Taylboys', demonstrates a warmth and affection for Elizabeth Vaux, as does Gilbert's own French inscription declaring, 'Jay Espoyr en Tempes Gylbert Taylboys'.

It seems likely that Bessie had come across members of the Parr family during her time at court. However, the friendship that evidently existed between her and its members was most likely established through Gilbert. The Tailboys family's legendary founder, the eleventh-century Ivo de Tailbois, had been created Baron of Kendal in Cumbria.[9] Kendal was the ancestral seat of the Parr family. According to sources which, as discussed previously, must be treated with some caution, Ivo was the founder both of Gilbert's branch of the Tailboys family and of the Parr family. His reputed descendants in Kendal, the de Lancasters, held Kendal for some time before it passed through an heiress to the le Brus family. Following the inheritance of Margaret le Brus, her granddaughter, Elizabeth de Ross, inherited the castle and lands in Kendal. She married William de Parr in the late fourteenth century, who was the first Parr to be associated with Kendal. Following his death in 1405, the castle passed through the Parr family to Sir Thomas Parr, the brother of the elder Sir William Parr, and then to Thomas's son, the younger William.[10] Whilst the descent from Ivo de Tailboys is suspicious, in the sixteenth century, as already discussed, it would have been largely accepted by both the Parr and Tailboys families, providing Bessie, Gilbert and the Parrs with a distant but, as far as they were concerned, very real kinship link. The Parr family also had connections in Lincolnshire similar to the Tailboys family's own. In 1527 or 1528 Catherine Parr travelled north to marry Edward Burgh of Gainsborough Hall in Lincolnshire, the grandson of the hall's incapacitated owner, Sir Edward Burgh. Sir Edward, who by the time of Catherine's arrival was considered to be a lunatic and 'distracted in memory', was the brother-in-law of Gilbert's father due to his first, childless marriage to Margaret Burgh. In addition to this, the two families, which were two of the most prominent in Lincolnshire, had other kinship links and associations. This included the Protestant 'martyr' Anne Askew, who married a kinsman of Gilbert's and was a neighbour and apparent associate of Catherine's during her time in the county. Catherine's mother, Lady Parr, visited her daughter during her brief first marriage, giving Bessie an opportunity to renew her acquaintance with her former colleague in the queen's household. In addition to numerous connections that Gilbert had with the Parrs, there were also links to Bessie's own family. Bessie's father, John Blount, served with the elder Sir William Parr as one of the king's Spears, with another link provided by the Earl of Essex, who was the captain of the Spears and would later become the father-in-law of the younger William Parr. A further connection can be seen with the marriage of Joan Vaux, the sister of Nicholas, to Richard Guildford. This marriage produced Sir Henry Guildford, the half-brother of Bessie's kinsman, Sir Edward Guildford and the master of the revels who assisted her early court career. What is made abundantly clear by the evidence both of Bessie's own manuscript of John Gower, and of Elizabeth Vaux's book, is that Bessie and Gilbert both knew and were on very friendly terms with the Parrs, Vauxs and Throckmortons, who were all closely related and played an important part in the upbringing of Bessie's son.

Sir William Parr of Horton, the uncle of Catherine Parr, had been knighted in 1513 during the king's French campaign.[11] He was a client of Cardinal Wolsey's, who secured for him the prestigious appointment of Fitzroy's chamberlain in 1525, making him the most powerful man in Bessie's son's household. The senior William Parr was a great promoter of his family. His nephew, Sir Nicholas Throckmorton, who was the fourth son of his half-sister, Katherine Vaux, found a position as Fitzroy's page.[12] Parr's nephew and namesake, William Parr the younger, was honoured as one of the companions to the duke, becoming such a friend of his that, in 1532, in relation to a dispute concerning his lands in Kendal, he complained that his authority in the area was questioned due to 'sundry wealthy and malicious persons, for the ill will they bear my lord of Richmond and me, infringe the said custom', which clearly suggests that his enemies were Fitzroy's enemies.[13] In addition to this, Sir James Leyburne, who was the steward of the Parr family's estates in Kendal, was appointed to the household by Parr.[14] Given the connection between Bessie and Gilbert and the Parr and Vaux families, the question must be asked whether the families' relationship came before Sir William Parr's appointment to Fitzroy's household or whether the Parrs and Vauxs specifically chose to cultivate Bessie, the mother of the child who was, effectively, their benefactor. This is a difficult question to answer. However, the fact of Bessie and Gilbert's friendship with the Vauxs and Parrs, coupled with the Parr and Tailboys families' kinship relationships, does suggest that Bessie may have played something of a role in promoting the interests of the Parrs to Cardinal Wolsey when the idea of her son's household was first mooted. This was not the case with the selection of Fitzroy's tutor.

The man chosen to be Fitzroy's first tutor was John Palsgrave, a Londoner, who had studied at the universities in Paris and London.[15] By the time of his appointment, he was around forty years old and had earlier served as the tutor to Henry VIII's sister, Mary. Evidently Palsgrave and his royal charge got on well as the princess appointed him as her secretary, allowing him to travel to France for her wedding in late 1514. Mary's husband, Louis XII, was dismayed at the number of English attendants that his new bride brought into his kingdom, immediately dismissing most of them, including John Palsgrave. With the support of his royal patron, he was able to commence study at the University of Paris. Mary remained involved in the scholar's career, writing from France to Cardinal Wolsey in 1515 to request Palsgrave's appointment as archdeacon of Derby or the living of Egglescliffe, both of which were refused him. Palsgrave may have had another connection to Mary Tudor. Although his origins are obscure, it has been suggested that he was a member of the Pagrave family of Norfolk.[16] If this was the case, Palsgrave's mother was a first cousin of Charles Brandon, Duke of Suffolk, Mary's second husband. In addition to his royal connections, he was a friend of Sir Thomas More, who acted as a patron to him. Palsgrave, although an all-round scholar, was particularly noted for his ability in the French language, producing a French grammar which was printed by Richard Pynson in 1530. His appointment as Fitzroy's tutor, which, as well as allowing him to keep three servants, also entitled him to sit on the child's council, was a prestigious one. For Palsgrave, who insisted that he was provided with apparel and other necessaries for his journey, the appointment came at an opportune time as he was burdened both with debts and the need to 'maintain my poor mother'.[17] Unlike the vast majority of Fitzroy's servants, his tutor was not chosen by Wolsey, with his appointment instead being proposed by Sir Richard Wingfield, who died in Spain in 22 July 1525. Given Wingfield's departure from the country on 18 April 1525, it is evident that thought had been given to Fitzroy's education some months before his elevation and that the matter had been settled by April at the latest. It has been suggested that Wingfield had promised to support Palsgrave financially when he took up the post, something that his sudden death rendered impossible. Wingfield, who had been a prominent courtier and diplomat also offered Palsgrave political protection in a largely Wolsey-appointed household, with his death leaving the tutor's position exposed.

The king personally sanctioned Palsgrave's appointment, interviewing him before he set off north. Palsgrave was at first enthusiastic about his appointment, declaring to Henry VIII in the gallery at Hampton Court that he would 'do my uttermost best to cause him to love learning and to be merry at it'.[18] Palsgrave believed in a gentle approach to teaching, something that he had in common with his contemporary, Roger Ascham, who would later be appointed as tutor to Fitzroy's half-sister, Princess Elizabeth. In his letter to the king written some time after his arrival at Sheriff Hutton, Palsgrave assured him that 'without any manner of fear or compulsion he [Fitzroy] hath already a great furtherance in the principles grammatical both Greek and Latin'. He also stated in a letter to his friend, Sir Thomas More, that in order to ensure that Fitzroy loved learning, he would stop work long before he became tired and instead 'devise all the ways I can possible to make learning pleasant to him, insomuch that many times his officers wot not whether I learn him or play with him, and yet have I already brought him to have a right good understanding in the principles of the grammars both of Greek and Latin'.[19] In spite of these early successes, Palsgrave was far from happy at Sheriff Hutton and took steps to make use of any powerful contacts that he had to improve his position, including

Bessie herself, whom he had presumably first come into contact with through her son's household.

Although direct evidence is largely lacking, it is clear that Bessie retained regular contact with her son and that she was fully acknowledged to have a role to play in his life. The only surviving letter actually addressed to Bessie was written by John Palsgrave during his time with her son and it illuminates much regarding the relationship between mother and son. In his letter, Palsgrave began by thanking Bessie for her 'favourable letter' before reminding her of his previous correspondence with her, noting that:

> Whereas I have in all my letters sent to your ladyship since my coming unto these parts certified you that I lived in perfect hope that, at the length, when the King's grace and my lord Cardinal should perfectly understand my diligent labours taken with my lord of Richmond's grace, and his great furtherance in good learning by reason of the same, that they would both be good and gracious unto me, and for my pains make me able to live according to the room they have set me in here.

Palsgrave evidently believed that Bessie held great influence with the king and cardinal. He further warned her that, unless she 'were good unto me [i.e. Palsgrave]', he would be forced to resign his post, something that would place the education of her child in peril. Bessie's 'favourable' letter to her son's tutor unfortunately does not survive, but, given that Palsgrave felt compelled to once again engage her in lengthy correspondence, the response cannot have been as fulsome as he had hoped. Just what she made of the tutor's bombardment of letters is not recorded but, as is clear from her later dealings with Lord Leonard Grey, Bessie could be an accomplished flatterer when she wished, assuring a listener of her willingness to favour them, whilst, in reality, following her own course and mind in the matter.

By the time he wrote his letter, Palsgrave had become embroiled in a dispute with Fitzroy's council and he sought to bring Bessie onto his side. In his letter he continued, relating the slights that had been done to his person since arriving in the north:

> Madam, I have sustained, since my coming unto Yorkshire a great deal more displeasure than you would know of, and that, not only in wanting of these things that were requisite for me to have, but also both for my necessity and honesty by reason of my poverty am maligned against. I am sore despised as VI sundry matters have been contrived against me, whereof yourself was as guilty [in respect of] many of them as I was, and that shall you evidently know, if it shall ever be my fortune to see you here and you to be at any convenient leisure.

The statement made by Palsgrave that matters had been contrived against him 'whereof yourself was as guilty [in respect of] many of them as I was' evidently refers to a common interest of Bessie and Palsgrave and can only mean Henry Fitzroy himself, something which must hint at the role that Bessie had been able to play in his early years. She had perhaps superintended his education, something that it is very clear she would have been capable of. Once he had related his misery to Bessie, the tutor then tried flattery, declaring that he intended to be indebted to no other person than herself and that he made his appeal only to her, declaring that:

> For, as for me, let them esteem me as they list, I will esteem myself, and endeavour me while I live to use as much faith and truth and honesty in my dealing as it should be in a man better that loveth perfect honesty to do. And, on my faith, if I thought it not honestly requisite for you to know these things, to the intent that you may substantially provide that the especial gifts of grace which God hath given unto my lord of Richmond's Grace (far above that which you yourself could think) be not by malicious and evil disposed persons corrupted, I would never have made motion of them to you.

Palsgrave claimed that Fitzroy's education and character were in peril and that it behoved his mother to take the part of his tutor to ensure that he was well brought up. He was, however, able to assure the boy's mother that 'to be plain with you, on my conscience my lord of Richmond is of as good a nature, as much inclined to all manner virtuous and honourable inclination, as any babe living'. All was evidently not lost, as far as Palsgrave was concerned, providing that Bessie determined to take action as a conscientious parent. He also sought to assure Bessie that Fitzroy's other parent, the king, was deeply involved in his upbringing, declaring that 'the King's Grace said unto me in the presence of Master Parr and Master Page I deliver of he [quoth he] unto you iij, my worldly jewel, you twain to have the guiding of his body, and you, Palsgrave, to bring him up in virtue and learning'. Palsgrave had made enemies in the household at Sheriff Hutton. He believed that Fitzroy's mind was being poisoned against him so that 'the babe shall begin to despise me, or [i.e. before] ever he know me, and conceive a hatred against me causeless, that hereafter it shall cause the gospel spoken of my mouth seem worse to him than a dream or fantasy; and to be plain with you, folks accustom him already to lie for their pleasure'. These claims were all too true.

The tutor ended his letter by begging Bessie to order the matter to be reviewed 'for it standeth you in hand'. Bessie was evidently entirely free to visit her son as Palsgrave begged her to come to Sheriff Hutton in person to review the situation for herself to use her 'secret wisdom' to 'try every man and person about him' and make her own decisions as to what was happening. He obviously vehemently believed in the virtue of his own position and that his charge's mother would wholeheartedly side with him and have the influence to see that a remedy was obtained. It was only in his closing sentences that the point of Palsgrave's letter became entirely clear, with the plea that the malicious attacks on him were caused only by his 'extreme poverty', something that 'shall you well know when so ever you be amongst us, which I would exhort you might be so shortly as might be possible'. Once at Sheriff Hutton, Palsgrave earnestly hoped that Bessie would engage herself in the study of 'how my poverty may be helped'. In case she could not think of a remedy, Palsgrave was, helpfully, able to remind her that 'it needeth me not to put you in mind how many spiritual prelates as well as bishops and abbots would not stick with you to grant you the advowsons of the best thing in their gift, or of any such thing as you thought would shortly fall void'. In the event that Bessie was able to obtain these livings for Palsgrave to supplement his income, he would, of course, 'apply my whole mind to advance my lord's grace in his learning'. He then ended on a note of flattery, comparing himself to Plutarch, the tutor of Trajan, a classical allusion which implied that Palsgrave saw in Fitzroy a future ruler.[20]

Bessie's response to Palsgrave's letter is not recorded. Palsgrave, almost alone amongst Fitzroy's council, was not appointed by Cardinal Wolsey and, as such, found himself politically isolated in the north. That he thought that Bessie would assist him was naive at best and it is clear that Bessie and her husband, along with her eldest son, relied on the patronage and support of the cardinal for their own advancement. Bessie also had strong connections within her son's household. Palsgrave's successor as tutor, Richard Croke, was a distant kinsman of hers, something that would have further served to alienate her from the grumbling academic. That Bessie refused to assist her son's tutor is apparent from the grudge that he later bore against both Bessie and Cardinal Wolsey. In around 1526 he drew up a list of the cardinal's 'achievements' which contained a large number of articles of complaint. These were discovered following a search of his rooms in around 1529. Of particular interest is the article which stated:

> We have begun to encourage the young gentlewomen of the realm to be our concubines by the well marrying of Besse Blont whom we would yet by sleight have married much better than she is and for that purpose changed her name.[21]

It is obvious from this that Palsgrave's letter to Bessie had contained more flattery than true sentiment and that she had offended him. Certainly, for all her status and wealth as Lady Tailboys, this may have been how she was perceived by many contemporaries, something of which Bessie was likely to have been aware. By bringing Bessie personally into his attack on the cardinal, Palsgrave was evidently acting upon a personal grudge, something that indicates that not only did Bessie refuse to act, but that, if she visited Sheriff Hutton at all, she most certainly did not show favour to John Palsgrave. The tutor, perhaps helped by the cardinal's own fall in 1529, survived the discovery of his articles, attaching himself to Thomas Cromwell, who was an up-and-coming minister and would later replace Wolsey as the king's chief advisor.[22]

Palsgrave comes across in his correspondence as a somewhat grasping and exasperating figure. However, given the difficulties that his successor, Richard Croke, later faced, it is clear that there was a concerted campaign at Sheriff Hutton to limit the influence that any tutor had on the young duke. In one of his letters to his friend, Sir Thomas More, Palsgrave complained that every day more people in the household would put pressure on Bessie's son:

> To bring his mind from learning some to hear a cry at a hare, some to kill a buck with his bow, sometime with grey hounds, and sometime with buck hounds. Some to see a flight with a hawk, some to ride a horse which yet he is not greatly cumbered with because of his youth, besides many other devises found within the house when he cannot go abroad.[23]

For a boy who modelled himself on his sporty father, it was always going to be an uphill struggle for Fitzroy's tutors to keep him at his books when there were other pastimes to be pursued. However, in the few short months that he was with his young charge, the tutor did make some progress, introducing him to classical texts, such as the works of Virgil.[24] Palsgrave – without the support of the other members of the council, Wolsey, Bessie or even his young charge himself, coupled with the distant, but fairly indifferent, support of the king – was never able to make a success of his position and, by February 1526, he had been supplanted as tutor by Richard Croke. He clung on to his position on Fitzroy's council, to the likely irritation of Sir William Parr and other members, until the end of the year.[25] Croke may well have been Wolsey's original choice for the role, something that, with the death of the influential Wingfield, meant that Palsgrave's removal, and Croke's appointment, was only a matter of time.

A further link between Bessie and her son can be seen in relation to the pair's relationship to the antiquary John Leland. Fitzroy was recorded by one sixteenth-century chronicler, to have 'loved' the antiquary, receiving a book from him designed to help him 'learn to write Roman letters great and small'.[26] The close relationship between the young duke and Leland suggests that the antiquary took a close interest in his education, something that may, perhaps, have been promoted by Bessie herself. She was evidently known to Leland as he visited South Kyme during her time there, presumably at the invitation of her and Gilbert. Bessie had ample opportunity to hear news of her son even when she was not actually with him. In the main, she must have been pleased with what she heard. Even allowing for a good deal of bias in reports of Bessie's son to his father and godfather, it is obvious that he was an able and quick-witted boy, with one of his councillors writing gushingly to Wolsey in October 1525 that he 'is a child of excellent wisdom and towardness, and for his good and quick capacity, retentive memory, virtuous inclination to all honour, humanity, and goodness, I think hard it would be to find any creature living of twice his age able or worthy to be compared to him'.[27]

In spite of his promise, Fitzroy's second tutor, Richard Croke, had grave concerns about his pupil's commitment to his studies and the behaviour of other members of his household. The Croke family had originally borne the surname Blount, abandoning it, according to local legend, due to the need of a member of the family to adopt an alias after being involved in a rebellion against Henry IV.[28] Although the last common ancestor of Richard Croke and Bessie Blount had lived in the fourteenth century, kinship ties were important in the Tudor period and the connection between them would have been known. Croke, as a humanist and friend of the scholar Erasmus, is also likely to have been acquainted with Bessie's, and his own, kinsman, Lord Mountjoy, who was also a great friend of Erasmus. Croke was an expert in Greek and had studied at the University of Cambridge, as well as a number of continental universities, including the University of Paris. He must have considered that educating one small child, plus a handful of carefully selected nobly born boys, would be a simple matter. However, he soon found, like Palsgrave, that his authority was considerably undermined. Within months, Croke was writing to the king to beg him to investigate the behaviour of Sir William Parr the elder and another member of the household, George Cotton, one of the gentlemen ushers.[29] He complained that Cotton and his brother entertained their friends and servants at Fitzroy's expense, making free use of his wine, beer and food from the kitchens. Parr was apparently also involved and the three were able to amend the household accounts to ensure that most of what they took was never recorded. Similarly, Croke complained that since his arrival, Parr had been absent for most of the time and that, even when he was present, he was busy with his own leisure pursuits of hawking and hunting. George Cotton was a particular thorn in the tutor's side, consistently undermining his authority – for example, refusing to allow Fitzroy to attend lessons before mass. Bessie's son was fond of the indulgent Cotton, learning from him to say 'Master, if you beat me I will beat you!' when Croke attempted to persuade him to apply himself to his lessons.[30] It is no wonder that Croke, constantly aware that his pupil was the king's beloved only son, found himself powerless to control his class. Cotton, for all of Croke's complaints about his behaviour, remained loyal to his master, remaining in Fitzroy's household until the young lord's death.[31]

To go so far as to report other members of the household to the king demonstrates that Croke was deeply unhappy with the situation at Sheriff Hutton. He sent a letter containing his articles, or complaints, to Wolsey at the same time. His first request was that, as well as being able to have access to his pupil one hour before mass and breakfast, he should be free to choose the time and duration of the lessons 'as I shall perceive most convenient', without any hindrance. In his second article, he complained that Fitzroy had been made by others to write, in his own hand, to abbots and other 'mean persons', contrary to Wolsey's instructions, often with such work occurring immediately after Fitzroy had eaten 'to the great dulling of his wits, spirits and memory, and no little hurt of his head, stomach, and body'. As far as Croke was concerned, his pupil should write only in Latin, with anything that he set his own hand to preferably being prepared for the king or the cardinal 'to the intent he might more firmly imprint in his mind both words and phrases of the Latin tongue, and the sooner frame him to some good style in writing whereunto he is now very ripe'. Croke wanted Wolsey to order which people Fitzroy should deem to write to, as well as what times of the week and in what language, in order to ensure that the rules were well understood. Equally, Croke wanted to ensure that he retained control of his pupil, stating that 'provided the said exercise of his hands and style in both the tongues be committed only to the discretion and order of me his schoolmaster: and that no man may force him to write unless I be there present, to direct and form his said hand and style'.

The third article concerned the boys that were taught with Fitzroy. He asked that Wolsey pass the authority over who was selected to join the schoolroom over to him alone 'so that they be straightly commanded to apply their learning at such times as I shall think convenient without maintenance of any man to the contrary'. He particularly asked that none be allowed to remain in the schoolroom whilst Fitzroy was at his lessons, unless Croke himself allowed it. The fourth article concerned the interruption of Fitzroy's learning, which had occurred 'for every trifle or resort to every stranger'. Croke asked for specific instructions that lessons would only be abandoned on the arrival of an important visitor, and then only because 'my said lord might by the advice of his Schoolmaster exhibit and make some show of his learning, like as he was wont and doth of his other pastimes'. Croke felt that this would 'greatly encourage him to his learning; to the which, because it is most laborious and tedious to children, his Grace should be most specially animated and encouraged'. Croke then made one final point, asking:

That no ways, colour, ne craft be taken to discourage, alienate, or avert my said lord's mind from learning, or to extinct the love of learning in his estimation, but that he be induced most highly to esteem his book of all his other studies. The which thing with other the premises obtained, I dare be bold to assure your Grace that his learning at the sight of your Grace shall with no little time, and much pleasure of himself, far surmount and pass the knowledge of his years, time, and age, no one except.[32]

Croke had high hopes for his pupil, but was concerned, as Palsgrave had been before him, of his lack of authority over the boy's daily routine. His complaints to the king and Wolsey did nothing to endear him to his fellow members of the household and, shortly after he sent the articles, he wrote again to Wolsey, complaining that Parr had threatened to destroy his credit at court.[33] Croke, convinced of his own righteousness, informed Wolsey that he was happy for Parr's complaints against him, together with his own complaints against Parr, to be heard by Fitzroy's council, or any three of them, providing, of course, that Parr was not one of their number. He once again complained that Fitzroy's overspending was due to Parr's negligence, as well as the great quantities of provisions which had been embezzled both to entertain the Cotton brothers' friends and to feed Parr's own family, who were not lodged in the household. Parr, who was understandably annoyed by the tutor's allegations, had responded by ordering Fitzroy that he was never to be alone with his schoolmaster, nor listen to him, save when he was actually reading aloud. Matters had reached such a head that Fitzroy would pay no attention to Croke's requests or threats, or the words of any of Croke's friends in the household. To add insult to injury, as far as Croke was concerned, Parr had appointed his nephew, the younger William Parr, to be Fitzroy's companion at matins and vespers – an office that, as the duke aged, could be influential. Croke finished his letter in an appeal to Wolsey's fondness for the boy, declaring that he feared that Fitzroy's disposition would be spoiled by those who cared only for their own pleasure and profit. Matters continued to deteriorate and Croke soon had cause to write to Wolsey to complain that one boy in particular, John Scrope, who was a kinsman of Sir William Parr's, was inciting the other boys against the tutor and calling him names, as well as ill-treating Croke's favourite, a boy who had been sent by the king to join the household and, as something of a teacher's pet, shared his lodging.[34] What the king thought of all these complaints is not recorded, although George Cotton's brother, Richard, would later be appointed comptroller of the household of Henry's legitimate son, Prince Edward, which suggests that the allegations were considered to have little substance.[35]

Given the accusations flying around the household, as well as the deep divisions between Fitzroy's officers and servants, it is not surprising that Wolsey sent Dr Thomas Magnus, Archdeacon of East Riding in Yorkshire, to attempt to straighten matters out, with the cleric immediately setting about rearranging the boy's household in a bid to reduce its cost, making redundancies and terminating the employment of some who were found to have committed offences.³⁶ Although Magnus baulked at the suggestion of reducing salaries without the king's official sanction, he was able to bring the household into better order. His activities were once again hampered by royal interference into Fitzroy's domestic affairs, with a number of dismissed servants taking their cases directly to the king, obtaining their reinstatements at a higher salary than before.

In spite of the difficulties in his household, Henry Fitzroy proved to be a quick and able pupil. An early letter of his, written as a New Year's gift for his father in 1527, still shows a childish hand:

> After most humble and most lowly request and petition had unto your grace for your daily blessing, please it the same to be advertised, I have received your most honourable and goodly New Year's gift, And give unto your said grace most lowly thanks for the same, humbly beseeching your grace to accept and take this my letter penned with mine own hand for a poor token at this time.³⁷

Fitzroy's schooling moved on quickly, with his next New Year's letter being written in an elegant italic script. The letter was intended to impress Fitzroy's royal father and the parallel guidelines which he used to regulate the height of his letters are still visible on the original.³⁸ The letter began with the usual filial request for a blessing, before assuring the king that he was applying himself entirely 'to the diligent appliance of all such sciences and feats of learning' as would give him pleasure. Rather hopefully, Bessie's son continued that, due to his diligence in his studies, he was 'making most humble and lowly intercession unto the same to remember me your most humble and lowly servant with on harness for my exercise in arms according to my learning of Julius Caesar'. Evidently, Fitzroy's tutors, supported by his father, had tried bribery in an attempt to persuade the boy to apply himself. This may not have been entirely successful since the boy was well used to receiving regular gifts from his indulgent father. In his privy purse expenses for 23 April 1530, for example, the king purchased arrows for his son. The following year he purchased a lute for him, both gifts that suggest that Henry was trying to mould his son into a second version of himself.³⁹ Henry kept an eye on his son's health, with his records demonstrating that he sent a physician to him in January 1532 when he was ill.⁴⁰ In the summer of 1528, during an outbreak of the lethal sweating sickness, Bessie's son was quickly removed to a secret place with only a few attendants in order to ensure that he was not exposed to the infection.[41]

Against expectations, Fitzroy gradually warmed to Richard Croke, with his old schoolmaster writing from Bologna whilst on a diplomatic mission in 1530 that he wished to be recommended to his 'dear lord and master', Fitzroy.[42] Croke also promised his former pupil that he would bring him a copy of some of the works of Caesar, as well as a model of a galley with five oars which he was sure would prove interesting since it was of a design that few had seen. Fitzroy wrote his tutor a glowing letter of recommendation, addressed to his father, when he left his household in late 1527.[43] Something of Bessie's gratitude to the tutor can perhaps also be seen in the king's insistence in July 1528 that Wolsey provide Croke with the living of Hurworth, which was in his grant 'by reason of old Mr Tailboys'.[44] Given that the living of Hurworth would, after Sir George Tailboys' death be Gilbert's to grant, it is likely that he would have been consulted in the proposal to benefit Croke, whom the king specifically wanted to benefit due to his good service as Fitzroy's schoolmaster. By the late 1520s, the boy was already conducting himself more like a man than a child, being at ease even when meeting grand dignitaries such as the Earl of Northumberland.[45] He kept a good Christmas at Pontefract castle in 1526, receiving visits from most of the local noblemen and gentry.[46] Fitzroy also cut something of a grand figure in the local area, giving aid to the priory at Haltemprice in Yorkshire, which by 1528 was in dire need of financial assistance. Although the priory had been in existence for some centuries, the monks flatteringly referred to Bessie's son as their founder.[47] The monastery was renowned for its possession of an arm of St George (something that would have appealed to Fitzroy as a member of the Order of the Garter), a piece of the holy cross and the girdle of St Mary, which was considered helpful to women in childbirth.[48] Fitzroy evidently had something of an interest in monasticism, sending commissioners to the monastery of Valle Crucis in 1534 following reports that the house was in difficulties. These concerns proved correct and Fitzroy's visitor, the Abbot of Neath, discovered the abbot and prior at war, both accusing the other of 'diverse crimes and excesses'.[49] That matters might not have been entirely as they seemed is evident from the fact that William Brereton, Fitzroy's high steward, received £40 from the abbot's replacement following his appointment.

In spite of his youth, Fitzroy intended to be no mere cipher in his own household. In a letter to his father of 21 July 1528, he confirmed that he had received his father's letters informing him that two of the king's servants (including Sir Edward Seymour, Henry Fitzroy's own master of horse) were to be promoted to offices and appointments that 'appertain unto my [Fitzroy's] gift and disposition in Dorsetshire'.[50] This request had caused something of a stir at Sheriff Hutton, with Fitzroy writing to his father to state that he had already given the offices away, something that he had been authorised to do by Wolsey:

> Whereupon, considering the great number of servants that I have, and that none of them in any wise have been rewarded with anything, since their coming unto me, I, therefore, hearing that the stewardship of my lands in Dorsetshire, and the stewardship of my lands in Somersetshire, were void, gave that office in Dorsetshire, with other small things appendant to the same, by the advice of my Council, to Sir William Parr, Knight, my Chamberlain, with the fee of an hundredth shillings, and the other stewardship in Somersetshire I disposed, in semblable manner, to my trusty and diligent servant, George Cotton, continually giving his attendance upon me, with the fee of six pounds thirteen shillings and four pence, in like manner as had the said Sir William Compton.

Although the letter was written by a secretary, it was signed by Fitzroy and he would in all probability have been made aware of its content. It must have rankled with the boy, who had by then reached his ninth birthday (the age that his half-brother, Edward VI, would eventually succeed to the crown), to find his authority undermined within his own household, particularly given that one of its members, Edward Seymour, had sought preferment direct from the king. This was not the last time that Henry interfered in his son's household, with one letter from the king to his son in 1534 expressing his surprise that Fitzroy had dismissed his cofferer, Sir George Lawson, from his service, and requesting that, at the least, the young duke should continue to pay him a pension.[51]

The king had great ambitions for his only son and, in 1527, Wolsey, who was particularly sceptical, wrote of 'the blind and doubtful overture' made by the Emperor Charles V's ministers to arrange a marriage between Fitzroy and the emperor's niece, Maria of Portugal, with the princess bringing as her dowry the duchy of Milan.[52] In spite of Wolsey's doubts, the king was eager to pursue such a grand alliance for his son, with Wolsey confirming to the king shortly afterwards that he would seek the emperor's assurance that he was serious in his offer to give Henry Fitzroy the duchy of Milan as his niece's dowry.[53] Henry's ambassadors to the emperor were also thrilled about the prospect of the match, writing excitedly that they believed Charles was on the verge of offering her hand in marriage and that she would come with a dowry of 400,000 ducats.[54] They had earlier opened the subject of a marriage alliance between Fitzroy and the Holy Roman Empire, being assured that he would certainly be offered a legitimate member of the imperial family and that 'we will offer you no bastard' – a very flattering offer for the king's illegitimate son.[55] As the cardinal had suspected, however, the match came to nothing, with Wolsey writing that same year to Henry that, after enquiries,

> I am surely ascertained that the Emperor mindeth nothing on earth less, than to give the said Duchy of Milan to the said Duke of Richmond, but is wholly determined to have and enjoy the same for himself; and that the overture thereof, made by Monsr. Buchans, otherwise called John Almain, was but to abuse Your Highness, and to suspend such treaties, as should be concluded between Your Grace and the French King.[56]

The marriage to Maria of Portugal, who, as well as being the niece of the emperor also later became the stepdaughter of the king of France, was not the only grand alliance suggested for Fitzroy, with rumours that Catherine de Medici, the future queen of France, and other noble or royal young ladies were being considered for him.[57] The emperor more sincerely offered one of the daughters of the king of Denmark, who were his nieces.[58] Interestingly, Henry VIII later made strenuous attempts to make the younger Danish princess, Christina, his fourth bride, until she rejected him with some finality, reputedly declaring that if she had two heads then one would be at the king's disposal.

Henry Fitzroy, by virtue of his position as the king's only surviving son, had an international prominence far above what would usually be expected of a king's illegitimate son (a position which can be contrasted with Arthur Plantagenet, Lord Lisle, who, in spite of being the illegitimate son of Edward IV, remained merely a crown servant during the reign of his nephew, Henry VIII). By early 1526 his cousin, James V of Scotland, who was the son of Henry VIII's sister Margaret, and his most senior legitimate male relative, was sufficiently concerned about the honours heaped upon his bastard cousin to attempt to open up direct contact with him, evidently to size him up. In early 1526 James wrote to Dr Magnus, who was present in Fitzroy's household and was familiar to the young king as a former English ambassador to Scotland. On 8 January 1526 Fitzroy's cousin wrote to Magnus, asking for 'three or four brace of the best ratches [small hounds] in the country, less or more, for hares, foxes, or other great beasts, with one brace of blood hounds of the best kind that are good, and will ride behind men on horseback'.[59] James's mother, Queen Margaret, fully supported her son's curiosity, writing her own letter to Magnus to confirm his request:

> We commend us unto you in our most hearty manner, praying you right effectuously that you will get and send to us three or four brace of the best ratches in the country, less and more,

for hares, foxes, and other great beasts, with a brace of blood-hounds of the best kind, that are good, and will ride behind men on horseback. And this we exhort you to do, as you will do us singular empleasure, and report special thanks of us therefore.[60]

Margaret, flatteringly, was happy to recognise Fitzroy as her kinsman, calling him our 'good nephew' in one letter to Magnus, before asking the diplomat 'affectionately to have us recommended unto him as we that shall entertain our dutiful kindness, as natural affection, aright towards him, as we that is right glad of his good prosperity, praying God the same continue'.[61] As a present for his Scottish cousin, Bessie's son sent ten pairs of hounds, as well as a letter of his own, to which the Scottish king replied. This was the first diplomatic manoeuvre that Henry Fitzroy was personally involved in and he acquitted himself admirably.

Henry Fitzroy's very existence as the only son of the king merited regular mentions in diplomatic dispatches. In March 1527, for example, the imperial ambassador reported to the emperor that Henry and Wolsey intended to make Fitzroy king of Ireland, something that had not been well received by those who heard of the plan due to the fear that 'it will be tantamount to having a second king of Scotland for this kingdom'.[62] That there may in fact have been some truth in this rumour is suggested by the ambassador's comment that 'the queen is very dissatisfied with these proceedings, though little of it is communicated to her'. Catherine was in regular contact with her nephew's ambassadors and was well able to express her anger to him. Once again, it is clear that Catherine was motivated by a fear for the position of her own daughter, with the ambassador continuing that it was feared that Mary would be forced to renounce her rights to Ireland to Fitzroy on her marriage. Rumours about Fitzroy being given Ireland as his own independent kingdom persisted until at least 1534.[63]

Although a young child, Henry Fitzroy's appointment in the north was not intended to be merely nominal. By the early sixteenth century, the north of England enjoyed a reputation that it was remote, poor and lawless, with the additional problem that, due to the border with Scotland, it was essentially a frontier area.[64] In order to govern the area effectively, it was necessary either for the king himself to take the expensive option of employing a standing army, or to rely on the great men of the north. Fitzroy's ancestor, Edward III, had taken the decision to appoint a Warden of the Marches but, as has been pointed out by one historian, 'to put the whole control of the North in the hands of one man was to take a very considerable risk'.[65] Accordingly, during the minority of Edward's successor, Richard II, the office was divided into three, with wardens appointed for the East, Middle and West Marches. The power of these wardens was severely curtailed by the existence of a number of semi-independent lordships, from the powerful Bishop of Durham to more minor noblemen. During the fifteenth century, the Lancastrian and Yorkist kings had attempted to work with the greatest of the northern noble families, the Percys and the Nevilles, in recognition of the fact that the king's orders had little authority in the area without their support. Richard III in the 1480s attempted to deal with the problem, creating a council in Yorkshire under the control of his nephew, the Earl of Lincoln, in 1484. Lincoln's authority lapsed, for obvious reasons, after Richard's defeat and death at the Battle of Bosworth Field but it appears that his successor, Henry VII, also relied upon family to control the north of his kingdom. At the time of his elevation, Fitzroy had received a number of properties that had previously belonged to his great-grandmother, Margaret Beaufort, Countess of Richmond, with his leading dukedom also referencing the indomitable mother of Henry VII. Henry VII, at the time that he came to the throne, had few relatives and relied on his mother both for advice and in relation to her administrative skills. In a note which was appended to a petition relating to Henry Fitzroy's administration of justice at Sheriff Hutton, it was declared:

> Mem. how that the like commission that my lady the king's grandam had was tried and approved greatly to the king's disadvantage in stopping of many lawful processes and course of his laws at Westminster Hall; and also his subjects thereby sustained great losses, mischances, charges and vexations thereby, and none gains commonly by any such commission but the clerks which for their proper lucres doth upon every light surmise make out processes, etc.[66]

Following his accession, Henry VIII made little attempt to regulate the governance of the north, relying instead on the long-standing system of wardens. When, in 1522, the Earl of Surrey was appointed as lieutenant-general for the Scottish war, he found the governance of the north to be in a poor state, something that spurred on Wolsey – who, as Archbishop of York and Bishop of Durham, had a special interest in the area – to find a solution. The power that Margaret Beaufort was given to hear legal matters and set up courts was evidently not entirely well received. However, it is clear that it was of assistance to Henry VII in his governance of his country and his son sought to emulate this with his own children, with Mary in the Welsh Marches and Henry Fitzroy in the north. There is strong evidence that Henry Fitzroy's council was involved in justice in the north, as a letter from Wolsey to Henry VIII in 1527 makes clear:

> I have also, Sir, as I was enclosing these my letters, been advertised from my Chancellor of Durham, of an heinous attemptate done

by Sir John [actually William] Lisle, and his son: who, committed
to ward at Newcastle by my Lord of Richmond's council, as well
for murder and felony, as for diverse other grievous offences, hath
not only broken the prison, wherein they were themselves, but also
other prisoners there, wherein was diverse outlaws kept, some for
felony, some for murder and treason. They be fled and escaped into
Scotland, and with them, as their issuing out of Newcastle, joined
20 other outlaws. By the reason of this attemptate, the said Sir
John Lisle hath not only forfeited his land; but his sureties, which
were bound that he should be true prisoner, hath forfeited the sum
of 500 pounds. I doubt not but Your Highness shall have many
cravers and suitors for the said forfeits; among whom it may like
your Highness to have in your gracious remembrance Sir William
Parr, who taketh great pain with my Lord of Richmond: the said
Sir John Lisle's land, or a good part thereof, shall be a very good
reward for him.[67]

Clearly Sir William Parr, on Henry Fitzroy's behalf, was making his presence
felt in the north. Fitzroy's council was also heavily dominated by Wolsey's
own followers, with a large number of the seventeen members, none of
whom ranked above a knight, being lawyers. The issue of Sir William Lisle
exercised Fitzroy's council for some time. They were able to use Fitzroy's
international prestige in their attempts to bring the fugitive to justice, with
the boy writing letters to both his cousin, James V of Scotland, and the
estranged husband of James's mother, the Earl of Angus, in an attempt to
persuade them to expel Lisle from Scotland.[68] Although Fitzroy received
polite responses, in accordance with his rank, his Scottish kinsmen were
unwilling to help, with Angus writing to say that he did not believe Lisle
to be in Scotland.[69] Fitzroy was used as the figurehead of the council, for
example writing letters to Sir Christopher Dacre in April 1526 to request
that the body of one William Ridley, which had been buried in Scotland,
was returned home.[70]

Fitzroy's council took their authority seriously and proved initially
very active in local governance. As has been pointed out, their authority
was greatly weakened by the tendency of litigants with a weak case
to go straight to the Star Chamber in London, bypassing the council's
attempts to impose justice in the north. With the fall of Wolsey
moves were made in the north to be rid of Fitzroy's council and,
eventually, the king agreed, downgrading Fitzroy's council simply to
his household council, although, pertinently, a number of its members
were appointed to serve on a new council in the north employed to
assist the Bishop of Durham in his governance of the area. By 1532
the experiment had clearly failed, with the Earl of Northumberland
being appointed as lieutenant in the north. In 1537 a new Council of
the North was created.

Even with the reduction of his authority in the north, Henry VIII still had high hopes for his son. On 16 June 1529, he left the north to return to London. On 22 June 1529 he was appointed to the prestigious post of lord-lieutenant of Ireland.[71] Fitzroy was not intended to play much of a direct role in Ireland, with a series of deputies being appointed during his time in office. For example, Sir William Skeffington was appointed to act as deputy in 1529,[72] whilst Bessie's later suitor, Lord Leonard Grey, also took the role during Henry Fitzroy's time as lieutenant.[73] It is clear that Fitzroy did take some interest in Ireland, with the king's privy purse expenses for 1 May 1530 recording that five shillings were paid 'in reward to a servant of my Lord of Richmond at his going into Ireland'.[74] He never set foot there himself, but his position as a near kinsman to the king was an important one in helping to maintain English control in the kingdom. The imperial ambassador Eustace Chapuys, for example, believed that the government considered Fitzroy to be an essential element in its strategy towards Ireland, recording in September 1534 that the Duke of Norfolk quarrelled with Thomas Cromwell, with Cromwell accusing Norfolk of being the cause of trouble in Ireland due to his reluctance to allow Fitzroy to travel to Ireland personally when he had been ordered to do so.[75] He was also apparently contacted by an Irish rebel, Thomas FitzGerald, who offered to surrender personally to him, again demonstrating that Fitzroy's role was no empty appointment, even if, in actual fact, he carried out none of the day-to-day running of affairs.[76] The gift of a pony from Fitzroy's deputy, Sir William Skeffington, recorded in the 1531 inventory of his goods is also very likely to have been an attempt to curry favour.[77] If so, it failed entirely, with Fitzroy passing the gift to his servant, George Cotton. Henry Fitzroy remained lieutenant of Ireland until his death. It is to be supposed that he would have taken a more active and direct role had he lived longer. When he was first appointed he was still only eleven years old and had a considerable amount of growing up to do, with the focus of his household primarily on London, Windsor and the court.

Bessie remained in contact with her son throughout his childhood. However, by the late 1520s she also had other family concerns to attend to.

# 16

# FAMILY MARRIAGES & FAMILY DISPUTES

Whilst Bessie established herself as a wife and mother in Lincolnshire, she also remained in contact with her family in Shropshire, as is evidenced by the places that her brothers found in their nephew's household.

During the early years of Bessie's first marriage, her parents turned their attentions to finding husbands for their four remaining unmarried daughters. Although the date of Anne's marriage does not survive, as the eldest unmarried daughter in the family, she is likely to have married first, particularly as she took Richard Lacon, a young protégé of her father's, as her husband. At the time of Richard's death in 1541, Anne had borne her husband at least eight children: Elizabeth died unmarried, whilst Eleanor married a local gentleman, William Banester, who, at least according to the Shropshire visitation made in the early seventeenth century, then married Eleanor's sister, Olivia, presumably after her death.[1] A daughter named Albora (for her youngest aunt) married twice, whilst a fifth daughter, Catherine, married a William Burgh. Three sons, Rowland, William and Edward, were born to Anne and Richard.[2] Rowland was five years old at his father's death,[3] whilst Edward can have been only a few months old at most, having been born in the year of his father's death. Richard Lacon's demise was apparently unexpected as, only the year before, he had served as sheriff of Shropshire for the first time. Although no date of birth survives for him, he must have been some years older than Anne, who was born in around 1504–06, as he served in France with his future father-in-law in 1513. He was, perhaps, born in the last few years of the fifteenth century. This is supported by the fact that his father, Sir Thomas Lacon, was still very much alive in 1533 when he served for the third time as sheriff of Shropshire.[4] Assuming that Anne bore a child every other year, this would give a date of marriage of around 1526. It is also clear that the visitation, with its omission of Edward Lacon, who presumably died in infancy, cannot be considered entirely accurate and it would be safe to assume that there were also further children that did not survive infancy. The date of Anne's marriage can therefore be pushed back to the early 1520s – perhaps around the same time that Bessie made her own first marriage. By then, Anne would have been in her late teens: a usual age for marriage for a girl of gentry status.

As discussed before, the Lacons of Willey were a solid gentry family of great local prominence. The backgrounds of Bessie's sister and her husband were similar. It is apparent from Richard Lacon's earlier association with John Blount that he had been groomed as a husband for one of his daughters. Anne and Richard were very distantly related. Back in the thirteenth century, when the two co-heiresses of Brian de Brompton inherited his estates, the younger married Edmund de Cornwall and brought Kinlet into the hands of the Cornwall and, later, the Blount families. The elder daughter, Margaret, married Robert de Harley. In the fifteenth century the heiress of Harley, Elizabeth Peshall, who was a descendant of this couple, married a Richard Lacon, bringing Harley into the Lacon family. The marriage of the younger Richard Lacon with Anne Blount therefore, effectively, reunited the Brompton patrimony for the first time since the thirteenth century when their son was named as heir to Anne's brother, George Blount.

Willey, the principal seat of the Lacon family, may have been occupied at the time of Anne's marriage by her father-in-law, necessitating a stay at another house held by the family – perhaps the manor at Harley. Alternatively, since Anne chose to live at Willey following her widowhood and second marriage, it may be that Richard's father ceded occupation of the larger manor on her marriage, allowing the couple to live there immediately. This is certainly not impossible as a number of members of the family do seem to have preferred to reside at Harley rather than Willey, in spite of the fact that Willey was, nominally at least, the family's principal seat.[5] Little now remains of the old hall at Willey as a new, classical-style hall was erected in the early years of the nineteenth century, with what remained of the older building being used for estate offices and stables.[6] The old hall, which was built in the sixteenth century, was a 'spacious building'. In the late seventeenth century, it was assessed for the Hearth Tax as having thirty-one hearths, suggesting a similar number of rooms. It must have been a comfortable home for Anne and her large family. The church at Willey, which was very closely associated with the lords of the manor there, was greatly altered during its 'restoration' in the late nineteenth century. In Anne's time it was primarily a Norman church with some fourteenth-century alterations, but there is little that she would now recognise in the building.[7] She took an active interest in the church at Willey, as befitted the lady of the manor. In 1557, for example, Anne and her second husband, Thomas Ridley, personally appointed a new rector. Their young son, George, was buried in the church there.

There can be no suggestion that Bessie's position, either as the king's mistress, or as the mother of his illegitimate son, played any part in Anne's match – save that, in all likelihood, Richard Lacon had originally been intended for her. It is also apparent that the two sisters remained close, with Anne's eldest daughter named for her aunt. Given the choice of name, Bessie may well have been her godmother. The match, which was arranged by Bessie's parents, was a very good one. Even long after she was widowed, Anne continued to be referred to in documents as the widow of Richard Lacon of Willey, in spite of her second marriage. In an account of the visit on 16 July 1554 of the Bishop of Worcester to the town of Much Wenlock (which was close to Willey), as written up by the vicar, Sir Thomas Botelar, it is clear that Anne's first marriage accorded her the status of a great lady in the local area:

16 July 1554 Memorandum. That the same day last above written my lord the Bishop of Worcester Dr Nicholas Heath, Lord President of the Marches of Wales coming with Justice Townesynde in company with him from Salop, and riding towards Bridgenorth, about two of the clock in the afternoon, was desired by the Burgesses of this Borough of Wenlock to drink, and so they did alight and drank, sitting in the house of Richard Lawley Gent. At the Ash, hanged and decked in the best manner the said Burgesses could, with clothes of Arras, Covering of Beds, Bancards, Carpets, Cushions, Chair Forms, and a Cupboard covered with Carpet and a cloth, whereon stood the silver plate whereof they drank, borrowed for the time of Mrs Agnes the wife of Mr Thomas Rydley, sometime wife of Mr Richard Lakyn of Willey; the table covered with Carpet cloth of diaper and napkins of the same, three dishes of Pears and a dish of old apples, cakes, fine wafers, wine white, and claret, and sack, and bread and ale for the waiters and servants without, at their pleasure, where my said Lord and Mr Justice sat the space of half an hour, and then arose, giving the said Burgesses great and gentle thanks for their cost and cheer, and so departed towards Bridgenorth.[8]

This was the best show that Much Wenlock could put on for the eminent visitors, and Anne's contribution was an integral and highly important one. Whilst she was not present at the 'banquet', it is probable that her second husband, Thomas Ridley, would have been.

Thomas Ridley, in spite of being bailiff of the franchises and liberties of Much Wenlock by 1554,[9] was not a match for Richard Lacon of Willey. He was, however, of a similar age to Anne, having been born by

1509 at the latest.[10] Ridley's exact background is unknown, although it appears that he was a member of the Ridleys of Alkington, a gentry family in Shropshire. At various times in his career he was based at Much Wenlock, Caughley and The Bold, a place very near to Kinlet. He would have been a neighbour to Anne and, although beneath her socially, may well have been known to her from childhood as her grandfather, Thomas Blount, was associated with Owen Ridley of Wolverhampton, a merchant of the Staple of Calais, in a bond made to Henry VII in 1500.[11] Owen was the father of Reginald Ridley, with whom Thomas Ridley associated, which suggests a familial link. Anne's husband can perhaps be identified as a son or nephew of the merchant.[12] Given the close physical proximity of the couple, the similarity of their age and the fact that Anne, as a wealthy and independent widow, had no need to take a second husband, it would seem highly probable that they made a love match. Certainly, after around thirty years of marriage, Ridley paid Bessie's sister the compliment of naming her as executor of his will. In addition to this, Anne rapidly bore her second husband two children, although only one, a daughter, Cecily, survived to adulthood. Ridley was something of an entrepreneur, taking a lease of an iron smithy in Much Wenlock in 1541, for example. He was an upstanding citizen and as well as his offices in Much Wenlock, he served as a member of parliament during the reign of Mary I, presumably due to the influence of Anne's brother, George, with whom Ridley travelled up to London. He was associated with his brother-in-law throughout the course of the parliament, with both opposing one of the government's bills. Following their marriage, Anne and Ridley settled at Willey and, after a brief period serving as an escheator in Shropshire during the early years of the reign of Elizabeth I, Ridley settled down to a comfortable retirement with Anne.

Even in the next generation, Anne's Lacon children seem to have taken a somewhat paternalistic view of Cecily, her daughter by Thomas Ridley. Cecily was first married to Thomas Jervoys, a gentleman of Worcester in 1573.[13] Her husband died in 1588 leaving a one-year-old son as his heir. Shortly afterwards, the queen granted young Thomas Jervoys' wardship to his mother's half-brother, Rowland Lacon, and Rowland's son-in-law, Francis Newport, in preference to Cecily and her second husband, George Wrottesley. That this was a contentious decision is clear from the fact that Cecily and her husband went to court to claim compensation for the loss of the use of the boy's estates. Although Cecily died in 1595, her second husband continued to attempt to obtain custody of his stepson's person and lands, finally being granted the wardship by 1600. In spite of his lower social standing, Thomas Ridley was accepted by the Blount family, with his brother-in-law George Blount agreeing to act with him as a co-trustee of Cecily's marriage settlement for her first marriage.[14]

Whilst Bessie's position as the king's mistress played no role in the choice of Anne's husband, it has been suggested that she had some influence over the marriages arranged for her sisters, Isabel and Rose.[15] Whilst, as will be seen, there is good evidence that Bessie played a major role in arranging Rose's marriage, she was not involved in Isabel's. Isabel, who was probably the fourth sister, was married in 1528. In the 1623 visitation of Shropshire, Isabel's husband was described as William Reade of Oatland. Oatlands Palace in Surrey, which was located between Weybridge and Walton on Thames, was a favourite of Henry VIII and the place where he chose to marry his fifth wife, Catherine Howard. He acquired the manor from the Reed family in 1538, exchanging the manor for former monastic lands.[16] The bargain was concluded, conveniently, by Henry's chief minister, Thomas Cromwell, who held the wardship of William Reed's heir, the young John Reed. Negotiations had begun in Isabel's husband's lifetime, apparently after Henry VIII took an interest in the hunting possibilities in the area.

During Isabel's marriage, William Reed, who was a gentleman, owned the house and lands at Oatlands, as well as property in nearby Long Ditton, with other lands in Surrey, Oxfordshire and the city of London.[17] He was based in Surrey and, as a neighbour of John Blount's sister, Katherine Smyth, may have first come to the family's attention through her. At the time of his death in 1534, Isabel and William were living at their house at Oatlands, which was very close to London and a number of royal residences. At the time of his marriage, William Reed was described as 'of Shepperton', again demonstrating that his sphere of interest was firmly in northern Surrey – very far from Bessie's own home in Lincolnshire.

Isabel's marriage settlement survives from July 1528, and demonstrates that John Blount was firmly in control of arranging his own daughter's marriage.[18] Under the terms of the agreement, which was signed by both John Blount and William Reed, and which concerned a marriage that was 'by the sufferance of god to be had and made', Reed promised John that he would 'before the 10th day of the month of June next coming shall marry and take to his wife the said Isabel and the same Isabel thereunto will agree and the said John by this promise in likewise covenant and promise to and in the same writing that the said Isabel Blount before the said tenth day of June shall marry and take to her husband the said William and the said William will thereunto agree'. John Blount obviously drove a hard bargain with his future son-in-law, perhaps helped in no small part by his new status as grandfather to the Duke of Richmond. He was able to extract a promise from Reed that, not only would he pay for his own clothing for the wedding, but that he would also pay for the bride's wedding dress, as well as all other associated costs of the wedding, such as 'all such meat and drink as shall be necessary for the day of the same marriage'. In addition to this, John ensured that Isabel's financial position was safeguarded in the event that she was widowed, with Reed agreeing to settle a 'sufficient and careful estate' of lands in the counties of Middlesex, Surrey and Kent on her, to the yearly value of £30 6s 8d. In addition to this, Isabel was to receive a further settlement following the death of Reed's mother, an event which would release the older woman's dower to benefit her daughter-in-law. Reed, who was the son of a knight and reasonably wealthy, was a good match for Isabel and the assumption must be that it was her relationship to Bessie and, more specifically, Henry Fitzroy, that recommended it to the Reed family. In 1528, when the king was already known to be having difficulty in divorcing Catherine of Aragon and had no legitimate sons, Henry Fitzroy was widely known to be a potential future king, something that very definitely increased the marriageability of Bessie's unmarried sisters. The provisions made for Isabel in the event of Reed's death were necessary, and her husband, who was already a widower, was some years older than her.[19] The prestige of the match, from the Blount family's point of view, was also limited somewhat by the fact that Reed already had a young son, John, to inherit the patrimony.

Whilst the geographical distance between the homes of the couple makes it very unlikely that they made a love match, the marriage between Isabel and William Reed proved to be a close one. Following their marriage – which, in spite of the eleven months given to arrange the marriage, almost certainly happened relatively rapidly – Isabel must have fallen pregnant almost immediately. She spent almost her entire brief marriage pregnant, bearing two sons and two daughters by the time of William Reed's death in September 1534. She was also pregnant again, as her husband made careful provision in his will for this unborn child, bequeathing the sum of one hundred marks to 'the child that my wife now goes with' towards its marriage should it prove to be a daughter.[20] If it was a son, it was to share with its elder brother, Reed's third son Anthony, the family lands in Long Ditton and the City of London, after the expiry of Isabel's own life interest. Henry, Reed's second son, but apparently his eldest by Isabel, also received a sum towards his marriage. Isabel received her dower, as well as a fifteen-year lease on Reed's house at Oatlands, which was the marital home, in return for a yearly rent to be paid to his eldest son. Reed's eldest daughter, Elizabeth, received the sum of £20, which, unlike the arrangement for his other daughters, was not given towards her marriage, suggesting that she was most likely his daughter from his first marriage and had already married. The other daughters, Anne and Joan, who are likely to have been Isabel's children, received one hundred marks towards their marriages.[21] Isabel, who must have found her life entirely taken up with raising her children, was probably the sister that Bessie knew the least well and their paths are unlikely to have crossed with any regularity. She is not mentioned in their mother's will, which was made on 2 January 1540 and, given the lack of mention of her in any later documents, the assumption must be that she died young, at least within a few years of her husband. That Oatlands, the manor in which she lived, was sold by her stepson's guardian, Thomas Cromwell, to the crown in 1538 would suggest that Isabel had died before then, although it is not impossible that the king dispossessed his former mistress's widowed sister in order to obtain a manor that he obviously coveted. The absence of any protest by the Blount family on Isabel's behalf does suggest that she was no longer alive.

Based on the evidence of the tomb, which shows a short scroll for the name of the third daughter, and the evidence of her own marriage, it would appear that Rose was the third sister and it can be assumed that she married a few years after Anne and before Isabel, which would suggest a marriage in the mid-1520s.[22] In the visitation of Shropshire carried out in 1623, it was recorded that Rose married William Grisling of the county of Lincolnshire.

Rose settled with her husband in the village of Asgarby, near Sleaford in Lincolnshire.[23] Asgarby, which by the late eighteenth century was little more than a hamlet with a fine church, was on the road to Boston and, as such, had reasonably good communications. Viscount Torrington, on his tour of Lincolnshire in 1791, for example, was able to reach the village on 'a fine gravelly road', something that many villages in the area lacked.[24] Little other detail survives of the village in an early period, although, significantly, it was less than ten miles from Bessie's home of South Kyme and the sisters must have been regular visitors to each other's residences.

William Grisling, in spite of his unusual name, is a difficult man to trace. A connection between the Lincolnshire (and Cornish) Grislings has been claimed with the more prominent Gresley family of Drakelowe on the Staffordshire and Derbyshire border.[25] The Gresley family, which was a wealthy one, owned lands spread across the West Country and Midlands, including, significantly, land at Boston in Lincolnshire. In Bessie's time, the head of the family was Sir William Gresley, who, like so much of the nobility and gentry, distinguished himself in France during Henry VIII's French wars, serving with her grandfather at Tournay. After his death, there was some dispute in the family, with the Gresley lands passing to his brother, George, who was made a knight of the Bath at Anne Boleyn's coronation in 1533, instead of his four sons by his second wife, Alice Tawke.[26] Interestingly, Sir George Gresley also twice served as sheriff of Shropshire, something that would have brought the family into contact with Bessie's. However, the claim, by a nineteenth-century biographer of the Gresley family that Sir William can be identified as the grandfather of Rose's husband (whom he considered the son of his son Anthony) is untenable. Sir William made his first marriage in 1496 or 1497 and his sons were born to his second wife. Anthony, who was the youngest of four sons, cannot have been born before around 1510 at the earliest, particularly since it is apparent that all four sons were still underage at their father's death in 1521.[27] Anthony could not therefore have been the father of Rose's husband. Another suggestion that Rose's husband was the son of Sir Thomas Gresley and his wife, Benedicta, is also inaccurate.[28] Sir Thomas Gresley was the father of William Gresley of Drakelow (described above), but his wife was named Anne. It was his son, William, who married Benedicta Vernon as his first wife, a marriage that was childless. Neither man can be identified as Rose's husband's father and any connection with the Gresley family must have been considerably more remote.

The 1562–64 visitation of Lincolnshire, which includes the genealogy of the Grisling family, made no mention of William Grisling's parentage, instead referring to Rose's relationship to Bessie and Henry Fitzroy. However, the 1592 visitation, which was also made up of information on the family supplied by Rose's son, has more detail. By 1592 the family were calling themselves 'Gresley', something that again suggests a link with the more prominent family. According to Rose's son, John, who was then living at Laceby in northern Lincolnshire, his father was the son of William Gresley of Saltash in Devon (now Cornwall).[29] He in turn was the son of a third son of Sir William Gresley of Leicestershire. Although these details are too vague to link Rose's Grislings with the Derbyshire Gresleys, they did own land in Lincolnshire and Leicestershire and it is probable that there was a distant connection, particularly given the prevalence of the Christian name William in both families.

Of considerably more interest is the assertion in the visitation of 1592 that Rose's husband, like his father, lived in Saltash in Cornwall. This is a very considerable distance from Lincolnshire. Given that, at the time of his marriage, William Grisling was described as being from Lincolnshire and the fact that the couple's eldest son certainly lived in Lincolnshire, it would seem probable that the move to Saltash was made later. There certainly was a Grisling family at Saltash in the sixteenth century. For example, when, in the late sixteenth century, Richard Carew made a survey of Cornwall, he recorded, with some wonder, details of a Saltash resident:

> In this town also dwelleth one Grisling, deaf from a long time, who, besides his merry conceits, of counterfeiting by signs (like the Roman pantomimi) any kind of occupation or exercise, had a strange quality to understand what you say, by marking the moving of your lips, especially if you speak deliberately, of any ordinary matter, so as (contrary to the rules of nature, and yet without the

help of art) he can see words as they pass forth of your mouth: and of this I have caused him to give often experiments.[30]

Carew, who had evidently never seen lip-reading before, found Saltash to be a town full of marvels, further noting the existence of a dog that cared lovingly for an old blind mastiff and 'a well in this town, whose water will never boil peas to a seasonable softness'.[31] The Grisling recorded by Carew was evidently a kinsman or descendant of Rose and William. A Peter Grisling was also a prominent resident of nearby Plymouth in 1625 when he complained to the justices of Devon that funds raised in the town for the redemption of people captured by the Turks had been misappropriated, a report that was taken seriously enough to be sent to the king's council in London.[32] The outcome of this complaint was not favourable for Peter Grisling, with an order being sent from the Privy Council in London following their investigation to commit him to gaol for 'falsely and slanderously accusing the Mayor and Commonalty of Plymouth of misappropriating charitable trusts'.[33] It seems that the Grislings had been a disruptive and anti-establishment force in Plymouth since even before Rose's time there.

In the mid-1530s, an earlier Peter Grisling of Plymouth found himself in trouble when he was part of a group of townsmen who were accused by a group of their fellow citizens of seditious beliefs, due to their adherence to traditional religious faith which was at odds with the tenets of the Henrician reformation.[34] It seems that there may have been more to this than simply religious difference and a number of their accusers, who, like Peter Grisling, were merchants, had earlier been associated with him 'when Peter Grislyng, merchant, James Horsewill, gentleman, John Coram, yeoman, John Grace, tailor, William Hawkyngs, merchant, and Lucas Cocke, merchant, all of Plymouth, were attached to answer for their conduct in beating and wounding John Jurdon of the same borough, so as to endanger his life'.[35] William Hawkins, who was the father of the Elizabethan sailor John Hawkins, was a particular enemy of Peter Grisling, with the pair, after their initial association in the assault on John Jurdon, clashing regularly.[36] William Hawkins, who was one of the leading men of Plymouth, had served as mayor in 1523–24. By 1535 Peter Grisling had been appointed to the prominent position of searcher of the port of Plymouth: effectively a customs officer. That year he brought a suit against the town which, although the details do not survive, was taken seriously enough for it to be heard by the Privy Council in London. The case, which saw Grisling pitched against the leading men of the town, including William Hawkins, was a bitter one, with Grisling, whilst the worse for wear for drink, calling the mayor of Plymouth, James Horsewell, 'a naughty heretic knave', words which could have been construed as treasonous given Horsewell's public office, as Hawkins pointed out.[37] It was perhaps lucky for Grisling that Hawkins assured the king's chief minister, Thomas Cromwell, that he did not consider the words to have been malicious, spoken as they were 'in his fury and in drink'. On his return to London, Peter Grisling refused to return to his hometown of Saltash, instead moving to Plymouth in the hope of obtaining a seat on the council there. When this proved impossible, he returned to Saltash and, towards the end of 1536, succeeded in persuading the Privy Council to banish Horsewell from Plymouth for a year and a day. The following year he became mayor of Saltash, immediately bringing the town into dispute with Plymouth with his claims for ancient harbour dues and a boat rent, as well as other ancient privileges. He used his position to pursue his personal vendetta against William Hawkins, continually summoning him to appear before the town court over which he presided. Matters only became quiet again when Hawkins appealed to the Star Chamber before being elected as mayor of Plymouth in 1538. With Thomas Cromwell's support, Hawkins and Horsewell were elected as members of parliament for their borough in the parliament of 1539. Trade rivalry in the town – which was, of course, at the centre of English trade in the sixteenth century – appears a likely cause for the dispute, although a personality clash is also likely. Rose and her husband apparently arrived at Saltash right in the middle of the dispute, perhaps even going with the intention of supporting their belligerent kinsman.

Rose's husband always referred to himself as 'Grisling' rather than 'Gresley' and this, coupled with the statement of his own son that his parents settled at Saltash, supports the view that Peter Grisling and other member of the family present in Devon and Cornwall during the reign of Henry VIII were his kinsmen. It has not proved possible to reconstruct details of their relationship. A John Grisling, who was appointed as mayor of Plymouth in 1512, was presumably Peter Grisling's father.[38] John was the name chosen for Rose and William's eldest son and, whilst this could have been for Rose's father, John Blount, it could equally have been a Grisling family name, suggesting that John Grisling and his son Peter could have been cousins of the Lincolnshire Grislings (or, perhaps, John Grisling was William Grisling's uncle).

Given the mobility of Rose's husband and son (both to Cornwall and to various residences in Lincolnshire), it appears that the Grislings had no family seat and they may have been only on the fringes of the gentry. In Henry VIII's accounts, he made a number of payments to a merchant named 'William Grisling'. For example, on 9 March 1531, Henry paid £20 12s 'to William Grisling mercer for xxv yards of Crimson satin and iij quarts at xvj s. the yard'.[39] The year before, the king had paid more than £11 to 'Walter Walsh upon his bill for that he laid unto to Locke of London and to Grislyn'.[40] Grisling was an unusual name and it is not improbable that Henry VIII's merchant can be identified as the husband of Rose Blount. Certainly, William Grisling took the time to make use of his wife's royal connections. On 27 October 1534 Henry Fitzroy wrote a letter to the king's chief minister, Thomas Cromwell, thanking him for 'your goodness the which ye all only for my sake have showed unto my friend William Grisling the bearer hereof'.[41] Clearly, Bessie's son was well enough acquainted with his uncle to seek to benefit him. They were also obviously in each other's company, with Fitzroy writing the letter at Grisling's request and then passing it to him by his own hand. Fitzroy's letter also further links Grisling to the West Country, with his comment that Grisling would also be bringing a testimonial under the seal of the town of Plymouth. Fitzroy's letter was written at Norwich Place, a royal house on the Strand in London. This demonstrates that Rose and her husband spent time in London, which accounts for Henry Fitzroy's familiarity with him.

There was a merchant active in London during Henry VIII's reign called William Grisling, who can in all probability be identified as Bessie's brother-in-law. Certainly, this William Grisling had connections with Bessie's circle and with Lincolnshire. Surviving legal cases in which he was involved show that he was associated with the Dymoke family, who were a prominent Lincolnshire family with which the Tailboys family were closely connected by marriage.[42] One case, which took place at some point between 1529 and 1532, showed a rather tenacious side to the merchant's character. According to surviving court documents, two years previously, one Thomas Benet, a merchant tailor of London, had become indebted to John Dymmok, who was a broker in London, for the sum of £20 sterling 'at which time the said Dymmok was indebted to one William Grisling mercer of London in the sum of xx li and for the payment thereof the said Dymmok delivered to the said Grisling the said obligation wherein the said Benet was bounden'. Grisling immediately commenced an action for debt against Benet, obtaining his condemnation. However, once it became clear that Benet was unable to pay, Grisling turned his attention to one John Fulwood, who had been unwise enough to provide surety for the original debt. John Dymmok of London remains unidentified but, given his highly unusual surname, the assumption must be that he was a member of the Dymoke family of Scrivelsby, giving him a family relationship to Grisling through Bessie and the Tailboys family that would account for Grisling's willingness to take on a debt owed to him rather than seeking direct payment of the sum from Dymmok himself.

Further evidence that demonstrates strongly that William Grisling, merchant of London, was Rose's husband can be seen in a second legal dispute. The merchant was involved in a legal case with Catherine Neville, the widow of Henry Burgh, a member of the Burgh family of Gainsborough in Lincolnshire, from which Catherine Parr, with whose family Bessie was well acquainted, also drew her first husband.[43] In this case William Grisling, 'citizen and mercer' of London, had been suggested by Cardinal Wolsey as one of the men suitable to hold property for Henry Burgh that was intended to form part of Catherine Burgh's jointure. With the fall of Wolsey in 1529, as well as Henry Burgh's sudden death in London, Grisling took the opportunity to make matters difficult for Catherine, with the widow taking her matter to court in an attempt to secure her jointure. The association both with a Lincolnshire family and with Cardinal Wolsey, coupled with the similarity of name between Rose's husband the merchant (including the unusual spelling of the surname), must strongly suggest that they were one and the same person. It is clear that William Grisling, merchant of London, moved in very similar circles to Bessie, which suggests that he can be identified as her brother-in-law and hints at how she may have come to be acquainted with him.

Merchants in the sixteenth century could be very wealthy and, even if they were not entirely accepted by some of the older gentry in England, they could live the life of a gentleman. Bessie and Rose's own grandmother had taken a merchant as her second husband and it is highly likely that Rose did so too, particularly given her husband's association with the port of Saltash. In the late sixteenth century, Richard Carew recorded that the town, which was by the sea and was on the top of a steep hill, was made up of between eighty and one hundred households.[44] It was prosperous, with a mayor and other officers. The town enjoyed a number of grants and privileges, particularly relating to shipping. Carew was in no doubt of the principal occupation of the town, recording that 'the townsmen addict themselves to the honest trade of merchandise, which endoweth them with a competent wealth'. It would appear that Rose married William Grisling whilst he was then a resident of Asgarby, close to Bessie's own home. He made a prosperous living from trade, perhaps even selling his goods directly to the king himself, and his business took him to Saltash and Plymouth for a time, probably to act in concert with other members of his family. Rose and her husband maintained strong links with her family. In her will, Rose's mother, Katherine, left a bequest of one hundred marks jointly to her daughter and her husband, to be paid in instalments.[45] Whilst it was Anne's husband, Richard Lacon, who was named as one of Katherine's executors (presumably mainly due to his close proximity to Kinlet), Katherine felt kindly enough about the Grisling family to provide that, in the event that her fifth daughter Albora remained unmarried (or married without the guidance of her sister Anne), her bequest of one hundred marks should instead be paid to 'the children of my said daughter Grysling'. William Grisling was involved with the family in other ways, being taken to court at some point in the late 1540s or early 1550s by Anne and Joan Reed, two of the daughters of his sister-in-law, Isabel Blount, following a complicated arrangement put in place by Isabel, Grisling and Katherine Blount following the death of Isabel's husband.[46] According to Anne and Joan,

Isabel had failed to pay the fifty marks which had been bequeathed to each of her daughters towards their marriage by their father. Instead, Isabel passed a number of chattels and other goods to Grisling in return for the promise of one hundred pounds sterling that he then paid to Katherine Blount. In acknowledgment of this, Katherine then promised to pay the one hundred marks when her granddaughters married. The case became increasingly muddled with the deaths of a number of the parties until, finally, when Anne and Joan sought their legacies through the courts, they came up against Bessie's brother, Sir George Blount, who swore that he would gladly pay the said sum if only Isabel's goods and chattels could be released from William Grisling's hold. Although the outcome of this case is not recorded, it is clear that William Grisling was able to command a position of some authority in the family, even if his interest was not always entirely benign.

That Bessie played a part in arranging Rose's marriage seems obvious: there is very little otherwise to link Rose to a fairly obscure merchant in Lincolnshire. The families also retained close links. Rose bore her husband four children, sons John, Thomas and William, and a daughter, Ursula.[47] Her eldest son, John Grisling, had three children: William (presumably named for his father), Ambrose and Elizabeth. Ambrose is a very unusual name and it is certain that Rose's grandson was named after Ambrose Dudley, Earl of Warwick, Rose's kinsman but also, even more significantly, Bessie's son-in-law from around 1552 until Elizabeth Tailboys' death in around 1560. It is highly likely that Ambrose Dudley would also have been Ambrose Grisling's godfather and his sister, Elizabeth Grisling, was perhaps the godchild of Elizabeth Tailboys. The name Ursula, which Rose chose for her only daughter and is again unusual, may have been selected as a compliment to Ursula Stourton, the second wife of Bessie's second husband, Edward Clinton, suggesting that Rose retained links with Bessie's Clinton family even after her death. Rose's son, John Grisling, received a substantial bequest in the will of Elizabeth Tailboys' first husband, Thomas Wymbish, who, as has been noted, was rather parsimonious with his wife. John received the sum of fifty shillings yearly for the duration of his life from the profits of the lands and tenements held by Wymbish in the city of Lincoln.[48] Such a pension strongly suggests that he was employed by Wymbish in some capacity. There were obviously continuing links between the two families and, of all her sisters, it was to Rose that Bessie remained closest. The two sisters were near-neighbours for some of their married lives and would have been regular visitors to each other's homes. Given the distance between Shropshire and Lincolnshire, Rose would have lodged with Bessie whilst she attempted to find a husband for her and negotiate her marriage. Such an arrangement was not uncommon and the widowed Catherine Parr, who later became Henry VIII's sixth wife and was well known to Bessie, later lived with her kinswoman,

Catherine Neville, at Sizergh Castle in Cumbria until a second marriage was arranged for her with her host's kinsman, Lord Latimer.[49] It was also common for a family to make use of better connected kin and acquaintances in attempting to arrange marriages. Correspondence survives between Catherine Parr's mother Maud Parr and Lord Dacre and his son-in-law Lord Scrope, for example, from the 1520s when Lady Parr was attempting to negotiate with the two men for a marriage between Catherine and the Scrope heir: a boy of a similar age to her daughter.[50] Lady Parr first made the approach to Lord Dacre, to whom she was related, whilst the pair were both with the court at Greenwich. Once she had secured the older man's consent to the match, she then set about contacting the boy's father, as did his grandfather, who wrote to Lord Scrope, declaring that he could not think 'that ye can marry him to so good stock as my lady Parr' before commenting on the family's great suitability. Lord Scrope, apparently resenting the intrusion of his father-in-law into such a personal matter, was unconvinced, sending Lady Parr a list of unreasonable demands which were clearly never intended to be met. Whilst the negotiations came to nothing, Lady Parr relied upon Lord Dacre at every step of the way to attempt to arrange the match for her daughter, clearly demonstrating the importance of prominent kin and patrons in any marriage negotiations. Bessie, as the wife of the well-connected Sir Gilbert Tailboys, and with her own solid court connections, was particularly well placed to identify potential husbands and to carry out negotiations on her sister's behalf. It may well be that Bessie, who must have left home for London when Rose was aged only around four or five, agreed to take responsibility for finding a husband for her due to the family turmoil that engulfed the Blounts following the death of her grandfather, Sir Thomas Blount, in 1524.

Sir Thomas Blount was evidently in ill health for some time before his death in 1524, making his will on 10 March 1523 in which he referred to himself as 'being aged and many Times sick in Body'.[51] He was, however, still well enough on 30 August 1523 to be appointed as one of the king's commissioners to collect the subsidies for Shropshire, something that demonstrates that he was still fully in control of his affairs.[52] His relationship with Bessie's father, John, had been troubled for some years and relations had evidently worsened as John became more independent in the first few decades of the sixteenth century. There is no doubt that Thomas favoured his second son, Edward, with whom he had served in France and who appears to have been singularly ambitious. He was eventually to marry an heiress, moving his family to Kidderminster, where they became particularly prominent, eventually effectively becoming the senior branch of the Blount family in Shropshire. In order to protect Edward's position, and, in all probability, to spite his eldest son, Sir Thomas spent the last few months of his life devising ways in which to frustrate the inheritance of Bessie's father.

At the same time that Sir Thomas Blount made his will, he also created a settlement in which he passed control of Kinlet and other lands into the hands of a number of trustees, including Sir William Compton, the king's favourite. Such settlements were common in Tudor times and remain a popular means of passing on wealth to the next generation in England today. However, whilst Thomas followed established practice in reserving a life interest in the lands for himself (effectively entitling him to occupy the properties and to their rents and profits, but giving him no absolute interest in them), the terms of his settlement can only have been directed as an attack on John Blount. Following his death, Thomas willed that the lands would remain in trust for a period of thirty years (a period presumably calculated to be long enough to ensure that John would not survive to achieve possession of his inheritance). During that period, the rents and profits from the lands would be paid to Thomas's trustees, whom he named as his second son Edward, his third son Walter (the future Walter Blount of Astley) and his friend Sir Thomas Mason, vicar of Kinlet, with the proviso that Edward was to be the lead trustee: 'so that the said Walter and Thomas be ordered and ruled in this the execution of my Will according to the mind and will of the said Edward and if not to suffer the said Edward only or such persons as the said Edward shall name and appoint at the time of his death'. The trustees were not intended to receive the full benefit of the trust fund and, from the rents and profits, Thomas ordained that his fourth son, Arthur, would receive an annual payment of five marks. Robert, the fifth son, received the same amount. Other pensions were also to be paid out of the trust fund, including one to Thomas's lawyer, John Adams, who perhaps devised the scheme. A final pension went to 'to the said Edward hereafter to be given xiijs iiijd of lawful English money of the said issues revenues and profits at the feast of saint Michael the archangel and the annunciation of Our Lady by even portions if the said John so long live'. Thomas's unmarried daughter, Joyce, received an annual sum, as well as a cash gift to be used towards her marriage. Thomas's three married daughters Anne, Elizabeth and Katherine also received cash sums, as did another daughter, Eleanor. Finally, Bessie's grandfather left sums for prayers to be said for his soul, and that of his wife and parents. He ordered that his three trustees could then exercise their discretion in distributing the remaining trust fund during the trust period with, presumably, the assumption being that the bulk would pass to Edward.

Bessie's father's absence was particularly noticeable in the terms of Thomas Blount's will, but it is clear that he was on his father's mind. Once the terms of the trust had been detailed, Thomas added the warning that:

If John Blount my son and heir apparent and his heirs do permit and suffer this my last will to be performed fulfilled and kept according to the word and intent of the same without any let vexation inquieting or interruption to be made by the said John Blount his heirs or any other person or persons in their name or in claiming by them or any of them or by their procurement abetting moving or storing or of any of them then I will that immediately after the said xxx years that the said William Compton knight with my other feoffees before named shall stand and be seized of the said manor etc. to the use and behalf of the said John Blount and the heirs male of his body lawfully begotten And if the said John Blount or his heirs or any other person or persons in his name or in claiming by him or his heirs or by his procuring moving or storing do let or hinder this my will or any part thereof to be performed and fulfilled according to the words or the intent of the same or for lack of issue of the body of the said John Blount lawfully begotten then the said William Compton knight and others before named at the end of the said xxx years do stand and be seized of and in the said manors etc. unto the use and behalf of Edward Blount my second son etc. and for lack of his heirs male to Walter Blount, then Arthur then Robert then to the right heirs of me the said Sir Thomas Blount.

Thomas evidently anticipated a legal challenge from the disgruntled John and, given that as the heir he expected to inherit his family's estates, the mere promise of the lands thirty years in the future were hardly likely to content him. It is almost certain that the trust was intended to be a deliberate provocation to John in the hope that he would challenge the will, and fail, allowing Edward to succeed to the family inheritance. Perhaps to rub salt into the wound still further, Thomas went on to make outright bequests to his other sons, leaving Edward and Walter land in Bewdley, for example. More personal bequests included his black gown to Roger Blount. In addition to this, Thomas's wife received a silver plate, as well as the chattels that he had received from her on marriage, including bedding, brass and pewter. As a testament to the relationship between Bessie's grandparents, Thomas also gave his wife 'a bed of damask with the curtains and hangings to the same and a feather bed of down with a pair of the best sheets and the best board cloth'. She was allowed to keep the best cup of silver in her husband's possession during her lifetime, with it passing to Edward's eldest son, Thomas Blount of Kidderminster, on her death. Edward received a bed and rich hangings, as well as his second best tablecloth, a salt of silver and a little pot of silver gilt. Walter received hangings, a salt of silver, a goblet of silver and a new tablecloth which had only recently been purchased. Edward was asked to deliver a bed each to his brothers, Arthur and Robert, as well as his sisters, Eleanor and Joyce, each bed fully made with hangings, pillows and sheets. Even the servants were remembered, with Thomas willing that all his household servants would receive their wages for a quarter of the year, as well as a black coat in which to mourn him. Even here, John Blount was not entirely forgotten, with Thomas adding the threat that, in the event that John, or anyone on his behalf, obtained a court judgment or an order from the king himself 'so that by mean of any of the promises my said will and intent thereof or any part of the said will is hindered and letted so that it is not performed according to the intent of the same', Sir William Compton and his other feoffees were to immediately declare that they held Kinlet for Edward Blount: doubtless the result that Thomas actually wanted to achieve. Edward also received the residue of his father's estate.

The will makes it clear that the relationship between John Blount and his father had entirely broken down by 1523. By disinheriting John, Thomas also disinherited Bessie and her siblings and there is no doubt that Bessie would have supported her father. The reference to an order from the king is also interesting and it seems likely that Bessie may have been one of the people that Thomas feared would use influence on John's behalf once the terms of the will became known. Everything about the will was designed to snub and provoke Bessie's father. Thomas named Sir William Compton, the king's favourite as one of the trustees of his will, empowering him to oversee the carrying out of his wishes. Compton was a patron of Edward Blount. At the time of Thomas's death, Edward was serving as deputy to the king's surveyor of the royal manor at Bewdley, whilst Compton is known to have been the king's surveyor by 1526.[53] Sir William Compton, who was born in 1482, has been described as an 'astonishingly successful early Tudor courtier'.[54] He was a formidable opponent to John Blount, as Thomas evidently knew. He had begun his career as a page to Henry VIII in his boyhood, developing a strong friendship with the future king. He rose rapidly after Henry's accession, becoming first a groom to the king's chamber and, by 1510, he had attained the intimate, and influential, post of groom of the stool. He later became chief gentleman of the bedchamber. Compton became very wealthy due to his association with the king and acquired so many crown offices that Henry had difficulty in remembering exactly what he had given him. He was also predatory in his acquisition of land, for example resorting to falsehoods in order to win the stewardship of Canford, after he had failed to persuade the manor's owner, the royal Countess of Salisbury, to marry him.[55] Almost certainly, he saw an opportunity to further his ambitions in involving himself in the Blounts' family disputes, especially since Edward Blount was firmly of his party. It has been suggested that Compton was a rival to Wolsey.[56] This can be seen both in Wolsey's attempt to prosecute the favourite for adultery with Lady Anne Hastings, and in his opposition to Compton becoming chancellor of the duchy of Lancaster in 1525. Compton was popularly considered to have considerable interest with the king, something that the cardinal also cannot have liked. It has been noted that, once Wolsey had established his dominant political position, the grants to Compton decreased. Bessie, through her submission to the cardinal's influence in her own life and that of her son, as well as accepting the marriage chosen for her, was very much Wolsey's creature, as was John Blount, who owed much of the favour that his family enjoyed to the position of Henry Fitzroy, who, as Wolsey's godson, was promoted by him. It is therefore not impossible that the division between Wolsey and Compton was played out on a small scale as part of the bitter family dispute between John and his father and brother. With Wolsey patronising John's family, it was only natural for Compton to take an interest in Edward, who no doubt expressed ill feeling towards his brother. It also appears that Thomas Blount's own deep-seated hatred of his eldest son was already in existence and he was pleased with any support that the king's favourite could offer in disinheriting him.

Not surprisingly, Compton was particularly disliked by Bessie's father, with a surviving letter from John in 1531 to his friend Thomas Cromwell, an up-and-coming minister of the king, complaining that thirty of his servants had been indicted on the orders of the favourite.[57] By the time that John wrote to the minister to 'recommend me unto you with hearty thanks for the great pain that you take with me' he was concerned that seven of his men still remained in pressing need, sending Cromwell their names. He asked Cromwell to intervene on his behalf and to discharge the matter from the authority of the sheriff of Shropshire, complaining that, in the county, 'I can have no favour by reason of my brother and other that were master Compton's servants'. It must have rankled with John Blount that Compton was able to wrest control of Bewdley from him following his father's death, and he decided to take no chances in 1531, sending Cromwell a 'token', as well as the promise of a gelding in the summer: a gift that would presumably only materialise in the event that the minister took action sufficiently to John's liking. He also assured the minister that 'I put my special trust in you in this matter and all others' as a mark of his esteem for his ally. Even beyond the grave, Sir William Compton was causing trouble for John Blount, since the king's favourite had died over two years before in the summer of 1528. The death eased some of the pressure and John was able to reclaim Bewdley soon afterwards, as well being back in enough favour in the shire to be appointed as sheriff of Shropshire before his own death some months later. It would seem not unlikely – given, in particular, Katherine Blount's later reliance on Cromwell in relation to local appointments – that Cromwell's hand was behind John's appointment as sheriff, in place of his enemy, Roger Holburro.

Luckily for John Blount, although Edward was able to call on powerful support in the form of the king's favourite following his father's death,

Bessie's parents were able to rely on the terms of their marriage settlement, which gave them a clear and incontrovertible right to Kinlet and the other Blount estates by giving them the remainder interest in the Blount lands, subject to Thomas Blount's prior life interest.[58] Bessie's parents once again resorted to litigation and were able to rely on the support of the trustees of their marriage settlement, including Lord Mountjoy, with a deed of recovery being made by the trustees on 25 February 1525 giving the couple the right to occupy the manor and, effectively, overturning the provisions of Thomas Blount's will. In February 1526 John secured the right to the livery of his father's possessions in Staffordshire, as well as those of his grandfather, Humphrey, and his wife.[59] This was a major victory for Bessie's parents, but it is clear that the anger festered. In his will, Thomas asked to be buried in the church at Kinlet and left sums from the sale of his cattle and sheep to purchase a slab of marble to be laid over his grave, with the images of both himself and his wife depicted on top. Kinlet church contains fine monuments to Thomas's father Humphrey, his son John, and John's son George Blount. There is, however, no record of Thomas Blount's burial and it is clear that he never received his marble tomb. This was John's revenge on his father, with his own particularly fine tomb taking the place that would otherwise have been occupied by the older man. John's position in Shropshire was unaffected by the troubles following his father's death. In November 1526 he was personally selected by the king to serve as sheriff of Shropshire.[60] He was also named as a member of a commission of the peace for Shropshire in January 1529.[61]

Bessie's father did not long survive his father, dying in February 1531. The death was evidently unexpected given that he was at that time serving as sheriff of Shropshire.[62] John, who had finally been knighted in 1529, was aged only in his late forties, with his heir, George, aged eighteen. John's early death and George's young age meant that Katherine Blount took over the running of her son's estates and his interests, as well as managing her own inheritance in Staffordshire. The succession from John to George was, however, somewhat easier than John's inheritance following his father's death, with the king confirming in March 1531 that George was to be steward of Bewdley and Cleobury Mortimer, as well as master of the hunt and rider of Wyre forest, keeper of Cleobury park and master of other parks and hunts in the area, on the same terms as they had been held by his father.[63]

Although her father's death must have been a shock, of even more immediate concern to Bessie was Gilbert's death, on 15 April 1530. The death of Gilbert, who was only in his early thirties, after only eight years of marriage must have been a shock for Bessie, especially given that her young son, George, who inherited his father's title and lands, was aged only seven. Given that Gilbert is known to have attended parliament the year before his death, and that he accepted a peerage at that time, it would seem probable that his death was unexpected. Gilbert was buried in the church at South Kyme and it would seem most probable that his death occurred at the manor there. During the years of her widowhood, Bessie based herself at the manor and she would have been with Gilbert at the end. She fulfilled her duties as a widow, commissioning a memorial to mark the grave that was intended for Gilbert, their young children who had died and, in due course, herself. As already discussed, Bessie paid for two memorial brasses depicting her and her husband kneeling in prayer. For reasons of economy, these were carved on the reverse of an earlier memorial brass apparently dating to the fourteenth century and made in Flanders, depicting a queen. Bessie also commissioned an inscription, which still survives in the church today:

Here lyeth the body of Sir Gilbert Taylboys, Lord Taylboys, Lord of Kyme Which married Elizabeth One of the daughters of Sir John Blount of Kinlet Knight. He departed forth of this world Ye 15th day of April An. Do. 1530 On whose soul God have Mercy, Amen.

As noted by Childe-Pemberton, Bessie's early biographer, 'this epitaph seems to suggest that the marriage of Gilbert Tailbois was the principal event of his life; and doubtless he was chiefly known to his contemporaries as the husband of Elizabeth Blount'.[64] It does indeed suggest something of Bessie's character that she used her husband's memorial brass to stress his links to her and her family, rather than focussing on any of his own achievements. Equally, however, Gilbert does appear to have been a fairly colourless young man. He was a good husband, but a poor son, given his willingness to take his inheritance during his father's lifetime. This was a policy that Bessie heartily supported and it is clear that, whilst she was prepared to assist and promote her own family – particularly her sister Rose – she had a considerably poorer relationship with her husband's. Given the number of children she produced and the fact that she and Gilbert were often together, Bessie must have mourned him. However, his death also ushered in a period of independence for her which was the first that she had known, and she relished the opportunity to make choices for herself.

# PART 4
# BESSIE THE WIDOW & BESSIE THE WIFE, 1530–c. 1539

## 17
## THE KING'S GREAT MATTER

Gilbert's death left Bessie independent and wealthy. Once her period of mourning for her husband was over, she was ready to go out into the world again. By 1530, life at court and in England as a whole was changing rapidly and, whether she liked it or not, Bessie found that she had a part to play in the King's Great Matter: his attempt to end his marriage to Catherine of Aragon.

Catherine of Aragon's last pregnancy occurred in 1518, ending with the birth of a stillborn girl a few months before Henry Fitzroy was born. It was not until 1527, however, that the king decided to take steps to end his marriage. By February 1526, at the latest, the king had become romantically interested in Anne Boleyn, the sister of his former mistress, who had returned to England from a time at the royal courts in Brussels and Paris some years before. That month, Henry arrived at a joust wearing the motto 'Declare I dare not' as the first external sign of his new love. At first, matters followed the usual course, with the king ardently pursuing the new object of his affections, bombarding her with letters when she returned to her family home of Hever Castle.[1] Anne had seen how the king had treated her sister: simply abandoning her when he lost interest in her. She therefore refused absolutely to become his mistress, even when he offered her the unprecedented (in England) position of his 'official mistress', writing that 'I promise you that not only the name will be done to you, but also to take you as my sole mistress, casting off all others than yourself out of mind and affection, and to serve you only'. Anne still refused, with the king eventually offering her marriage, a position that she was prepared to accept, signifying her acquiescence with the present of a jewel representing a 'ship in which the lonely damsel is tossed about'. With Anne's acceptance, Henry set about attempting to rid himself of his first wife, with a secret ecclesiastical court opening in May 1527 to try the validity of his marriage.

Henry always maintained that his decision to end his marriage to Catherine was due to the union's fundamental invalidity due to Catherine's position as his brother's widow, something that he argued had been beyond the pope's power to dispense. If Henry had hoped that his divorce could be quickly dealt with in England, he was disappointed. Within days of the secret court opening, Catherine of Aragon had learned of what was happening and written to her powerful nephew, Emperor Charles V, for support. Even aside from the attack on his family's honour that the proposed repudiation of his aunt represented, Charles had a more personal reason to oppose the divorce. His own wife was the daughter of his aunt, Maria of Aragon, who had married her deceased sister's husband. Due to the failure to maintain secrecy, Henry was forced to adjourn his court on 31 May 1527. Worse news for the king followed soon afterwards when he heard that the emperor had sacked Rome and was holding the pope as a virtual prisoner. Anxious not to displease Catherine's nephew, the pope, Clement VII, refused to give judgment either way in the case as time dragged on. Even when he was finally persuaded to send a papal legate, Cardinal Campeggio, to England, the cardinal had secret instructions not to give judgment but to delay matters as much he could. On his arrival in England in late 1528, Campeggio also set about trying to 'persuade the Queen to a Divorce; and dissuade the King from it, as having either way the end he proposed; yet he failed in both'.[2] Catherine refused absolutely to consider the suggestion that she become a nun, instead making a very public appeal to the king at a legatine court which opened at Blackfriars in June 1529.[3] When Campeggio found that he could delay no more, he stood up in court and revoked the case to Rome, returning home rather hurriedly.

It was Cardinal Wolsey, with whom Bessie and her family were so associated, who bore the brunt of the king's anger. Wolsey had never had a good relationship with Anne, whom he referred to as a 'serpentine enemy' and the 'Night Crow'.[4] However, the pair had been forced to work together in an attempt to secure the divorce. With the failure of the Blackfriars court, it became apparent to everyone that the pope would never grant Henry his divorce. Finally, on 9 October 1529, Wolsey was charged by the king with taking orders from a foreign power (the pope) and forced to surrender the great seal and his position as chancellor. Wolsey's authority over Henry Fitzroy ended at that time as, within a few short weeks, the Duke of Norfolk was boasting to the imperial ambassador that the king had asked him to take on the role of guiding Fitzroy's education.[5] Any remaining involvement that Wolsey had in Bessie and Gilbert's lives would also have ended at this time. Wolsey did not long survive Bessie's husband. In spite of continual rumours that he would engineer a return to power, the cardinal died a broken man at Leicester on his way to face trial for treason on 29 November 1530. In the years leading up to his fall, Wolsey had been attempting to negotiate a French alliance for Henry, with provision for the king to take a French bride.[6] If he had still been in power at the time of Gilbert's death, it seems not unlikely that he might have put forward another candidate for Henry's hand who was considerably closer to home.

In 1530 the relationship between Bessie and Henry had been over for several years. Bessie was still only aged around thirty-two years old, a similar age to Anne Boleyn, who was probably born in 1501. A description of Henry VIII in 1531, when he was forty, describes him as having a face that was 'angelic rather than handsome; his head imperial and bald, and he wears a beard, contrary to English custom'.[7] Henry was evidently rather touchy about his hair loss, but he still had an athletic body and remained active at sports. Certainly, in 1531 he was very far from the bloated and aged tyrant that he would later become and in all probability Bessie was still highly attracted to him. Bessie was considered to compare highly favourably to her rival, Anne Boleyn. In a report of the meeting between Henry VIII and Francis I of France at Calais in late 1532, the Venetian ambassador recorded that 'Madame Anne is not one of the handsomest women in the world, she is of middling stature, swarthy complexion, long neck, wide mouth, bosom not much raised, and in fact has nothing but the English king's great appetite, and her eyes, which are black and beautiful'.[8] Bessie was still widely regarded as a beauty, with her appearance conforming more to contemporary ideals of beauty than the swarthy Anne. She also had one great advantage over the king's love in that she was already the mother of his son, who was described by the Venetian ambassador as 'a youth of great promise, so much does he resemble his father'.[9] It is perhaps telling that, in the same report, made in November 1531, the ambassador referred to Bessie as 'the widow of one of his Peers', which indicates that he had evidently carried out some research into her current marital position. He was certainly not the only person to take an interest in Bessie during the years of the king's divorce.

Speculation was rife on the continent that Bessie was to be the beneficiary of the king's decision to end his marriage. During a dinner between John Barlow, Dean of Westbury, and a member of Charles V's council, whilst the Dean was visiting Flanders in June 1532, the conversation turned to the divorce.[10] The dean's companion, Loys de Heylwigen, mentioned a report that the king intended to marry a lady of a noble house in order to legitimise by subsequent marriage a son that she had borne him. The dean quickly moved to assure him that this was incorrect, and that the king intended to marry a second lady. Heylwigen refused to believe this, stating that the king's love for a woman other than his wife must be for the mother of his son. When Heylwigen pressed the dean on the two ladies, Barlow was forced to admit that Bessie was indeed beautiful, eloquent and gracious, although commenting that Anne Boleyn was also a beauty. To this, Heylwigen responded that perhaps the king had been bewitched by potions. It was evidently far-fetched that Henry would consider divorcing a wife as noble as Catherine of Aragon for anyone other than the beautiful mother of his son.

Bessie had a number of advantages over Anne Boleyn, if the king had cared to look at them. He always maintained that he would have been happy to remain in his marriage to Catherine, if only it could be proved valid. However, as far as Henry was concerned, the fact that Catherine had been the widow of his brother made this impossible. Unfortunately for Henry, as a number of contemporaries were quick to point out, the king's intention of marrying Anne Boleyn, the sister of his former mistress, made something of a mockery of this argument. The king's cousin and great opponent Reginald Pole later wrote in a discourse on the divorce addressed to Henry:

> Now what sort of person is it whom you have put in the place of your divorced wife? Is she not the sister of her whom you first violated, and for a long time after kept as your concubine? She certainly is. How is it, then, that you now tell us of the horror you have of illicit marriage? Are you ignorant of the law which certainly no less prohibits marriage with a sister of one with whom you have become one flesh, than with one with whom your brother was one flesh? If the one kind of marriage is detestable, so is the other. Were you ignorant of this law? Nay, you knew it better than others. How do I prove that? Because at the very time you were rejecting he dispensation of the pope to marry your brother's widow, you were doing your very utmost to get leave from the pope to marry the sister of your former concubine.[11]

When looked at objectively, Bessie made considerably more sense as a second wife than Anne Boleyn. The two women were of a similar age and rank (at least taking Bessie's Tailboys marriage into account). Bessie was generally considered the more beautiful, whilst both were well educated and accomplished. Bessie had the trump card: she was already the mother of the king's son. Counting against Bessie, of course, was the fact that, unlike Anne Boleyn, who stood by her virtue when the king pressed her to become him mistress, she had already yielded to him and had a somewhat dubious reputation due to this, as John Palsgrave's articles against Wolsey show. However, even if she stopped short of a sexual relationship with the king, Anne was hardly prim and proper in the way that the king's third wife, Jane Seymour, presented herself to him at the time of their courtship. In one surviving letter from Henry to Anne he commented that he was 'wishing myself (especially of an evening) in my sweetheart's arms, whose pretty duckies [breasts] I trust shortly to kiss'. Also, the couple's daughter, Elizabeth, was conceived in the weeks before their marriage in January 1533. A greater disadvantage in marriage to Bessie would be that it would suggest that the king had admitted defeat and was concerned that the difficulties that he had had in producing a legitimate son might have been due, at least in part, to his own problems, rather than simply blaming Catherine of Aragon. It would suggest that the king despaired of siring another healthy boy. However, balanced against this must be the king's obvious fondness for Fitzroy and the boy's great promise. It is hardly surprising that contemporaries talked of Henry marrying Bessie.

Although Henry Fitzroy was, of course, illegitimate, there was a precedent in the immediate royal family which suggested that he could be legitimated by his parents' subsequent marriage. John of Gaunt, the third surviving son of Edward III, had enjoyed a longstanding affair with Katherine Swynford, a lady of his household, during his marriage to his second wife, Constance of Castile. During the liaison, Katherine bore her lover four children, all of whom were given the surname of 'Beaufort' after one of their father's continental possessions. The family were openly acknowledged by their father. In 1396, John 'for the love he had to his children, he wedded their mother the lady Katheryn of Ruet, whereof there was much marvel both in England and in France, for she was but of base lineage, in regard to the two other wives'.[12] This scandalous marriage did not, in itself, legitimise the couple's children. This was a twofold process, requiring both the pope's consent in order to remove the stain of bastardy from the four children in the eyes of the Church, and also an Act of Parliament, which was passed in 1397, legitimising them under English law.[13] The statute of 1397 made the four Beauforts as legitimate as their elder half-brother, the future Henry IV, who was the son of John of Gaunt's first marriage. Henry IV, after attaining the crown, attempted to alter this position by inserting a clause into the 1397 statute confirming that the Beauforts were legitimate in all matters, save with regard to the inheritance of the throne. Given that it does not appear that this insertion was enacted by parliament, its legality was highly dubious. In any event, John of Gaunt's marriage to Katherine Swynford when their children were already adult was sufficient to allow their descendant, Henry VII, to claim the throne through them. In addition to this, the Tudor family had originally obtained much of their prestige from their ancestress, Catherine of Valois, the mother of Henry VI, who had borne children in an illicit relationship with a squire, Owen Tudor, during her son's minority. No details of the marriage survive and the legitimacy of their children must therefore be open to question. Furthermore, their eldest son, Edmund, who was the father of Henry VII, was given the Christian name of Edmund Beaufort, a man whom Catherine had taken strenuous efforts to marry before being forced to abandon him by her son's council. It is not impossible that Catherine's relationship with Owen had been necessary to ensure that she did not bear a child out of wedlock.[14]

Bessie had a role to play in the divorce simply by virtue of the fact that she was the mother of the king's only son, with Gilbert's death in April 1530 freeing her to be an active participant if matters moved in her favour. The question must be asked whether Bessie, or her friends, did indeed make an attempt to make her Henry's queen in the months following Gilbert's death. As has already been noted, Bessie enjoyed close and friendly links with the Parr family and their kin, the Vauxs and the Throckmortons. The head of the Throckmorton family, Sir George, who was the brother-in-law of the elder Sir William Parr, was a gentleman with conservative religious leanings who sat as a member of parliament for Warwickshire in the parliament of 1529.[15] Throckmorton, who had served as an esquire of the body and a member of the king's Spears alongside John Blount, was probably well known to his daughter, Bessie. A further, less direct link was provided by the fact that Throckmorton's father determined to go on a pilgrimage to the holy land in 1518, apparently emulating that undertaken by Richard Guildford, who was the uncle of his son's wife, and also, of course, the father of Bessie's kinsman, Sir Edward Guildford.[16] Bessie was acquainted with his son, Nicholas, through his position in her son's household. She showed the boy considerable favour in the years following Gilbert's death, giving him two pairs of Fitzroy's outgrown hose during her clear-out of her eldest son's wardrobe.[17] During the parliament, Throckmorton actively opposed all anti-papal measures and showed himself in great opposition to the king's new chief minister, Thomas Cromwell. Throckmorton and a group of like-minded gentlemen dined regularly at the Queen's Head Tavern, where they unwisely discussed their views. The group have been described by a modern historian as 'the core of an opposition group' and their activities quickly came to the government's attention, with Throckmorton being summoned to a personal interview with the king. It was at this interview that Throckmorton bravely, but unwisely, attempted to dissuade Henry from marrying Anne Boleyn, declaring that 'it is thought you have meddled both with the mother and the sister' in relation to the king's rumoured relationship with other members of the Boleyn family. Nothing concrete could be proved against Throckmorton, although it was suggested that he was associated with Sir Thomas More and John Fisher, Bishop of Rochester, who were leading opponents of the king's divorce. Interestingly, in autumn 1533 Throckmorton wrote to Cromwell to advise him that he had decided to cease his interference in politics and would return home.[18] However, he did not stay out of trouble enough to avoid the Tower in 1536 following the Pilgrimage of Grace.

At first glance, Throckmorton's political meddling had no link to Bessie. However, he was later to play something of a role in bringing Henry VIII together with his sixth wife, Throckmorton's niece, Catherine Parr. In 1540, Throckmorton had found himself in trouble again after becoming involved in a boundary dispute with Thomas Cromwell over the manors of Coughton Court and Owsley. Cromwell reported Throckmorton to the king, accusing him of denying the king's supremacy over the Church. Throckmorton was, unsurprisingly, committed to prison, with his wife sending to her relatives for assistance once again. According to a near-contemporary source, the *Legend of Throckmorton*, Throckmorton's niece, Catherine Parr, who was then married to Lord Latimer, a nobleman who remained out of favour with the king due to his involvement in the Pilgrimage of Grace, took up the call on his behalf. Catherine, who was apparently even then renowned as 'a woman rare, her like but seldom seen', was prevailed upon by her aunt to go to the king personally:

> She, willing of herself to do us good,
> Sought out the means her Uncle's life to save;
> And, when the king was in the pleasing mood,
> She humbly then her suit began to crave.
> With wooing times denials disagree,
> She spake, and sped: my Father was set free.[19]

This is the first recorded meeting between Henry VIII and his sixth wife. It went well and Throckmorton soon found himself released. Interestingly, the meeting took place during the final months of Henry's disastrous marriage to Anne of Cleves. It is not impossible that the king's interest in Catherine was noted by her family and, when the king was once again free following the end of his fifth marriage, Catherine was pushed in his direction. Certainly, Henry's courtship of Catherine moved quickly and appears to have been largely beyond her control, with the king's sixth wife attempting to make her own marriage at the time of Thomas Seymour, a man that she was in love with. Catherine's second husband, Lord Latimer, had died by March 1543.[20] By 16 February of that year, which must have been close to the unrecorded date of Lord Latimer's death, if not before it, Henry had made his interest in Catherine known by purchasing fine clothes for her.[21] The couple were married on 12 July 1543. This can only be conjecture, but it does appear that the Throckmortons and Parrs played some role in pushing Catherine Parr towards the king. She was highly reluctant to take on the role, commenting when Henry first raised the possibility that 'it were better to be your mistress than your wife'.[22] This may, in itself, have been a reference to Bessie, given Catherine's familiarity with her. Since the Parrs and their kin were later to have a successful candidate as the king's wife, it is surely not at all improbable that they had had an earlier candidate during the years of the divorce, and that this was their kinswoman and friend, Bessie Blount.

It has recently been commented that Sir George Throckmorton 'dared to go much further than almost anyone else among the religiously conservative gentry in the early 1530s in his opposition to Henry VIII's break with Rome and concurrent casting aside of Queen Katherine'.[23] Certainly, Throckmorton was very vocally bold in expressing his disapproval of the king's actions, although there is little evidence of direct action. However, it would seem odd if he had not followed up some of his words with physical actions. He certainly remained close to his cousin William Peto, who was a Franciscan Observant friar who preached openly against the divorce in the king's presence before fleeing to Antwerp in 1533.[24] Peto, along with other leading opponents to Henry VIII's policy towards religion, all urged Throckmorton strongly to maintain his opposition. Dangerously for the family, Throckmorton's brother, Michael, would later enter the service of the king's cousin and greatest opponent, Reginald Pole, who was made a cardinal by the pope thanks largely to his opposition to the king. Following his arrest in 1536, Throckmorton was released in early 1537, only to be returned to the Tower later that year. Throckmorton's wife, Katherine Vaux, wrote to her brother, the elder Sir William Parr, to request his counsel in what should be done to assist her husband.[25] Parr evidently used some influence, with his brother-in-law finally being released in 1538. It may be that Throckmorton and his associates intended Bessie as a potential alternative candidate as queen in the event that Catherine of Aragon was cast aside. If that was the case, they reckoned without the king's personal feelings in the matter.

Although the evidence of her New Year's gift in 1532 indicates that Henry still thought warmly of his former mistress, Bessie was not in so much favour that she was able to obtain the wardship of her second son, George, with the king instead selling the rights to his wardship and marriage to Sir William Fitzwilliam, future Earl of Southampton.[26] This does not necessarily mean that she lost custody of her son. However, it did mean that decisions concerning George's lands, and the income from them, as well as the choice of his bride, no longer fell to her, something that tended to be resented by Tudor mothers, for good reason. Bessie's own sister, Anne, would later make strenuous efforts for their brother, William, to secure the wardship of her own eldest son after her first husband's early death.[27] Bessie was a noticeable omission from the king's list of New Year's gifts in 1534. Of the ladies that the king had honoured with presents in 1532, only four were missed off the next extant gift list, including Bessie, suggesting that she was no longer quite as favoured as she had previously been.[28] Mary Boleyn still featured, which suggests that there was no blanket ban on former royal mistresses, although, given the earlier speculation that the king intended to marry her, coupled with Anne Boleyn's conspicuous lack of a son after a year of marriage, it is perhaps not surprising that Bessie was omitted.

Although the king was apparently no longer interested in Bessie, she remained very attractive to men, both personally and due to her wealth and position. Following Sir William Skeffington's sudden death in 1535, the king's first cousin, Lord Leonard Grey, was appointed to act as Henry Fitzroy's deputy in Ireland, visiting the country in an attempt to maintain order.[29] Although this was obviously some years in the future in 1532, it is not impossible that the peer had already taken an interest in Ireland in the hope of making his reputation, something that would have helped draw him towards Bessie. Grey, who was the younger brother of the Marquis of Dorset, had always enjoyed favour with his royal cousin. He had something of a martial reputation as in 1512, when his eldest brother was appointed as chief captain of the king's troops in Spain to assist in the war against France, Grey accompanied him.[30] Grey was also one of the men who accompanied the king to the Field of the Cloth of Gold in 1521. Lord Leonard Grey was on the lookout for a wealthy wife. In May 1532 Grey was enjoying a hunting trip in Lincolnshire when he decided to call in at South Kyme to visit Bessie, whom he knew from court.[31] Bessie, perhaps unwittingly, brought Grey's attention towards her by giving him 'very good cheer' during his visit, causing her guest to take her aside quietly so that he could enter into 'communication with her in the way of marriage'. This was evidently something of a shock to Bessie who had, after all, merely been trying to receive the king's cousin hospitably. Her answer does not survive but she went so far as to give her suitor hope that his feelings were reciprocated. On the basis of his visit, Grey was convinced that Bessie was the woman for him, writing that very night from South Kyme to the king's chief minister, Thomas Cromwell, to request his support for his suit and to assure him that 'I could be well contented to marry with her, God and the king pleasing, than with any other lady or gentlewoman living'. Bessie, with her beauty, accomplishments and wealth, had obviously made an impression. He begged that Cromwell would raise his suit with both the king and the Duke of Norfolk, who had taken on Wolsey's godfatherly role with her son, and to ask them both to write to Bessie pressing his suit on his behalf. As an added incentive to induce the minister to act, Grey sent a gift of £5. As even greater evidence of his keenness, he also sent Cromwell blank paper for his letters to the king and Norfolk.

The evidence of Grey's letter suggests that he was a particularly ardent suitor and, alone at South Kyme, Bessie must have had a difficult time attempting to dampen his enthusiasm for the match. On the face of it, it was a very good match for her. Although Grey, as a younger son, was not particularly wealthy, he was a member of one of the noblest and most prominent families in the land. The Grey family was an ancient one which had risen dramatically in the second half of the fifteenth century following the marriage of Dame Elizabeth Grey (née Woodville) to Edward IV. Elizabeth's first marriage had produced two sons, the eldest of whom, Thomas Grey, was created Marquis of Dorset by his stepfather. The first marquis received considerable favour under Edward

IV. In spite of a downturn in his fortunes following the deposition of his half-brother, Edward V, and the reign of Richard III, he re-established himself during the reign of his brother-in-law, Henry VII. The Grey family remained linked to the royal family in subsequent generations, with Leonard Grey's nephew, Henry, marrying the king's niece, Frances Brandon, in 1533, the year after his unsuccessful pursuit of Bessie. Whilst socially Grey was a good match for Bessie, he was also around twenty years older than her, something that may have disinclined her to accept him, coupled with the fact that he was also somewhat hot-headed, eventually ending his life on the executioner's block for treason in 1541. As an independent widow of means, Bessie had no need to marry again. The lukewarm way in which she responded to her suitor's overtures must therefore indicate that she did not have a liking for him.

Soon after his visit to South Kyme, Grey returned to his own home. He had been encouraged by Bessie's reception of his marriage proposal and thought that Cromwell's intervention would secure her for him. Cromwell did as he was bid and, perhaps using the paper which Grey sent, wrote dutifully to Bessie, recommending her suitor to her.[32] This letter failed to sway Bessie, who was emboldened enough by Grey's removal from her house to give a more direct answer. Grey remained undaunted and wrote once again to Cromwell, begging him to try again, for 'I had rather obtain that matter than to be made lord of as much goods and lands as any one noble man hath within this realm and wherefore I heartily desire you for your good continuance in the same'. Grey pointed out that the king had confirmed that he did not object to the match, although, reading between the lines, he was somewhat ambivalent towards it, certainly not going so far as to command Bessie to marry his cousin. Grey had evidently begun to feel that his earlier bribe to Cromwell had not been quite adequate, assuring him in his second letter, which was written six weeks after his first, that 'I promise you I would do a service for you, as one friend might do reasonably for another'. Regardless of the pressure brought to bear on her by Grey and the rather lukewarm support that he received from the king and his chief minister, Bessie was not to be swayed, refusing resolutely to marry Lord Leonard Grey, however much in love with her he professed to be. Bessie knew her own mind and, whilst not averse to the possibility of a second marriage, she was not prepared to rush into matrimony unless she had a liking for her suitor, regardless of his status. The Grey affair also provides strong evidence that Henry VIII's romantic interest in Bessie had not been reawakened by Gilbert's death. His agreement to the match must demonstrate that he had no plans to marry Bessie himself, in spite of the advantages that this offered in providing an immediate Prince of Wales.

Following his return from the north, Fitzroy spent much of his time at Windsor Castle, a residence conveniently situated for access to London and a favourite of his father's. Although Fitzroy had always enjoyed the company of noble boys of his own age, in late 1529, following the fall of Cardinal Wolsey, the Duke of Norfolk began to take an interest in Bessie's son, placing his own son, Henry Howard, Earl of Surrey, in the household. According to Norfolk himself in a conversation with the imperial ambassador shortly after Wolsey's fall:

> I told you that I was on many accounts delighted to see my son making so much progress in his studies, and following the path of virtue, and since it is but proper that friends should communicate to each other their most secret affairs and thoughts, I do not hesitate to tell you my ideas on this subject. The king has entrusted to me the education of his bastard son, the Duke of Richmond, of whom my own son may become in time preceptor and tutor, that he may attain both knowledge and virtue, so that a friendship thus cemented promises fair to be very strong and firm.[33]

Norfolk was content to take on something of the role that Wolsey had played in the boy's life, particularly, as he confided to Chapuys at the time, because it was intended that his daughter should marry Fitzroy. Like Wolsey, Norfolk took a considerable interest in the day-to-day working of the young duke's household, being understood by contemporaries to be largely responsible for appointments there. For example, in late 1533, the Archbishop of Canterbury wrote to Anne Boleyn's brother, Lord Rochford, to request that he ask his uncle, Norfolk, to prefer the bearer of the letter to the post of Fitzroy's secretary, making it clear who truly wielded the power in Fitzroy's ducal establishment.[34] Similarly, in May 1536, Sir George Lawson, a retainer of Fitzroy's, wrote to Norfolk concerned that the elder duke's anger at him would cause him to lose his place with Bessie's son.[35] Leonard Grey's first letter, in which he asked Cromwell to recommend him to the king and the Duke of Norfolk, also makes it clear that Norfolk became Bessie's patron, in the same way that Cardinal Wolsey had formerly been, ensuring that she retained her protection and ability to influence matters at court. This can also be seen in the fact that Norfolk took George Blount's wardship in 1531 after the death of Sir John Blount.

Henry Fitzroy and Surrey soon became close friends. The earl later provided details of the pair's daily life at the castle in a long sonnet composed shortly before his execution for treason in 1547, which began:

> So cruel prison how could betide, alas!
> As proud Windsor? Where I in lust and joy,
> With a king's son, my childish years did pass,
> In greater feast than Priam's sons of Troy.[36]

Life at Windsor between 1529 and late 1532 was idyllic, even allowing for some poetic licence. According to Surrey, there were dances with 'ladies bright of hue', with whom the boys would entertain themselves following the rituals of courtly love, 'where each of us did plead the other's right'. When not amusing themselves with the ladies, the boys practised their martial skills in gravelled courtyards 'on foaming horse with swords and friendly hearts'. They took part in

> Games of nimbleness and strength,
> Where we did strain, trained with swarms of youth,
> Our tender limbs, that yet shot up in length.

The boys roamed in grassed courtyards and 'secret groves', as well as riding through the forests at the hunt, accompanied by their hounds. They were firm friends, with Surrey wistfully recording

> The secret thoughts, imparted with such trust;
> The wanton talk, the divers changes of play;
> The friendship sworn, each promise kept so just,
> Wherewith we past the winter nights away.

Surrey was the person to whom Bessie's son was closest and the quiet years at Windsor were, in all probability, the happiest of both men's short lives. For Surrey, certainly, Windsor was remembered as a 'place of bliss!' Presumably Bessie, who had enjoyed access to her son at Sheriff Hutton, would have been free to visit if she chose. This is supported by the evidence of gifts of Fitzroy's outgrown clothes made by her, and also by the clothes received from Fitzroy by her younger son, George Tailboys.

During the years that Henry Fitzroy was growing up at Windsor, Bessie remained, for the most part, in Lincolnshire, presumably spending her time running her household and raising her younger children.[37] The years following Gilbert's death were a time of great change in England as Henry's attempts to obtain a divorce progressed. Following the end of the Blackfriars trial in 1529, Henry VIII and Anne Boleyn had continued to work busily towards the divorce, with the king finally separating from the queen in the summer of 1531. Whilst Henry had always preferred to secure his divorce from the pope, as the years passed it became increasingly obvious that Clement would never grant his request. It was Anne who first drew the king's attention to a more radical solution, providing copies of William Tyndale's *Obedience of a Christian Man* and the anti-clerical work *The Supplication of Beggars* by Simon Fish, amongst other reformist texts. Henry was willing to listen to anti-papal sentiment, making his first move against the pope in the praemunire manoeuvres of 1530 and 1531.[38] In the summer of

1530 Henry prosecuted a number of clerics for prioritising papal law above that of the king. Whilst the case was adjourned, in the autumn and winter it was extended into an attack on the entire southern clergy. At a convocation in January 1531, the clergy were compelled by Henry to recognise him as 'Supreme head of the Church of England, as far as the law of Christ allows'. Although qualifications introduced into the title by the clergy meant that it had little force, it was still a shocking move, with the imperial ambassador commenting that Henry had effectively declared himself 'Pope in England'. The next few years saw increasing anti-papal sentiment in England, culminating in the appointment of the reformist-leaning Thomas Cranmer, a Boleyn family chaplain, as Archbishop of Canterbury early in 1533. As soon as Cranmer's appointment had been sanctioned by the pope, Henry and Anne were able to reveal the fact that they had been secretly married since January 1533, with the new archbishop quickly pronouncing on the invalidity of Catherine of Aragon's marriage. A pregnant Anne Boleyn was crowned queen of England on 1 June 1533.

Anne Boleyn had high hopes that she would bear a future king of England, something that must have led to some degree of friction with Fitzroy, who had, after all, been talked about as a potential successor to the crown. There is little direct evidence for Henry Fitzroy's relationship with Anne Boleyn. Obviously, their interests were somewhat opposed, with Fitzroy's hopes for the future depending on Henry's second wife not producing a legitimate son. One twentieth-century historian, for example, posited from this that, based on Anne Boleyn and Fitzroy's conflicting interests, 'we are not surprised to learn that Richmond was later on the worst of terms with Anne Boleyn'.[39] One piece of evidence that supports a view that they had a hostile relationship can be seen in the fact that, in the afternoon of 2 May 1536, the day of Anne's arrest on suspicion of adultery, Fitzroy went to see his father to ask for his blessing.[40] Henry VIII, having decided to rid himself of his second wife, was evidently in a highly emotional state. On seeing his son, he burst into tears and informed him that 'both he and his sister, meaning the Princess [Mary], ought to thank God for having escaped from the hands of that woman, who had planned their death by poison'. Fitzroy must have been somewhat alarmed to hear this news from his usually composed father. Another contemporary, Charles Wriothesley, later recorded that Fitzroy had died from an apparently slow-acting poison administered to him by the queen and her brother.[41] Henry's and Wriothesley's claims will be examined in more detail later, but suffice it to say that, on the face of it, the fact that such a claim could be given credence does not suggest that stepmother and stepson had a particularly warm relationship. A gift that the future queen had given Fitzroy to mark his return from Yorkshire also appears to have been less than generous: a bay horse, which was in such poor condition that Fitzroy quickly gave it away.[42]

Anne Boleyn is remembered for her fiery temper and sharp tongue, which she is known to have unleashed on members of her own family, such as her father, Sir Thomas Boleyn, her sister, Mary, and her uncle, the Duke of Norfolk. Her hostility towards Henry's daughter, Princess Mary, is well known, with Henry's second wife making comments that she would bring down the pride of the girl's unbridled Spanish blood. There is no evidence, however, that she ever publicly attacked Fitzroy. In fact, what little surviving evidence there is suggests that they might have had a warmer relationship than is commonly supposed. Even the poor quality of the horse that she gave Fitzroy could have been accidental, with the boy immediately making a gift of it to avoid any embarrassment in the event that his father's fiancée saw just what a poor specimen she had provided. A gift of a saddle of spruce leather and black velvet which she made to Fitzroy at the same time was considerably better received, remaining within the boy's possessions.[43] Any woman meeting the ten-year-old son of her fiancé for the first time would have a difficult time selecting presents for him. Anne, at least, picked gifts that Fitzroy was likely to like, demonstrating that she had made enquiries. Bessie herself had previously given the boy horses. Although, by the early 1530s, Fitzroy must have had some hopes of the throne, he knew that he was illegitimate and such aspirations were fraught with legal difficulty. Even if Henry produced a legitimate son, Fitzroy could look forward to a future as one of the premier peers in England and the founder of a noble dynasty of his own.

Anne Boleyn was an astute politician. She bore a grudge against Cardinal Wolsey from the time that he broke her secret betrothal to Henry Percy, the heir to the Earl of Northumberland, in 1522 or 1523.[44] In the early days of the divorce, she was prepared to work with the king's chief minister, sending him warm letters and, even, a tablet of gold when he was ill at Christmas 1529. The fact that she later settled her score with Wolsey – when her old suitor, by then the Earl of Northumberland, was sent to arrest the cardinal – demonstrates that a gift from Anne was no guarantee of favour. However, there is some evidence that Anne's gifts to Fitzroy were more warmly received (with the exception, of course, of the horse). Certainly, they are evidence that, during Anne's time as queen, what must have been a fairly difficult relationship for them both was not overtly hostile. In the inventory of his possessions commissioned after his death, for example, Fitzroy was found to possess 'a great jug with a cover gilt, with letters H and A crowned, and ii ears of serpents' which had been part of the king's New Year's gift to him in 1536.[45] Since this gift proudly symbolised the relationship between Henry and his queen, it would have been a tactless gift if Fitzroy's relations with Anne were not known to be cordial. Even more tellingly, in the same inventory it was recorded that Anne's New Year's gift for 1535 to Fitzroy had included 'a bonnet furnished with buttons, and a little brooch'.[46] This was well received with a note in the inventory stating that the bonnet remained 'in my lord's grace hands, and never delivered to his treasure'. The fact that Fitzroy chose to keep the bonnet and, presumably, wear it, suggests that his relationship with Anne – who was, after all, also his future wife's first cousin – was reasonably warm. Even Anne's acquisition of Collyweston, a manor house that Fitzroy had been granted at the time of his elevation and which he is known to have made personal use of, does not appear to have been hostile. In November 1535, when the queen's interest in the manor was first made known, Fitzroy merely protested that he had already offered his servant the office of keeper of the park there, and that he was concerned that he should be able to retain this honour: hardly the protests of someone outraged at the loss of a house to an enemy.[47] The Act granting him the house was later repealed by parliament, giving it to the queen for life instead.[48] A further, rather more tenuous, link was provided by the fact that Fitzroy's high steward, William Brereton, who was one of his most trusted officials, was also one of the men accused of adultery with Anne after her fall.[49] Whilst the charges against Anne were clearly false, she obviously must have had some association with all of the men in order for the charges to be formulated. Whilst Brereton was the most incongruous of the five men with whom Anne was accused (with the other four all being in regular attendance at court), the fact that two other men, Sir Thomas Wyatt and Sir Richard Page, were also arrested but not charged does suggest that it was necessary for the charges to be reasonably believable, even if they were hardly plausible. Brereton must therefore have been an acquaintance of the queen's even if – as is likely from the fact that, unlike the other men, she never spoke of him whilst she was imprisoned in the Tower – she had very little connection with him.

Whilst Anne's enmity towards Princess Mary is understandable, given the danger that the elder half-sister posed to her own daughter, Fitzroy's readily acknowledged bastardy made him less of a threat. Mary was declared illegitimate by the terms of the first Act of Succession of 1534, which settled the crown on the children of Henry and Anne, making Anne's daughter, Elizabeth, who was born in September 1533, heiress to the crown. No mention was, of course, made of Fitzroy in the Act although its terms did actually benefit him. Mary had always been Fitzroy's greatest rival by virtue of her position as the king's legitimate daughter. With her illegitimacy, Henry Fitzroy actually outranked her, ranking only below his father, his stepmother and their daughter who, as a female infant, was very unlikely to have held the throne in the event of Henry VIII's early death. Princess Mary perhaps summed up best the idea that Fitzroy, as a bastard, was no threat to the legitimate offspring of the king whilst Henry lived. Unsurprisingly, she refused to recognise Elizabeth as heir to the throne, instead declaring that she was content to call her sister, since her father acknowledged her as his child, in the same way that she called Fitzroy brother. Of Henry VIII's two older children, Fitzroy, in spite of being the boy, was considerably less of a threat to Elizabeth than Mary, something which may have caused the queen to cultivate his favour. Interestingly, Fitzroy was one of the knights present at a chapter of the Order of the Garter at Greenwich on St George's Day 1536, at which Anne Boleyn, who had been lobbying for her brother to receive the honour of membership, was publicly slighted by the election of Nicholas Carew, a supporter of the king's new love, Jane Seymour.⁵⁰ However, there is no evidence that Fitzroy gave any personal support to either candidate. Certainly, by 1536, when Anne Boleyn had failed to produce a son after three years of marriage, it would not be surprising if Fitzroy quietly supported her rather than the possibility of the king making a new marriage to the younger and potentially more fertile Jane Seymour.

Anne had also managed to tie Fitzroy more firmly to her own family interests: a sign that she was attempting to cultivate his friendship. Although he had earlier had grand plans for his son's marriage, the hope of legitimate sons by Anne and, perhaps, the expense in arranging such a match had put Henry off the idea. At one stage, during the early years of the divorce, he had apparently considered marrying Fitzroy to his half-sister, Princess Mary, a match to which the pope might have consented, providing that the couple's father then abandoned his own divorce.⁵¹ However, for Henry, whose main interest in the divorce was to enable him to marry Anne Boleyn, this was not really a solution. Shortly after Fitzroy's return from the north, when Anne Boleyn was firmly ensconced in the king's affections, the suggestion was made that he should marry Mary Howard, the daughter of the Duke of Norfolk and a first cousin of Anne Boleyn. Mary Howard, as a daughter of one of England's premier peers and of a similar age to Fitzroy, was actually a very suitable bride. She was also the niece of the Duke of Buckingham, who had been executed for treason earlier in the reign. Buckingham had been a descendant of the youngest son of Edward III and, as such, had on occasion been spoken of as a possible claimant for the crown. She was therefore the best possible English match that Fitzroy could make, albeit very far from the Princess of Portugal, or other foreign princesses that had once been spoken of as possible brides for the young duke. The suggestion of the match had first been raised in late 1529 when Norfolk – who had already betrothed his eldest daughter to his first choice of son-in-law, the son of the Earl of Derby – was first approached.⁵² He was not entirely enthusiastic, however, as, when his eldest daughter died not long after her marriage, it was only the fact that he had an available sister to marry his son-in-law that stopped Norfolk breaking Fitzroy's betrothal to allow Mary to marry her deceased sister's husband.⁵³ Whilst Mary later claimed that the king had made the marriage, given Henry's lack of enthusiasm for the match after Fitzroy's death, coupled with a later claim by Mary's mother, the Duchess of Norfolk, that it was Anne Boleyn who had arranged the match, this would seem to be correct. Anne was close to her cousin, having her with her at court after she became queen and it must have appealed both to see a kinswoman so well married and to tie Fitzroy's family interests to her own. Matters moved relatively quickly and, by March 1531, the imperial ambassador was referring to Fitzroy as Norfolk's son-in-law, suggesting that marriage negotiations had been fully concluded.[54] Given Fitzroy's youth, it is very unlikely that he would have had any say in his choice of marriage partner. Equally, Bessie, who ranked far below the Duke of Norfolk, is unlikely to have had any input in the negotiations, although, as Leonard Grey's correspondence shows, there is some suggestion that she allowed her life to be somewhat governed by the duke, suggesting that she would not have been entirely displeased by the match. Also, whilst the marriage would, to some extent, help to link Fitzroy's family concerns to Anne Boleyn's, it would also have served to potentially divert Norfolk's support from Anne's: in the event of Henry VIII's early death, Norfolk was highly likely to prefer his son-in-law as monarch than an infant great-niece.

Henry Fitzroy and Mary Howard married on 25 November 1533 in a ceremony that was conducted at court. Although both parties to the marriage were in their late teens, they were not permitted to live together and it was an established fact that, at the time of Fitzroy's death, Mary remained a virgin, something that caused her considerable grief when she attempted to claim her widow's dower from the king. Mary later wrote that Fitzroy's death had caused her 'sorrow and discomfort',[55] words which sound phrased more to conform to conventional notions of a widow's conduct that any real devastation at the loss of her young husband. However, the couple were close enough for Mary to want to take keepsakes from her husband's possessions following his death, with it being recorded in his inventory that some silver spoons had been delivered into the duchess of Richmond's hands.[56]

As early as the summer of 1532, there were rumours that Henry had not entirely abandoned plans for his son to have an international prominence, in spite of his acquiescence to the marriage pushed by Anne Boleyn, with claims that he intended to send Fitzroy and Surrey to France.[57] It was intended that Fitzroy would play an important role in Henry's peace with France, journeying to the French court with a suite of sixty gentlemen to 'remain there for greater security of the matters treated between them'.[58] By the end of October, it had been agreed that Fitzroy would indeed accompany his father to France for his interview with the French king, and that the boy would then travel to the French court to take up a position in Francis I's service.[59] By the end of 1532, Fitzroy was thirteen years old and ready to take a greater prominence in diplomatic affairs. As well as his resemblance to Henry VIII being commonly remarked upon, contemporaries gushed that he was both handsome and entirely accomplished.[60] Following the meeting between the two kings at which Fitzroy, as the king's only son, played a prominent role, he remained at Boulogne.[61] Fitzroy nominally offered the French king his service and was lodged at the French court at great expense as a sign of the friendship between the two monarchs.[62] He was well treated and granted some prominence. In April 1533, for example, when an English herald arrived bearing the robes of the Order of the Garter for two members of Francis's court who had been recently elected, it was decreed by Francis that he and Fitzroy, who were both members of the Order, would celebrate the elections on St George's Day, the date on which chapters were held.[63] Fitzroy was sent to stay in the household of the French king's three sons, a significant honour.[64] Bessie's son was no doubt gratified by his reception in France, with Francis publicly embracing him on his arrival and assuring him that 'he thought himself now to have four sons, and esteemed him no less'.[65] Fitzroy's stay in France was destined to be short and, in August 1533, the Duke of Norfolk arrived to bring him and Surrey home to England, in order to allow Bessie's son's marriage to be celebrated.[66] On 25 September 1533 the Chronicle of Calais recorded that Fitzroy and Surrey 'came to Calais out of France, were they had been almost xii months'.[67] Bessie's son enjoyed his time with the French court and thought well of the country, writing to his father's chief minister in the summer of 1534 when it was proposed that the king should again meet with his French counterpart on the continent, to ask if he could be a member of the party.[68]

Fitzroy retained his prominence during Anne Boleyn's time as queen, attending parliament in early 1534, for example.[69] In April of the same year he attended a chapter of the Garter at Greenwich with his father. In late 1534, the Admiral of France arrived in England on a diplomatic visit. Whilst he caused offence by being ambivalent about meeting with Anne Boleyn, he was evidently keen to meet the king's only son, being entertained by Henry Fitzroy during his visit to London.[70] In February 1536, shortly after the queen suffered a miscarriage of a son, Henry granted his only surviving son the lordship of Raskall in Yorkshire, which was worth £44 or £45.[71]

As Henry Fitzroy grew up, the king required him to play a more adult role in English affairs. In May 1535, when he was approaching his sixteenth birthday, he witnessed the executions of three Carthusian monks who had denied the king's supremacy as head of the church.[72] There was some sympathy for the three men in London and they were referred to by the imperial ambassador as 'all men of good and sound doctrine, as well as exemplary life and reputation'. The execution, which is the first that Fitzroy is recorded to have witnessed, must have been quite an experience for the young lord as he watched the men dragged through the streets before their execution. Fitzroy stood close to the scaffold with the Duke of Norfolk and Anne Boleyn's father and brother, something which again does not suggest any great estrangement between Bessie's son and the queen. The execution was something of a court event, with many courtiers coming to view the spectacle, some of them masked to obscure their faces from the crowd. This was not the only execution that Fitzroy was called upon to witness. On 19 May 1536 he, along with his uncle, the Duke of Suffolk, and most of the king's council, assembled on Tower Green before eight o'clock in the morning to witness the execution of Anne Boleyn herself, who had been convicted on rather improbable evidence of adultery and incest.[73] Fitzroy's thoughts on the death of his stepmother are not recorded, although he is unlikely to have been pleased to hear that the very next day his father had become betrothed to the sister of his former master of horse, Sir Edward Seymour, with the new queen coming from a famously fecund family.

# 18

# LADY CLINTON

Bessie was evidently not keen to marry the king's cousin, Lord Leonard Grey. That this was due to a personal disinclination to marry Grey is clear by the fact that, from the mid-1530s, Bessie was the wife of dashing and up-and-coming Edward Fiennes-Clinton, Lord Clinton.

The Clinton family was an ancient one, with the first recorded member, Geoffrey de Clinton, appointed as lord chamberlain and treasurer to Henry I in the eleventh century.[1] Although Geoffrey's descendants died out, his brother left issue, with the family obtaining a peerage during the reign of Edward III.[2] The family's lands were widely spread throughout England, holding the manor of Folkestone in Kent, as well as substantial estates in Warwickshire, for example. Their family name derived from the manor of Glinton in Northamptonshire which was also one of their possessions.[3] They adopted the surname 'Fiennes' or 'Fynes' following the marriage of John, fifth Lord Clinton, to Elizabeth Fiennes, daughter of Lord Dacre of the South.[4] The Fiennes family claimed descent from William I, a royal lineage which may account for the decision of the Clintons to annex the name Fiennes to their own, with both surnames being used interchangeably by family members for centuries. Bessie's own husband's name can be most accurately given as Edward Fiennes-Clinton, although he generally used the name Clinton which was, of course, the title of his peerage. This was also the surname by which Bessie's daughters by Clinton were known. By the late fifteenth century, the head of the family was John, seventh Lord Clinton, who was Bessie's husband's grandfather. This Lord Clinton accompanied the prominent courtier Sir Edward Poynings to aid Margaret of Savoy, the regent of the Netherlands, in her war with the Duke of Guelders in 1500. He, like most of the English nobility, also served in France with Henry VIII in his campaign of 1513–14. John, Lord Clinton, died in 1514, leaving his lands and title to his twenty-four-year-old son, Thomas.

Thomas, Lord Clinton, did not long enjoy his inheritance, dying suddenly of the sweating sickness on 7 August 1517.[5] This illness, which was a peculiarly Tudor disease, struck fear into the people of England due to its deadly nature and the fact that it tended to strike the young and healthy. According to a contemporary, Edward Hall, 'this malady was so cruel that it killed some within three hours, some within two hours, some merry at dinner and dead at supper'. Thomas Clinton actually died whilst he was visiting court, along with a number of other courtiers. This was during Bessie's time there and she may well have remembered her future husband's father. She would certainly have recalled that particular outbreak of the sweating sickness which caused the king to withdraw from society, keeping 'himself ever with a small company' and banning festivities that Christmas for fear of infection.[6] Thomas had married Jane, the illegitimate daughter of his father's friend, Sir Edward Poynings. He left a five-year-old son, Edward, who, according to one early biographer, 'was, in the age he lived, one of the most eminent persons this nation then produced'.[7]

Bessie's second husband, Edward Clinton, would later attain a great deal of prominence in England, although, at the time of his marriage to Bessie, he was very far from the peak of his career. He was made a knight of the garter during the reign of Edward VI, for example.[8] He enjoyed something of a martial reputation, serving with the navy in Scotland in 1544, as well as fighting with the king's brother-in-law, Edward Seymour, when he marched on Edinburgh. Like Bessie's brothers, George and William, he would later serve with the king in his campaign at Boulogne. He was once again associated with his brother-in-law, George Blount, when both men were prominent at the funeral of Henry VIII. Clinton was very capable and, even more importantly, adaptable, acting as a trusted official for all three of Henry VIII's surviving children – something which was no mean feat in the troubled years of the mid-sixteenth century. Mary I relied on him to such an extent in the quelling of Wyatt's rebellion early in 1554 that she appointed him as lieutenant-governor of London with his own army when she left the capital after the rebellion had been defeated.[9] He also received a pension from Philip of Spain on his marriage to Queen Mary, although he was evidently not entirely accepted by the government, with Mary's chancellor, Stephen Gardiner, casting suspicion on him in May 1554, something that was probably due to his known Protestant leanings.[10] Clinton remained in favour under Elizabeth I, being regularly appointed as a justice of the peace for the important county of Surrey within months of her accession, for example.[11] He was appointed as Lord High Admiral of England during the reign of Edward VI, a position that he held on and off and with which he became very associated. In 1572 he became Earl of Lincoln. He married twice more after Bessie's death, leaving Elizabeth FitzGerald, who was the 'fair Geraldine' of a sonnet written by Henry Fitzroy's friend, the Earl of Surrey, as his widow. Clinton outlived

Bessie by over forty years, dying in 1585 as one of the most prominent and respected men in England.

Following his father's early death, Clinton's grandfather, Sir Edward Poynings, purchased his wardship from the king.[12] Poynings, who had no legitimate children, was determined to provide for his illegitimate offspring, leaving his daughter, Lady Clinton, fine silk hangings in his will, which was proved in December 1521.[13] He also left bequests to Clinton's two sisters, Isabel and Barbara. He did not forget his grandson in the will, confirming that Clinton should be allowed to remain with his mother, to whom an annuity would be paid during his childhood. Generously, he gave Clinton free choice over his marriage. This was an unusual concession in the sixteenth century, when families usually expected to be fully involved in marriage negotiations and demonstrates the high level of confidence that Poynings had in his grandson. The fact that Clinton bore his grandfather's Christian name suggests that he had always had some involvement in his upbringing and that he respected his grandson's intelligence and ability to choose wisely. In 1532 Clinton was one of the noblemen who accompanied Henry VIII and Anne Boleyn in France to meet with the French king, a mark of his rising prominence.[14] This was followed on 1 June 1533 by his appointment as a cupbearer at the coronation feast of Anne Boleyn.[15]

Why did Bessie choose to abandon the independence of widowhood to embark on matrimony for a second time? Dr Murphy, the biographer of Bessie's son, suggested that the match was not made at the king's commandment and that, instead, the couple were brought together by a desire to unite their Warwickshire lands.[16] Whilst it is true that both had landed interests in Warwickshire, it seems more likely that this was the means by which the couple came to meet, rather than the driving force behind the union. Lincolnshire was the focus of Bessie's life by the 1530s and, given the fact that Clinton also settled there after the marriage and worked to become a leading magnate in the county, it seems highly unlikely that the match was driven by a desire to establish a power base in another county altogether. Almost certainly, the couple had another, simpler reason for their marriage.

Clinton was born in 1512 and was therefore around fourteen years younger than Bessie. A surviving drawing of him from around the time of his marriage shows him to have been a handsome young man with a pleasant face, dark hair and a prominent nose. He and Bessie made a striking couple. Clinton was in his early twenties when Bessie first came across him. Given the fact that Bessie had already refused a higher-status suitor in the king's cousin, Leonard Grey, coupled with the fact that she had no financial or social need to take a further husband, it is almost certain that she and Clinton made a love match. Certainly, Bessie bore her husband three daughters in quick succession.

The terms of Clinton's grandfather's will also made it clear that his marriage was his own choice, demonstrating that his family would not have been involved in suggesting or arranging the match. Bessie's Gower manuscript contains an interesting verse inscribed in the margin under the name 'the Lorde Clyntone'.[17] After Clinton's name, in a different hand, someone wrote 'Elesabyth Talboys', before the first hand continued:

> Your enemy to the most
> Take your part whatever shall
> Though it be churls oft whisper

Neither name is a signature, and it would seem highly likely that it was Bessie who wrote her lover's name during their courtship, with Clinton then writing hers beneath.[18] This would mean that it was Bessie herself who supplied the verse. The verse is cryptic and does seem to suggest flirtation with the playful way in which Bessie described herself as Clinton's enemy before suggesting that she would take his part in anything. On another page someone also added the romantic line 'I have been ever as you do know', although the identity of the writer is not known.[19] It would also be tempting to ascribe this as referring to Bessie and Clinton's courtship. Henry VIII and Anne Boleyn are known to have playfully written passages into a book during their courtship. The evidence of Bessie's book suggests that this was a practice that she and Clinton followed and that, unlike her first match, she made a love match with him.

As with Bessie's first marriage, the date of her second is not recorded. She was first noted as the wife of Lord Clinton in a grant made to her personally by the king of three tuns of Gascon wine yearly from the port of Boston in Lincolnshire, a grant which is likely to have been of great use to her in supporting her household.[20] The grant was made on 12 February 1535. Given that Bessie bore Clinton three children and that she probably died in 1539, a marriage date of 1535 or, perhaps, a year or so earlier, would seem probable. In November 1535 Clinton was finally granted the livery of the lands in his inheritance by the king, effectively taking control of them as a full adult.[21] The coincidence of this grant only eight months after Bessie was first recorded as his wife also supports the fact that their marriage was relatively recent, with marriage always being recognised as one of the ways in which a young man could assert his claims to independent adulthood. Clinton began to be appointed to commissions for the peace for Lincolnshire from July 1536, demonstrating his increased interest in the county, which can only have been associated with his marriage.[22] He was regularly appointed to this role during his marriage to Bessie.[23]

Following their marriage, Clinton set about establishing himself as a power in Lincolnshire, using Bessie's home of South Kyme as his base.

As well as making regular appearances on commissions of the peace, in 1539 he was also appointed as a commissioner to search and defend the Lincolnshire coast in preparation for a potential foreign invasion.[24] Clinton was not averse to using underhand methods to extend his wealth. In 1526 Bessie and Gilbert had entered into an agreement to pay the not insubstantial sum of £7 a year for land stocked with sheep and cattle in Coningsby.[25] After Gilbert's death, Bessie retained the lands, apparently with no complaint until she married Clinton and the rent payments abruptly stopped. In spite of repeated entreaties by the landowner to Bessie herself, no payment was made, suggesting strongly that Clinton took over most of the finances in the marriage, with Bessie surrendering much of her independence. In addition to this, Clinton retained a presence at court, for example sitting as one of the peers at the trials of Anne Boleyn and her brother, Lord Rochford, in May 1536.[26] He was not, during his marriage to Bessie, particularly wealthy. In the subsidy of July 1536, which was based on an individual's wealth, Clinton was assessed at having to pay only £5 for the first payment due, whilst, in comparison, Henry Fitzroy's payment was £90.[27] Given the frequency with which she bore children during her second marriage, it is likely that Bessie regularly travelled with her husband when he made visits to court or to his other lands and estates.

Bessie bore her second husband three daughters. There is no evidence of any other children. The meticulous way that her husband later recorded the birth of his eldest son by his second wife in Bessie's Gower manuscript, which extended so far as noting the time that the baby was born,[28] strongly suggests that, if Bessie did bear any other children who did not survive infancy, none was a son (as, presumably, their birth would also have been recorded). Given the short duration of her second marriage, it would seem most probable that the three daughters were the only issue. The evidence of Clinton's eldest surviving son by his second wife suggests that Bessie's husband was an indulgent parent. Clinton's son, Henry, who later became the second Earl of Lincoln, was renowned for his quarrels with his Lincolnshire neighbours and his generally spoiled behaviour.[29] One particular quarrel was with his nephew, Sir Edward Dymoke, the son of Bessie's daughter Bridget, which began in around 1582. By the late sixteenth century, the Dymokes had inherited South Kyme and other Tailboys family property from the marriage of Gilbert's sister Anne to the first Sir Edward Dymoke, Bridget's father-in-law. Henry Clinton was adamant that the family's inheritance of South Kyme had been at his family's behest, claiming that it had come to the Dymokes through Bessie and then his father, rather than strict heredity. There was no legal basis to Clinton's claim but he continued to pursue it for some years, involving the queen's chief minister, Lord Burghley, in his quarrel. Clinton pursued a vendetta against his nephew and his family, eventually assisting another disgruntled family member, Dymoke's sister,

Mary Shute, in reporting Lady Dymoke to the government for speaking of prophecies. This was found to have no substance, but it is a mark of Henry Clinton's unruly personality that his own son later testified that his father had forced him to seek the lease of land in Horncastle from the king merely because he knew that it was desired by Sir Robert Dymoke. Henry Clinton died in 1616, still making enemies. He has been described as a 'madman' and this may be accurate.[30] What is abundantly clear is that he had a strong sense of entitlement that may well have come from the indulgence of his father in childhood.

Bessie can have played only a very limited role in raising her three younger daughters. It is very unlikely that any of them remembered her, and Clinton's second wife, Ursula Stourton, played the role of mother to them. All three girls grew up to make good marriages to members of the Lincolnshire gentry. Bridget, the eldest, married Robert Dymoke of Scrivelsby, who, as outlined above, came from one of the most prominent local families. The second daughter, Katherine, married William, Lord Burgh, the head of another great Lincolnshire family. Finally, Margaret, Bessie's youngest child, married Charles, Lord Willoughby of Parham, the grandson of Gilbert's turbulent brother-in-law, Sir Christopher Willoughby, and his wife, Elizabeth Tailboys. It is interesting to note that two out of Bessie's three daughters married descendants of Gilbert's sisters, whilst the middle daughter married into the Burgh family with which the Tailboys family had great links. Partly this can be seen as part of Clinton's policy of establishing himself as a Lincolnshire lord and allying himself with the local nobility and gentry. However, the connections had initially been Bessie's and it is not at all impossible that these marriages to Tailboys family members reflected her own wishes for her daughters – anchoring them to a society within which their mother had come to feel at home. With the death of Bessie's eldest daughter, the childless Elizabeth Tailboys, the Tailboys family estates also passed to the families of Gilbert's sisters, allowing Bessie's Clinton daughters to retain a connection with their mother's old home at South Kyme and to make use to the wealth of the Tailboys family.

Clinton found himself deeply involved in the greatest crisis of Henry's reign: the uprising known as the Pilgrimage of Grace. During the summer and autumn of 1536, a number of rumours were circulating throughout England regarding the king's religious policies and the great changes that he had wrought, such as the break with Rome and the beginning of the dissolution of the monasteries. Not unsurprisingly, given the king's appropriation of much monastic property in the mid-1530s, one rumour stated that the king wished to confiscate all the jewels and ornaments of the parish churches – perhaps as a precursor to the dissolution of the churches as well.[31] The dissolution of the monasteries had seen a marked increase in bureaucracy and by the end of September 1536 there were three sets of royal commissioners at work in Lincolnshire.[32] The first was there to dissolve the smaller monasteries in the county, the second to levy a tax subsidy and the third to make a general enquiry into the clergy and, in particular, their fitness for their role and their moral and political leanings. All levels of society resented the commissioners, which gave them common cause against the king's policies. The county suddenly and shockingly erupted into violence on 1 October when the vicar of Louth, a town in Lincolnshire to the north of South Kyme, angrily denounced the commissioners from his pulpit. Following the service the townspeople assembled in order to walk in procession behind the church's three silver crosses. The crowd was tense and when a yeoman called Thomas Foster commented 'go we to follow the crosses for and if they be taken from us we be like to follow them no more', the resentment burst into the open. A cobbler of the town, Nicholas Melton, who adopted the alias Captain Cobbler, took charge and, following his lead, a large crowd gathered again outside the church after evensong, taking the keys to the church from the churchwarden 'for saving of the church jewels'. The following day the townsmen gathered again at the church and agreed to ring the common bell in alarm.

The events at Louth were the spark that lit the Lincolnshire rebellion. Within hours, the townsmen had captured an official of the Bishop of Lincoln, who had had the misfortune to arrive in Louth just as the rebellion got under way. As the rebellion spread, they also managed to capture two of Cromwell's servants. Once Louth was up in arms, the rebellion spread rapidly throughout Lincolnshire, with the king's commissioners being attacked at Caister on 3 October, with only Lord Burgh escaping by means of a fast horse.[33] The rebels actively sought gentlemen and noblemen to act as their captains and the boundary between free support and duress became blurred. Sir William Skipwith, a neighbour of Bessie's and the father of her second son's future bride, for example, went, according to the report of Captain Cobbler, to Louth of his own free will.[34] However, given the fact that he was helped on the road to Louth by a party of rebels, this seems doubtful. Equally, the king's commissioners who were captured at Louth wrote to the king to confirm that they had been met there by 20,000 of the king's 'true and faithful subjects'. This was very far from how the king viewed matters at Windsor when he first heard reports of the uprising on 4 October. By 6 October around 40,000 men had gathered at Lincoln under the banner of the five wounds of Christ. Horncastle had risen on 3 October and at the same time warning beacons were burned along the south side of the Humber which could be seen from Yorkshire. On 7 October the rebels read out their list of demands at Lincoln, which included an end to taxes except in times of war, that the church be allowed to enjoy its ancient liberties and that no more abbeys be suppressed. The rebels also wanted England to be purged of heresy, with the reform-minded bishops, such as the Archbishop of Canterbury himself, deposed and exiled. Finally, they asked that the king agree to take only noblemen as his councillors – a measure aimed at Thomas Cromwell. Henry's response was full of fury, complaining that he was being dictated to by 'the rude commons of one shire, and that one of the most brute and beastly of the whole realm'.[35] With no proper leaders, the Lincolnshire commons eventually dispersed, having received none of the concessions that they had asked for. Matters were not over as, on 7 October, the town of Beverley in Yorkshire rose in support of the Lincolnshire rebels. Soon the whole of Yorkshire had risen, led by the gentleman Robert Aske and a number of members of the nobility. The Yorkshire rebels, who referred to themselves as on a pilgrimage of grace, proved more organised and thus more dangerous to the king and it was only with great difficulty that it was finally quelled.

Bessie and her husband were at South Kyme on 1 October when the rebellion broke out; they were hosting a hunting party at which Gilbert Tailboys' cousin, Sir Thomas Percy, was in attendance.[36] News of the rebellion broke up the party, with Percy immediately returning to his mother's house, where he was sworn to the rebels' cause. Whilst his guest decided to rebel, Clinton threw in his lot with the king from the start. On the very day that the rebellion broke out in Louth, Clinton sent word to Lord Hussey to inform him of the danger.[37] Hussey, who later became deeply involved on the rebels' side and sympathised with them, delayed until the morning of 4 October to respond, sending a message to Clinton at South Kyme, where his messenger found that he had already gone. Whilst the peers and gentlemen tended to be very mobile during the rebellion (either on the side of the king or the rebels), the women remained at home, which strongly suggests that when Lord Hussey's messenger arrived early on the morning of 4 October, it was Bessie who greeted him. She would have remained in her house with her children for the period of the rebellion. She was very lucky that it was only Lord Hussey's messenger who arrived at South Kyme looking for Clinton and not a party of rebels. The Lincolnshire and Yorkshire rebels were certainly not above menacing the families of the men that they sought as their captains. Lord Hussey's wife was confronted by a braying mob early in the rebellion, who threatened to burn down her home and destroy her family if her (already sympathetic) husband did not immediately join with them.[38] Bessie's acquaintance Catherine Parr, who was living with her second husband, Lord Latimer, at Snape Castle in Yorkshire, found herself twice the subject of a mob's anger. Early in the Yorkshire rebellion a mob of rebels surrounded her house, forcing her husband to take their oath before riding away with them as both their prisoner and their leader.[39] When Latimer later defected to the king, a mob once again arrived at Snape, forcing their way inside and abusing Catherine and her stepchildren and servants, before making inventories of their goods. Latimer was in no doubt of the danger his family was in, writing at the time to his friend Sir William Fitzwilliam that 'I learn the Commons of Richmondshire, grieved at my coming up, have entered my house at Snape and will destroy it if I come not home shortly. If I do not please them I know not what they will do with my body and goods, wife and children.'[40] That Bessie was in actual danger during the early days of October is clear from the rumour reported by Robert Carre of nearby Sleaford, which he evidently found credible, that on 5 October both South Kyme manor and Gainsborough Old Hall (the home of the defiant Lord Burgh) had been burned by the rebels.[41] It was probably only the fact that South Kyme did not lie close to the rebel's route from Louth and towards the major towns of Lincoln and Horncastle which prevented the main force from bearing down on Bessie and her children. Nevertheless, she would have been aware of the very real possibility that the local commons would rise in support of the rebellion, something that did indeed prove true when Clinton attempted to raise a force. Bessie and her servants and elder children would certainly have made preparations to fortify the manor as best they could, although even a barricaded door would provide little protection if the rebels were determined to enter to 'persuade' the absent Clinton to join with them.

Whereas on the breaking up of Bessie's hunting party Clinton immediately threw his lot in behind the king, and their guest Thomas Percy sympathised with the rebels, Bessie's exact allegiance is not recorded and is open to speculation. Bessie's religious connections were mixed. One family of Lincolnshire neighbours, the Ayscoughs (or Askews), who lived at South Kelsey, first settled in the county following the marriage of John Ayscough of Yorkshire with Margaret, the daughter of John Tailbois of Stallingborough, a family connection for Bessie.[42] Their grandson, Sir William, who died in 1541, was the father of the famous Protestant martyr Anne Askew. Anne, who was connected to a number of Bessie's acquaintances, such as Catherine Parr and her cousins Lady Lane and Lady Tyrwhitt when she came to London, may well have been known to Bessie. It has been suggested that she had already been known to Catherine Parr, for example, during the future queen's first marriage to the son of Lord Burgh. In addition to this, Anne's sister was married to the steward of the Duke of Suffolk and her brother was a member of the king's household: both connections that had the potential to bring her to the attention of Bessie following her marriage to Gilbert. Anne's husband was a 'Thomas Kyme of Lincolnshire'. He has been identified as a member of the Kyme family of Stickford, who were descended from the de Kyme family which had originally held South Kyme. As such, Anne was also a relative of Gilbert's by marriage which, although the marriage was far from happy, was a further link, particularly as, after being thrown out of her home by her husband, Anne went to stay at Ewerby Thorpe near Sleaford, not far from South

Kyme.[43] Anne Askew proved to be a dangerous connection for the aristocratic women who patronised her due to her great promotion of her reformist religious beliefs. After leaving Lincolnshire, she came to London. In March 1545, she was arrested and, during her interrogation, spoke openly of her hostility towards the mass. She was arrested again in May and, this time, was interrogated under torture by the king's Lord Chancellor.[44] Interestingly, both the younger William Parr and Bessie's kinsman John Dudley were brought in to assist in the interrogation, something which, due to their known Protestant leanings, cannot have been easy for them. Anne herself turned on them, declaring 'that it was a great shame for them to counsel contrary to their knowledge'. Anne was interrogated closely on her relationship to Catherine Parr and other ladies, something that was the precursor to a plot against the queen which nearly brought her to the Tower for heresy.[45] Anne Askew was executed following conviction on the same charge. Her family would at least have been known to Bessie and it is not impossible that she also knew Anne herself. This does not, of course, mean that she shared her beliefs and Bessie's friendship connections, as was common in the mid-sixteenth century, were mixed.

Bessie also had firmly traditional links. Her daughter, Bridget Clinton, married into the Catholic Dymoke family in Lincolnshire. Her husband, Sir Robert Dymoke, who was born in 1537 and was a similar age to Bridget, is remembered as a Catholic martyr. Sir Robert and Bridget were indicted for hearing mass on 24 July 1580.[46] Sir Robert was, by that time, in very poor health and had been confined to his house due to paralysis. This did not stop the Bishop of Lincoln coming personally to him to enquire about rumours that Dymoke and his family followed the Catholic faith. As suspected, he was found to be staunch in his faith and, regardless of his illness, was carried off to prison in Lincoln, where he died later in 1580. Clearly Bridget followed her husband's faith and, whilst Bessie died when her daughter was a very small child, it is not impossible that this was also the faith that her mother adhered to.

Another factor which suggests that Bessie might have had more traditional views can be seen in the adherence during the Pilgrimage of Grace of the wider Tailboys family. A Thomas Tailboys, who was a member of the Raithby Tailboys family, was also caught up in the rebellion, later testifying that a number of priests from Louth had travelled to Bolingbroke, which was close to his home.[47] Tailboys was present at this meeting, reporting that the priests resolved to rebel, stating that 'they would not be so ordered nor examined in their learning'. Although the Raithby Tailboys family were only very distant kin (at best) to the South Kyme Tailboys family, the coincidence of their unusual surnames would have raised the suspicions of contemporaries. More dangerously for Bessie, a clergyman named Thomas Ratford testified that he was staying with her mother-in-law, the elder Lady Tailboys, at

Goltho when he first heard news of the rebellion, presumably during discussions in the household.[48] When he set out for his home he was met by two armed men who ordered him to join the rebels at Horncastle the next day. The elder Lady Tailboys' chaplain, who was known as Sir Edmund, was one of the rebels' leaders, menacing the inhabitants of Barlings Abbey to provide his band with provisions.[49] 'Sir Edmund' had evidently joined with his mistress's grandson, Mr Willoughby, who was described by one informant as the grand captain of the whole host. Bessie and her mother-in-law had decidedly frosty relations and little can perhaps be posited of her own religious beliefs from the elder lady's clear support for the rebel's cause. However, it is certain that many of Bessie's relatives, friends and neighbours were caught up in the rebellion and it is not impossible that she also sympathised. Certainly, the case of Lord Latimer, who joined the rebels, and his wife Catherine Parr, who was an adherent of the religious reform movement, makes it very clear that husbands and wives need not necessarily have supported the same position. When the priory at South Kyme was suppressed a few years after the rebellion, the prior received a sum in compensation in recognition of him being an honest priest. It has been suggested that this might have been at Bessie's intercession, a not unreasonable assumption given her court connections and the fact that she knew the prior personally.[50] The evidence suggests that Bessie had traditional religious beliefs.

Clinton was not particularly pious and had little common cause with the Lincolnshire rebels in October 1536. As a newcomer to the county he was also not tied by kinship loyalties in the same way as Bessie (who had, of course, been in Lincolnshire rather longer) and his neighbours. In 1543 he was upbraided at the same time as Lord Cobham by the Privy Council for having been caught eating meat and keeping an open board during Lent, both practices barred by the traditional Church.[51] He remained in favour, being one of the barons appointed to lead an Irish gentleman, Donoghe O'Brien, into the queen's closet at Greenwich to receive a peerage in July 1543.[52] It is perhaps fair to say that he followed the king's own religious doctrine. He attended parliament as one of the peers in May 1540 when he helped pass a bill relating to the dissolution of the monasteries.[53] Admittedly, in October 1535, when Thomas Cromwell's commissioners visited the priory at Folkestone in Kent in relation to the potential dissolution of the house, Clinton, who owned the nearby manor, claimed to be the priory's founder, something which could suggest some degree of traditional religious belief.[54] However, given that the house, which was apparently in great decay, was a prime candidate for dissolution, it would seem more likely that Clinton sought to be involved in its fate more in the hope of benefitting from a grant of its property and lands than for any religious motive. Clinton, like most members of his class in Henrician England, took an active interest in the property of dissolved religious houses, regularly making suit to the king for their grant.[55] In April 1538 he received the grant of a twenty-one-year lease of the lands of the dissolved monastery of Barlings in Lincolnshire, which had passed to the king following the attainder for treason of the abbot, who had been deeply involved in the Pilgrimage of Grace.[56] This was Clinton's reward for his loyalty to the king during the uprising. In December 1538 Clinton's wealth was further augmented by a lease of land belonging to the former priory of Sempringham in Lincolnshire, which was close to South Kyme. In January 1539 Clinton and Bessie were jointly the beneficiaries of a royal grant of lands belonging to the dissolved priory of Haverholme in Lincolnshire.[57] Bessie's inclusion in this grant is evidence that the king's affection for her remained, in spite of the loss of her son over two years earlier. At the same time, she and Clinton received the actual building and site of the dissolved priory of Sempringham.

As soon as word reached South Kyme of the trouble at Louth, Clinton raised a force of 500 men who, unfortunately, immediately deserted, causing him to flee accompanied by only a single servant.[58] Clinton rallied his stepson, George, Lord Tailboys, with both peers being summoned to attend the king in October 1536.[59] Bessie's brother, William, also served the king during the rebellion, joining the retinue of Sir Adrian Fortescu.[60] Clinton was employed as a messenger by the king, writing to Cromwell on 7 October to inform him that the day before, he had delivered Henry's letters to the Earl of Huntingdon, before setting out immediately for Nottingham, assuming that he would find the Earl of Shrewsbury there.[61] Sadly the Earl had already gone and Clinton set out again. He was hampered both by poor communications and bad weather and found that he could not cross the river that night. At 7 a.m. on 7 October a no doubt exhausted Clinton reached the earl, who was staying in Sherwood Forest.[62] Whilst Clinton found the earl receptive, his was a largely abortive mission, with Shrewsbury writing to Henry that day to inform him that many of the men to whom the king had addressed letters had defected to the rebels, and Clinton had taken the decision not to attempt to deliver them. Only Sir Robert Dymoke, Sir Robert Tyrwhitt and Lord Burgh were reported to be loyal. Clinton's loyalty was conspicuous. At the trials of a number of the rebellion's leaders, including Lord Hussey and Robert Aske, who was the leader of the Yorkshire rebellion, he sat as one of the judges who sentenced them to death.[63] It was his loyalty during the Pilgrimage of Grace which caused his career to prosper, ultimate ending with his ennoblement as Earl of Lincoln many years after Bessie's death.

The choice of the name Katherine for her second daughter by Clinton demonstrates that Bessie retained strong links to her own family and it is reasonable to assume that her own mother stood as godmother to her daughter. Bessie's mother, Katherine, had been rather shadowy during

Bessie's early career but, following the death of her husband, took up a dominant position in the family. This tended to be common in the case of aristocratic and gentry widows.[64] Although it was George Blount, in March 1531, who received a number of royal grants confirming his inheritance of offices that had belonged to his father, his mother remained largely in control of family affairs.[65] A letter from Katherine to Thomas Cromwell survives from 1533, in which she begged the minister for his help in relation to a debt that she owed to one Master Kitson for 400 marks.[66] Bessie's mother wrote from Kinlet that 'I must beseech you to be good master unto me as you have been at all times. Where it pleased you to take the pain to make an end betwixt Master Kitson and me for iiij hundred marks'. According to Katherine, Cromwell had previously arranged that the Duke of Norfolk would take on the debt to Kitson, due to the fact that he held George's wardship. Katherine thought that the matter had come to an end, and was therefore horrified to discover that, after she paid £100 to Norfolk for him to transfer George's wardship to her, the liability for the debt was once again transferred to her, with Norfolk sending her 'word that Kitson will have his money at Candlemas, or else to enter into the land'. The outcome of Katherine's suit is not recorded, but she remained on friendly terms with Cromwell, suggesting that he resolved matters to her approval.

In 1536, Katherine stepped out into the world of politics in order to assist her eldest son, campaigning for his election to parliament. Katherine's letter, one of only four of her missives to survive, provides a fascinating insight into local electioneering:

Pleaseth it your mastership to be advertised, that at the coming down of the king's writ into Shropshire to the sheriff to choose the knights for the parliament, there were of the worshipful of the shire with the justices that sent unto me and willed me to make labour that my son, George Blount, should be one of them, and so I did, my son being at the court; and, moreover, the shire laboured the sheriff that the election should not be appointed at Shrewsbury, because the plague reigned there so sore, but in any wise the sheriff would it should be there, to the intent that the inhabitants burgesses, with the franchise of the town, should assemble themselves to choose one Trentham: and so they assembled themselves riotously, that the worshipful of the shire were not content (saying their voice cannot be heard), and had much to do to keep the king's peace. Whereupon they titled their names and went to the sheriff, willing him to return George Blount, for they would have no other; but in any wise he would not, because the under-sheriff is a dweller in the said town: and then the gentlemen delivered their names to this bearer, being a honest gentleman, to make report, who can advertise you more plainly than I can write (to whom it may please you to give credence), beseeching you to be good master unto my son in this as you have been unto me, and all those that mine be, at all times. And we can do no more but pray for you daily; as we do, as knoweth God, who send you much comfort.[67]

The election was not a fair one, but neither were Katherine's attempts to secure the election of her son, who was uninterested in local affairs, preferring to spend his time at court in London where he was a member of his nephew's household. Katherine was hardly impartial and it seems likely that her attempts to persuade the minister to overturn the election in George's favour may not have been received entirely favourably in Shropshire. It is very clear that Katherine had a close relationship with the minister, and that this also extended to her family. She paid him for his support, with a fee of forty shillings paid by her to Cromwell in November 1536.[68]

In 1540, Katherine wrote again to Cromwell, this time seeking his assistance for the bearer of her letter, one Philip, who in spite of being 'a very honest man and well beloved', had become involved in a dispute with the secretary of the king's bench over some wheat.[69] The matter escalated with the son of Philip's opponent 'knowing that the said Philip with an honest man with him went to dinner to a gentleman cast off his gown and took a sword in his hand and ran after the said Philip and when he out-took the said Philip said nothing to him but then remember how thou handlest my father and then withal strake at his head'. According to Katherine, Philip was only saved from being killed when his companion grappled with his opponent, warning Philip to flee. Katherine begged a favour of Cromwell in her letter, asking him to 'be good lord unto this bearer for the safeguard of his life'. In addition to this favour, Katherine also asked the minister to be 'good lord to a son-in-law of mine one Richard Lacon which is wrongfully troubled and vexed by one Sir Richard Brereton as shall plainly appear before your lordship and other of the king's most honourable council'. Clearly Katherine made it her business to learn of local affairs and troubles and report them to the king's chief minister. She was held in high enough regard by Cromwell to be able to ask favours from him when required, which suggests strong links that probably had their roots in the minister's earlier friendship with John Blount.

Katherine's links to Cromwell were echoed in her daughter's own connection with the chief minister. Bessie had lost her patron when Wolsey fell and it appears that both she and Clinton had some dealings with the king's new chief minister. In July 1538, for example, Cromwell lent Clinton the substantial sum of £100, which was repaid promptly in December of that year.[70] The following September, Bessie's husband showed his regard for the minister by sending him the present of some falcons and a tassel. The pair did business together, with Cromwell purchasing some of Clinton's manors in Kent in December 1539.

With all but Albora of her daughters well married by John Blount's death, Katherine busied herself with providing for her sons' futures. Although George Blount was eighteen at the time of his father's death, he was made a ward of the Duke of Norfolk.[71] By 1533, George had formed a romantic attachment to Constance, one of the daughters of Sir John Talbot, which progressed to such an extent that his indulgent mother 'bought my son of my lord [i.e. Norfolk], and must give him a hundred pounds to the intent that I would marry my son to his comfort, and so I have bargained with Sir John Talbot, for my son'. To emphasise the altruistic nature of this bargain on her part, Katherine, who wrote to Thomas Cromwell to explain her dealings, declared that 'I have no penny of profit by the wardship of my son'. Katherine was one of the contracting parties to the young couple's marriage settlement in March 1536, the year of their marriage, negotiating with Sir John and his wife Margaret.[72] Katherine's dominance in the Blount family is evident from the fact that she had retained full control over her own inheritance, stating in the contract that George was the heir of John Blount 'and also son and heir apparent of the said Dame Katherine'. Katherine consented to settle some of her property on the couple from her own inheritance. In addition to this, Blount family property was promised, after the life interests of first Anne Croft, Bessie's grandmother, and then Katherine had come to an end. Katherine drove something of a hard bargain, as she was able to extract the condition that, in relation to any property in her inheritance in England, the lands would pass first to George's male heirs. In the event that he left no sons, the property would pass to his brother, William, and his male heirs, and then to the third brother, Henry, and his sons. Only in default of all these potential heirs would the property pass to George's daughters, a potentially very valuable concession to the Blount family. Another concession designed to assist her younger sons was that Katherine was left able to bequeath lands from her inheritance worth £40 a year, something that would make a reasonably substantial bequest for a younger son. Both younger sons were specifically mentioned in a clause allowing Katherine 'liberty to grant give or bequeath other lands and tenements also parcel of the premises of her own inheritance to William Blount and Henry Blount her two younger sons to the close yearly value of ten pounds to either of them for time of their life only'. Constance's potential inheritance as one of her parents' co-heiresses was also safeguarded in the agreement. This, coupled with the fact that Constance's parents paid sums of money to Katherine, demonstrates that she drove a hard bargain. George's marriage was long-lasting and evidently happy, with the couple being buried together in Kinlet church. His mother may well have felt that, in spite of the financial difficulties that releasing her son from wardship had brought her, it was money well spent.

The business of providing for her younger sons was evidently on Katherine's mind as she negotiated the settlement with the Talbots as, on 21 February, shortly before she entered into the marriage settlement on George's behalf, she wrote to Thomas Cromwell from her 'poor house at Kinlet' to request a grant of the property of 'certain abbeys and priories' that she had heard rumoured the king intended to take into his hands: 'and if it please his grace so to do I would desire you to be so good master to me as to help that I might take some of them for my two younger sons'.[73] Again, the result of this suit does not survive, but Henry Blount later found employment in the minister's household, suggesting a fondness for his mother. William Blount was later appointed one of Katherine's executors in her will, and both younger sons received a number of bequests, in spite of her promises in George's marriage settlement.[74]

George Blount continued to prosper long after the death of his nephew and sister. Like his mother, George took a personal interest in monastic property during the dissolution of the monasteries in the hope of personal enrichment. In April 1536, Sir Simon Harcourt, a descendant of the founder of Ranston Priory in Staffordshire, wrote to Thomas Cromwell offering money to both him and the king in return for the priory being exempted from dissolution.[75] In the event that this failed, he offered to buy the property as it adjoined his lands in the county. He was right to be concerned about the priory's fate, with Henry, Lord Stafford, writing later the same month to request that Cromwell would persuade the king to grant it to him since it was within four miles of his house and because he had a large number of children to support. He offered to match any other bid for the property, ending his letter by saying that he was concerned because he had 'heard that George Blount endeavours to obstruct my suit'.[76] George, as the uncle of the Duke of Richmond, was a strong contender for the grant, for which he was lobbying hard. The very next day, Stafford also wrote to the Earl of Westmorland requesting his assistance against Bessie's brother who 'makes great suit to have the abbey of Rantone, that I sue for'.[77] In spite of George's hopes, he was unsuccessful in his bid, with Cromwell supporting Stafford's claims. However, the fact that he took action to secure the priory in the face of considerable opposition is clear evidence of George's local prominence. In January 1537 he acted as a good government servant, with the Bishop of Coventry and Lichfield reporting to Cromwell that George had detained a friar, who had dissipated the goods of his monastery and returned to secular dress without authority, whilst they awaited instructions from Cromwell.[78] In 1549, for example, he was prominent enough for his name to crop up in the interrogations following the arrest of

Thomas Seymour, the uncle of the then king, Edward VI, who was later beheaded for treason. Luckily for George, the confession of Wightman, a servant of Seymour's, merely stated that his master was in opposition to Bessie's brother in relation to a law case which only 'touched his own private gain', rather than for any political links.[79] It appears that in this matter George was in the right, with Seymour's own servant agreeing in relation to the case that, with regard to his master, 'wherein the law, by his own counsellor Mr Weston, was declared to be merely against him: But it prevailed nothing to say in those Things; for if he had once conceived Opinion by his own Persuasions, neither lawyer nor other could turn him'. George also regularly served as a member of parliament for Shropshire into the reign of Elizabeth I.[80]

George Blount had a somewhat irascible reputation in Shropshire. According to local legend, 'sheer force of character and a desire for revenge seem to have given him the power to haunt the district for many years after his death'.[81] According to this story, George was so offended by his daughter's marriage that, as well as disinheriting her, he swore that he would haunt her and her descendants. In the years after his death it was reported that his ghost would appear suddenly by a pool which has now dried up on the Kinlet estate. He rode suddenly from the pool on horseback, scattering the local women who were washing their clothes. Occasionally, George would reputedly also appear in a coach drawn by four white horses before driving straight into Kinlet Hall and into the dining room as the occupants ate their dinner. Local legend reported that it was fear of George which caused the old hall to be pulled down in the early eighteenth century, with a new hall being built a little further away from the church and George's earthly remains. Eventually, a group of clergymen exorcised the ghost by locking his spirit into a bottle before placing it under his monument. To add spice to the story, a bottle was indeed found in the church in the late nineteenth century, although enquiries later discovered that this contained photographic material rather than anything supernatural. A large part of this ghost story must be connected with the fact that George's elaborate tomb in Kinlet church, whilst a fine monument, is rather creepy. The figures of George and his family kneel on the top half of the tomb, staring straight out at a visitor, whilst in a cage beneath the tomb there lies the representation of a cadaver. Even in his lifetime George was not always well liked, with his great uncle, Sir Edward Croft, complaining to Cromwell in April 1537 that George was refusing to pay two fee-deer for which he was bound, one in summer and one in winter, as part of Bessie's brother's office as keeper of the forest of Wyre.[82] During John Blount's time this tribute had evidently always been made, with the loss of his deer an added blow to Sir Edward, who found the flesh of a red deer beneficial to his health on account of his age. Later that same year, George was the subject of a complaint that the scholar Dr Henry King made to Cromwell, complaining that after he had been released from an unjust imprisonment, he had found that his goods had been detained by Bessie's eldest brother, who had proved very loath to release them.[83]

George Blount's only son, John, died in childhood from choking on an apple.[84] Following this tragedy, George took the decision to pass Kinlet and his other estates over to his nephew, Rowland Lacon. He died in 1581 and Rowland settled at Kinlet, leaving it to his son, Sir Francis Lacon, on his death in 1610.[85] Sir Francis proved to be something of a spendthrift, even selling Willey, the Lacon family's ancestral home, in 1618. However, Kinlet and other Blount possessions survived to be passed to his daughter, Anne, who married into the Childe family. Their descendants were still in possession of Kinlet in the early twentieth century. The inheritance of Rowland Lacon is generally characterised as a decision taken by Bessie's brother to disinherit his daughter, Dorothy, due to the fact that she married beneath her.[86] Her first husband was a gentleman, although certainly not a match for the heiress to the Blounts of Kinlet. However, there is some evidence that, in fact, relations may have been rather more friendly. Dorothy obviously did not bear a grudge against her cousin, bearing a son in February 1582, shortly after the death of her father, who was named Rowland Purslow, presumably after her affluent cousin.[87] She survived her father by some years, making a second marriage after her first husband's death and leaving children.[88] Perhaps the simplest explanation for her exclusion from what would naturally be considered to be her inheritance was that her father required a male heir, and that it was well understood that the lands and other inheritance were fully his to bequeath as he saw fit. The terms of his marriage settlement had, of course, precluded the succession of a daughter to his mother's inheritance whilst there were male heirs living (although this would also have precluded Rowland Lacon, the son of a daughter, from inheriting).

Bessie's second brother, William, also prospered in the service of his nephew. However, claims that he lived to sire his own family are false. In the early twentieth century one member of the Blount family claimed descent from him, suggesting that he had married a Joan Packington and had a son named Thomas and a daughter named Elizabeth, who married a Richard Jenks of Shropshire.[89] A further son, John, apparently died in infancy. This information evidently came from that collected in a visitation of Kent carried out between 1619 and 1621, which described a family which was descended from William Blount of Waddesley and Glose in Shropshire and had settled at Charlton in Kent.[90] The arms displayed by the family were those of Bessie's family, distinguished by a 'mullet', which is a mark in heraldry used to denote descent from a third son.[91] Whilst this does indeed appear to support the assertion that Bessie's brother was the founder of the family, conclusive proof to the contrary is provided by the visitation taken in London in 1568, which describes the same family.[92] Here William Blount of Wadeley, who married Joyce Pakington, was also noted to have had three children. His eldest surviving son Thomas had, by 1568, produced seven children of his own, with one at least, a daughter named Hester, having already married. Given the fact that Bessie's brother William was probably born in around 1514 or 1515, it would be almost impossible for him to have had a married granddaughter when he was fifty-three years old. It seems more likely that the absence of any spouse or family noted for William in either the Shropshire or the Worcestershire visitations taken in the sixteenth and seventeenth centuries was correct and that he died unmarried and childless. He certainly died young, with his sister Anne acting as his executor in the late 1540s. William Blount of Wadeley can probably be identified as the third son of Humphrey Blount, Bessie's great-uncle, William Blount of Glazeley. Bessie's third brother, Henry, married and produced a family, with a son, George, who was named after his uncle, and settled at Bewdley. Like his cousin, Dorothy, he apparently bore no grudge against Rowland Lacon for taking the Blount inheritance, in his will making a bequest to William Lacon, Rowland's brother, and to his goddaughter, William Lacon's daughter, Ellen.[93]

Bessie, of course, had played a great role in establishing the careers of her three brothers by establishing them in the household of her eldest son, Henry Fitzroy. As Fitzroy grew to manhood, Bessie, her husband and family looked forward to his future prominence and the role that they would play in this. Yet even before the turmoil of the Pilgrimage of Grace, Bessie had suffered a devastating blow with the premature death of her eldest son.

# 19
# BESSIE'S THREE SONS

The death of Anne Boleyn and the king's rapid remarriage to Jane Seymour once again opened up the troubled matter of the succession in England. The first Act of Succession in 1534 had bequeathed the crown to the legitimate issue of Henry VIII and Anne Boleyn and, at the time of Henry's marriage to Jane on 30 May 1536, the two-year-old Princess Elizabeth was legally heir to the throne. This was obviously unsatisfactory for Henry, both on account of the child's sex and her age, as well as the fact that her mother had been publicly shamed as an adulteress and had had her marriage annulled. Whilst Henry never doubted that the intelligent red-headed child was his daughter and, of course, knew the lack of truth in the charges laid against Anne, he was not prepared to leave the throne to Elizabeth. Later that summer, therefore, parliament passed a second Act of Succession, confirming the legitimacy of the king's third attempt at matrimony with a 'right noble, virtuous, and excellent lady'.[1] The Act confirmed that Henry's marriage to Anne had been invalid and that Elizabeth, like her elder half-sister Mary, was illegitimate and barred from the succession. To confirm the point about Mary, whose supporters had hoped that she would be declared legitimate in the wake of her stepmother's fall, Catherine of Aragon's marriage was also confirmed as invalid. The Act stated that Henry's heirs were to be the children of his 'most dear and entirely beloved lawful wife queen Jane' and, if Jane produced no sons, Henry would be succeeded by the sons of a subsequent legitimate wife, with Jane's daughters then taking priority. Given that, in the summer of 1536, Henry and Jane had no children and the new queen showed no signs of pregnancy, the Act in fact left the succession entirely open with no actual heir to the throne in existence. As recognition of this, in a revolutionary move, the Act provided that, in default of legitimate children, Henry could nominate his own heir.

Princess Elizabeth, like her half-sister before her, keenly felt her drop in status, with the infant noting to her governess, 'how haps it yesterday

Lady Princess and today but Lady Elizabeth?'[2] Although Fitzroy was not
expressly mentioned in the Act, it was assumed by everyone, probably
correctly, that the provision allowing Henry to nominate his own heir
would be exercised in his favour in the event that Jane produced no
child. Fitzroy was certainly in everyone's thoughts and, as early as 6 June
1536, the imperial ambassador, Eustace Chapuys, reported in cipher
that there was a great deal of speculation about the succession: 'The
Earl of Sussex stated the other day in the Privy Council in the king's
presence that considering the Princess [Mary] was a bastard, as well
as the duke of Richmond, it would be advisable to prefer the male to
the female for the succession to the Crown. This opinion of the Earl
not having been contradicted by the king might hereafter gain ground
and have adherents.'[3] Henry made no move to quash the rumours that
Fitzroy would be declared heir to the throne. Even the Emperor Charles
V recognised Fitzroy's importance, flatteringly addressing a letter to him
in May 1536.[4]

Henry had probably always viewed Fitzroy as his insurance policy.
As early as April 1527, Henry VIII's ambassadors to the emperor,
when attempting to win Maria of Portugal as a bride for Fitzroy, had
commented that, in the event that her betrothal to the Dauphin of
France (the traditional title for the heir to the throne in that country) was
broken, they would need to 'seek another Dauphin for the daughter',
something that was a clear hint that Fitzroy was a potential heir to the
English throne.[5] Henry's insistence over the summer of 1536 that Mary
recognise her own illegitimacy before she could be reconciled with him,
something that she was ultimately forced to do, is also likely have been
intended to benefit Fitzroy. After all, to paraphrase the Earl of Sussex: if
all the king's children were bastards why not just choose the boy?

Hopes were high over the summer of 1536 that Fitzroy would
be named as heir to throne. However, the young man was, perhaps,
the victim of his own success. His existence showed the king that he
could father a surviving son and he remained determined to produce
a legitimate heir. Catherine of Aragon had become pregnant within
weeks of her marriage, whilst Anne Boleyn had actually been in the
early stages of pregnancy at her wedding. It was therefore confidently
expected that Jane Seymour would rapidly produce a child. In the
early autumn of 1536, at the time of Mary's return to court, Jane was
believed to be pregnant. When Henry declared publicly of his daughter
that 'some of your were desirous that I should have put this jewel to
death', Jane replied, 'that had been great pity to have your chiefest
jewel in England', to which the king answered, patting Jane's stomach,
'nay, Edward, Edward'.[6] This turned out to be a false alarm and it
was not until the early weeks of 1537 that Jane actually conceived
Prince Edward. It is improbable that Henry would actually have named
Fitzroy as his heir unless he was on his deathbed as he always retained

hopes of legitimate sons. When the third Act of Succession was passed in 1545, however, the crown was left first to Prince Edward, then to any children by the king's sixth wife (or a later legitimate wife), with the still illegitimate Princesses Mary and Elizabeth then restored to the succession. If Henry Fitzroy had lived Henry would almost certainly have placed his illegitimate son over his illegitimate daughters. Fitzroy, who would in all probability have taken the role of Edward VI's regent, would have succeeded to the crown as Henry IX in 1553 on his half-brother's premature death. It is also not impossible that an adult son of Henry VIII, who might already have fathered his own sons, might have been preferred to a nine-year-old boy on Henry VIII's death in 1547. Unfortunately, this must only be speculation, but there was certainly a period in the early summer of 1536 when Bessie had hopes of one day becoming the mother of a king.

For the partisans of Fitzroy's eldest half-sister, there were further worrying reports following her reconciliation with her father which was, in part, engineered by Queen Jane. On 8 July 1536, Chapuys reported that, following the reconciliation,

> It was naturally expected – nay, it was the common belief among the people of England – that after the Boleyn catastrophe the king, her father, would immediately proclaim the Princess presumptive heiress to the crown. But if such was ever his intention, he must have changed his mind since, for a statute has lately been made and promulgated, purporting that should the king have no legitimate male children, he can appoint whomsoever he chooses to succeed him on the throne, such appointment and declaration having the same validity and vigour as if it had been made by his own Parliament.[7]

Chapuys was able to reassure his master, the Emperor Charles V, who was Mary's first cousin, that 'There is, however, no fear for the Princess losing her right to the throne of England, for the king's bastard son, – I mean the duke of Richmond, – cannot, according to the prognostication of his physicians, live many months, having been pronounced to be in a state of rapid consumption.' This is the first report that Fitzroy was in poor health, with Chapuys's informants assuring him that the young man's condition was by then extremely worrying. Fitzroy's illness had come on suddenly, with no indication that he was in ill health when he attended the execution of Anne Boleyn. The terms of the second Act of Succession also make it highly likely that he was not then known to be dying, as does the fact that shortly before his stepmother's execution Fitzroy benefitted from some of the spoils, being appointed Chamberlain of Chester and North Wales, an office vacated by one of Anne's 'lovers'.[8] Fitzroy also attended the opening session of parliament on 8 June, walking in procession close to the king himself.[9] Given that this was the parliament which passed the second Act of Succession, it seems highly improbable, given the speculation about Fitzroy's succession, that he was visibly failing. In all probability, he first became ill in the last weeks of June, since his illness was apparently already well advanced by 8 July. He was notably absent from a quadruple wedding that was held at Shoreditch on 3 July between various children of the earls of Oxford, Westmoreland and Rutland, which nearly the entire court attended, including the king himself.[10] Although at first kept strictly secret, by mid-July news of Fitzroy's illness had begun to leak out, with John Husee, the agent of Fitzroy's great-uncle, Arthur Plantagenet, Lord Lisle, reporting on 18 July that 'my lord of Richmond [is] very sick, Jesus be his comfort'.[11] Evidently, Bessie's son's life was already despaired of. During the early days of his sickness, life in his household went on much as before, with Fitzroy's kitchen expenses showing that as wide a range of provisions were purchased as usual.[12] However, from 17 July the amount of provisions purchased dropped sharply, with a further drop from 19 July, which suggests that some of his attendants may have been sent away – perhaps to preserve secrecy regarding his condition.

By 22 July Chapuys was reporting that the king had no hope of Fitzroy's life, something that the ambassador believed was particularly devastating to him due to the fact that he had intended to name his son as his heir.[13] Henry's despair may also account for the fact that he and Jane Seymour left London for Dover around that time, reaching Rochester on 19 July, Sittingbourne the following day, then Canterbury. They were at Dover on 23 July. Bessie's whereabouts are not recorded. Given the fact that her brothers were still within her son's household, she would certainly have known of his illness, even if she was not specifically informed. She was probably at South Kyme in July. Certainly, she is known to have been there on 1 October 1536, only a few months later. There is evidence that Fitzroy was thinking of his maternal family in the last weeks of his life. In an inventory prepared after his death it was recorded that his half-brother George had been given a coat of green taffeta and velvet, which had been delivered personally by Fitzroy's closest attendant, George Cotton.[14] This was not the only small bequest which Fitzroy, who as a minor was not able to make a will, had expressed a wish to make. The closest people in his life were included, with Surrey and Mary Howard also receiving small gifts. Interestingly, in the inventory a number of pieces of plate, including a basin, ewer, two pots and two salts were delivered to 'my lady's grace'.[15] As has been convincingly suggested by Dr Murphy, the fact that Mary Howard was already mentioned by name in the inventory does tend to suggest that she was not the lady in question.[16] Since a similarly titled person in the 1531 inventory is highly likely to be Bessie, she can probably also be identified as the recipient of these small keepsakes of her lost son, something which again demonstrates just how close their relationship was.

Henry Fitzroy died in the morning of 23 July 1536 at St James's Palace in London.[17] The news leaked quickly, with the imperial ambassador Eustace Chapuys writing, rather uncharitably, later that day that the death was no bad thing for the interests of Princess Mary.[18] Less than two weeks later he qualified this remark by adding that 'few are sorry for his death because of the Princess'.[19] Word of his son's death was, of course, brought directly to Henry VIII. The king's reaction appeared bizarre both to his contemporaries and to later observers and Fitzroy's recent biographer has suggested that it 'seems to have been close to the emotional hysteria produced by Anne Boleyn's second miscarriage'.[20] This miscarriage had of course also resulted in the loss of a son. Henry Fitzroy's body remained where he had died for eight days until preparations could be made for his funeral.[21] As a duke and the highest-ranking peer in England, quite apart from being the king's only son, Fitzroy could expect a grand funeral not far off the scale of that accorded to Prince Arthur – Bessie's likely earliest childhood memory. For Henry, however, quite apart from his personal grief for his son, he also had the political fallout from the death to contend with. Henry had always maintained that his failure to produce a legitimate son was due to the invalidity of his marriages: first to Catherine of Aragon, the widow of his brother, and then to Anne Boleyn, who was the sister of a former mistress and may also have been pre-contracted to marry Henry Percy – something that could have invalidated her marriage to Henry. To lose his son – who was, after all, also his proof of his own virility – was a political disaster and cast doubts on all his future hopes for the succession and his chances of siring a legitimate son by his new wife. Faced with this, Henry ordered that Fitzroy's funeral be conducted as secretly as possible, with the body carried in a covered wagon and hidden under straw, with only two liveried officers of his household in attendance at a distance. Henry allowed Fitzroy's father-in-law, Norfolk, to make the arrangements, agreeing to the duke's request that Fitzroy be interred with members of the Howard family at Thetford Priory – a safe distance from London.[22] As it turned out, Norfolk, who was undoubtedly deeply fond of his son-in-law, did not have the stomach for arranging such a dishonourable burial. Although George and Richard Cotton, two of Fitzroy's most trusted attendants, disguised the body in a lead coffin, they were unable (and, perhaps, unwilling) to obtain a closed cart, with the body being conveyed quietly, but not very secretly, out of London.

It would never have been possible to keep news of Fitzroy's death secret, however quietly he was buried, as Henry came to realise in the weeks after his son's death. By 5 August, he had had second thoughts about the dishonourable burial that he had ordered for his son, with

Norfolk writing hurriedly that day to Cromwell, concerned that he had heard rumours that the king was displeased with him. Norfolk was entirely confused, and not a little alarmed, declaring of the rumour that the king had said he deserved to be in the Tower that 'when I shall deserve to be there Tottenham shall turn French'. His initial thought was that the king was displeased with him for not carrying out the burial secretly enough, and it was only later that he learned that, in fact, the king was angry at the lack of ceremony given to his son. Once the initial shock was over, Henry regretted his hasty panic. In September of that year the king personally organised a reward to Fitzroy's officers and servants, something that demonstrates his gratitude for their attendance on the young man.[23]

Henry's grief at the loss of his son did not, however, extend so far as generosity towards the boy's widow, with the king immediately disputing the validity of the unconsummated marriage in the hope of withholding her generous widow's dower. Although the marriage was unconsummated, it had been made between two people above the age of consent and was therefore valid as far as the Church was concerned. Whilst Archbishop Cranmer voiced his certainty over the match in a letter to Cromwell in January 1538, neither he nor anyone else was prepared to directly contradict the king, instead confirming that he would consult with learned men to see if they were of the contrary opinion.[24] Mary pressed her suit for years, growing increasingly frustrated, for example writing to Cromwell in January 1538 that 'I beseech your good lordship to help me, a desolate widow, that by your good means I may obtain my right, and to be a suitor to his highness for me for the same'.[25] She never remarried although attempts were later made to arrange a match for her to Sir Thomas Seymour, something which suggests that she may not have been entirely adverse to taking a second husband. Her main focus in the years following Fitzroy's death was to obtain her dower, with her father writing to Cromwell in an attempt to tug on his heartstrings, recording that 'my daughter of Richmond doth continually, with weeping and wailing, cry out on me to have me give her licence to ride to London to sue for her cause, thinking that I have not effectually followed the same'.[26] Henry VIII also left it to Norfolk to spend a substantial sum from his own pocket on building the boy a tomb sufficient for his rank.[27] Even the king's son's tomb was not safe from Henry's religious policies, with his body and tomb being moved to Framlingham church following the dissolution of Thetford Priory.

News of Fitzroy's death leaked out very quickly. By mid-August it had reached Rome.[28] Charles Wriothesley, a contemporary with court connections, recorded in his chronicle that 'It was thought that he was privily poisoned by the means of Queen Anne and her brother Lord Rochford, for he pined inwardly in his body long before he died; God knoweth the truth thereof.'[29] Henry VIII also reportedly believed that Anne had intended to poison both Fitzroy and his half-sister, Princess Mary.[30] One recent writer has suggested that, whilst Fitzroy's death might have been a 'timely coincidence', its close proximity to the Lincolnshire uprising in October 1536 suggests that it was not a natural death.[31] Under this analysis, it is suggested that Fitzroy had been at Collyweston with a large army intended for Ireland, which, if he had not fallen ill, could have been diverted by him to assist the rebels in Lincolnshire, with the implication that he would claim the crown. In this, it was considered that Bessie, who of course was influential in Lincolnshire, was involved. If this point of view is accepted then Fitzroy's death does begin to look suspicious, with it being suggested that the relatives of Henry VIII's new wife, Jane Seymour, had the most to gain as Fitzroy's death cleared the way for Jane's children.[32] Henry VIII was also apparently involved and it was pointed out that it was not the first time that Henry turned on someone close to him. Poison appears to have been the suggested cause of death in this analysis, with the commentator claiming that Fitzroy had been ill for only three weeks before his death and that it cannot therefore be compared to that which would later kill Fitzroy's younger half-brother, Edward VI. Another recent commentator has suggested that Fitzroy was poisoned, although this time alleging that Henry VIII himself ordered the death, having heard that Fitzroy and his mother intended to lead the Lincolnshire uprising to depose the king.[33]

These suggestions can be entirely discounted. Fitzroy had already parted with Collyweston before Anne Boleyn's death and there is no evidence that he was ever provided with an army, regardless of regular suggestions that he might one day go to Ireland in person. In addition to this, there is no firm evidence that Fitzroy sided with the rebels, although what limited evidence there is does suggest some interest in monasticism. Given the fact that the king allowed his commissioners to be unprotected in Lincolnshire in late September 1536, it appears highly unlikely that he had received word of any organised rebellion in July which caused him to order to death of his son. Whilst Bessie herself had a great deal to gain from Fitzroy becoming king, there is no evidence that she ever contemplated treason. In fact she had no reason too. Whilst he lived, Henry Fitzroy was always Henry's only acknowledged son. In the summer of 1536, Jane Seymour was newly married. Whilst it does appear that she and Henry had a false alarm in the autumn of 1536, there is no evidence that she actually conceived until early 1537, meaning that any attempt by the Seymours to protect her offspring was premature. Jane herself was also not so concerned about the future prospects of her own children: she is known to have spoken up for Princess Mary on a number of occasions, eventually helping in bringing about the reconciliation between father and daughter. Edward Seymour had been a member of Fitzroy's household and, whilst there is no evidence that he was particularly close to him, it seems a step too far to accuse him of murder. Given the lack of evidence of Bessie playing any role in the Pilgrimage of Grace, it is also highly unlikely that she had been one of its instigators – such behaviour would have become known in the interrogations of the rebels, regardless of how conspicuously loyal her husband was to the king. After all, her mother-in-law's sympathy for the rebels came to light.

The assertion that Henry Fitzroy was involved in the Pilgrimage of Grace, with the notion that he intended to lead the rebellion against his father before his rather convenient death, is also highly improbable. All the evidence suggests that the Lincolnshire rebellion was a spontaneous movement, brought about by a particular set of circumstances and, initially at least, led by lower members of society, such as 'Captain Cobbler'. The Yorkshire rebellion, which was informed by that in Lincolnshire, was rather more aristocratic, but neither can be identified as a cohesive movement to remove the king. If they had intended to depose the king, it is unlikely that the rebels would have negotiated with him, preferring instead to sweep south towards London, a route on which they undoubtedly would have encountered some popular sympathy for their cause. Even with Fitzroy's death it is unlikely that the rebels' tactics would have changed much. There were many other men in England with royal blood, after all. Alternatively, the discontented Princess Mary could have potentially made a useful figurehead. Further evidence, more personal to Fitzroy, strongly discounts any involvement. George Cotton, Fitzroy's governor, joined Cromwell's nephew at Ware early in the rebellion, accompanied by twenty men that he had mustered to assist in the king's cause.[34] Cotton, who was one of only two officers to attend Fitzroy's funeral, was very close to his master, and if Fitzroy had been involved in any traitorous plots before his death it is likely that Cotton would have been privy to them. Whilst, after Fitzroy's death, Cotton might have abandoned any allegiance he had to the rebels, it is very unlikely that he would have been so quick to join with the king only eight days after the rebellion broke out when, at the time, the rebels arguably still had the upper hand in Lincolnshire. Even more compellingly, we have Fitzroy's own statement as to whether he would consider being disloyal to the father who had done so much for him and was certainly considering making him his successor to the crown. In November 1536 Lord Darcy, who was heavily involved in the rebellion, had a conversation with Thomas Treheyes, the Somerset herald of arms.[35] During the course of their discussion, Darcy commented that:

> When Thomas FitzGarrad did rebel in Ireland he sent word to the Duke of Richmond, whose soul God pardon, that if he would receive him he would yield to him. And the Duke answered fully wisely and said: By my faith! If I were sure to get him his pardon I

would be glad to receive him; but he that will lay his head on the block may have it soon stricken off.

Fitzroy's comments exhibit a great disinclination to commit treason. Henry Fitzroy, as the king's only living son and a very credible successor to the throne, as well as being the premier peer in England, simply had too much to lose to risk laying his head on the block.

There is also evidence that Fitzroy died of natural causes which must, in any event, be the most likely conclusion given that only one contemporary source actually attributed his death to foul play. In early February 1553, Fitzroy's younger half-brother, the fifteen-year-old Edward VI, contracted a feverish cold. On 1 March, he was forced to open parliament with a ceremony in the great chamber at Whitehall Palace, rather than going in person to Westminster as was customary.[36] Edward had still not recovered by Easter, with his symptoms gradually growing alarming. Interestingly, on 30 May 1553 the imperial ambassador, Jehan Scheyfve, commented to Charles V that:

> The king of England is wasting away daily, and there is no sign or likelihood of any improvement. Some are of the opinion that he may last two months more, but he cannot possibly live beyond that time. He cannot rest except by means of medicines and external applications; and his body has begun to swell, especially his head and feet. His hair is to be shaved off and plasters are going to be put on his head. The illness is judged to be the same as that which killed the late Earl of Richmond.[37]

Scheyfve obviously had informants who were in attendance upon the young king as he was able to give a very detailed account of his last illness. Although he was mistaken in calling Fitzroy 'Earl of Richmond', rather than 'Duke', it does appear that he was otherwise very well informed. Edward's death came only seventeen years after Fitzroy's and many at court, including in all probability some of the physicians and apothecaries called in to advise, would have known both half-brothers. Fitzroy was apparently in good health on 19 May 1536 when he was called upon to witness his stepmother's execution. Equally, on 8 June 1536 a parliament which he personally attended confirmed his possession of Baynard's Castle in London.[38] He died only six weeks later of a disease which was said by a contemporary, Chapuys, to be consumption. Whilst there is very limited information on Fitzroy's final illness, what there is does indeed accord with the death of Edward VI, with the boy king going from robust health to death in only a matter of months. Like Fitzroy, Edward's death has been commonly attributed to consumption, again suggesting a similarity of symptoms as far as contemporaries were concerned.

If Fitzroy did indeed suffer from the same condition as his younger half-brother then he was afflicted with a particularly gruesome death. By late April 1553, Scheyfve was reporting that Edward had only been able to show himself once in recent days, appearing in the gardens at Greenwich Palace to display a body that was wasting away.[39] Edward's symptoms had, by then, become highly unpleasant, with the report that, when he coughed, 'the matter he ejects from his mouth is sometimes coloured a greenish yellow and black, sometimes pink, like the colour of blood'. By mid-June the king was deeply afflicted by fever which never left him, sometimes increasing to a 'violent hot fever' that caused the king yet more agony.[40] By that time the matter that he coughed up gave off a great stench and his doctors despaired of his life. He was unable to keep any food or liquid down and his legs began to swell, forcing him to remain in his bed. By 19 June 1553 Scheyfve reported of the monarch that 'his state is such that the king himself has given up hope, and says he feels so weak that he can resist no longer, and that he is done for'.[41] His suffering was far from over and, by 24 June 1553, he was incontinent and barely able to move. In addition to this, it was noted that 'his nails and hair are dropping off, and all his person is scabby'.[42] The agony was finally over on 6 July 1553, when the young king finally died.

Dr Loach pointed out in her biography of Edward VI that, whilst in the reign of Mary I it was claimed that he suffered from consumption, there was simply no evidence of the previous ill health which would support the diagnosis of such a slow-progressing condition.[43] According to Scheyfve, Edward VI's physicians were 'perplexed' by his illness 'and do not know what to make of it', which strongly suggests that the disease should not be identified as tuberculosis (i.e. consumption), which was well known and common in an increasingly urban society.[44] In addition to this, Loach pointed out that reports of Edward's condition, which mentioned coughing but little blood, do not accord with the general symptoms attributable to a consumptive. Instead, all accounts of the king's final illness focus on his fever and the fact that he was coughing up infected matter which was foul-smelling. According to Loach, 'theses symptoms strongly suggest that Edward developed a chronic infectious disease in the chest, in technical terms a suppurating pulmonary infection'.[45] This seems highly probable as such an infection would begin with a feverish cold, before developing into bronchopneumonia. This would eventually lead to septicaemia, an infection to which Edward's symptoms strongly point, and which would cause kidney failure and, ultimately, death. Although no account of Fitzroy's own symptoms survive, the fact that a healthy young man was struck down in a very short space of time, coupled with the obvious belief by some contemporaries that Edward VI suffered from the same condition, does suggest that something of the symptoms suffered by Edward must have been seen in Fitzroy. The most likely cause of his death must therefore be a chest infection and septicaemia: the same illness which, in all probability, claimed the life of Edward VI. If this is the case, Bessie's son must have suffered terribly in his final weeks and it is no surprise that his father kept him closeted away from the prying eyes of the court.

The loss of her eldest son, upon whom her hopes for the future rested, must have been a great blow to Bessie. She had played a distant, but very real, part in raising her son and had built a relationship with him during his short life. It was only Bessie's own early death which prevented her from suffering a similar tragedy in relation to both her two younger sons, George and Robert Tailboys.

George, Lord Tailboys, showed every sign of growing into a man of great promise. In July 1536, when he was thirteen years old, he took his seat in parliament for the first time as Lord Tailboys of Kyme.⁴⁶ Although Bessie did not hold her son's wardship, she remained close to him and he may have spent much time in her custody. In February 1537, for example, she and George received the joint grant of the offices of bailiff of the manor or lordship of nearby Tattershall Castle, as well as being appointed as keepers of the great park and chase there and other areas within the manorial estate.⁴⁷ Given Bessie's love of hunting, this must have been a welcome grant and was perhaps one that she petitioned the king personally for. It also made sound local sense for Bessie and George to take on the governance of Tattershall Castle which, after all, was so close to South Kyme that it could be seen from there – ensuring that no new power was introduced into the Tailboys family's sphere of influence. By the late 1530s George was granted more autonomy in his own affairs, with a report made to the king of his lordship of the strategically important, but dilapidated, Harbottle Castle, recommending that George should either be compelled to repair the castle or that the king should take it into his own hands and pay the young lord compensation.⁴⁸ Whilst George remained a minor, his affairs were under the ultimate control of Sir William Fitzwilliam, who had newly been ennobled as the Earl of Southampton and who served as Lord Admiral following Fitzroy's death. Fitzwilliam had been granted George's wardship following Gilbert's death and, whilst Bessie is likely to have retained custody of her son, it was the Admiral's decision whom he should marry.

Bessie was still living in February 1539, although she had died by January 1540. It is therefore probable (although not certain) that she was aware of the marriage made for her second son. If so, there was a certain circularity to the match which may have amused her. In a letter written on 3 January 1538 to his employer, Lord Lisle, John Husee, who was then resident at court, wrote to update the peer on court gossip, informing him that:

> My lord of Wiltshire is again now in the Court and very well entertained. The election lieth betwixt Mrs Mary Shelton and Mrs Mary Skipwith. I pray Jesu send such one as may be for his Highness' comfort and the wealth of the realm. Herein I doubt not but your lordship will keep silence till the matter be surely known.⁴⁹

'Mary' Shelton almost certainly refers to Margaret (or Madge) Shelton, a cousin of Anne Boleyn and a probable mistress of the king. The return to court of her uncle, Thomas Boleyn, Earl of Wiltshire, may have had something to do with her influence at court. The second lady mentioned in what was obviously a highly confidential piece of gossip was Margaret (rather than Mary) Skipwith, the daughter of Sir William Skipwith, a Lincolnshire gentleman. Muriel St Clare Byrne, in her commentary in relation to this letter suggested that Henry was casting an appreciative eye on both ladies, evidently to make one of them either his mistress or, perhaps, his wife.[50] In January 1538 Henry was between queens, with the premature death of Jane Seymour leaving a vacancy for the office. Although he was busily negotiating for a foreign alliance, it is not impossible that he also considered the possibility of another English match, a course that he had already taken twice before. In his negotiations with Christina of Denmark, a niece of the emperor, it was concluded by Henry's ambassadors to be advantageous that she resembled one Mistress Shelton, again demonstrating that the king's interest in one at least of the two ladies mentioned by Husee was reasonably well known.

Decisions relating to George's marriage were at Fitzwilliam's discretion due to the fact that he held his wardship. On 17 April 1539 Margaret's uncle, Sir Thomas Heneage, wrote to Cromwell to confirm the king had given his consent to a match between Margaret and George, commanding that it would be well to have them married as soon as possible.[51] Matters were evidently conducted with some secrecy, with John Husee informing his master on 26 April 1539 that 'it hath been shewed me that Mrs Skipwith shall marry the Lord Tailboys. This it shall please your lordship to keep secret till you hear more.'[52] The reason for this secrecy, or even Lord Lisle's interest in the match, is unclear, particularly as on 15 May 1539 Husee deemed it important enough to inform Lady Lisle that 'the Lord Tailboys is married' with no further comment.[53] St Clare Byrne commented in her analysis of the Lisle Letters that Henry's interest in the marriage could have been merely due to the fact that George, as a minor heir, was still under royal control. However, she also speculated that the reference to Margaret Skipwith as a potential love interest for Henry, coupled with the king's interest in her marriage and the secrecy with which it was conducted, 'perhaps justify the suspicion that the youthful George was happy to follow obligingly in his father's footsteps for the sake of an attractive young wife and the enjoyment of his own inheritance at sixteen, instead of having to wait until he was out of wardship at the age of twenty-one'.[54] Although evidence for Margaret's relationship with the king is scant, this does indeed seem highly probable. She was one of a select party of ladies invited by Henry to view his fleet at Portsmouth in August 1539, an event which included gifts, cheer and entertainment laid on for the ladies, although the king himself was not present.[55]

Margaret was a very beautiful and accomplished woman (very similar to her mother-in-law, Bessie). She certainly inspired devotion in her second husband, Peter Carew. Carew, who knew George when the pair were in Calais together at the end of 1539 to welcome Anne of Cleves, came into contact with his friend's young bride on their return to England. He later declared that he fell deeply in love with Margaret whilst at court, finding himself 'wrapped in Venus bands, and stricken with Cupid's darts'.[56] Following George's death, Margaret attended court regularly, where Carew proceeded to court her. Margaret was, at first, entirely uninterested in Carew, who, as a younger son, had no great prospects. However, in a move similar to that employed by Lord Leonard Grey when he sought to make Bessie his bride, Carew enlisted the support of Henry VIII himself:

> The king at first seemed to strain courtesy at the matter, neither would have any good liking thereof: nevertheless, in the end, he did so consider of the worthiness and nobility of the gentleman, that he did not only grant his request, but also wrote his most earnest letters unto the lady in his behalf, and promised also to give with that marriage a hundred pound land to them and to the heirs of their bodies.[57]

Henry's interest and, in particular, his financial outlay is interesting and again suggests a past connection between him and Bessie's daughter-in-law, as his continued good relationship with Bessie after the end of their affair also indicated. Margaret was finally persuaded to accept Carew, a decision which may have been assisted by the death of his elder brother. The couple were married on the day of the coronation of Edward VI. That very day the romantic Peter Carew jousted in a tournament, wearing Margaret's glove upon his headpiece to show his devotion as Ulysses to his Penelope.[58] Margaret Skipwith outlived her second husband, marrying for a third time in 1579 before dying in 1583. If Margaret Skipwith was indeed Henry's mistress, she was not the only one of Bessie's daughters-in-law to whom the king's eye turned, with rumours in the 1540s that the king would make Mary Howard his mistress.

As well as the king's interest in Margaret after George's death, there were further similarities in her match to George Tailboys and Bessie's to Gilbert. With his marriage, George Tailboys was able to take on a more active role in his inheritance and in public affairs, and his guardian, the Earl of Southampton, arranged for him to be one of the noblemen who accompanied him to Calais in December 1539 to receive the king's affianced bride, Anne of Cleves, on her journey to England, something that was a very significant honour.[59] He was one of the noblemen to meet the new queen outside Calais, before escorting her to the last English possession on the continent.[60] As a minor, George had no control of his property, something that was rectified by a private Act of Parliament in which he was granted the use of his lands and the ability to settle a dower on his wife 'at the humble suit, petition, and special instance of the said Earl [of Southampton], and also for the good and faithful service that the said Gilbert the late Lord Tailboys and his ancestors hath done unto his highness and his progenitors'.[61] The Act itself is an unusual one and the king and Fitzwilliam had no need to relinquish control of George's property for another five years. The enactment is very similar to that provided for Bessie at the time of her marriage to Gilbert and also to the evidence of Elizabeth Carew's letter to Cromwell which stated that the king had provided for her at her marriage. It is highly probable that Margaret Skipwith, like her mother-in-law before her, had indeed been a mistress of the king's and that George, like his father before him, provided a convenient and willing spouse when the king looked around to reward a former love. Just what Bessie would have thought about this is not recorded, if indeed she was still alive to witness the wedding in May 1539.

George sadly did not long survive his marriage, dying, like his half-brother, in his late teens, in September 1540. As will be discussed, Bessie was almost certainly no longer living at that time and so was spared the loss of another son. George had been a well-liked and pleasant young man, with his guardian, the Earl of Southampton, writing in a letter to the king 'thus having none other news to signify, but that your Majesty hath lost a great treasure of my Lord Tailboys, whom if worldly goodness would have preserved, would to God I have bestowed and spent all I have under your grace in this world to have him alive, for in mine opinion a more toward and likely gentleman to have done your Majesty service had ye not within your realm: but the will of God must be fulfilled'.[62]

Very little information survives about Bessie's third son, Robert Tailboys, who succeeded his brother as Lord Tailboys and was the last person in the direct male line of the ancient family. Given the fact that his signature is included in Bessie's Gower manuscript, it would seem likely that mother and son were close.[63] His age is not known although, based on the dates of his elder brother's birth and his father's death, he must have been born between 1524 and 1530, meaning that, at the time of his death in 1542 he was still a minor. Since there is so little information recorded about him, a date closer to 1530 would seem likely. The loss of all three of Bessie's sons in their teenage years was an all too common disaster in Tudor families and one echoed in the fate of the king's own two sons, Henry Fitzroy and Edward VI. It has been speculated that both of Bessie's younger sons died of consumption.[64] Given that he was well enough to travel to Calais at the end of 1539, it would appear that, like his half-brother, George was not the victim of a long illness, making consumption unlikely. The cause of his death is actually entirely unrecorded. No information survives about Robert's death.

For Bessie, the loss of Henry Fitzroy would have been the biggest blow of her life. As he grew up and the king continually failed to produce a legitimate son, Bessie must have become increasingly hopeful that she would one day live to see him reign as king. In this, she was disappointed. With the loss of her eldest son, Bessie's prominence receded and the last years of her life are obscure.

# THE DEATH OF BESSIE BLOUNT

Following Henry Fitzroy's death, Bessie slowly faded into obscurity, with her contemporaries taking little interest in a woman who was no longer the mother of the king's son. In spite of this, and regardless of the fact that the date of Bessie's death was not even recorded, it is possible to reconstruct something of the last few years of her life.

There is some evidence that Bessie had cause to consult a physician in the years before she died. In the Tudor period, there were three types of medical practitioner: a physician, who was responsible for diagnosing conditions and prescribing medicines; a surgeon, who performed more menial tasks; and an apothecary, who made up the medicines.[1] The physician would be a university graduate and relied on ancient Greek philosophy, as well as the knowledge of the ancient world as the basis of his profession. A central belief was that the body contained four humours, with ill health caused by an imbalance in these elements. In spite of their learning and the evident authority that they possessed, it has been pointed out that 'hardly any of the medicaments available in medieval times had a specific value in treating disease and there was therefore a strong tendency to put as many ingredients as possible in a medicine in the hope of doing some good'.[2] After 1512 it was necessary for physicians to be licensed by their local bishop, something which must have provided some reassurance for Bessie and other patients. The system was, however, largely unworkable and a number of scholars set themselves up as physicians with only a very limited ability to heal or cure anybody.

The evidence for Bessie's own medical treatment is contained within a small manuscript volume which is held by the British Library and inscribed as 'Hugo Glyn Dr in physic his medicines practice in physic 1555'.[3] In a separate entry on the same page it also confirms that 'this book was writ by Hugo Glyn Dr of Physic'. The book contains a number of prescriptions and details of cures compiled (although not necessarily all prescribed) by Dr Glyn. Anyone driven to seek some of the cures included in the book must have been desperate. For example, the cure for scrofula, or 'king's evil', advised the patient to boil the fat of a serpent and apply it, mixed with some other ingredients, to the body with cotton.[4] An alternative cure, for the same condition, recommended boiling the feet of a toad when the moon was in an auspicious position. There were cures for patients with 'stinking breath'[5] or who had lost their voices.[6] The dung from a gander was required to help draw out a thorn or a splinter,[7] whilst to cure scabies required the relatively tame procedure of stamping garlic and onions in water and washing the scabs with the resulting mixture.[8] A rather more imaginative cure recorded that 'to gather fleas together anoint a staff with the grease of a deer, fox, or bear or badger or hedgehog: make a hole in the frame of a great hour glass in the top and bottom, put in a great stick, anoint it with turpentine the fleas will stick fast about it'.[9] The entry for this particular remedy confidently stated that it was 'Proved'. The remedies contained in the book were not entirely medicinal, with one providing advice on how to remove ink stains from linen.[10] Interestingly, on one of the early pages of the book, there was a recipe for 'the young lady Taylboys' for a pain in her head.[11]

It is obviously necessary to identify this young lady Tailboys. Hugo Glyn, a Welshman, who was the owner and compiler of the manuscript, was a somewhat colourful character who, in 1556, was appointed as one of the proctors of the University of Cambridge.[12] His contemporary, John Caius, who was also a doctor of medicine, refounded Gonville Hall at the university as a new college which bore both his name and its original: Gonville and Caius College. Dr Caius was responsible for compiling the statutes for his new foundation, including the prohibition that no one could be elected as the master, a fellow or a scholar who 'is deformed, dumb, blind, lame, maimed, mutilated, a Welshman, or suffering from any grave or contagious illness, or an invalid, that is sick in a serious measure'.[13] The prohibition against Welshmen in a list which otherwise deals with physical complaints is noticeable. It has been suggested that Caius included his prohibition against Welshmen due to his relations with Glyn, who had been a fellow of the college before leaving the university to practise medicine in Wales shortly after Caius became master. Glyn had been an active member of the college, donating a number of valuable volumes to the library only six weeks before his hasty departure.[14] He had obtained his first degree in 1548 or 1549, following this with a master's degree and then a doctorate a few years later.[15] He practised medicine in Chester in the 1550s, although it is improbable that he would have been practising during Bessie's own lifetime, so he was almost certainly not the physician to treat her. This does not necessarily mean that the prescription in the notebook was not for Bessie, however. It has been suggested that the notebook was compiled by Glyn during his medical studies, something which suggests the information contained within would not necessarily have related to his own practice.[16] This is supported by the fact that some prescriptions are known not to have been Glyn's own work, such as that of a Dr Francis which is contained on one page of the notebook. There are also multiple cures listed for the same ailment, such as the cure for king's evil, which suggests more than one physician's work was included. On one page there was a reference to a 'Cordial Henry Octavi',[17] which suggests a remedy created during the lifetime of Henry VIII, who died in 1547, some years before Glyn began to practise. Chester, where he practised, also had no particular significance for any of the four sixteenth-century women called Lady Tailboys, again demonstrating that Glyn was not likely to have been their physician.

It is necessary to demonstrate who the young Lady Tailboys was. Bessie's mother-in-law, the elder Elizabeth Tailboys, did not die until 1559. Bessie's daughter, who was also Elizabeth, Lady Tailboys, had not acquired a higher title through marriage by 1555, suggesting that she could have been the patient to have consulted Glyn. In the Latin petitions which she commissioned the scholar Roger Ascham to prepare on her behalf in 1554 and 1555, for example, she was referred to as 'Lady E.T.', demonstrating that she was still known as Lady Tailboys, rather than Lady Dudley.[18] However, in 1555, when the book was compiled, there were in fact three women known as Lady Tailboys: Elizabeth Gascoigne (Gilbert's mother), Bessie's daughter Elizabeth, and Margaret Skipwith, the widow of Bessie's son George, who retained her title until her death. Given that there were then two young Lady Tailboyses it seems more probable that the prescription dates to a time when there was only one young Lady Tailboys. This would be during Bessie's marriage to Gilbert, her widowhood and, perhaps, during her marriage to Clinton when she was occasionally still known by her previous title. Bessie is the most plausible candidate for Glyn's young Lady Tailboys, with the prescription probably dating to between 1522 and 1535 or, perhaps, up to 1539 when George Tailboys married. One note of caution is that it is just possible that the prescription was given to Margaret Skipwith between 1539 and 1542 (after Bessie's death but before the younger Elizabeth's inheritance of the Tailboys title). However, on the balance of probabilities, it is more likely to have been Bessie's.

Bessie suffered from headaches serious enough to cause her to take medical advice from a physician who either prescribed or was associated with men who prescribed some of the more unusual remedies included in the notebook, which, even in the sixteenth century, would hardly have been considered to be mainstream. Bessie's prescription was comparatively gentle, advising her to comb her hair with a violet liquid. She also received a recipe for 'a perfume for the head'. Bessie may have had a lucky escape as, ominously, on the very next page of the book, there was a note on how to 'open the head', a procedure which would have had to be carried out without anaesthetic in the sixteenth century.

The evidence of Dr Glyn's notebook suggests that Bessie was in some ill health during her lifetime. She certainly died young. It used to be thought that the reference in the diary of a London contemporary, Henry Machyn, from 1551 referred to Bessie when it said 'the iiij day of September died my lord Admiral [i.e. Clinton's] wife in Lincolnshire, and there buried'.[19] This in fact refers to Clinton's second wife, Ursula Stourton. With Henry Fitzroy's death, the notice that contemporaries paid to Bessie began to dwindle and the date or cause of her death was not recorded. She had died by June 1541 when a grant was made by the king to Clinton and his wife Ursula of a manor in Lincolnshire.[20] In June 1541 Bessie would only have been around forty-three years old, so she clearly died young, at most only around eight years after her second marriage. The last certain recorded references to her also date from early 1539. In January 1539 Bessie and Clinton jointly received a grant of some monastic property from the king.[21] On 6 February 1539 Bessie and her eldest surviving son, George, were jointly the beneficiaries of a further grant in relation to Tattershall Castle.[22] There is no certain further reference to Bessie in surviving records, demonstrating that she must have died between 6 February 1539 and June 1541.

There is one further potential reference to Bessie which needs to be discussed when the time of her likely death is analysed. The king's fourth wife, Anne of Cleves, arrived in England at the end of December 1539 and was married early in the New Year. In advance of her arrival, the king appointed a household for her, with the great ladies appointed to attend the new queen as her principal servants being the king's niece Lady Margaret Douglas; Bessie's daughter-in-law, the Duchess of Richmond; the Countess of Sussex; and Ladies Howard and Clinton.[23] The question must be asked – was this 'Lady Clinton' Bessie, or was it her mother-in-law, Jane, Lady Clinton. Bessie's earlier biographer, Childe-Pemberton, believed it to be Bessie.[24]

In November 1535 it was recorded in a grant to Clinton that his grandmother, Anne, Lady Clinton, and his mother, Jane, Lady Clinton, were still alive, with Jane by then the wife of Sir Robert Wingfield.[25] Anne, Lady Clinton, can be discounted as one of Anne of Cleves' great ladies on account of her age. Jane, Lady Clinton, however is very likely. Although she was Bessie's mother-in-law, she was actually similar in age to her due to the age difference between Bessie and her young husband. Clinton and his mother had a poor relationship, with his mother writing to her friend, Lady Lisle, in November 1538 that 'I am sorry that my son can so little good that he hath not seen your ladyship since your being at London, for is a token that he hath little love to me'.[26] The cause of this animosity is not known. It might, perhaps, have related to Lady Clinton's second marriage, or even Clinton's own match with Bessie, who, as an older woman and a former mistress of the king, was not necessarily an ideal daughter-in-law. Bessie, of course, did not have the best record of being friendly with her mothers-in-law. During her second marriage, to the diplomat

Sir Robert Wingfield, Lady Clinton resided mainly at Calais, which accounts for her friendship with Lady Lisle, the wife of the governor of the city.[27] Wingfield died in March 1539, with his widow remaining in Calais.[28] Lady Clinton would therefore have been very well placed to have secured an appointment with Anne of Cleves, who arrived in Calais in December 1539 in order to cross the Channel to England. The last mention of Lady Clinton in the Lisle Letters, in which she had previously been mentioned with some regularity, was in August 1539, something which would again suggest that she returned to England with the new queen in December.

Further evidence that the Lady Clinton in question was his mother rather than his wife can be seen in Clinton's own conduct. On May Day 1540, he took part in a great court joust at Westminster.[29] Although the king's jousting days were long behind him, he and his fourth wife, Anne of Cleves, witnessed the spectacle before the entire company moved to Durham Place for a feast and entertainments. The sports lasted the best part of a week, with Clinton an active participant. The evenings were spent in feasting and merriments, frequented by the ladies of the court. Some period of mourning was expected of a Tudor husband, which would preclude an appearance in a tournament in the weeks after a wife's death. Even Henry VIII shut himself away for a time after Jane Seymour's death, although, within days of her loss, his ambassadors had begun making discreet enquiries about available foreign princesses. If Bessie was the Lady Clinton who served Anne of Cleves, this would arguably place her death between May 1540 and June 1541, making it all the more surprising that she received no further royal grants after February 1539.

Whilst it is possible that Bessie did indeed serve Anne of Cleves, the evidence suggests that it was, in fact, Jane, Lady Clinton, who acted as the queen's great lady, something that would have been more tactful than the king placing his former mistress with his new bride. This is further supported by the fact that Bessie was not included in her mother's will, which was drawn up on 2 January 1540, the day after Henry VIII's first meeting with Anne of Cleves. In her will, Katherine mentioned all her children except Isabel and Bessie. Isabel died before 1540 and Bessie's exclusion would suggest that she was also already deceased. There is one mention of a person connected with Bessie which almost certainly clears up the mystery of what became of Bessie Blount.

In her will, Katherine referred to 'Margaret christchild of my daughter Lady Elizabeth'. The logical conclusion would be that she was referring to one of her daughter's godchildren. However, this seems unlikely given the fact that this Margaret's full name was not given, something that would be unusual for someone who was not a blood relation. Bessie's youngest child was Margaret Clinton and this reference almost certainly relates to her. Evidently Katherine, who did not leave anything to Bessie's other children, had a special reason for including Margaret. This was almost certainly linked to Bessie's death.

Death in childbirth was all too common for women in the sixteenth century, with two of Henry VIII's wives and his own mother succumbing to it. Whilst it more commonly afflicted women during their first confinement, it was by no means limited to the first birth, with Queen Elizabeth of York dying following her eighth confinement in 1503, for example. The evidence of Dr Glyn's notebook suggests that Bessie was not in the best of health and, by the late 1530s, she was rather old to be bearing children with regularity. Assuming that she married Clinton in 1535 and died in 1539, her first daughter would have been born in, perhaps, 1536, with the second in 1537 or 1538 and the last in 1539. This would be a birth approximately every eighteen months which, to a woman in poor health, who was by then approaching forty and had already borne around six children to the king and her first husband, would have placed a considerable strain on her. The Clinton title was an ancient one and Edward Clinton had no brothers, hence the need for a male heir, and Bessie's would have been aware that, at around fourteen years older than her husband, she had little time in which to deliver one. The birth of two daughters in succession would have pushed her to immediately try for a son, something that Clinton, along with all men of his class, desired. Certainly, he was excited enough about the birth of his eldest son by his second wife to record the birth in Bessie's Gower manuscript, something that was not done for the birth of any of his other children. A woman who had already reached forty and was in ill health and worn down by regular childbearing would have all too easily fallen a victim to complications either during the birth or an infection following it.

The reference to Bessie's youngest child as her 'christchild' in Katherine Pershall's will supports the suggestion that Bessie did, indeed, die in childbirth. The idea of a death in childbirth held a particular religious significance in the early modern period, particularly following the advent of Protestantism when people who had died a good death were commonly referred to as saints. One historian has recently commented that 'women's death in childbed held a special significance: in the early modern period such women became intimately connected to a set of interrelated ideas about Eve's sin and all women's punishment for that transgression, Mary's giving birth to Christ, and a Protestant mother's spiritual instruction to her children'.[30] The Virgin Mary was seen as the woman who redeemed the female sex following Eve, as well as a source of redemption in general. Under this analysis, it is pointed out that a virtuous woman in the early modern period in which Bessie lived was a domesticated version of the Virgin Mary, with maternity as an essential part of this: 'thus, women who died during or just after enduring such suffering became peculiarly revered, particularly within their own families, such "sainted sisters" showed their sisters how they should live and how they should die'.[31] This fits with an analysis of Katherine Pershall's will as revering the memory of a daughter who had made a good death and, effectively, redeemed her past sins to be recalled, by her family at least, as a holy or saintly figure. That this was an idea current in the early modern period can be seen in a sonnet by John Milton, who wrote in the mid-seventeenth century regarding a vision that he had had of his wife, who had died in childbirth within a year of their marriage. In Milton's poem, his wife came to him:

> Methought I saw my late espoused saint
> Brought to me, like Alcestis, from the grave.
> Whom Jove's great son to her glad husband gave,
> Rescu'd from death by force, though pale and faint.
> Mine, as whom wash'd from spot of child-bed taint
> Purification in the old Law did save,
> And such, as yet once more I trust to have
> Full sight of her in Heaven without restraint,
> Came vested all in white, pure as her mind:
> Her face was veil'd; yet my fancied sight
> Love, sweetness, goodness, in her person shin'd
> So clear, as in no face with more delight.
> But O, as to embrace me she inclin'd,
> I wak'd; she fled; and day brought back my night.[32]

Milton's wife – the circumstances of her death being alluded to in the poem – appeared as a redemptive figure. In Christianity, of course, Christ redeemed everyone in the world, something which again fits with Katherine's description of Bessie's youngest child as a 'christchild': through childbirth and the mother's death, the baby redeemed the mother's past sins. Bessie, of course, was well known to have committed sins with the king, something about which the evidence suggests her parents may not have been entirely happy. Death was a very real risk for all women embarking upon childbirth and it is therefore not surprising that they may have looked for inspiration in the deaths of those who did prove unlucky. For women, death in childbirth can arguably be compared to death in battle for a man. Like a soldier, a woman in childbirth was doing her duty (in her case, ensuring the continuation of her husband's family into the next generation). Soldiers were (and remain) often revered for their good death in battle and the evidence of the will suggests that Bessie met her own good death which, whilst drawing her life to an end prematurely, did at least serve to redeem her in the eyes of her contemporaries, something which, given the claim by one acquaintance that she had encouraged women into concubinage, may have been badly needed. It is perhaps pushing the evidence too far to suggest that the reference to Margaret as a 'christchild' might even suggest that she was born by a Caesarean birth, with such children being referred to by contemporaries by such terms as 'not of woman born', 'the fortunate' and 'the unborn', for example.[33] Given that the operation, which was known from antiquity onwards, had a particularly spiritual nature, such an interpretation of the reference in Katherine's will is not impossible. Such operations were performed only on deceased mothers when the midwives believed that the baby was still living and, thus, could be baptised before their death. These children were not expected to survive and rarely did so, leading to a special religious significance. As one historian has commented, 'no other medical procedure was so directly linked to spiritual salvation or damnation'.[34] The operation, although rare, was well known in Bessie's time, with the later sixteenth-century physician Francois Rousset writing a treatise advocating the operation's performance on living women, whom he believed could survive the procedure.[35] Henry VIII's third wife, Jane Seymour, was commonly believed by contemporaries to have undergone the procedure in 1537, with a contemporary ballad declaring that 'they opened her two sides, and the baby was found'.[36] Given that the queen survived the birth by more than a week, and was well enough to attend her son's christening, this is impossible. However, it is not entirely impossible that the religious significance evidently accorded to Margaret in her grandmother's will might have hinted at the child being one of 'the fortunate', surviving the death of her mother before she was even born. This can only be speculation, but the reference to Margaret in Katherine Pershall's will does make it a possibility.

Another recent historian has considered the accounts of the lives of fairly ordinary women which were produced in the seventeenth century:

> Works such as this would combine with accounts of women dying well in childbirth in order to encourage women in their vital role within Early Modern society as producers of heirs and nurturers of children. Thus a woman relying upon accounts of other women in death for courage in facing the prospect of her own death had a choice. She could turn to accounts of good deaths, with their assurances that women could die well and thus receive the admiration of family, friends and all those who read of their lives, or she could seek guidance from the many spiritual conduct books of the period, or she could peruse accounts of the death of sinful women, reassured that even the most despicable of criminals could make some attempt to die well in the last minutes of their lives.[37]

Bessie, by dying in childbirth, died well. It is therefore not at all surprising that her mother would have wished to commemorate this, even going so far as to ascribe a particular religious symbolism to her lost daughter, and to the child who was the cause of her mother's death. This interpretation fits very well with the analysis of later accounts of the deaths of early modern women, which were prepared on behalf of their families, where the woman was 'exalted posthumously as a reflection of the virtue of her family as a whole, rather than as a separate entity in her own right'.[38] The only plausible interpretation of the omission of Bessie from her mother's will, coupled with the description of her youngest daughter as her 'christchild' is that, sadly, Bessie, like so many women of her time, died either during or after the birth of her child, bringing the life of the fairest, and one of the most accomplished, women of her time to a premature end when she was only aged around forty or forty-one years old at some point between 6 February 1539 and 2 January 1540.

Details of Bessie's burial and her funeral are unknown. It is surprising that Bessie was not buried at South Kyme as she had evidently intended to be when she commissioned Gilbert's memorial, which also included her own memorial brass. It would therefore seem probable that she died away from home. Given her own court connections and Clinton's rising career, London would be a plausible location. A search for a grave for Bessie in London has, however, proved fruitless. White Friar's church in London was founded in 1241. In the choir, it was recorded that a Henry Blunt Esq. and an Elizabeth Blunt were buried.[39] Sadly this Elizabeth cannot be identified with Bessie as the church was dissolved in November 1538, when Bessie is known to have certainly still been alive. This does not preclude London as a location for her death as church records are sparse from the early sixteenth century and a number of churches no longer exist in the city, particularly following the great fire in 1666. However, it does sadly appear that the grave of Bessie Blount, Lady Tailboys and Lady Clinton, has disappeared.

After her death, Bessie's possessions were inherited by her successors as Clinton's wives. Bessie's Gower manuscript, which was one of her most treasured possessions, remained associated with Edward Clinton during his second marriage, with his third wife, Elizabeth Fitzgerald, then taking possession and adding her own signature to a number of pages.[40] The book eventually passed to Bessie's daughter, Katherine Clinton, who in turn passed it to Edward Dymoke, the son of Bessie's daughter, Bridget.[41] Bessie's death went entirely unrecorded by her contemporaries, as was to be expected following the early death of her eldest son. Only her eldest daughter, Elizabeth Tailboys, survived as an unacknowledged reminder of the love affair between Henry VIII and Bessie Blount.

Bessie Blount left little trace in the records of her time. We never know what she was thinking at any given moment and there are no recorded instances of her speech. However, from what survives, it is clear that she was a remarkable and passionate woman. Whilst still only a teenager, Bessie won the affection of the most powerful, and handsome, man in England. She retained his love for some years and always retained his affection. Bessie took a pragmatic approach to her first marriage, grasping the opportunity for social advancement that it offered whilst displaying a staunch character in her dispute with her mother-in-law. Following Gilbert's death, Bessie demonstrated that she was not interested only in her social position (as John Palsgrave had cruelly suggested in his articles against Wolsey). She turned down the king's cousin, Lord Leonard Grey, who had much to recommend him, instead making what must have been a love match with a considerably younger man. The indications are that both of Bessie's marriages were happy, given the number of children that she produced. She was a good mother and, although not given much input into Henry Fitzroy's upbringing, she remained in contact with him and involved in his life. Her other children (save her three youngest) knew her better, with Robert, her youngest son, having his name inscribed into her Gower manuscript.

Bessie Blount was highly educated and one of the most accomplished women of her day, being viewed as a potential rival to Anne Boleyn for a brief period. Who knows, perhaps Bessie Blount, the mother of Henry IX, might have been remembered today as having as forceful a character as Margaret Beaufort. She was for a time the mother of the king's only son, entitling her to a certain prominence and position in society. Bessie Blount and her boy are one of the great 'what ifs' of English history.

# NOTES

## Chapter 1: The Blounts of Kinlet

1. Burke 1833:355–356.
2. Grazebrook and Rylands 1889:51.
3. Camden 1701:581.
4. Eyton 1857:240.
5. Bod MS Blakeway 22 f.8.
6. Eyton 1857:242.
7. Quoted from Eyton 1857:244.
8. Bod MS Blakeway 22 f.9.
9. Quoted from Bod MS Blakeway 22 f.12.
10. Bod MS Blakeway 22 f.12.
11. Bod MS Blakeway 22 f.14.
12. Bod MS Blakeway 22 f.15a and Anderson 1864:285.
13. Bod MS Blakeway 22 f.15a.
14. Eyton 1857:255.
15. Bod MS Blakeway 22 f.26.
16. Maddern 2005:19.
17. Fleming 2005:51.
18. Griffiths and Thomas 1998:18–24.
19. Pedigree from Childe-Pemberton 1913:262–263.
20. Petition of Gruffuth Vaghan ab Eygnon and Maud, his wife, to the Prince of Wales (*Calendar of Ancient Petitions Relating to Wales*, pp531–532).
21. Wright 1826:218 and Burke 1852:256.
22. Southern and Nicolas 1827:470.
23. PROB 11/16 Will of Sir Richard Croft.
24. Quoted from Childe-Pemberton 1913:43–44.
25. Childe-Pemberton 1913:42.
26. Southern and Nicolas 1827:472.
27. Edward, Earl of March and Edmund, Earl of Rutland, to their father, the Duke of York, June 1454 (*Excerpta Historica* 1831:8–9).
28. Edward, Earl of March and Edmund, Earl of Rutland, to their father, the Duke of York, c.1454 (Ellis 1825:9–10).
29. Edward IV's collection of books is detailed in his Wardrobe Accounts (Nicolas 1830).
30. Southern and Nicolas 1827:472.
31. Hall's Chronicle 1809:301.
32. Warkworth's Chronicle (Dockray 1999:86) and the contemporary *History of the Arrival of Edward IV in England, and the Final Recovery of the Kingdoms from Henry VI AD 1471* p82 both record that Edward of Lancaster did not die in battle, instead being killed while fleeing.
33. BL Harleian MS 433 f.89 (printed in Horrox and Hammond I 1979) notes the grant to Sir Richard Croft. This was made either in the brief reign of Edward V or during the reign of his successor, Richard III. Betham 1802:417 discusses Croft's role as high sheriff of Herefordshire during Edward IV's reign.

## Chapter 2: Bessie's Parents

1. Bod MS Blakeway 22 f.25.
2. Bod MS Blakeway 22 f.25 and f.25v.
3. Shrewsbury Record Office 3365/67/63v refers to John Blount of Bitterley and William Blount of Glazeley acknowledging a bond to the prior of the monastery at Wenlock. Both Bitterley and Glazeley are in Shropshire and it is highly likely that they were Thomas Blount's brothers.
4. Bod MS Blakeway 22 f.27.
5. Childe-Pemberton 1913:25.
6. John Blount of Bitterley was associated with Thomas Blount in a number of surviving documents (such as Shrewsbury Record Office 3365/67/63v which records that Thomas Blount of Kinlet, knt., John Corbet of Kinlet, gent., and John Blount of Bitterley, gent., acknowledged their bond to Thomas Trentham and Thomas Trentham

Jr., of Shrewsbury, for £50 to be paid at the Feast of the Ascension next following). As discussed above, they were probably brothers.

7. The location of John and Katherine's marriage is recorded in the *Inquisition Post Mortem* of Humphrey Pershall (or Peshall) taken at Stafford on 7 September 1502 (printed in Parshall 1915:108–109). There is a contradictory statement in the Staffordshire *Inquisition Post Mortem* taken for Sir Thomas Blount which states that the marriage occurred at Kinlet on 1 August 1491 (PRO E150/1032/2). Given that the document stating Bewdley is more contemporary with the marriage, coupled with the fact that Bewdley was an unusual (but entirely plausible) location for a Blount marriage, it would appear more likely that Kinlet is the mistake, based on the fact that Kinlet was the family home of the Blounts and would be expected as the location for the marriage. Alternatively, the couple may have been betrothed at Bewdley and married at Kinlet.

8. PRO E150/1032/2.

9. Details of Bewdley are contained in Burton 1883:3–15.

10. The 1831 census (Purcell 1998). The 'Blunts' were considerably less prominent than their earlier Blount cousins, with occupations such as shoemaker, basket maker and labourers.

11. Bridgeman 1883:79.

12. PROB 11/111 George Blunte of Bewdley's Will.

13. PRO C2/Eliz/B19/52.

14. Thomas Blount's Will (Shropshire Archives 3320/62/7).

15. Burton p7. Also Colvin 1982:281 points out that the manor is known to have been let from the middle of the sixteenth century although the house remained at the disposal of the Council in the Marches of Wales. It is not improbable that a similar arrangement existed in Bessie's time, particularly given the strong association of her family with Bewdley.

16. Colvin 1982:280.

17. Moule 1837:141.

18. Colvin 1982:279.

19. Moule 1837:141.

20. Barrett pp82–84.

21. Leland quoted from Burton 1883:11.

22. The 1612 manorial survey is taken from Burton 1883:7–9.

23. Printed in Childe-Pemberton 1913:269–272.

24. *Inquisition Post Mortem* for Sir Humphrey Pershall (printed in Parshall 1915:109).

25. Phillips 1999:4.

26. Norton 2010:27.

27. Phillips 1999:4–5.

28. BL Harl MSS 1415 f.133 Visitation of Staffordshire 1583 notes the name of Humphrey Pershall's wife. Anne Egerton apparently commonly used the diminutive 'Agnes', but was actually called Anne (she is called Anne in Staffordshire Record Office D1798/HM Chetwynd/99).

29. Parshall 1903:3.

30. Collections 1917:272.

31. Extract from the Plea Roll for Trinity 5 Ed IV (*Collections* 1901:138).

32. Murphy 1997:30.

33. Quoted from Murphy 1997:30.

34. Extract from the Plea Roll for Michaelmas 3 Edward IV (*Collections* 1901:129).

35. Parshall 1903:2.

36. Parshall 1915:51.

37. Parshall 1915:106.

38. Adams 1922:x.

39. Ibid.

40. Gnossal Parish Register (Adams 1922).

41. Quoted from Hone 1906:187.

42. Extract from the Plea Roll Easter 3 Edward IV (*Collections* 1901:126).

43. Extract from the Plea Roll 33 Hen VI (*Collections* 1901:109).

44. Murphy 1997:28.

45. Extract from the Plea Rolls Easter 9 Edward IV p163.

46. Norton 2010b details Margaret Beaufort's marriage.

47. Bagley 1985:1–7.

48. Seacombe 1821:235.

49. Murphy 1997:26.

50. Childe-Pemberton 1913:29.

51. Norton 2010b.

52. Crowland Chronicle Continuations p502.

53. Ballad of Bosworth Ffeilde (printed in Hales and Furnivall 1868:252).

54. 'Grant for life, to Hugh Peshale, knight of the king's body, of an annuity of 20 l.' Dated 7 August 1486 (printed in Campbell 1873 I:536).

55. Details of Henry VII's Parliament 1485–86 (*Collections* 1917:272).

56. Ibid. p536 and Writ under the Great Seal at Easter 1486 'to Hugh Peshal, at 20 l. a year, for term of his life' (Campbell 1873 I:406).

57. Hugh's role as sheriff is recorded in a 'Pardon for Isabel Pershall, 1491' taken from Henry VII's Patent Roll (Parshall 1915:110).

58. Grant to Hugh Persalle, knt., Sheriff of Stafford, 1488 (Campbell 1873 II:391).

59. Ibid. p110.

60. Pearsall, Pearsall and Neall 1928:751.

61. Hugh Peshall's Will PROB 11/8.

62. Richard Pershall's age is noted in Sir Humphrey Pershall's *Inquisition Post Mortem* (printed in Parshall 1915:107).

63. Childe-Pemberton 1913:37.
64. Harwood 1806:98.
65. Actually 1494.
66. Pennant 1811:96–97.
67. Alice Chetwynd's petition is quoted in Rowney 1981:333.
68. Murphy 1997:26.
69. Rowney 1981:333.
70. Rowney 1981:286 notes that in 1490 Sir Humphrey Stanley had been sent by the council of the duchy of Lancaster to investigate a weir built at Barton-under-Needwood in Staffordshire to confirm whether it affected the royal mill there.
71. Jones and Underwood 1995:154.
72. Bond 1909:189.
73. Hewitt 1867:222–225.
74. Details of the arrangement of the marriage and the marriage settlement are contained in PRO C1/385/10 John Blount and Katherine Blount *v.* Edward Blount and Walter Blount (Detention of deeds relating to various manors).
75. Details of the monetary inflation of the Tudor period can be found in Norton 2009b.

## Chapter 3: Bessie Blount of Kinlet

1. For example, Sir Humphrey Blount's Will (Bod MS Blakeway 22 f.25) and Bessie's brother, Sir George Blount's Will (PROB 11/63).
2. Four letters of Katherine Blount's survive: two were written at her own family manor of Knightley and two at Kinlet (Katherine's letters are printed in Parshall 1915:113–119). Two of her letters are also printed by Wood 1846 II:102–103 and 167–168. Unlike her husband, she did not specify Kinlet as the place of her burial in her will, instead requesting 'my body to be buried upon burial in such place as mine executors shall think most convenient' (PROB 11/28).
3. Baldwyn-Childe 1916:iii.
4. Bod MS Blakeway 22 f.7.
5. The Shropshire Gazeteer (1824:218–219).
6. Baldwyn Childe 1916:iii.
7. Shropshire Parish Registers, Kinlet (Fletcher 1920).
8. Parish registers (Fletcher 1920:3).
9. Bod MS Blakeway 22 f.3.
10. Quoted from Baldwyn Childe 1916:iv.
11. Leighton 1901:42.
12. Baldwyn-Childe 1916:iv.
13. Obituary for Revd J.B. Blakeway (1826:278–278).
14. Ibid. 278.
15. Bod MS Blakeway 22 f.3.
16. Ibid. f.4.
17. The identification of the children on the tomb is considered in great detail in Norton 2011 (forthcoming).

18. PRO E150/852/1 states that George was eighteen at the time of his father's death in 1531, giving a birth date of 1513.
19. PRO C1/385/10 John and Katherine Blount *v.* Edward and Walter Blount.
20. Vaughan 1882.
21. *Visitation of Shropshire* p401.
22. Burke 1866:428 and Burke and Burke 1847:1041.
23. *The Leominster Guide* p323.
24. PRO C1/731/21.
25. PROB 11/76 Will of Margaret Blounte, Widow of Netleye.
26. *Annales Rerum Anglicarum* for January 1465 (in Dockray 1999).
27. Bridgeman 1883:81.
28. Ibid.
29. PROB 11/67 Will of Robert Pigott of Chetwynd, 1584.
30. Shropshire Archives 665/513.
31. Purton 1868:202–203.
32. Burke 1836:526.
33. Owen and Blakeway 1825:290.
34. This was also suggested by Purton 1868:203.
35. Childe-Pemberton 1913:20 and Murphy 2002:18.
36. Details of George Blount's settlement in favour of Rowland Lacon are mentioned in George Blount's Will PROB 11/63. The settlement is printed in Childe-Pemberton 1913:276–278.
37. Bridgeman 1883:78–83.
38. PROB 11/111 George Blunte of Bewdley's Will.
39. Lady Lisle's attempts to secure positions at court for her daughters, Anne and Katherine Bassett, first with Anne Boleyn and then Jane Seymour, are detailed in her correspondence (the *Lisle Letters*).
40. *The Register of Thomas Boteler* p115.
41. *The Register of Thomas Boteler* p110.
42. This is the context of the phrase 'sucking child' in the Bible (Isaiah 49:15).
43. Bindoff 1982 III p198.
44. Ibid.
45. Quoted from Childe-Pemberton 1913:198.
46. Marriage Settlement between William Reed of Shepperton and Isabel Blount (Somerset Archive and Records DD\WHb/2986).
47. William Reed's Will PROB 11/25.
48. Isabel Stanley's Will is transcribed and translated in Pearsall, Pearsall and Neale 1928:752.
49. Elizabeth Blount's Will PROB 11/13.
50. PRO C1/165/60.
51. Isabel Stanley is referred to as Dame Elizabeth Pershall in a court case brought by Mary Judd, the daughter of her second husband, John Russhe, and her husband,

Thomas Judd of Wickford (PRO C1/530/20).
52. BL Add MS 42013 f.106.
53. Margaret's Ordinances for a royal birth are printed in Leland 1774 IV from p179. The king's mother had an interest in ceremony that extended right up to death. She also produced ordinances for royal mourning (BL Add MSS 45133 f.141v).
54. Beauchamp Pageant f.22b (printed in Dillon and Hope 1914:88).
55. f.1 (ibid. p88).
56. Thomas Blount's Will (Shropshire Archives 3320/62/7).
57. f.1b (ibid. p4).
58. PRO C1/165/60 (John Salter and Elizabeth his wife *v.* John and William Blount, Chancery case, refers to Dame Elizabeth as Thomas Otteley's executor).
59. Thomas Blount's Will (Shropshire Archives 3320/62/7) refers to his daughter Elizabeth Monynton.
60. Windsor 1975:11.
61. *The Register of Thomas Boteler*, the vicar of Much Wenlock, who was acquainted with Anne, always refers to her as Agnes.
62. For example PRO C1/1168/55 and C1/1141/4.
63. See chapter 4 for a greater discussion of this document.
64. Thomas Blount's Will (Shropshire Archives 3320/62/7).
65. Joyce Blount's marriages are noted in Bod MS Blakeway 22 f.27.
66. Thomas Blount's Will (Shropshire Archives 3320/62/7) notes the names and birth order of his sons.
67. Humphrey Blount's Will is described in Bod MS Blakeway 22 f.25.
68. PRO C241/275/195.
69. PRO C241/275/106.
70. Writ printed in Campbell 1873 II:243.
71. PRO C1/343/27.
72. Rowney 1981:300.
73. Rowney 1981:300–302.
74. Murphy 1997:19.
75. PRO C1/530/20.
76. Isabel Stanley's Will (Pearsall, Pearsall and Neale 1928:752).
77. Thomas Blount's *Inquisition Post Mortem* 1524–25 (printed in Childe-Pemberton 1913:270).
78. Bod MS Blakeway 22 f.27.
79. Shrewsbury Record Office 3365/67/63v.
80. Details of the history of Bitterley can be found in Anderson 1864:303.
81. PRO C1/731/21 and PRO C1/751/1.
82. Rowney 1981:376.
83. Parshall 1915:108.
84. Humphrey's *Inquisition Post Mortem* is printed in Parshall 1915:109.
85. PRO C1/222/94.
86. Murphy 1997:30.

87. Wrottesley 1883 notes the property in Stafford. Staffordshire Record Office D948/3/99 Writ to Escheator of Staffordshire to have valuation made of estate of Richard Pershall a minor, heir to Humphrey Pershall, a tenant in chief notes Richard's position as Humphrey's heir.
88. PRO C1/186/1 and C1/186/5.
89. Wrottesley 1883.
90. Murphy 1997:37.
91. *Letters and Papers, Foreign and Domestic, of the Reign of Henry VIII* (henceforth L&P), vol. I, n969 p490 (47).
92. Richard Pershall's *Inquisition Post Mortem* of 17 November 1524 is printed in Parshall 1915:109.
93. Staffordshire Record Office D1798/HM Chetwynd/99.
94. Murphy 1997:13.
95. Ibid.
96. Burton 1883:75 (List of Rectors and Patrons of Ribbesford).
97. Childe-Pemberton 1913:40.
98. Murphy 1997:55.
99. Noake 1851:141–142.


## Chapter 4: Bessie's Childhood

1. This is discussed in more detail in Norton 2011 (forthcoming).
2. Cranage 1900:320.
3. PRO C1/1141/27–31.
4. PRO C1/1141/27–31 states that William paid sums to George Wood to purchase the wardship for £200 from the king, who had already apparently granted it to Lord St John.
5. PRO C1/1141/4. The document is damaged and the surname of 'Richard' does not survive. However, given that Anne had no other close relative named Richard, it is certainly her husband.
6. PRO C1/1168/55.
7. PRO C1/1141/28 Wode's reply to Agnes Laken's suit.
8. This was the belief of her descendant, Bessie's earliest biographer, Childe-Pemberton (1913).
9. Lewis 1999:34.
10. As Wood (1846:168) pointed out, one of the letters is unsigned and was only identified as being by Katherine due to the place that it was written and, pertinently, the handwriting.
11. Bod MS Blakeway 22 f.24. These gifts are mistakenly attributed to Sir John Blount in Churton 1800:443–444.
12. Baldwin Childe 1916:xiv.
13. John Palsgrave to Bessie Blount, Lady Tailboys, mid-1520s (quoted from Childe-Pemberton 1913:164).
14. Plomer 1909. Details of Pynson's work can be found in Plomer 1927. Russhe may also have taken an interest in the style of the

books and *Dives and Paupers* is notable for the new typeface used: distinguishable by an angular finish to the letter 'h'.

15. Plomer 1909:109. This identification has recently been followed tentatively by Gillespie 2006:100.

16. In 1467, 1470, 1475, 1476, 1477 and 1485 (Palmer 1856).

17. Davis 1999:77. Further biographical details of John Russe can be found in Richmond 1996:129.

18. PRO C1/221/3.

19. PRO C142/8/41 *Inquisition Post Mortem* for John Russe of Suffolk.

20. PROB 11/11 John Russhe's Will.

21. Russell 1868:74.

22. Plomer 1909:117.

23. Stow 1615:460.

24. Jones and Underwood 1995:62.

25. Margaret's Act of Attainder is from *Rotuli Parliamentorum* V, p250.

26. Rotuli Parliamentorum VI p244.

27. BL Harl MS 433 f.165 (printed in Horrox and Hammond 1980).

28. Ibid. f.174b.

29. Gill 1999.

30. List of Bailiffs of Great Yarmouth in Palmer 1856.

31. Gill 1999:83.

32. PRO C1/352/11.

33. PRO C1/530/20.

34. Thomas Judd of Wickford's Will (PROB 11/25).

35. *Dives and Paupers* was a weighty religious text built on the framework of the Ten Commandments with 255 chapters for each of the ten books and written in the early fifteenth century (Pfander 1933).

36. Pollard 1970:207.

37. Pynson's claim is in PRO C1/349/40. The document was also transcribed and printed in Plomer 1909.

38. PRO C1/269/66. Transcribed in *Pynson's Dealings with John Russhe* 1918.

39. PRO C1/203/14.

40. Crane 1919:10.

41. Morgan 1933:227.

42. Margaret Beaufort, for example, was a great patron of early printers and also published her own translations of certain religious works (Norton 2010b).

43. Bessie's signature is in the edition of Chaucer's Troilus in JRL 12005. A discussion of the other surviving editions of this work and their gentry status owners is in Gillespie 2006:75.

44. Lewis 1999:34.

45. Ibid. p26.

46. Ibid. pp26–27.

47. Printing was first developed on the continent. The earliest English printer, William Caxton, printed his first work in England in 1477 (Hindley 1979:239).

48. Orme 2005:65.

49. *The Book of the Knight of the Tower* p19.

50. Ibid. p19.

51. Ibid. p22.

52. Ibid. p24.

53. Ibid. p26.

54. Ibid. p30.

55. Ibid. p32.

56. No record of a husband for Albora survives. She was unmarried at the time of her mother's death, with Katherine Pershall making detailed provision for her eventual marriage in her will. The details recorded by the Visitation of Shropshire in 1583 (BL Harl MSS 1415 f.134) supports this as, of the daughters of John Blount, only Anne, Elizabeth and Albora are given by name. Isabel is not recorded at all and Rose is merely described as 'Nupta William Gresley'. It seems likely that Albora was either still alive or a recent memory at Kinlet, something which explains her inclusion. The lack of a husband is telling and, unlike her sisters, who are described in relation to their husbands, she is merely described as 'Albora filia Johanis'.

57. Schoole of Vertue (Furnivall 1868:242).

58. Details of the Astley tombs are in *A Guide and History of the Parish Church of St Peter Astley Worcestershire*.

59. For example, in his will Robert Blount left a bequest to the children of his sister Joyce (Barnard 1930:102).

60. Pogue 2006:32.

61. Report on Thomas Blount, Captain Thomas Lea and Sir Christopher Blount, 1 February 1600 (Salisbury MSS XI p98).

62. Adams 2002:331–339.

63. Northumberland's conversion earned the criticism of his daughter-in-law, Lady Jane Grey, as set out in the *Chronicle of Queen Jane and Two Years of Queen Mary*.

64. Adams 2002:338.

65. Adams 2002:229.

66. L&P XIII pt I 1509 (Thomas Blount and others to Cromwell, 31 July 1538).

67. Lord Robert Dudley to Thomas Blount, 9 September 1560 (Adlard 2007:32).

68. List of West Midlands Gentry who served in the Low Countries Expeditionary Force, 1585 (in Adams 2002:349).

69. The list of vicars of Kinlet is taken from Baldwin Childe 1916:xiv.

70. Strype 1824:269–270. The Earl of Shrewsbury's letter detailing Kellet's interrogation of Kellet is in Lodge 1791:88.

71. Klein 1998:20–30.

72. The young children's book (Ashmolean MS 61) (printed in Furnivall 1868).

73. The Schoole of Vertue, and Booke of

Good Nourture for Chyldren, and Youth to Learne theyr Dutie by (printed by Wyllyam Seares, and written by F. Seager) (printed in Furnivall 1868).

74. The Babees Book *c*.1475 (Furnival 1868:251–253).

75. The Schoole of Vertue (Furnivall 1868:226–232).

76. A fifteenth-century courtesy book (printed in Chambers 1914).

77. Ibid. p11.

78. The accounts of the fifth Earl of Northumberland for 1512 record the purchase of wax 'for all manner of lights of wax' (1770:13).

79. *The Book of the Knight of the Tower* p83.

80. A fifteenth-century courtesy book (Chambers p14).

81. The great feast at the Intronization of the Reverend Father in God George Nevell, Archbishop of York (printed in Warner 1791:94).

82. John Russell's Boke of Nurture p4.

83. Details of Bewdley's market and fairs are taken from Brown pp89–93.

84. The higher status Earl of Northumberland, in his accounts for 1512, recorded the employment of two rockers and a child to attend in the nursery (1770:46).

85. Thomas Blount's appointment is recorded in BL Harl MS 433 f.85 (printed in Horrox and Hammond 1979).

86. Burton pp32–33.

87. Churton 1800:113 prints a document concerning the visit of the Bishop. He prints Arthur's letter to Oxford University on pp499–500.

88. Murphy 1997:22.

89. Details of Catherine's landing, wedding and time in Ludlow are described in 'The Receyt of the Ladie Kateryne'.

90. Ibid. p7.

91. Camden 1701:580.

92. Leland 1906:50.

93. Wright 1869:v.

94. Ludlow churchwarden accounts for 1540 (printed in Wright 1869:7).

95. The Receyt of the Ladie Katherine p82.

96. Ibid. p77.

97. Hobden.

98. Murphy 1997:22.

99. Arthur's funeral is described in detail in 'The Receyt of the Ladie Katherine' pp81–87.

100. Ibid. p87.

101. Ibid. pp92–93.

102. Elizabeth of York's privy purse expenses p103.


**Chapter 5: Maid of Honour to the Queen**

1. L&P I, 279.

2. L&P I, 713 and 664.

3. For example, L&P I, 791, 886, 1770.

4. L&P I, 918.

5. Murphy 1997:42.

6. Hall's Chronicle I, p14.

7. Sanderman 1912 provides a detailed account of the Spears.

8. BL Cotton MS Titus A XIII f.186–189.

9. Arthur Plantagenet's appointment as a Spear is recorded in BL Add MS 21481 f.158 (printed in Sanderman 1912:14).

10. L&P I, 1974.

11. In a letter from Anne Basset to her mother, Lady Lisle, in 1540, she explained that the king said of the attendants to his fourth wife 'that he would have them that should be fair' (*Lisle Letters* VI 34).

12. Hayward 2007:155.

13. Murphy 1997:46.

14. Hobden 2001:4.

15. BL Add MS 28585 f.43.

16. Freeth 2000–2001a:305.

17. Freeth 2000–2001b:404.

18. Dowden 1990.

19. Hayward 2007:172.

20. Hall's Chronicle 1904:303.

21. John Husee to Lady Lisle, 17 September 1537 (*Lisle Letters* IV 1981:163–164).

22. Sneyd 1847:41–2.

23. Schellinks 1993:47.

24. Schellinks 1993:56.

25. Journal of Frederick, Duke of Wirtemberg, 1592 (Rye 1865:6).

26. Ibid. p7.

27. Ibid.

28. Privy Purse Expenses Henry VIII p22. It is clear that this was Bessie's uncle as the previous entry in the privy purse expenses detailed payments made to watermen for conveying Henry from Greenwich to Hampton Court (p22). Thames Ditton, where Smythe and his wife are buried, is less than a mile from the palace.

29. Ibid. p23. Thomas Ogull was able to spend 5*d* a piece for the boys.

30. Ibid. p23. Payments for the clothes were made in February 1530.

31. *Lisle Letters* IV 1981:151.

32. Childe-Pemberton 1913:50.

33. Rowney 1981:24.

34. PRO E36/215 f.340.

35. Murphy 1997:43.

36. Southern and Nicolas 1827:473.

37. Samman 1988:27.

38. List of the noble persons who accompanied Henry VIII to the Field of the Cloth of Gold in Rutland Papers pp35, 38.

39. Rutland Papers pp31–32.

40. PRO E101/418/5 f.21.

41. Dame Jane Guildford is listed as one of the ladies receiving their wages from Elizabeth of York's privy purse in March

1503 (presumably their final payment following the queen's death) (Privy Purse Expenses of Elizabeth of York p99).

42. Hall's Chronicle p12.

43. PRO E36/215 King's Book of Payments f.270.

44. Murphy 2001:7.

45. PRO E36/215 f.301 and f.336.

46. Quoted from Sneyd 1847:25.

47. John Husee to Lady Lisle, 17 September 1537 (*Lisle Letters* IV 1981:163).

48. John Husee to Lady Lisle, 2 October 1537 (*Lisle Letters* IV 1981:167).

49. Hanham 2003:244.

50. PRO E36/215 f.250.

51. For example, Sir Edward Cobham, one of John Blount's fellow Spears, received a year's advance as recorded in Henry VIII's household book. In January 1514 Sir Richard Candysshe received a similar advance (BL Add MS 21481, f.124, printed in Sanderman 1912:13 and 14).

52. For example PRO E36/215 f.310 for April 1514 and f.318 for May 1514.

53. PRO E101/418/5 f.31.

54. PRO E101/417/6 f.18.

55. PRO E101/417/6 f.85.

56. PRO E101/418/5 f.4.

57. PRO E101/418/5 f.6.

58. PRO E101/418/5 f.14.

59. PRO E101/417/6 f.6.

60. Hayward 2007:159–168.

61. John Husee to Lady Lisle, 2 October 1537 (*Lisle Letters* IV 1981:167–168).

62. John Husee to Lady Lisle, 17 July 1537 (*Lisle Letters* IV 1981:151–2).

63. Ordinances for the Household Made at Eltham, 1526 (in *A Collection of Ordinances and Regulations* 1790).

64. Ibid. p142.

65. Nicolo di Favri to Francesco Gradenigo, 23 January 1513 (Mumby 1913:160).

66. Ibid. p146.

67. Ibid. p154.

68. Ibid. p156.

69. Privy Purse Expenses of Elizabeth of York p48.

70. Somerset 1984 discusses the role of a lady in waiting in the Tudor court in detail.

71. Somerset 1984:14.

72. Shaw 2005:160 discusses the training expected to be given to the daughters of the gentry in the household of a social superior or equal.

73. Palsgrave received wages as 'My lady Princess' schole master' in 1513, for example (PR E36/215 f.255, f.280).

74. A Declaration of the particular ordinances of fares for the diets to be served to the king's highnesse, the queen's grace, and the sides, with the household, as hearafter followeth (the diet for the king and queen) (A Collection of Ordinances and Regulations 1790:174).

75. A Diett for the three next messes to be served at one table, to the queen's lord chamberlayne; and for seven messes of ladyes, and gentlewomen, sitting in the said great chamber, in all ten messes of the like fare (*A Collection of Ordinances and Regulations*, 1790:182–183).

76. Intronization Wilhelmi Warham; Archiepiscopi Cantuar. Dominica in Passione, Anno Henrici 7. Vicessiom, & Anno Domini 1504. Nono die Martii in Warner 1791:107.

77. Somerset 1984:6.

## Chapter 6: Court Life

1. Anne Boleyn's relationship with Henry Percy is contained in Cavendish 1962:59–64.

2. Burke 1883:131.

3. Hitchins 1824:602.

4. Visitation of the County of Cornwall in 1620 (Vivian and Drake 1874:169).

5. List of the Sheriffs of Cornwall in Polwhele 1816:109.

6. Cornwall Record Office AR/19/37/1,2.

7. Penrhos, Abergavenny formed part of the dower of the Countess of Pembroke in c.1353, for example (*Calendar of Ancient Petitions, Wales*, p357).

8. Smart 1868:50.

9. Stephenson 1894:66–68.

10. Stephenson 1894:67.

11. Collins 1768:244.

12. *Inquisition Post Mortem* for Henry Grendon and Elizabeth his Wife, 28 May 1446 (*Calendar of Inquisitions Miscellaneous* VIII p113).

13. William Lacon in 1452, Sir Richard Lacon II in 1477, 1487 and 1498, Sir Thomas Lacon in 1510, 1515 and 1533, Richard Lacon III (Bessie's brother-in-law) in 1540, Rowland Lacon in 1571 and Sir Francis Lacon in 1612 (Register for Willey iv).

14. PRO c1/1141/4.

15. *The Register of Sir Thomas Botelar* p109.

16. The Badges of the Captains in the King's Army, 16 June 1513 (L&P I, 4253).

17. Quoted from Mumby 1913:4.

18. Henry to Erasmus, 17 January 1507, for example (Mumby 1913:66).

19. William, Lord Mountjoy to Erasmus, 27 May 1509 (Mumby 1913:126–127).

20. Giustinian 1854:72.

21. Nicolo Sagudino, Secretary of Sebastian Giustinian to Alvise Foscari, 3 May 1515 (Giustinian 1854:78).

22. Ibid. p78.

23. Venetian Ambassador Extraordinary, the Magnifico Piero Pasqualigo's Letter of 30 April 1515 (Giustinian 1854:87).

24. Ibid. pp90–91.

25. Compendium of the Report of Sebastian Giustinian concerning his legation in England, delivered in the Senate on the 10 October 1519 (Giustinian 1854:312).

26. Hayward 2007 describes Henry's clothes.

27. Hayward 2007:113.

28. Chapuys to Charles V, 19 May 1536 (Norton 2011a:217).

29. Hayward 2007:113.

30. Ibid. p312.

31. Ibid. p221.

32. Ibid.

33. Giustinian 1854:76.

34. Nicolo Sagudino to Alvise Foscari, 3 May 1515 (Giustinian 1854:80).

35. BL Harleian MS 1419A f.200–205v.

36. Taken from Falkus 1974:51.

37. For example, in Princess Mary's privy purse expenses, there are references to both Mary's and her half-sister Elizabeth's minstrels (Madden 1831:24).

38. BL Add MS 7100 f.37.

39. Payments to Mary's music tutors are recorded in April 1536 in her privy purse expenses (Madden 1831:26).

40. Childe-Pemberton 1913:38.

41. Childe-Pemberton 1913:85.

42. London, 10 July 1517 (Giustinian 1854:97).

43. London, 30 September 1516 (Giustinian 1854:296).

44. Hobden 2001:9.

45. Chappell 1867:371.

46. Chappell 1867:379.

47. Chappell 1867:279–380.

48. Chappell 1867:380.

49. Tucker 1969:336 and Norton 2009a:9–10.

50. There are a number of biographies of Catherine of Aragon, including Tremlett 2010, Fox 2011 and Mattingly.

51. Tremlett 2010:70.

52. Quoted from Chappell 1867:376.

53. Catherine of Aragon to Ferdinand of Aragon, 29 July 1509 (Mumby 1913:132).

54. Charges of the English Navy for the First Three Months, 17 April – 8 July 1512 (Spont 1897:11). The pomegranate was Catherine's emblem, whilst the rose was Henry's.

56. Childe-Pemberton 1913:55.

57. Bodleian MS Blakeway 22, f.23v.

58. Appointments for the War, 1512 (L&P I, 3231).

59. The Badges of the Captains in the King's Army, 16 June 1513 (L&P I, 4253).

60. Sandeman 1912:16 and 26.

61. Sandeman 1912:16.

62. Summary of letters from Paulo da Lodi, 19 September 1513 (CSP Venetian, 312).

63. Catherine of Aragon to Henry VIII, 16 September 1513 (Mumby 1913:219).

64. L&P I, 41.

65. Samman 1988:8.

66. Compendium of the Report of Sebastian Giustinian concerning his legation in England, delivered in the Senate on 10 October 1519 (Giustinian 1854:314).

67. 'A ballet of ye deth of ye Cardynall' (printed in MS Ballads, Temp. Hen.VIII)

68. Roy 1812:23.

69. Why Come Ye Not to Court? (Skelton p347).

70. One of Wolsey's chief residences.

71. Another London residence of the cardinal.

72. Skelton pp350–351.

## Chapter 7: Court Pageantry

1. Somerset 1984:15.

2. Her literary interests show Bessie to have delighted in the themes of courtly love and chivalry.

3. Nicolo Sagudino to Alvise Foscari, 3 May 1515 (Giustinian 1854:81).

4. Henry VII and Elizabeth of York had four sons: Arthur, Henry VIII, an unnamed son who died at birth and Edmund, who died in infancy.

5. The Justes of the Moneths of May and June (printed in Hazlitt 1866:128–9).

6. Hall's Chronicle, I p15.

7. Samman 1988:98.

8. Samman 1988:99.

9. Luis Caroz to Ferdinand of Aragon, 29 May 1510 (Mumby 1913:142).

10. Compendium of the Report of Sebastian Giustinian concerning his legation in England, delivered in the Senate on 10 October 1519 (Giustinian 1854:312).

11. The Wardrobe Book of the Wardrobe of the Robes Prepared by James Worsley in December 1516, Edited from British Library MS Harley 2284 (printed in Hayward 2007) p371.

12. Ibid. p392.

13. Williams 1998:75.

14. Privy Purse Expenses of Henry VIII p43.

15. Privy Purse Expenses of Henry VIII p67.

16. Privy Purse Expenses of Henry VIII p50. Henry purchased four bows for Anne.

17. In Henry's privy purse expenses for 1529–32 there are also a number of payments made for keeping hawks, for example that made in 1529 for meat for two hawks at 2*d* a day (Privy Purse Expenses of Henry VIII 1827:3).

18. Privy Purse Expenses of Henry VIII p87.

19. Chapuys, 17 July 1531.

20. Privy Purse Expenses of Henry VIII p55. Mary's servant sent Henry a buck, the assumption being that it had been killed by her during a hunting trip.

21. The Duke of Estrada to Isabella of Castile, 10 August 1504 (Mumby 1913:49).

22. Williams 1998:47.

23. Compendium of the Report of Sebastian Giustinian concerning his legation in England, delivered in the Senate on 10 October 1519 (Giustinian 1854:312).

24. Herbert p121.

25. Account Books of John Heron, 1494 (Anglo 1960–61:14).

26. Account Books of John Heron, 1498 (Anglo 1960–61:33).

27. Privy Purse Expenses of the Princess Mary, December 1536 (Madden 1831:3).

28. Privy Purse Expenses of Henry VIII p98.

29. George Wyatt's Life of Queen Anne (in Norton 2011a:18).

30. Ibid. p18.

31. Privy Purse Expenses of Henry VIII record that Anne lost over £12 at bowls in May 1532. Henry also lost large sums in the same year to both Sir Thomas Boleyn and Francis Bryan (pp216, 211 and 278).

32. Catherine of Aragon to Ferdinand of Aragon, 29 July 1509 (L&P I, 368).

33. There are a number of records of masques during Henry VII's reign; for example, in 1494 the king paid a sum 'to Peche for the disguising in rewarde' (Account Books of John Heron in Anglo 1960–61:28).

34. Somerset 1984:16.

35. Henry VIII's Inventory p167.

36. Henry VIII's Inventory p168.

37. Ibid.

38. Hall's Chronicle I p15.

39. Ibid.

40. Samman 1988:143.

41. Samman 1988:454.

42. Samman 1988:146.

43. Samman 1988:445.

44. Nicolo di Favri of Treviso Attached to the Venetian Embassy in England, to Francesco Gardenigo, 24 September 1514 (CSP Venetian, 505).

45. Ship Launch, October 1515 (CSP Venetian, 662).

46. Hall I p143.

47. The costumes and participants in the New Year 1515 masque are described in Revel Accounts, no. 7, 25 December 1515 (L&P II, pt I, 1501). The fact that the revel accounts list four costumes for men and four for ladies makes it clear they refer to the same masque as Hall.

48. Scarisbrick 1991:193.

49. Anne of Denmark's Jewel Inventory (Scarisbrick 1991:209).

50. Ibid. p211.

51. Henry refers to this gift in one of his letters.

52. A summary is contained in O'Conor 1818:357 (manuscript LXXVI Crown Jewels).

53. Payments for the cloth in May 1540 (Madden 1831:90).

54. Inventory of the Jewels Belonging to the Lady Mary, Daughter of King Henry VIII, 1542–46 (in Madden 1831).

55. Elizabeth I's Inventory (Collins 1955:269, 278).

56. Ibid. p532.

57. Hayward 2007:178.

58. Taken from 'List from May 1536 of assorted property left in a chest in the chamber over the kitchen' belonging to Lady Rochford (transcribed in Rowley-Williams 1998:305).

59. Taken from 'Plate, Apparel and Jewels which were the Lady Rochford's' (presumably made after her death and transcribed in Rowley-Williams 1998:299).

60. Taken from 'Record of bedding received into the royal wardrobe after Jane Parker's death' (transcribed in Rowley-Williams 1998:300).

61. Inventory of the Regalia and Gold Plate of Henry VIII (Palgrave 1836:259).

62. Ibid. p262.

63. Ibid. p282.

64. Ibid. p284.

65. The Inventory of King Henry VIII (Society of Antiquaries MS 129 p4).

66. Ibid. p5.

67. The Inventory of King Henry VIII (BL Harley MS 1419) p179.

68. Ibid. p183.

69. Nicolo Sagudino, Secretary of Sebastian Giustinian to Alvise Foscari, 3 May 1515 (Giustinian 1854:80).

70. Venetian Ambassador Extraordinary, the Magnifico Piero Pasqualigo's Letter of 30 April 1515 (Giustinian 1854:90.

71. James Howell to Captain Thomas Porter, Madrid, 10 July 1623 (Howell 1655:131).

72. Pepys, 28 May 1667 p6.

73. Herbert p270.

74. Schellink 1993:149.

75. Somerset 1984:17.

76. Nicolo Sagudino to Alvise Foscari, 3 May 1515 (Guistinian 1854:81).

77. Compendium of the Report of Sebastian Giustinian concerning his legation in England, delivered in the Senate on 10 October 1519 (Giustinian 1854:313).

78. Antonio Giustinian and Antonio Surian, Venetian Ambassadors in France, to the Signory, 4 June 1519 (CSP Venetian, 1230).

79. Murphy 2001:12.

80. Don Luis Caroz to Miguel Perez de Almazan, 28 May 1510:138–141). Caroz also suggests the possibility that Lady Anne was wooed by William Compton but considered it more likely that Compton wooed her on behalf of the king.

81. Murphy 2001:13.

82. Dewhurst 1984 discusses Catherine of Aragon's pregnancies.

83. Henry VIII to Ferdinand of Aragon, 1 November 1509 (in Falkus 1974:20).

84. The Doge and Senate to Andrea Badoer, Ambassador in England, 22 December 1509 (CSP, Venetian 25).

85. Receipt of letters from Andrea Badoer, 20 April 1510 (CSP, Venetian 63).

86. Catherine of Aragon to Ferdinand of Aragon, 27 May 1510 (CSP, Spanish II, 43).

87. Dewhurst 1984:50.

88. Starkey 2004:117–118 sets out this phantom pregnancy in detail.

89. Reading to the Senate of Letters from the ambassador in England, Andrea Badoer, 15 January 1511 (CSP Venetian, 95).

90. Hall's Chronicle I p72.

91. L&P I, 1491.

92. Quoted from Chappell 1867:382.

93. L&P I, 1513.

94. Wages were paid in June 1513 for 'Wm. Lambert, keeping the wardrobe of the late Prince Henry from 24 Dec, last to 4 May' (L&P II pt I, 1461). Lambert was apparently kept in his office following the prince's death in the hope that a new prince would soon be born who would require his services.

95. Wriothesley's Chronicle I p6.

96. L&P I, 1862.

97. Wolsey to Bishop Fox, 30 September 1511 (Mumby 1913:144).

98. Receipt on that morning through the Duke of Ferrara of a letter, 8 October 1513 (CSP Venetian, 329) and James Bannisius, Imperial Agent, to the Lord Albert of Carpi, 8 October 1513 (CSP Venetian, 331).

99. Vetor Lippomano to ?, 1 September 1514 (CSP Venetian, 479).

100. Andrea Badoer to the State, 8 January 1515 (CSP Venetian, 555) claims that the child was stillborn and dead on 8 January 1515. However, Peter Martyr to Lud. Furtado, 31 December 1514 (L&P I, 5718) claimed that the premature birth had already taken place.

101. PRO E36/215 f.449.

102. Peter Martyr to Lud. Furtado, 31 December 1514 (L&P I, 5718).

103. London 20 February 1516 (Giustinian 1854:181).

104. Lorenzo Pasqualigo, Merchant of Venice in London, to his brothers Alvise and Francesco, 31 October 1515 (CSP, Venetian 661).

105. Ibid. p182.

106. London, 28 February 1518 (Giustinian 1854:161).

107. Francesco Chieregato to the Marquis of Mantua, 1 August 1517 (CSP Venetian, 942).

108. Sebastian Giustinian to the Signory, 6 June 1518 (CSP Venetian, 1038).

109. Pace to Wolsey, 5 July 1518 (State Papers, I, 2).

110. Silvester, Bishop of Worcester to Henry, 27 August 1518 (L&P I, 4398).

111. i.e. in Henry's own hand, rather than through a secretary.

112. Henry VIII to Cardinal Wolsey, July 1518 (State Papers, I, 1).

113. Dewhurst 1984 disputes this, finding no evidence of Catherine suffering any miscarriages. However, Henry's words concerning Catherine having a dangerous time when she was still relatively early in her pregnancy does support an assertion that she suffered miscarriages during her marriage.

114. Sebastian Giustinian to the Signory, 25 October 1518 (CSP Venetian, 1093).

## Chapter 8: Bessie's Literary Interests

1. For example, BL Egerton 1991 f.143 and f.214v.

2. f.143 contains a reference to 'the Lord Clinton'. 'Elizabeth Clynton' signed the manuscript on f.34 and f.94. The writing for this signature is considerably different to other surviving examples of Bessie's handwriting and is therefore more likely to relate to Clinton's third wife.

3. f.1v (discussed in Meyer 1889:49 and attributed to Sir Edward Dymoke).

4. f.2.

5. Leach 2009:12–14 (part 1) details the dispute between Bessie's stepson and her grandson.

6. Pearsall 2010:80.

7. BL Egerton 1991 f.142v.

8. Ibid. f.6.

9. Ibid. f.7v.

10. Pearsall 2010:90.

11. Equally, by the nineteenth century it was described as a 'superb MS' (Sims 1854:440).

12. Backhouse 1995:181.

13. Pearsall 2010:95.

14. Carley 2004:64.

15. F.2v and f.207.

16. Henry VIII's Inventory (no. 14026).

17. Pearsall 2010:96.

18. Ibid.

19. Such as f.143.

20. Echard 2010a:2.

21. Echard 2010b:116–117.

22. Macaulay 1901:vii.

23. Gower 1901:2.

24. Butterfield 2010:165.

25. Gower 1901:36.

26. Gower 1901:45.

27. Gower 1901:68.

28. Watt 2010:197.

29. Watt 2010:201.

30. JRL 12005.

31. Gillespie 2006:110.
32. BL Egerton 1991 f.34 and 94.
33. For example, the letter 'h' in both the signature and Bessie's writing on f.143 of BL Egerton 1991 are very similar, as are the rounded letters used for both.
34. JRL 12005 f.1 and f.60.
35. Ibid. f.17v.
36. Ibid. f.12v.
37. Ibid. f.64.
38. Ibid. f.6v–7.
39. Gillespie 2006:75.
40. Coghill's introduction in Chaucer 1971: xi.
41. Ibid. xviii.
42. This is a modern translation from Coghill's edition of Chaucer (1971:4). The original is:

> And byddeth ek for hem that ben desespeyred
> In loue that neuere nyl recouered be.
> And ek for hem that falsely ben apeyred.
> Thorugh wykked tonges be it he or she
> Thus biddeth god for his benignite.
> So graunte hem soone out of this world to pace.
> Than ben desespeyred out of loues grace

Quoted from Chaucer 1888:3 (Furnivall's edition)

43. The original version:

> Criseyde was this lady name al right.
> As to my dome in al Troyes cyte.
> Nas noon so faire for-passyng euery wryght.
> Sp angelyk was here natyf beaute.
> That lyk a thing immortal semed she.
> As doth an heunysh parfit creature.
> That down were sent in scorning of nature

Quoted from Chaucer 1888:4 (Furnivall's edition)

The modern translation quoted in the text is from Chaucer 1971:7.
44. For example, Henry VIII declared in one letter to Anne Boleyn that he had been 'for the whole year stricken with the dart of love' (printed in Norton 2011a:42).
45. Southall 1964:142–150.
46. The extracts from Troilus and Crysede in the Devonshire Manuscript are discussed in Seaton 1956:55–56.
47. Southall 1964:144.
48. Plomer 1909:122.
49. Hellinga 2010:122.
50. Hellinga 2010:158.
51. *Dives and Paupers* is discussed in Pfander 1933.
52. Pfander 1933:308.
53. Quoted from Pfander 1933:310.
54. HMC Fourth Report 1881:102.
55. HMC Fourth Report 1881:102.
56. Lincolnshire Pedigrees (Maddison 1904:947) lists Gilbert's sisters and their marriages.
57. It is not listed in a catalogue of books relating to Mary, Queen of Scots, in Johnston 1906. Sharman 1889:15–16 refers to the note in the Ashburnham book as suggesting that it belonged to Mary. However, it is not included in any inventory of the Scottish queen's goods.
58. Henry VIII's Inventory (no. 3527).
59. Hazlitt 1904:199.
60. Book Prices 1898:40. The book is also described in Ashburnham Sale Prices 1897.
61. Warton 1824:329.
62. James 2008:304.
63. 'He desyreth exchange of lyfe' by Thomas Vaux (Brydges 1810:11).
64. 'A lover disdained, complaineth' by Thomas Vaux (Brydges 1810:73–74).
65. Barnard 1930:103 and Pogue 2006:32.

## Chapter 9: The King's Mistress

1. BL Cotton Caligula DVI f.155.
2. Journal of Frederick, Duke of Wirtemberg, 1592 (Rye 1865:7).
3. Gunn 1988 describes Suffolk's rise to power and his life.
4. Letters of Margaret Duchess of Savoy, 1513 (printed as an appendix to the Chronicle of Calais, p73).
5. Gunn 1988:29.
6. Details of Elizabeth Carew and her marriage are found in Mitchell 1981.
7. Hobden 2001:7 asserts that Elizabeth Carew was Henry's mistress. The evidence supports this.
8. The Wardrobe Book of the Wardrobe of the Robes Prepared by James Worsley in December 1516, edited from British Library MS Harley 2284 (printed in Hayward 2007) p369.
9. Ibid. p373.
10. Ibid. p387.
11. Ibid. p393. Green velvet and purple velvet supplied to Catherine for stomachers.
12. Ibid. p394.
13. Ibid. p387.
14. Ibid. p382.
15. Ibid. p381.
16. Ibid.
17. Privy Purse Expenses of Henry VIII, for example. On 22 November 1530 Henry

bought crimson satin for Anne (p95). In December 1530 he paid for furs for Anne's gowns (p101). On 10 May 1531 he bought crimson cloth of gold for Anne (p133).

18. 'Itm paid to my Lady Carow for cards for my Ladies grace' (17 May 1537, 22s 6d) (Madden 1831:29).

19. Mary's Privy Purse Expenses (Madden 1831:7 and 51).

20. In her accounts for January 1537, Princess Mary gave 7s 6d to the nurse of Lady Carew's daughter who was her goddaughter (Madden 1831:11).

21. Elizabeth, Lady Carew, to Lord Cromwell, 1539 (Wood 1846, III pp110–111).

22. Mitchell 1981:27.

23. Mitchell 1981:42.

24. Fraser suggested this, for example.

25. Bessie's daughter, Elizabeth Tailboys, received a bequest in Sir Charles Brandon's will (printed in Clay 1908:217). Interestingly, Sir Charles Brandon's mother's identity is unknown. There is no suggestion that it was Bessie. Sir Charles had a full sister, whom he addressed as sister in his will, whilst Elizabeth Tailboys was merely described by name. His sister was Frances, wife of Sir William Sandon (Turk 1909:38). He also named his very distant Brandon cousins, the Sackfords, in his will (for details of the relationship between the Brandons and Sackfords, see the Visitation of the County of Huntingdon, 1613), and if the Blounts had been his maternal family, he could have been expected to also name them, given their involvement in the life of Bessie's known illegitimate son.

26. *Register of Thomas Botelar* p115.

27. Murphy 2001:23.

28. Account of the manors of Viscountess Lysle, 15 May 1513 (L&P I, 4071).

29. L&P I, 5523.

30. London, 10 July 1517 (Giustinian 1854:97).

31. Hart 2009:12.

32. BL Add MSS 21481 f.162 (printed in Sandeman 1912:15).

33. There is no further mention of the Spears after December 1515 (Sandeman 1912:3).

34. Murphy 2001:26.

35. Articles Ordained by King Henry VII for the Regulation of his Household, 31 December 1494 (in *A Collection of Ordinances and Regulations* p109).

36. L&P II pt I, 73.

37. Grant to Sir Thomas and John Blount, Squire to the Body, 16 February 1519 (L&P II, pt I, 79).

38. PRO C1/389/2 names John as the master of the game in Wyre Forest. It can be dated to between 1515 and 1518.

39. Murphy 1997:55.

40. Bernard 1981:757.

41. Privy Purse Expenses of Henry VIII p16.

42. List of Noblemen and others attending the Field of the Cloth of Gold (L&P II pt I, 703).

43. Murphy 1997:56.

44. Hall, II p49.

45. Quoted from Elton 1976:220.

46. The later sixteenth century writer, Nicholas Harpsfield, who was particularly hostile to Anne Boleyn repeated the rumour that Henry had enjoyed an affair with Elizabeth Boleyn. He was well aware of the relationship with Mary Boleyn p236.

47. Fuller 1952:614 notes the gift to Jane of Henry's picture. Details of the bag of gold coins are contained in L&P X 245 (Chapuys to Charles V, 1 April 1536).

48. Ibid.

49. The gift is noted in one of Henry's love letters to Anne (letter 1 in Norton 2011a:41).

50. Herbert p270.

51. Henry's VIII'S Inventory p90.

52. Childe-Pemberton 1913:113.

53. Norton 2009a.

54. Henry VIII's Inventory (BL Harley MS 1419) p184.

55. Chapuys to Charles V, 3 September 1533 (Norton 2011a:166).

56. Ibid. p246.

57. L&P X 374 (Chapuys to Antoine Perrenot, 18 May 1536).

58. Ibid.

59. Rowley-Williams 1998:9.

60. Quoted from Rowley-Williams 1998:30.

## Chapter 10: Mother of the King's Son

1. Samman 1988:14.

2. Journal of Frederick, Duke of Wirtemberg, 1592 (Rye 1865:14).

3. Journal of Frederick, Duke of Wirtemberg, 1592 (Rye 1865:16).

4. Samman 1988:59.

5. The visit of the Emperor Charles V to England, 1522 (Rutland Papers p86).

6. Ibid. p80.

7. Samman 1988:27.

8. Eltham Ordinances, 1526 (in *A Collection of Ordinances* p145).

9. Samman 1988:62.

10. PRO E36/215 f.259.

11. Ibid. f.275.

12. Ibid. f.284 and 285.

13. Ibid.295.

14. Ibid. f310–311.

15. Ibid. f340 shows the court at Dover on 1 October 1514.

16. Ibid. f.343.

17. Samman 1988:15.

18. Murphy 1997:56. Murphy points out that the age of six was a significant one

for royal sons, with Fitzroy's half-brother, Edward VI, recording in his journal that he was raised with women until the age of six when he began his studies.

19. Samman 1988:352.

20. Hall I, p168.

21. Lambeth, 5 October 1518 (Giustinian 1854:224).

22. Lambeth, 5 October 1518 (Giustinian 1854:225).

23. Hall I, p171.

24. Sebastian Giustinian to the Signory, 10 November 1518 (CSP Venetian, 1103).

25. Advices from England, 13 December 1518 (CSP Venetian, 1123).

26. Hayward 2007:167.

27. Chapuys to Charles V, 29 May 1533 (Norton 2011a:161).

28. John Husee to Lord Lisle, 23 May 1537 (St Clare Byrne 1981:142).

29. The attempts to provide Jane with quails are discussed in Norton 2009a. The sources relating to this are contained in the *Lisle Letters*.

30. Morant 1768:56–57.

31. Oxley 1965:74.

32. Morant 1768:57.

33. Lease by the advice of John Daunce knt. and John Hales to John Smyth of Blackmore, 18 February 1529 (Nichols 1855:x).

34. Parkyns 1816:80.

35. Blackmore is not included in the list of monasteries stayed at by Henry VIII and Catherine of Aragon between 1509 and 1529 in Samman 1988 Appendix III.

36. Oxley 1965:73.

37. Samman 1988:17.

38. Hume p96.

39. Samman 1988:29.

40. PRO E101 622/31.

41. Samman 1988:17.

42. This can be surmised from the fact that his privy purse expenses contain a sum 'paied to the gardyner of Beawlie in rewarde for bringing glasses with waters to the kings grace' (Privy Purse Expenses of Henry VIII, p5).

43. Williams 1998:8.

44. Touch me not.

45. Wyatt 1858.

46. Rowley-Williams 1998:62.

47. Generally a young woman's virginity was seen as something in need of protection in the sixteenth century. For example, the scholar Luis Vives was of the view that young girls should not leave the house unless absolutely necessary.

48. Hayward 2007:200.

49. Rowley-Williams 1998:67.

50. L&P I, 1652.

51. Murphy 1997:59.

52. Murphy 2001:30.

53. Although commonly used to refer to illegitimate children, the prefix 'Fitz' need not necessarily refer to illegitimate children and was used more broadly for sons in general during the medieval and Tudor periods. Henry II, for example, was known as Henry FitzEmpress before his accession due to the high rank of his mother.

54. Mattingley.

55. Murphy 1997:60.

## Chapter 11: Mother of the King's Daughter?

1. Hart 2009:47.

2. PRO Durham 3 Inquisition Post Mortem Portfolio 177 (*Inquisition Post Mortem* for Robert Tailboys).

3. Murphy 2001:32.

4. Bindoff 1982:419.

5. Ibid.

6. The king held the wardship of heirs until they came of age and could bestow these on favoured courtiers. There is no evidence that Henry or Wolsey held Gilbert Tailboys' wardship (*Prerogatives Regis* (of the King's Prerogatives) in Statutes of the Realm I p226).

7. Lincolnshire Pedigree of the Talboys family from Cotton MS Faustina CX (Maddison 1904:946).

8. Ibid. p946.

9. Will of Sir Robert Talboys (*Testamenta Vetusta* II 1826:420).

10. *Inquisition Post Mortem*, Durham, of Sir George Taylboyse (Forty-Fourth Annual Report of the Deputy Keeper of the Public Records p517).

11. Henry's grandmother, Lady Margaret Beaufort did not, as commonly supposed, serve as regent for her grandson. She took a less official role in assisting him in the appointment of his council (Norton 2010b).

12. Hill 1870:197 and *Antiquarian Researches of the Archaeological Institute* 1848:295.

13. Cockayne 1910.

14. L&P XIV pt I 905.

15. Cole 1897:81.

16. Senderowitz 2003:328.

17. Quoted from Hodgson 1827:65–66.

18. Hodgson 1827:66.

19. PRO C1/1167/74.

20. PRO E305/10/E82.

21. Worcestershire Record Office 705:134/1531/77/69.

22. Hodgson 1827:87.

23. APC II, 6 February 1547 p16.

24. APC III, 13 June 1550 p48.

25. APC III, 17 July 1550 p83–84.

26. Thomas Wymbish's Will PROB 11/36.

27. Letter CLXXVI in Ascham 1865:419.

28. Letter CLXXXIV in Ascham 1865:429.
29. A proven ability to bear sons was desirable in a wife. For example, Edward IV used it as a means of justifying to his mother, Cecily Neville, his marriage to the widow Elizabeth Woodville, the mother of two healthy sons.
30. Wimbish *v.* Tailbois (Plowden 1792).
31. Wimbish *v.* Willoughby (Plowden 1792).
32. Sir Charles Brandon's Will is contained in Clay 1908:216–217.
33. Wilkinson 2009:40.
34. Hoskins 1997 details the grants in detail.
35. Wilkinson 2009:79.
36. Wilkinson 2009:87.
37. Bundesen 2008:26
38. Henry VIII to Wyatt (BL Harl MS 282, f.26) and L&P XIII pt I 640.
39. Bundesen 2008:74.
40. Bundesen 2008:75.
41. Hoskins 1997.
42. Naunton 1824:10.
43. Bundesen 2008:75.
44. Deut. 33:22.
45. Wyatt 1858.
46. Samman 1988:354.
47. Samman 1988:11. This average is based on an analysis of Henry VIII's progress of 1528.
48. Parkyns 1816:80.
49. *Proceedings of the Society of Antiquaries of London*, 17 November 1864 – 20 June 1867 pp77–79.
50. Samman 1988:23.
51. Leland 1770:686.
52. Herbert 1870:270.
53. Murphy 2001:35.
54. Quoted from Murphy 2001:35.
55. Sir William Poulet to Cromwell, 9 October 1534 (State Papers I, 26).
56. Wilkinson 2009:65.
57. Wilkinson 2009:66.

## Chapter 12: First Marriage

1. Bindoff III p419.
2. Creasey 1825:274.
3. Newton 1995:9.
4. Thompson 1856:381.
5. Newton 1995:11.
6. Newton 1995:13. It should be noted that a great many families claimed descent from some unspecified 'relative' of William I. Most of these claimed lineages are unlikely to be genuine, although the fact that they were believed does highlight the status of the families in the medieval period.
7. Newton 1995:17.
8. Hill 1870:1870.
9. Armstrong 2008:35 claims that Ivo's first wife, Elgiva, daughter of Aethelred II, married him after the Conquest and produced two sons. However, given that Aethelred II died in

1016, this claim is improbable. It is rendered even less likely by the fact that all the children of Emma of Normandy, Aethelred's final wife, whom he married in 1002, are accounted for. Unless she was an illegitimate child (which is unlikely due to Aethelred's age at his death and the prestige of his second wife which would make it difficult to acknowledge illegitimate offspring) Elgiva would have to be the daughter of Aethelred's first wife and therefore born at some point before 1002. She is unlikely to have borne children at the age of nearly seventy.
10. Ingulph's Chronicle of the Abbey of Croyland p143.
11. Croyland Chronicle p143.
12. Armstrong 2008 discusses the Raithby Tailboys family.
13. Armstrong 2008:52.
14. Magna Court Roll 1486. Robert Tailboys failed to attend and was fined 12 pence. He was also fined in 1487 for non-attendance (documents printed in Armstrong 2008:59).
15. Page 1928:285.
16. Maddison 1904:945.
17. Page 1928:288.
18. William Tailboys is listed as one of the men who was in Scotland with the queen in August 1461 (*Paston Letters* II p46).
19. William Tailboys to Viscount Beaumont (*Paston Letters* I pp96–98).
20. Petition to parliament of 1559 (Hodgson 1827:63).
21. Newton 1995:17.
22. L&P XIV pt II 780 refers to a lease held by Sir George Tayleboys and his wife, Isabella.
23. The elder Elizabeth Tailboys' father, Sir William Gascoigne was the son of Jane Neville, who was the daughter of John Neville. He was the son of Mary de Ferrers, daughter of Joan Beaufort.
24. Pedigree from BL Cotton MS Faustina CX (printed in Maddison 1904).
25. Harris 2004:31.
26. The documents for the case are C1/1074/5–9.
27. Murphy 2001:32.
28. Richardson 1941:60.
29. Statutes of the Realm 1 p226 (*Prerogatives Regis*).
30. Bindoff III p419. Redesdale was a Tailboys manor, although, due to its proximity to the Scottish border, had only a very low value. In 1436, during one of England's many wars with Scotland, it was assessed to be worth less than seven pounds (Hodgson 1827:61).
31. L&P I 380.
32. PRO C142/31/41.
33. L&P I 2979. The other men granted custody of Sir George were John Constable,

Dean of Lincoln, Sir William Tyrwhitt, Sir Robert Dymmoke, Sir Robert Tyrwhitt, Philip Constable, John Hennege, John Fulneby and Thomas Hennege.

34. He was almost certainly already over twenty-one by 1517 (as discussed in a previous chapter). In any event, there were no grounds for his wardship given that his father was still alive. The king only had authority to take the wardship of heirs who had inherited their property until they came of age (*Prerogatives Regis* in Statutes of the Realm I).

35. Maddison 1904:947.

36. Maddison 1904:946.

37. Hill 1870:195.

38. The Testament of Sir Robert Sparke of Goltho, 13 May 1528 (Foster 1918:80–81).

39. Samman 1988:201.

40. L&P IV pt II 2972.

41. Cavendish 1825:58.

42. L&P I 3446.

43. Childe-Pemberton 1913:123.

44. Newton 1995:18.

45. A brief description of the brass was recorded by Gervase Holles p186. In theory, Gilbert's brass ought to be easy enough to identify. We have a description of the image and know its exact size. It is likely to be a palimpsest, as Bessie's is. A search of the catalogues of brasses in public collections (such as Stephenson 1926) has, however, not served to identify any brasses that could potentially be Gilbert's. It may still exist in private hands although it is more likely that it is no longer extant.

46. Newton 1995:50.

47. The inscription is contained with a manuscript of the *Horae Beate Virginis* which was in the Ashburnham Library (Book Prices 1898:40).

48. Sir Robert Tailboys' Will is printed in *Testamenta Vetusta* II p420. His *Inquisition Post Mortem* notes that he owned nearly sixty manors, churches and pastures, as well as many hundreds of acres, demonstrating that he was a very substantial landowner (Armstrong 2008:105).

49. Will of Elizabeth, Lady Greystock in *Testamenta Vetusta* II p492.

50. Hart 2009:46.

51. L&P III pt II 2145 (Commission of the Peace March 1522).

52. L&P III pt I 1379.

53. L&P IV pt I 390 (Commission of the peace in May 1524), L&P IV pt I 1002 (Commission of the peace in February 1526), L&P IV pt II 5083 (Commission of the peace in three areas of Lincolnshire in December 1528).

54. L&P III pt II 3282, L&P III pt II 3504.

55. L&P III pt II 3583 (Sheriff Roll,

November 1523) L&P IV pt I 819 (Sheriff Roll, 10 November 1524), L&P IV pt I 1795 (Sheriff Roll, November 1525).

56. L&P IV pt III 6042.

57. Henry Percy, Earl of Northumberland, to Thomas Arundel, one of the gentlemen of Wolsey's privy chamber 1527 (Cavendish 1825 II p246).

58. Chapter 34: Elizabeth Uxe Gilbert Taylboys 1523 (The Statutes of the Realm III).

59. Bindoff III p419.

60. Ibid.

61. L&P III pt II 2356.

62. Nicolas 1826:29.

63. The Act is quoted from Nicolas 1826:30.

64. Nicholas 1826:30.

65. Nicholas 1826:34.

66. L&P I 2214.

## Chapter 13: Married Life

1. Childe-Pemberton 1913:127.

2. Sir George Tailboys is described as 'of Goltho' in the document granting custody of his person and lands to Wolsey and other (L&P I 2979).

3. Hobden 2001:10.

4. Emery 1985 details the surviving tower at South Kyme.

5. Creasey 1825:279.

6. *Torrington Diaries* II p357.

7. Leland VII 1744:36.

8. Creasey 1825:280.

9. Oliver 1837:18.

10. Oliver 1837:18.

11. Thompson 1856:385.

12. Emery 1985:317.

13. Emery 1985:319.

14. Johnson 2002:55–59 describes the links between the South Kyme tower and Tattershall castle.

15. Johnson 2002:59.

16. L&P IV pt I 1298.

17. L&P IV pt I 1533.

18. Torrington Diaries II p357.

19. Ibid.

20. Creasey 1825:290

21. Ibid.

22. Ibid.

23. Creasey 1825:280.

24. James 1986:226.

25. James 1986:227.

26. James 1986:230.

27. Ibid.

28. Sir Christopher Willoughby's Complaint to the king, 1534 (L&P VII 224).

29. Suffolk complained to Wolsey of Willoughby's occupation of Eresby (L&P IV pt II 3997), to which Willoughby responded that he had entered peaceably (L&P IV pt II 4184).

30. John Copuldike to the Duke of Suffolk, 23 February 1534 (L&P VII 223).

31. James 1986:234.

32. Childe-Pemberton 1913:183.

33. Elizabeth, Lady Tailbois to Cardinal Wolsey, 11 June 1528 (West Yorkshire Archive Service WYL 230/3788). It is also printed in Wood II pp40–43.

34. PRO C1/1156/14.

35. L&P IV pt II 2972.

36. Holles p66–7. Their younger son, William Tailboys, refers to the chapel as the chapel of his father and mother in his Will of 24 September 1577 (printed in Armstrong 2008:104).

37. PRO C1/1156/14.

38. L&P X 1008.

39. Elizabeth, Lady Tailbois to Mr Thomas Heneage, 1 April 1529 (Wood II pp43–45).

40. It is clear that Bessie travelled to court given that Lady Tailbois was able to report what Bessie had said to 'old Blesby' whilst he was still in London with Gilbert.

41. It was also Anne's marriage money that was the subject of the legal case between the elder Lady Tailboys and her brother over claims that Sir Robert Tailboys had bequeathed her outstanding marriage portion to her for Anne's marriage.

42. Leach 2009:11.

43. L&P V 119. Interestingly, Dr Magnus, one of Henry Fitzroy's chief officers was included as one of the men charged with holding the lands and person of George Tailboys, demonstrating continuing links between Bessie's eldest son and her husband's family.

44. William Tailboys' will is printed in Armstrong 2008:104. His wish to be buried in Lincoln Cathedral in his parents' chapel is testament to his good relationship with them. His grave, which is marked by a stone slab, lies beside his parents' more ornate tomb in the cathedral.

45. The Inventories of John Tailboys of Raithby, 1579 and Robert Tailboys of Raithby, 1576 are printed in Armstrong 2008.

46. Sir William Tailboys' will is printed in Armstrong 2008:104.

47. Maddison 1883:22.

48. Ibid.

49. PRO E328/204.

50. Noble 1878:44.

51. Creasey 1825:285 and *The History of the County of Lincoln* pp275–276 detail the opening of the vault.

52. Creasey 1825:283.

53. Newton 1995:18.

54. Oliver 1837:17.

55. Hayward 2005:127 discussed New Year's gifts in 1529. Bessie's gift is known from the reward given to her servant by the king on New Year's Day 1529 for bringing her gift (L&P V 307).

56. Childe-Pemberton 1913:199.

57. PRO E101 420/15 f.3.

58. Ibid. f.2.

59. E328/204.

60. L&P IV pt II 2972.

## Chapter 14: Henry Fitzroy, Duke of Richmond & Somerset

1. SP1/35 f.160.

2. PRO E36/171.

3. For example, in Wolsey's accounts in *Collectanea Curiosa* p314 Wolsey gave a salt of silver and gilt for the christening of a child to which Henry was godfather.

4. An Account of Plate, Gold and Silver, made for Cardinal Wolsey, from the ninth year of Henry VIII, unto the nineteenth year (*Collectanea Curiosa* p321).

5. 1536 Inventory (Nichols 1855:5).

6. Henry Fitzroy's Council to Wolsey, 25 December 1525 (Nichols 1855:xxx).

7. Dr Magnus to Wolsey, 13 September 1526 (Nichols 1855:xxxi).

8. Henry Fitzroy to Wolsey, March 1529 (Murphy 2001:63).

9. Order of the Creation of the Duke of Richmond (from MS Cotton Tiberius E VIII) (printed in Nichols 1855:lxxx).

10. *Notes and Queries* 5th series XI. Note by JTF p333–334.

11. *Legend of Throckmorton* p11.

12. Longleat Misc MSS 17 f.13v–14.

13. Ibid.f.17v–18

14. Ibid. f.17v.

15. Ibid. f.22.

16. Hall's Chronicle I p320.

17. Wolsey to Henry VIII, May or June 1525 (State Papers I:161).

18. Ashmole 1715:525.

19. L&P IV pt I 1399 (John Arundel to Wolsey, 9 June 1525).

20. Lorenzo Orio to the Doge and Signory, 12 June 1525 (CSP Venetian III 1037).

21. Lorenzo Orio to the Doge and Signory, 29 June 1525 (CSP Venetian III 1052).

22. Letter of Lorenzo Orio, 29 June 1525 (CSP Venetian III 1053).

23. Fiddes 1726:348.

24. Fitzroy's half brother, Edward VI, noted in his diary that it was at six that he was removed from the company of women to begin his education.

25. Ashmole 1715:523.

26. Longleat Misc 17 f.5v.

27. Stow 1842:147.

28. Programme for the creation of the Duke of Richmond, The Marquis of Exeter, the Earls of Rutland and Cumberland, and the

Viscounts Fitzwalter and Rochford, at the Palace of Bridewell, on Sunday the 18th of June, 1525 (printed in Nichols 1855).

29. L&P IV pt I 1431.
30. Longleat Misc 17 f.3v.
31. Murphy 2001:48.
32. This precedence was specifically stated in a patent created at the time of his elevation (L&P IV pt I 1431).
33. L&P IV pt I 1500 (16 July 1525).
34. L&P IV pt I 1510 (22 July 1525).
35. L&P IV pt I 1431.
36. L&P IV pt III 5748.
37. Nichols 1855:xvi. These grants were restated by parliament in 1530–31 (Statutes of the Realm III p338).
38. Fitzroy's acquisition of Collyweston was restated by parliament in the Act noted above in 1530–31 (Statues of the Realm III p338). This part of the Act was repealed in 1535–36 and the manor granted to Anne Boleyn for life (Statutes of the Realm III p621). Perhaps as compensation, Fitzroy then received Baynard's Castle in London (Statutes of the Realm III p688).
39. Murphy 1997:97.
40. Longleat Misc 17 f.108v.
41. SP1/35 f.149–160.
42. Longleat Misc 15 and 16 *passim*.
43. BL MS Harl 589, f.192 (printed in Nichols 1855:xxv).
44. Longleat Misc 17 f.96v.
45. Accounts from 16 June 1525 to 31 December 1525 (Nichols 1855:xxvi).
46. The Regulations and Establishment of the Earl of Northumberland p29.
47. Henry Fitzroy's Council to Cardinal Wolsey, 5 November 1525 (Nichols 1855: xxx).
48. Nichols 1855:xxvii.
49. Longleat Misc 17 f.96v and f.18v.
50. Longleat Misc 17 f.21v–22.
51. Ibid. f.9v.
52. Murphy 2001:35.
53. Book Prices 1897:40.
54. Epitaph to Sir George Blount from his tomb in Kinlet church (printed in Blakeway 1908:149).
55. Lord Tailboys is noted as one of the gentlemen who dined with Anne of Cleves in a letter of the Earl of Southampton and Wotton to Henry VIII in December 1539 (State Papers VIII pp208–213).
56. Reception of the Lady Anna of Cleves at Calais, 1539 (MS Harl 296, f.171 printed as an appendix to the Chronicle of Calais, p123).
57. The Ceremonies and funeral solemnities paid to the corpse of King Henry VIII in Strype Ecclesiastical Memorials II pt II p301. George carried the tenth banner, that of St Edmund.

58. L&P X 749 (Henry, Lord Stafford to the Earl of Westmoreland, 28 April 1536) notes that George was one of the Duke of Richmond's servants.
59. L&P XIII pt II 1184 (A list of 'Gentlemen most mete to be daily waiters upon my said lord and allowed in his house' includes Henry Blount who can most probably be identified as Bessie's brother).
60. PRO C1/1141/27 and PRO C1/1141/28.
61. L&P XI 164.
62. Longleat Misc 17 f.7v–17.
63. L&P IV pt I 2151.
64. 1536 Inventory.
65. Ibid.
66. Letter of Lorenzo Orio, 29 June 1525 (CSP Venetian III 1053).
67. A Tour of England: Mario Savorgnano to ?, 25 August 1531 (CSP Venetian IV 682).
68. Richard Sampson to Wolsey, 3 September 1525 (State Papers I:162).
69. BL Harl MS 252 f.26.
70. L&P XII pt II 186.

## Chapter 15: Henry Fitzroy in the North

1. BL Egerton 1991, f.34.
2. For example three letters of Sir Nicholas Vaux to Cardinal Wolsey (Appendix to the Chronicle of Calais, pp80–84).
3. List of the noble persons who accompanied Henry VIII to the Field of the Cloth of Gold (Rutland Papers p31).
4. Henry VIII'S privy purse expenses p42.
5. Norton 2010a:228–230.
6. Nichols 1857:10.
7. Edward, Prince of Wales, to Princess Mary, 20 May 1536 (Nichols 1857:10).
8. As an aside, Throckmorton's reference to his cousin as his 'Valentine' is interesting. It has been suggested that the reference made in a letter of 1477 by Margery Brews to John Paston in which she referred to her correspondent as 'my right welebeloved Voluntyne' is the first known written example of the phrase, indicating that Throckmorton's use of the term was an early one (Margery Brews to John Paston, February 1477 in Paston Letters III p170).
9. Hill 1870:187.
10. Nicholson 1861:84.
11. James 2008:37.
12. *Legend of Throckmorton* p11.
13. Farrer 1923:62–63.
14. James 2008:40.
15. Carver's introduction in Palsgrave 1937: ix.
16. Carver 1937:xv.
17. SP1/55 f.14.
18. John Palsgrave to Henry VIII (Childe-Pemberton 1913:159).
19. John Palsgrave to Thomas More (James

2008:44).

20. Printed in Childe-Pemberton 1913:169.

21. L&P IV pt III 5750.

22. Carver xliii.

23. Letter of John Palsgrave, quoted from Carver xxxi.

24. Carver xxxi.

25. For example, Palsgrave along with fellow members of the council wrote to Wolsey on 9 April 1526 from Sheriff Hutton regarding a fraud committed by Fitzroy's yeoman purveyor, Simon Prior (L&P IV I 2081).

26. Holinshed's Chronicle IV p283.

27. Sir William Frankelyn to Wolsey, 10 October 1525 (Childe-Pemberton 1913:148–149).

28. Croke 1823:391.

29. L&P IV pt I 1947 (Richard Croke to Henry VIII, 1 February 1526).

30. Nichols 1855:xxxix.

31. Cotton is named as the 'rider of the great horses' in the list of officers in the household at Fitzroy's death (printed in Nichols 1855: lxxii). The Cotton brothers were the only members of Fitzroy's household permitted to accompany his body to his burial place at Thetford Abbey, something which suggests their close relationship with him (L&P XI 233 Norfolk to Cromwell, 5 August 1536).

32. Croke to Wolsey (Ellis, third series I p333).

33. Croke to Wolsey, 6 February 1526 (L&P IV pt I 1954).

34. James 2008:43.

35. BL Arundel MS 97 f.122v.

36. L&P IV pt II 2861 (Sir William Bulmer and Sir Thomas Tempest to Wolsey, 8 February 1527).

37. Henry Fitzroy to Henry VIII, 14 January 1527 (Kitching 1972:9).

38. Henry Fitzroy to Henry VIII, 31 January 1528 (Kitching 1972:9).

39. The gifts are contained in Henry VIII's privy purse expenses pp40 and 131.

40. Henry VIII's privy purse expenses p189.

41. Magnus to Wolsey, 7 October 1528 (L&P IV pt II 4828).

42. L&P IV pt III 6406 (Croke to Fox, 26 May 1530).

43. L&P IV pt II 3520 (Fitzroy to Henry VIII, 26 October 1527).

44. L&P IV pt II 4562 (Russell and Hennege to Wolsey, 28 July 1528).

45. L&P IV pt II 4828 and L&P IV pt II 3689 (Northumberland to Wolsey, 26 December 1527).

46. L&P IV pt II 2801 (Magnus to Wolsey, 14 January 1527).

47. L&P IV pt II (Brian Higdon to Wolsey, 6 February 1528).

48. L&P X 364 (Visitation of Monasteries, 1536).

49. Leyson Thomas, Abbot of Neath to William Brereton, 17 February 1534 (Ives 1976:91). Ives 1976:28–9 provides a commentary on the investigation.

50. Henry Fitzroy to Henry VIII, 21 July 1528 (State Papers I, 164).

51. L&P VII 684 (Henry VIII to Henry Fitzroy, 18 May 1534).

52. Wolsey to Henry VIII, 1527 (State Papers I p234).

53. Wolsey to Henry VIII, 24 August 1527 (State Papers I p266).

54. L&P IV pt II 3272 (Ghinucci, Lee and Poyntz to Wolsey, July 1527).

55. L&P IV pt II 3051 (Lee and Ghinucci to Wolsey, 17 April 1527).

56. Wolsey to Henry VIII (State Papers I p269).

57. For example, L&P IV pt II 2876, the king's ambassadors to Rome suggested to the pope that Catherine de Medici would be a good match for Fitzroy.

58. CSP III pt II 220 (Mendoca to Mary of Hungary, 21 October 1527).

59. James V to Dr Magnus, 8 January 1526 (Childe-Pemberton 1913:152).

60. Wood II p20.

61. Queen Margaret to Dr Magnus, late 1525 (Wood I p368).

62. CSP III Pt II 37 (Don Inigo de Mendoca, imperial ambassador to England, to Charles V, 18 March 1527).

63. L&P VII 1107 (Charles V to his Ambassadors in France, 31 August 1534).

64. Details of the north and the attempts to govern there are contained in Brooks 1966.

65. Brooks 1966:4.

66. Printed in Pollard 1914:200.

67. Cardinal Wolsey to Henry VIII, 1527 (State Papers I p208).

68. L&P IV pt II 3383 (The Council of the North to Henry VIII, 24 August 1527).

69. L&P IV pt II 3358 (Earl of Angus to Henry Fitzroy, 18 August 1527).

70. L&P IV pt I 2110 (Sir Christopher Dacre to Lord Dacre, 17 April 1526).

71. Quinn 1935:175.

72. Carew Manuscripts 1867, 32.

73. Acts not Extant in the Printed Books (Carew Manuscripts 1867, 234).

74. Henry VIII's Privy Purse Expenses p42.

75. CSP Spanish V pt I 87 (Chapuys to Charles V, 10 September 1534).

76. L&P XI 1086.

77. Longleat Misc 17 f.98.

## Chapter 16: Family Marriages & Family Disputes

1. Visitation of Shropshire p308.

2. Only Rowland and William are listed in the 1623 visitation. However, Edward's

birth is noted in the *Register of Thomas Boteler* (p115). It seems probable that he died in infancy. The will of George Blount of Bewdley, another nephew of Bessie refers only to his cousin's Rowland and William Lacon (PROB 11/111).

3. Blakeway 1908:128.

4. Register for Willey v.

5. For example, the fine brass to a member of the Lacon family in Harley church suggests that they occupied the manor there during their lifetime. The parish register for Harley (which does not extend as far back as the early sixteenth century) also notes that a member of the family, Francis Lakyn, son of William Lakyn, was baptised in Harley church on 16 January 1608 (*Register of Harley* p1).

6. Register for Willey vi.

7. Register for Willey viii.

8. *Register of Thomas Botelar* p110.

9. *Register of Thomas Botelar* records that he was bailiff in late 1554 (p110) and that he was still bailiff in 1560 (p113).

10. Bindoff III p198.

11. Calendar of the Close Rolls Henry VII, I no. 1222.

12. Bindoff III p198.

13. Decrees Court of Wards and Liveries, Michaelmas Term, November 1590 (in Wrottesley 1903:393).

14. The marriage settlement is discussed in Wrottesley 1903:394.

15. Childe-Pemberton 1913:198 erroneously claimed that both Rose and Isabel married Lincolnshire gentlemen. In fact, only Rose did.

16. Brayley p382.

17. William Reed's Will PROB 11/25.

18. Somerset Archives DD\WHb/2986.

19. Visitations of Surrey p68 note that William Reed's first wife was the daughter of a man named Stede and was the mother of his heir, John Reed. No children by Isabel are mentioned in the visitation.

20. PROB 11/25 William Reed's Will.

21. Anne and Joan Reed later took legal action against Rose's husband over sums owed to them by Katherine Blount, suggesting that they were Isabel's children.

22. This is supported by the fact that two of Rose's grandchildren appear to have been born between 1552 and 1560. A date of birth for their father, Rose's son, is therefore likely to be in the 1520s. See below for a discussion of Rose's grandchildren which highlights their likely birthdates.

23. The 1562–64 Visitation for Lincolnshire records that Rose's son, John Grisling, was then living at Asgarby (p57).

24. Torrington Diaries II p342.

25. Madan 1899:66.

26. Madan 1899:65.

27. This can be inferred by the fact that it was their mother and her second husband, Sir John Savage, who disputed the inheritance of her brother-in-law in favour of her sons with Cardinal Wolsey (Madan 1899:65).

28. Murphy 1997:69.

29. Visitation of Lincolnshire 1592.

30. Carew 1811:267.

31. Ibid.

32. Justices of Devon to the Council, 22 April 1625 (CSP Domestic, Charles I, 78).

33. Order from the Privy Council, 31, May 1625 (Calendar of Plymouth Municipal Records p238).

34. Whiting 1991:117.

35. Copy of exemplification of the record of proceedings in the Common Please at Westminster, 19 Henry VIII (Calendar of the Plymouth Municipal Records, p43).

36. Williamson 1927:20–24.

37. L&P X no. 52 (John Elyot and William Hawkins to Thomas Cromwell, 7 January 1536).

38. Jewitt 1873:82.

39. Privy Purse Expenses of Henry VIII p117.

40. Privy Purse Expenses of Henry VIII p74.

41. Quoted from Nichols 1855:xcvii.

42. PRO C1/633/31.

43. PRO C1/610/2.

44. Carew 1811:266.

45. PROB 11/28 Katherine Pershall's Will.

46. PRO C4/93/78.

47. Visitation of Lincolnshire 1592. Ursula is not mentioned in the 1562–64 visitation, although her brothers are. This would seem to be an oversight. It is highly unlikely that Rose was still of childbearing age in 1564.

48. Thomas Wymbish's Will Prob 11/36.

49. Norton 2010a:34–36.

50. The negotiations between Lady Parr, Lord Dacre and Lord Scrope are discussed in Norton 2010a:19–23. Their letters are in Nicholson 1861:90–3.

51. Sir Thomas Blount's Will (Shropshire Archives 3320/62/7).

52. L&P III pt II 3282.

53. Childe-Pemberton 1913:192.

54. Bernard 1981:755.

55. Bernard 1981:764.

56. Bernard 1981:776.

57. Sir John Blount to Thomas Cromwell, 1531 (SP1/68 f.116).

58. The terms of the marriage settlement are recited in Thomas Blount's *Inquisition Post Mortem* (printed in Childe-Pemberton p271).

59. L&P IV pt I, 2002.

60. L&P IV pt II 2672 (Sheriff List, November 1526).

61. L&P IV pt III 5243.

62. L&P IV pt III 6721.

63. L&P V 166.

64. Childe-Pemberton 1913:188.

## Chapter 17: The King's Great Matter

1. The letters are printed in Norton 2011a.
2. Herbert 1649:231.
3. Cavendish 1962:114–116.
4. Cavendish 1962.
5. CSP Spanish IV pt I 228 (Chapuys to Charles V, 9 December 1529).
6. Herbert 1649:215.
7. CSP Venetian IV 694 (Report of England, made to the Senate by Lodovico Falier, 10 November 1531).
8. CSP Venetian IV 824 (Summary of the Interview between the kings of England and France, 31 October 1532).
9. CSP Venetian IV 694 (Report of England, made to the Senate by Lodovico Falier, 10 November 1531).
10. L&P V 1114.
11. Quoted from De C. Parmiter 1967:3–4.
12. Froissart p191.
13. The Act of Parliament is contained in Myers 1969:169. This notes that the pope's consent had already been obtained.
14. Details of Catherine of Valois' life are found in Norton 2010b:31–38 and Norton 2011b.
15. Lehmberg 1970:18.
16. Marshall 2009:33. Sir George Throckmorton was married to Katherine Vaux, the niece of Joan Vaux who was the second wife of Sir Richard Guildford.
17. Longleat Misc MS f.21v and 22.
18. Lehmberg 1970:180.
19. *Legend of Throckmorton* pp6–8.
20. L&P XVIII pt I 199.
21. L&P XVIII pt I 266.
22. Gordon p15.
23. Marshall 2009:31.
24. Marshall 2009:38–9.
25. Marshall 2009:51.
26. George's wardship is noted in an Act of Parliament of 1539 concerning the marriage of George Tailboys and Margaret Skipwith (printed in Maclean 1856:246).
27. PRO C1/1141/27.
28. L&P VII 9.
29. For example, a parliament held at Dublin in the twenty-eighth year of Henry VIII's reign was before Grey 'Deputy to Henry, Duke of Richmond and Somerset, Lieutenant of Ireland' (Carew Manuscripts 234).
30. Chronicle of Calais pp8–9.
31. Lord Leonard Grey to Thomas Cromwell (PRO SP1/70, f.56).
32. PRO SP/70 f.144.
33. CSP Spanish IV pt I 228 (Chapuys to Charles V, 9 December 1529).
34. L&P VI 1229 (Cranmer to Lord Rochford, 6 October 1533).
35. L&P X 935 (Sir George Lawson to the Duke of Norfolk, 21 May 1536).
36. Surrey's sonnet is printed in Croke 1823, II pp164–165.
37. Leonard Grey's correspondence and the fact of her own second marriage clearly place her at South Kyme.
38. Guy 1982.
39. Derrett 1963:7.
40. CSP Spanish V pt II 55 (Chapuys to Charles V, 19 May 1536).
41. Wriothesley I p53.
42. Longleat Misc MS f.97v and f.98.
43. Longleat Misc MS f.102v.
44. Norton 2008.
45. 1536 Inventory p13.
46. 1536 Inventory p12.
47. L&P IX 779 (Henry Fitzroy to Cromwell, 6 November 1535).
48. Statutes of the Realm III c60 1535–36.
49. Brereton also held a number of lands in farm from Fitzroy, demonstrating further links between the two men (L&P X 878).
50. L&P X 715.
51. Murphy 2001:107.
52. CSP Spanish IV pt I 228 (Chapuys to Charles V, 9 December 1529).
53. CSP Spanish IV pt I 460 (Chapuys to Charles V, 15 October 1530).
54. CSP Spanish IV pt II 664 (Chapuys to Charles V, 22 March 1531).
55. Mary, Duchess of Richmond to Thomas Cromwell, 1538 (Wood II p375).
56. 1536 Inventory p10.
57. For example, CSP Venetian IV 782 (Carlo Capello to the Signory, 21 June 1532) and CSP Venetian IV 795 (Carlo Capello to the Signory, 6 August 1532).
58. CSP Spanish IV pt II 1028 (Captain Thouard to Mr D'Yve, 12 November 1532).
59. CSP Venetian IV 823 (Carlo Capello to the Signory, 31 October 1532).
60. Ibid.
61. CSP Venetian IV 824.
62. CSP Venetian V 1036 (Giovanni Antonio Venier and Marin Giustinian, Venetian Ambassadors in France, to the Doge and Senate, 5 December 1532).
63. CSP Venetian IV 876 (Marin Giustinian to the Signory, 22 April 1533).
64. L&P VI 1616 (Montmorency to the Bishop of Auxerre, 8 December 1532).
65. L&P V 1627 (Richard Tate to Cromwell, 11 December 1532).
66. CSP Venetian IV 973 (Marin Giustinian to the Signory, 25 August 1533).
67. Chronicle of Calais p44.
68. L&P VII 904 (Henry Fitzroy to Cromwell, 30 June 1534).
69. Nichols 1855:lxvi.
70. CSP Spanish V pt I 112 (Chapuys to the High Commander, 18 November 1534).
71. L&P X 380.

72. CSP Spanish V pt I 156 (Chapuys to Charles V, 5–8 May 1533).

73. Wriothesley's Chronicle I p41.

## Chapter 18: Lady Clinton

1. Collin's Peerage II p181.

2. The Will of William, Lord Clinton, dating from 1354 survives (*Testamenta Vetusta* I p55).

3. Craik 1924:6.

4. Craik 1924:7.

5. Hall's Chronicle I p165.

6. Ibid.

7. Collins Peerage II p193.

8. Ashmole 1715:527.

9. CSP Spanish XII (Count d'Egmont and Simon Renard to Charles V, 8 March 1554 P140).

10. CSP Spanish XII p315 for the pension and p261 (M. de Courrieres and Simon Renard to Charles V, 22–25 May 1554) for the suspicion in which Clinton was held by Gardiner.

11. Calendar Assize Records. The earliest appointment is no. 1 (February 1559) and the latest no. 1483 (July 1584).

12. Murphy 1997:123.

13. *Testamenta Vetusta* II p579.

14. Collins Peerage II p193.

15. L&P VI 562.

16. Murphy 1997:74.

17. BL Egerton 1991 f.143.

18. Clinton's name is clearly not his signature, which is well known from surviving letters and appears on f.100 of BL Egerton 1991 f.100 in two places (one cut off).

19. BL Egerton 1991 f.72.

20. L&P VIII 291.

21. L&P IX 914.

22. L&P XI 202.

23. For example, L&P XII pt I 1104 (July 1536), L&P XII pt II 1150 (November 1537) and L&P XIII pt I 1519 (July 1538).

24. L&P XIV pt I 398.

25. Murphy 1997:75.

26. L&P X 876.

27. L&P XI 139.

28. BL Egerton 1991 f.2.

29. Leach 2009:13.

30. Leach 2009:13.

31. L&P XI 389.

32. Dodds and Dodds 1915 details the Pilgrimage of Grace.

33. L&P XI 216 (Lord Burgh to Henry VIII, 3 October 1536).

34. L&P XI 321.

35. Henry VIII's response to the rebels (St Clare Byrne 1968:141–142).

36. L&P XII pt I 467.

37. L&P XI 852 (Lord Hussey to the Council).

38. L&P XI 341 (Lord Hussey to the Council).

39. L&P XII pt I 4.

40. L&P XII pt II 74–75.

41. L&P XI 969.

42. Leach 2009:69.

43. Thompson 1856:381–387.

44. Anne Askew's interrogation is described in The Examinations of Anne Askew by John Bale 1831:5–7. She also left her own account (Askew 1831:10–20, 22 and 27–8).

45. Norton 2010a:135–152).

46. Leach 2009:13.

47. L&P XI 975.

48. L&P XI 828.

49. L&P XI 805.

50. Childe-Pemberton 1913:230.

51. APC I p114.

52. Carew Manuscripts 178.

53. Spelman 1698:123.

54. L&P IX 669 (Richard Layton to Cromwell, 23 October 1535).

55. For example, his attempts to obtain a property owned by Christ Church, Canterbury was noted in a letter from the prior to Cromwell on 17 March 1538 (L&P XIII pt I 528).

56. L&P XIII pt I 887.

57. L&P XIV pt I 191.

58. CSP Spanish V pt II 104 (Chapuys to Charles V, 7 October 1536) and L&P XI 714 (Chapuys' Nephew to the Queen of Hungary, October 1536).

59. L&P XI Appendix 9.

60. L&P XI 580.

61. L&P XI 590 (Edward, Lord Clinton to Cromwell, 7 October 1536).

62. L&P XI 587 (George, Earl of Shrewsbury to Henry VIII, 7 October 1536).

63. L&P XII pt I 1199.

64. Harris 1990:262.

65. L&P V 166.

66. Katherine Blount to Cromwell, 20 January 1533 (Parshall 1915:112–113).

67. Katherine Blount to Cromwell, 1 June 1536 from Knightley (Parshall 1915:114–115).

68. L&P XI Appendix 16 (Cromwell's Fees).

69. Katherine Blount to Cromwell, 16 January 1540 (Parshall 1915:117–119).

70. L&P XIV pt II 782 (Cromwell's Accounts).

71. George's wardship is described in Katherine Blount's letter to Thomas Cromwell of 1533 (printed in Parshall 1915:112–113).

72. BL Add MS 46457 f.56–62.

73. Katherine Blount to Cromwell, 21 February 1536 (Parshall 1915:116).

74. PROB 11/28 Katherine Blount's Will.

75. Greenslade 2006:17.

76. L&P X 741 (Henry, Lord Stafford, to

Cromwell, 27 April 1536).

77. L&P X 749 (Henry, Lord Stafford to the Earl of Westmoreland, 28 April 1536).

78. Roland, Bishop of Coventry and Lichfield to Cromwell, 15 January 1537 (Strype 1822:272).

79. Confession of Wyghtman, Servant to the Lord Admiral, no.2, 10 January 1549 (Haynes 1740:68–70).

80. Willis 1750.

81. Hole 1941:148.

82. L&P XII pt I 928 (Sir Edward Croft to Cromwell, 13 April 1537).

83. L&P XII pt II 296 (Dr Henry Kyng to Cromwell, July 1537).

84. Childe-Pemberton 1913:255.

85. Register for Willey iv.

86. Bridgeman 1883:83.

87. Bridgeman 1883:82.

88. The Visitation of Worcester p19.

89. Blunt 1911 Appendix 6.

90. The Visitation of Kent 1898.

91. May 1908:10.

92. The Visitation of London p28.

93. Will of George Blount of Bewdley PROB 11/111.

## Chapter 19: Bessie's Three Sons

1. The second Act of Succession is printed in Williams 1967:452–4.

2. Colwell 1888:310.

3. CSP Spanish V pt II p61 (Chapuys to Charles V, 6 June 1536).

4. CSP Spanish V pt II p572.

5. L&P IV pt II 3051 (Lee and Ghinucci to Wolsey, 17 April 1527).

6. Colwell 1888:309–310.

7. CSP Spanish V pt II 71 (Chapuys to Charles V, 8 July 1536).

8. John Husee to Lord Lisle, 13 May 1536 (*Lisle Letters* III 695).

9. Murphy 1997:173.

10. Wriothesley's Chronicle I p40.

11. John Husee to Lord Lisle, 18 July 1536 (*Lisle Letters* III 748).

12. IHR Longleat Miscellaneous Manuscript 16.

13. CSP Spanish V pt II 77 (Chapuys to Charles V, 22 July 1536).

14. 1536 Inventory p2.

15. 1536 Inventory p10.

16. Murphy 1997:294.

17. Wriothesley's Chronicle I pp53–54.

18. L&P XI 148 (Chapuys to Granvelle, 23 July 1536).

19. L&P XI 221 (Chapuys to Secretary Perrenot, 3 August 1536).

20. Murphy 2001:176.

21. L&P XI 221 (Chapuys to Secretary Perrenot, 3 August 1536).

22. L&P XI 233 (Norfolk to Cromwell, 5 August 1536).

23. L&P XI 516.

24. L&P XIII pt I 78 (Cranmer to Cromwell, 14 January 1538).

25. Mary Howard to Cromwell, January 1538 (Wood II p376).

26. Norfolk to Cromwell, 6 April 1538 (Wood II p376–377).

27. L&P XIV pt II 815.

28. CSP Venetian V 118.

29. Wriothesley's Chronicle I pp53–54.

30. CSP Spanish V pt II 55.

31. Hobden 2001:25.

32. Hobden 2001:27.

33. Denny 2005:75–79.

34. L&P XI 607 (Richard Cromwell to Cromwell, 8 October 1536).

35. L&P XI 1086 (Darcy and Somerset Herald, November 1536).

36. Loach 1999:159.

37. CSP Spanish XI Jehan Scheyfve to Charles V, 30 May 1553 p45.

38. L&P X 1087.

39. CSP Spanish XI (Jehan Scheyfve to Charles V, 28 April 1553 p35).

40. CSP Spanish XI (Jehan Scheyfve to Charles V, 15 June 1553 p54).

41. CSP Spanish XI (Jehan Scheyfve to Charles V, 19 June 1553 p57).

42. CSP Spanish XI (Jehan Scheyfve to Charles V, 24 June 1553 p66).

43. Loach 1999:161.

44. CSP Spanish XI (Jehan Scheyfve to Charles V, 28 April 1553 p35).

45. Loach 1999:162.

46. L&P XI 104.

47. L&P XII pt I 539.

48. L&P XII pt I 595.

49. *Lisle Letters* V 1086.

50. *Lisle Letters* V pp11–13.

51. L&P XIII pt I 795 (Sir Thomas Hennege to Cromwell, 17 April 1538). Re-dated to 1539 in L&PXIV 790.

52. *Lisle Letters* V 1394.

53. *Lisle Letters* V 1414.

54. *Lisle Letters* V 12.

55. The Ladies of the Queen's Privy Chamber to Henry VIII, 4 August 1539 (*Lisle Letters* V 1512).

56. The Life and Times of Sir Peter Carew p44.

57. Ibid. pp45–6.

58. Ibid. p46.

59. L&P XIV pt II 572.

60. L&P XV 14.

61. The Act of Parliament is printed in MacLean 1856:244–6.

62. The Earl of Southampton to Henry VIII (MacLean 1856:246).

63. BL Egerton 1991 f.13v.

64. Childe Pemberton 1913:251 and Murphy 1997:190.

Chapter 20: The Death of Bessie Blount

1. Roberts 1964:8.
2. Roberts 1964:8.
3. BL Sloane MS 398 f.1v.
4. BL Sloane MS 398 f.70v.
5. Ibid. f.69.
6. Ibid. f.68v.
7. Ibid. f.70V.
8. Ibid. f.70v.
9. Ibid. f.118.
10. Ibid. f.164v.
11. Ibid. f.17.
12. Fuller 1840:189.
13. Brooke 1985:69.
14. Cule 1970:186.
15. Cule 1970:187.
16. Cule 1970:190.
17. Ibid. f.153.
18. Ascham 1865:419, 429.
19. Machyn p9.
20. L&P XVI 947.
21. L&P XIV pt I 191.
22. L&P XIV pt I 403.
23. L&P XV 21.
24. Childe Pemberton 1913:242.
25. L&P IX 914.
26. Lady Jane Clinton to Lady Lisle, 19 November 1538 (*Lisle Letters* V 1276).
27. The two women were close, with a number of surviving letters to Lady Lisle asking her to pass on a greeting to Clinton's mother (including *Lisle Letters* II 390 and 436, III 771a, V 1201, 1277).
28. Lady Grenville to Lady Lisle, 31 August 1539 (*Lisle Letters* V 1531) asks Lady Lisle to send greetings to Lady Clinton, demonstrating that she had remained in Calais.
29. Stow 1842:167.
30. McPherson 2006:182.
31. Ibid. p183.
32. Milton's Methought I saw My Late Espoused Saint Brought to Me, Like Alcestis, From the Grave' pp215–216.
33. Blumenfeld-Kosinski 1990:2.
34. Ibid.
35. Ibid. p39.
36. The Ballad of the Death of Queen Jane (Leach 1955:478-9).
37. Becker 2003:105.
38. Becker 2003:107.
39. Stow 1842:148.
40. BL Egerton MS 1991 f.34 and f.94 bears the signature 'Elyzabeth Clynton'. F.92v contains a damaged signature of someone named 'Fitzgerald', the maiden name of Clinton's third wife.
41. BL Egerton MS 1991 f.1.

# BIBLIOGRAPHY

Place of publication for printed sources London unless otherwise
stated.

MANUSCRIPT SOURCES

*The Bodleian Library, Oxford*
MS Blakeway 22, Notes on Kinlet by the Reverend J.B. Blakeway.

*British Library*
Additional MS 7100, Extracts from Household Books of Henry VIII.
Additional MS 28585, f.43, Letter containing the comments on Bessie's appearance by the
Dean of Westbury.
Additional MS 42013, f.104–106, Nineteenth-century drawings of the tombs of Isabel
Cornwall, Humphrey Blount and Sir John Blount at Kinlet.
Additional MS 45133, f.141v, Ordinances for Royal Mourning.
Additional MS 46457, f.56–62, Marriage Settlement of George Blount and Constance
Talbot.
Arundel MS 97, Book of Household Expenses of Henry VIII.
Cotton MS Caligula DVI, f.155, Letter from Charles Brandon, Duke of Suffolk to Henry
VIII, 15 October 1514.
Cotton MS Titus A XIII, The Spears of Honour.
Egerton 1991, John Gower's *Confessio Amantis.*
Harleian MS 252, f.26 Letter of Henry VIII to Sir Thomas Wyatt.
Harleian MS 1415, Visitation of Staffordshire, 1583.
Harleian MS 1419A, Inventory of the Wardrobe of Henry VIII.

*Cornwall Record Office*
AR/19/37/1,2, Marriage settlement for John Arundell, son and heir of Sir John Arundell,
and Elizabeth, daughter of Gerard Danet, Esquire, 6 December 1525.
*Institute of Historical Research*
Miscellaneous Manuscripts from the Archives of the Marquis of Bath at Longleat
(Microfilm, Reel 2):
15. Book of Kitchen Expenses of Henry Fitzroy, Duke of Richmond and Somerset,
Natural Son of Henry VIII and Elizabeth Blount. March 1527 – September 1528.
16. Book of Kitchen Expenses of Henry Fitzroy, Duke of Richmond and Somerset,
Natural Son of Henry VIII and Elizabeth Blount. October 1535 – August 1536.
17. Inventory of the Wardrobe Etc. of Henry Fitzroy, Duke of Richmond and Somerset,
taken 23 June 1531.

*John Rylands Library, University of Manchester*
JRL 12005, Chaucer's *Troilus and Crysede.*

*Public Record Office (The National Archives)*
C1/165/60, Early Chancery Proceedings. John Salter and Elizabeth, his wife, daughter of Thomas Otteley, of Shrewsbury *v.* John and William Blount, sons and executors of Dame Elizabeth Blount, executrix of the said Thomas Otteley and grandmother of the said Elizabeth.
C1/186/1, Early Chancery Proceedings. John Blounte and Kateryn, his wife, daughter and heir of Hugh Pessale, knight, son and heir apparent of Humfrey Pessale, esquire *v.* Humfrey Pessale, esquire, aforesaid, John Harecourte and William Lowe.
C1/186/5, Early Chancery Proceedings. John Blounte and Kateryn, his wife, daughter and heir of Hugh Pessale, knight, son and heir apparent of Humfrey Pessale, esquire *v.* The same and Nicholas Sutton, John Morton and William Gybbons.
C1/203/14, Early Chancery Proceedings. Thomas Grey and Dame Isabell his wife, executrix and late the wife of John Russhe *v.* The mayor, aldermen and sheriffs of London regarding an attachment for debt by John Elman, executor of Henry Mathewe, citizen and tailor.
C1/221/3, Early Chancery Proceedings. Elizabeth, late wife of John Russe, of Yarmouth *v.* Simon Gerard and Thomas Sowter.
C1/222/94, Early Chancery Proceedings. John Russh and Isabel, his wife, daughter of Sir John Stanley, Knight, and previously the wife of Sir Hugh Peshale, knight, son and heir apparent of Humfrey Peshale, esquire *v.* Humfrey Peshale, esquire.
C1/269/66, Early Chancery Proceedings. Richard Pynson, bookbinder and printer *v.* The mayor, aldermen and sheriffs of London: An action of account by Thomas Grey and Isabel, his wife, executrix and previously the wife of John Rushe, and John Wellys, his executor.
C2/Eliz/B19/52, Early Chancery Proceedings, George Ballarde and his wife Margery *v.* John Bullock and his wife Dorothy. Bill of revivor. Lands in Bewdley, Worcestershire, late the estate of Sir George Blount.
C241/275/106, Chancery Certificates of Statute Merchant (Debtor Thomas Blount of Kinlet. Creditor Roger Grove merchant of London).
C241/275/195, Chancery Certificate of Statute Merchant (debtor Thomas Blount of Kinlet, knight, and John Blount, his son and heir apparent. Creditor Eustace Knylle, merchant of London).
C1/343/27, Early Chancery Proceedings. Mary, daughter of Thomas Otteley, deceased *v.* John and William Blount, executors of Dame Elizabeth Blount.
C1/349/40, Early Chancery Proceedings. Richard Pynson, of London, printer *v.* Isabel, wife of Sir Thomas Grey, knight, late the wife of John Russhe, esquire, and John Welles, gentleman.
C1/352/11, Early Chancery Proceedings. John Russhe of London, gentleman, son and heir of John Russhe *v.* Dame Isabell Persall.
C1/385/10, Early Chancery Proceedings. John Blount, esquire, son and heir of Thomas Blount, knight, and Katherine, his wife *v.* Edward and Walter Blount.
C1/389/2, Early Chancery Proceedings. John Blount, esquire, master of the game in Wyre Forest *v.* Roger Halborowhe, of Wolverley, yeoman.
C1/530/20, Early Chancery Proceedings. Thomas Judd of Wickford, and Mary, his wife, daughter of John Russhe, deceased *v.* Thomas Blount, knight.
C1/610/2, Early Chancery Proceedings. Katherine Burghe, executrix and late the wife of Henry Borughe, esquire, sometime Wolsey's servant, and formerly the wife of Walter Strycland, knight *v.* William Grysling, citizen and mercer of London.
C1/633/31, Early Chancery Proceedings. John Fulwood *v.* The sheriffs of London. Action of debt by William Gryslyng, mercer of London, upon complainant's surety bond for Thomas Benet of London, merchant tailor, indebted to John Dymmok, broker, a creditor of the said William.
C1/731/21, Early Chancery Proceedings. Margaret, late the wife of Jasper Balthazar, foreigner, and daughter of John Blount of Bitterley, deceased *v.* George Abyngdon and Elizabeth, his wife, executrix and late the wife of the said Blount.
C1/751/1, Early Chancery Proceedings. John, son and heir of John Blount of Butterley, and of Elizabeth, his wife, daughter and heir of John Eye, and of Eleanor, his wife *v.* George Abyngton, fourth husband of the said Elizabeth, and Richard, his brother.
C1/1074/5–9, Early Chancery Proceedings. Elizabeth Tailboys *v.* Sir William Gascoigne.

C1/1141/4, Early Chancery Proceedings. Agnes Laken, administratrix of the goods of Richard Laken *v.* William Jenyns.

C1/1141/27–31, Early Chancery Proceedings. Agnes late the wife of Richard Laycon, and sister and executrix of William Blount, knight *v.* George Wood, gentleman.

C1/1156/14, Early Chancery Proceedings. George Sayntpoll and Thomas Halle, Executors of Richard Sayntpoll *v.* Elizabeth, Late Wife of George Taylbus, Knight.

C1/1167/74, Early Chancery Proceedings. Thomas Wymbysshe and Elizabeth Taylboys, his wife *v.* Richard Unnyngton and John Calcoke.

C1/1168/55, Early Chancery Proceedings. George Wode *v.* Agnes Laken.

C2/Eliz/B19/52, Early Chancery Proceedings. George Ballarde and his wife Margery *v.* John Bullock and his wife Dorothy. Lands in Bewdley, Worcestershire, late the estate of Sir George Blount.

C4/93/78, Early Chancery Proceedings. Anne and Joan Redde *v.* William Gryslyng.

C142/8/41, Inquisition Post Mortem for John Russe of Suffolk.

C142/31/41, Inquisition for George Tailboys (idiot), Lincoln.

Durham 3 Inquisition Post Mortem Portfolio 177. For Robert Tailboys.

E36/171, f.71–71v, Memorandum delivered to my Lord Cardinal's grace by me Robert Amadas.

E36/215, King's Book of Payments.

E101/417/6, Warrants Connected with the Great Wardrobe.

E101/418/5, 6–8 Hen VIII. Warrants Connected with the Great Wardrobe.

E101/420/15, Henry VIII's New Year's Gifts List, 1532.

E101/622/31, Accounts relating to Beaulieu, Essex.

E150/852/1, Inquisition Post Mortem, Shropshire for Sir John Blount (anno. 23 Henry VIII).

E150/1032/2, Inquisition Post Mortem, Staffordshire for Sir Thomas Blount (anno. 17 Henry VIII).

E199/9/19, Inventory of goods in Sir Peter Carew's house, and order for them to be handed over to Lady Tailboys, his wife.

E305/10/E82, Exchange Henry VIII with Thomas Wymbish and Lady Elizabeth Talboys his wife.

E328/204, Indenture of Agreement concerning Sir Gilbert Tailboys, deceased. 3 March 1535.

PROB 11/8, Will of Sir Hugh Peshall.

PROB 11/11, Will of John Russhe.

PROB 11/13, Will of Dame Elizabeth Blount.

PROB 11/16, Will of Sir Richard Croft.

PROB 11/25, Will of Thomas Judd of Wickford.

PROB 11/25, Will of William Reed of Weybridge.

PROB 11/28, Will of Katherine Blount.

PROB 11/36, Will of Thomas Wymbysh.

PROB 11/63, Will of Sir George Blount.

PROB 11/67 Will of Robert Pigott of Chetwynd.

PROB 11/76, Will of Margaret Blounte, Widow of Netleye.

PROB 11/111, Will of George Blunte of Bewdley.

SP1/35, f.149–160, Information on the Duke of Richmond's Household.

SP1/55, f.14, Instructions for Sir William from John Palsgrave.

SP1/68 f.116, John Blount to Thomas Cromwell.

SP1/70 f.56, Lord Leonard Grey to Thomas Cromwell, 24 May 1532.

SP1/70 f.144, Lord Leonard Grey to Thomas Cromwell, 2 July 1532.

*Shrewsbury Record Office (Shropshire Archives)*

665/513, Marriage Settlement of Thomas Pigott and Dorothy Eyton, 20 February 1573.

3320/62/7, Will of Sir Thomas Blount 1524.

3365/67/63v, Bonds in Statute Merchant 1509.

*Somerset Archive and Records*

DD\WHb/2986, Marriage settlement of William Reed of Shepperton and Isabel Blount.

*Staffordshire Record Office*

D948/3/99, Writ to Escheator of Staffordshire for a valuation of the estate of Richard Pershall, a minor.

D1798/HM Chetwynd/99, Rental of Humphrey Peshall and Anne his wife of Hopton.

*West Yorkshire Archive Service, Leeds*
WYL 230/3788, Letter from Elizabeth, Lady Tailboys to Cardinal Wolsey, 11 June 1528.

*Worcestershire Record Office*
705:134/1531/77/69, Charter of Thomas Wymbyshe of Kyme, County Lincoln, Esquire, 25 December 1546.

PRINTED PRIMARY SOURCES

*A Collection of Ordinances and Regulations for the Government of the Royal Household, Made in Divers Reigns From King Edward III to King William and Queen Mary* (1790).
*Acts of the Privy Council, vols I–III*, Dasent, J.R., ed. (1890–1891) (APC).
Adams, P.W.L. (ed.), *Staffordshire Parish Registers: Gnosall Parish Register* (1922).
Adlard, G. (ed.), *Amye Robsart and the Earl of Leycester* (Teddington, 2007).
Anglo, S. (ed.), *The Court Festivals of Henry VII: A Study Based on the Account Books of John Heron, Treasurer of the Chamber* (Bulletin of the John Rylands Library 43, 1960–61).
Ascham, R., *The Whole Works of Roger Ascham, vol. I pt II*, Giles, Dr., ed. (1865)
Askew, A., 'The Examinations and Confession of Anne Askew' in *Writings of Edward the Sixth, William Hugh, Queen Catherine Parr, Anne Askew, Lady Jane Grey, Hamilton and Balnaves* (1831).
'The Babees Book, or a "Lytyl Reporte" of How Young People Should Behave' in Furnivall, F.J. (ed.), *Early English Meals and Manners* (1868).
Bale, J., 'The Examination of Anne Askew' in *Writings of Edward the Sixth, William Hugh, Queen Catherine Parr, Anne Askew, Lady Jane Grey, Hamilton and Balnaves* (1831).
Botelar, T., *The Register of Sir Thomas Botelar, Vicar of Much Wenlock* (Transactions of the Shropshire Archaeological and Natural History Society 6, 1882).
Brydges, E. (ed.), *The Paradise of Dainty Deuices* (1810).
*Calendar of Ancient Petitions Relating to Wales*, Rees, E., ed. (1975, Cardiff).
*Calendar of Assize Records: Surrey Indictments Elizabeth I*, Cockburn, J.S., ed. (1980).
*Calendar of the Carew Manuscripts, Preserved in the Archepiscopal Library at Lambeth 1515–1574*, Brewer, J.S. and Bullen, W., ed. (1867).
*Calendar of the Close Rolls, Henry VII, vol. I* (1955).
*Calendar of Inquisitions Miscellaneous Preserved in the Public Record Office, vol. VIII 1422–85*, Knighton, C.S., ed. (Woodbridge, 2003).
*Calendar of State Papers, Domestic Series, of the Reign of Charles I, 1525, 1526*, Bruce, J., ed. (1858).
*Calendar of State Papers, Spain, vols II–XII*, Bergenroth, G.A., De Gayangos, P., and Tyler, R., eds (1866–1949).
*Calendar of State Papers and Manuscripts, Relating to English Affairs, Existing in the Archives and Collections of Venice, and in Other Libraries of Northern Italy, vols II, III, IV and V*, Brown, R., ed. (1867–1871).
*Calendar of the Manuscripts of the Most Hon. The Marquis of Salisbury's, Part XI* (1906).
*Calendar of the Plymouth Municipal Records*, Worth, R.N., ed. (Plymouth, 1893).
Camden, W., *Camden's Britannia Abridg'd with Improvements, and Continuations, to this Present Time, vol. II* (1701).
Campbell, W. (ed.), *Materials for a History of the Reign of Henry VII*, 2 vols (1873).
Carew, R., *Carew's Survey of Cornwall*, Dunstanville, F., de, ed. (1811).
Cavendish, G., *The Life of Cardinal Wolsey, vol. II*, Singer, S.W., ed. (1825).
Cavendish, G., *Thomas Wolsey Late Cardinal, His Life and Death*, Lockyer, R., ed. (1962).
Chambers, R.W. (ed.), *A Fifteenth Century Courtesy Book* (1914).
Chaucer, W., *Troilus and Criseyde*, Furnivall, F.J., ed. (1888).
Chaucer, W., *Troilus and Criseyde*, Coghill, N., ed. (Translated into modern English) (1971).
*The Chronicle of Calais in the Reigns of Henry VII and Henry VIII to the Year 1540*, Nichols, J.G., ed. (1846).

*The Chronicle of Queen Jane and Two Years of Queen Mary*, Nichols, J.G., ed. (Felinfach, 1996).

Clay, J.W. (ed.), *North Country Wills* (1908).

Cole, R.E.G., *History of the Manor and Township of Doddington, Otherwise Doddington-Pigot, In the Count of Lincoln and Its Successive Owners, With Pedigrees* (1897).

*Collectanea Curiosa: Or Miscellaneous Tracts, Relating to the History and Antiquities of England and Ireland*, vol. II (Oxford, 1781).

*Collections for a History of Staffordshire*, vol. IV New Series (William Salt Archaeological Society, 1901) 'Extracts from the Plea Rolls, 34 Henry VI to 14 Edw IV, Inclusive', Wrottesley, G., ed.

*Collections for a History of Staffordshire* (William Salt Archaeological Society, 1917) 'Henry VII's Parliament, 1485–6'.

Collins, A.J. (ed.), *Jewels and Plate of Queen Elizabeth I: The Inventory of 1574: Edited from Harley MS. 1650 and Stowe MS. 555 in the British Museum* (1955).

Colwell, T., in *Historical Manuscripts Commission, Twelfth Report, Appendix, Part IV: Manuscripts of his Grace the Duke of Rutland*, vol. I (1888).

*Crowland Chronicle Continuations: Ingulph's Chronicle of the Abbey of Croyland with the Continuations by Peter of Blois and Anonymous Writers* (1854).

Davis, N. (ed.), *The Paston Letters* (Oxford, 1999).

Dillon, Viscount and St John Hope, W.H. (eds), *Pageant of the Birth, life, and Death of Richard Beauchamp Earl of Warwick K.G. 1389–1439* (1914).

Dockray, K. (ed.), *Edward IV: A Source Book* (Stroud, 1999).

Ellis, H. (ed.), *Original Letters Illustrative of English History*, vol. I first series, vol. I third series (1825–46).

Ellis, H., (ed.), *The Visitation of the County of Huntingdon, From the Authority of William Camden, 1613* (1849).

*Excerpta Historica* (1831).

Falkus, C. (ed.), *The Private Lives of the Tudor Monarchs* (1974).

Farrer, W. (ed.), *Records Relating to the Barony of Kendale*, vol. I (Kendal, 1923).

Fletcher, W.G.D. (ed.), *Shropshire Parish Registers Hereford Diocese*, vol. XVII (Shropshire Parish Register Society, 1920).

*The Forty-Fourth Annual Report of the Deputy Keeper of the Public Records* (1883).

Foster, C.W. (ed.), *Lincoln Wills Registered in the District Probate Registry at Lincoln*, vol. II 1505 – May 1530 (Horncastle, 1918).

Froissart, J., *The Chronicle of Froissart*, vol. VI, Berners, Lord, ed. (1903).

Gairdner, J. (ed.), *The Paston Letters*, 3 vols (Westminster, 1896).

Giustinian, S., *Four Years at the Court of Henry VIII. Selection of Despatches Written by the Venetian Ambassador, Sebastian Giustinian, and Addressed to the Signory of Venice, Jan 12th 1515 to July 26th 1519*, 2 vols, Brown, R., ed. and trans. (1854).

Gower, J., *The Complete Works of John Gower*, vol. II, Macaulay, G.C., ed. (Oxford, 1901).

Grazebrook, G., and Rylands, J.P. (eds), *The Visitation of Shropshire, Taken in the Year 1623 by Robert Tresswell, Somerset Herald, and Augustine Vincent, Rouge Croix Pursuivant of Arms*, Parts I and II (1889).

Hales, J.W. and Furnivall, F.J. (eds), 'Ballad of Bosworth Ffeilde' in *Bishop Percy's Folio Manuscript, Ballads and Romances*, vol. III (1868).

Hall, E., *Chronicle Containing the History of England* (1809).

Hall, E., *Henry VIII*, 2 vols, Whibley, C., ed. (1904).

Harpsfield, N., *A Treatise on the Pretended Divorce Between Henry VIII and Catherine of Aragon*, Pocock, N., ed. (1878).

Haynes, S. (ed.), *A Collection of State Papers, Relating to Affairs in the Reigns of King Henry VIII, King Edward VI, Queen Mary, and Queen Elizabeth, from the Year 1542 to 1570 Transcribed from Original Letters and Other Authentick Memorials, Never Before Publish'd, Left by William Cecill Lord Burghley, and Now Remaining at Hatfield House* (1740).

Hayward, M. (ed.), *Dress at the Court of King Henry VIII* (Leeds, 2007).

Hazlitt, W.C. (ed.), *Remains of the Early Popular Poetry of England*, vol. II (1866).

Herbert, E., *The History of England under Henry VIII* (1870).

*Historical Manuscripts Commission, Fourth Report* (1991).

*History of the Arrival of Edward IV in England, and the Final Recovery of the Kingdoms from Henry VI AD 1471* in Giles, J.A. (ed.), *The Chronicles of the White Rose of York*,

Part I (1845).

Hodgson, J., *A History of Northumberland,* Part II vol. I (Newcastle upon Tyne, 1827).

*Holinshed's Chronicles of England, Scotland and Ireland,* vol. IV (1809).

Holles, G., *Lincolnshire Church Notes,* Cole, R.E.G., ed. (Lincoln, 1911).

Hone, N.J. (ed.), 'Court Rolls of Gnossall, Staffs' in *The Manor and Manorial Records* (1906).

Hook, J., *The Life and Times of Sir Peter Carew,* Maclean, J., ed. (1857).

Horrox, R. and Hammond, P.W. (eds), *British Library Harleian Manuscript 433,* vols I and II (Gloucester, 1979).

Howell, J., *Epistolae Ho-Elianae: Familiar Letters Domestic and Forren,* vol. I (1655).

Ives, E.W. (ed.), *Letters and Accounts of William Brereton of Malpas* (Old Woking, 1976).

Johnston, G.P. (ed.), *A Catalogue of Rare Books Relating to Mary Queen of Scots and of Rare Editions of the Writings of George Buchanan* (Edinburgh, 1906).

Kipling, G. (ed.), *The Receyt of the Ladie Kateryne* (Oxford, 1990).

Kitching, C.J. (ed.), *Tudor Royal Letters: The Family of Henry VIII* (1972).

Landry, G., de la Tour, *The Book of the Knight of the Tower,* Vance, A., ed. (Dublin, 1868).

*The Legend of Sir Nicholas Throckmorton,* Nichols, J.G., ed. (1874).

Leland, J., *The Itinerary,* vols V and VII, Hearne, T., ed. (Oxford, 1744).

Leland, J., *The Itinerary in Wales of John Leland,* Smith, L.T., ed. (1906).

Leland, J., *Joannis Lelandi Antiquarii De Rebus Britannicis Collectanea,* vol. I (1770).

*Letters and Papers, Foreign and Domestic, of the Reign of Henry VIII,* vols I–XXI, Brewer, J.S., Gairdner, J., and Brodie, R.H., eds (1862–1932).

*The Lisle Letters,* 6 vols, St Clare Byrne, M., ed. (1981).

Lodge, E. (ed.), *Illustrations of British History, Biography and Manners in the Reigns of Henry VIII, Edward VI, Mary, Elizabeth and James I,* vol. II (London, 1791).

Machin, H., *The Diary of Henry Machyn: Citizen and Merchant-Taylor of London from A.D. 1550 to A.D. 1563,* Nichols, J.G., ed. (1848).

Madden, F., (ed.), *Privy Purse Expenses of the Princess Mary* (1831).

Maddison, A.R. (ed.), *Lincolnshire Pedigrees,* vol. III (1904).

Milton, J., *The Poetical Works of John Milton,* vol. IV, Hawkins, E., ed. (Oxford, 1824).

*MS Ballads, Temp. Hen. VIII* (Notes and Queries 5th Series vol. XI, 1879).

Mumby, F.A., ed., *The Youth of Henry VIII: A Narrative in Contemporary Letters* (Boston, 1913).

Myers, A.R. (ed.), *English Historical Documents,* vol. IV: 1327–1485 (1969).

Nichols, J.G. (ed.), *Inventories of the Wardrobes, Plate, Chapel Stuff, etc. of Henry Fitzroy, Duke of Richmond, and of the Wardrobe Stuff at Baynard's Castle of Katharine, Princess Dowager* (1855).

Nichols, J.G. (ed.), *Literary Remains of King Edward the Sixth* (1857).

Nicolas, N. H. (ed.), *Privy Purse Expenses of Elizabeth of York and Wardrobe Accounts of Edward the Fourth* (1830).

Northumberland, Fifth Earl of, *The Regulations and Establishment of the Household of Henry Algernon Percy, The Fifth Earl of Northumberland, at his Castles of Wresill and Lekinfield in Yorkshire Begun Anno Domini M.D.XII* (1770).

Norton, E. (ed.), *Anne Boleyn: In Her Own Words and the Words of Those Who Knew Her* (Stroud, 2011a).

*Obituary for Rev. J.B. Blakeway* (The Gentleman's Magazine vol. 96, 1826).

O'Conor, C. (ed.), *Bibliotheca MS. Stowensis: A Descriptive Catalogue of the Manuscripts in the Stowe Library,* vol. I (Buckingham, 1818).

Palgrave, F. (ed.), *The Antient Kalendars and Inventories of the Treasury of his Majesty's Exchequer,* vol. II (1836).

Palsgrave, J., *The Comedy of Acolastus,* Carver, P.L., ed. (1937).

Pennant, T., *The Journey from Chester to London* (1811).

Pepys, S., *Leaves from the Diary of Samuel Pepys* (New York).

Plowden, E. (ed.), *The Commentaries, or Reports of Edmund Plowden, of the Middle-Temple, Esq; An Apprentice of the Common Law,* Part I (Dublin, 1792).

Pollard, A.F., (ed.), *The Reign of Henry VII from Contemporary Sources,* vol. III (1914).

*Privy Purse Expenses of Elizabeth of York,* Nicolas, N.H., ed. (1830).

*The Privy Purse Expenses of King Henry the Eighth from November 1529 to December 1532,* Nicolas, N.H., ed. (1827).

Purcell, C., *1831 Census of Bewdley: An Index of Names With Trades* (Bewdley Historical Research Group, Occasional Paper No.2, 1998).

*The Registers of Harley, Shropshire*, Horton, T.R., ed. (Shropshire Parish Register Society, vol. XXIII, 1899).

'The Register for Willey', in *Shropshire Parish Registers, Diocese of Hereford*, vol. XVI, Fletcher, W.G.D, ed. (Shropshire Parish Register Society, 1915).

*The Regulations and Establishment of the Household of Henry Algernon Percy, the Fifth Earl of Northumberland, at his Castles of Wresill and Lekinfield in Yorkshire Begun Anno Domini MDXII* (1770).

*Rotuli Parliamentorum; ut et Petitiones et Placita in Parliamento*, vols V and VI (1767).

Roy, W., 'A Satire Upon Wolsey and the Romish Clergy', in Park, T. (ed.), *The Harleian Miscellany: A Collection of Scarce, Curious, and Entertaining Pamphlets and Tracts, as well in Manuscript as in Print*, vol. 9 (1812).

Russell, J., 'Boke of Nurture', in Furnivall, F.J. (ed.), *Early English Meals and Manners* (1868).

*Rutland Papers: Original Documents Illustrative of the Courts and Times of Henry VII and Henry VIII*, Jerdan, W., ed. (1842).

Rye, W.B. (ed.), *England as Seen by Foreigners in the Days of Elizabeth and James the First Comprising Translations of the Journals of the Two Dukes of Wirtemberg in 1592 and 1610* (1865).

St Clare Byrne, M. (ed.), *The Letters of King Henry VIII* (1968).

Scarisbrick, D. (ed.), *Anne of Denmark's Jewellery Inventory* (Archaeologia 109, 1991).

Schellink, W., *The Journal of William Schellinks' Travels in England 1661–1663*, Exwood, M. and Lehmann, H.L., eds (1993).

Seager, F., 'The Schoole of Vertue, and Booke of Good Nourture for Chyldren, and Youth to Learne Theyr Dutie By', in Furnivall, F.J. (ed.), *Early English Meals and Manners* (1868).

Sharman, J. (ed.), *The Library of Mary, Queen of Scots* (1889).

Skelton, J., *The Complete Poems*, Henderson, P., ed. (1931).

Sneyd, C.A. (ed.), *A Relation, or Rather a True Account, of the Island of England; With Sundry Particulars of the Customs of These People, and of the Royal Revenues Under King Henry the Seventh About the Year 1500* (1847).

Spont, A. (ed.), *Letters and Papers Relating to the War with France 1512–1513* (1897).

Starkey, D. (ed.), *The Inventory of King Henry VIII: Society of Antiquaries MS 129 and British Library MS Harley 1419: The Transcript*, vol. I (1998).

*State Papers Published Under the Authority of His Majesty's Commission*, vols I and VIII (1830–49).

*Statutes of the Realm*, vol. I and III (1810–17).

St Clare Byrne, M. (ed.), *The Letters of King Henry VIII* (1968).

Stow, J., *The Annales or Generall Chronicle of England* (1615).

Stow, J., *A Survey of London Written in the Year 1898*, Thomas, W.J., ed. (1842).

Strype, J. (ed.), *Ecclesiastical Memorials, Relating Chiefly to Religion, and the Reformation of It, and the Emergencies of the Church of England Under King Henry VIII King Edward VI and Queen Mary I* (Oxford, 1822).

*Testamenta Vetusta*, vols I– II, Nicolas, N.H., ed. (1826).

Torrington, John Byng, Viscount, *The Torrington Diaries*, 2 vols, Andrews, C.B., ed. (New York, 1970).

*The Visitation of Kent, Taken in the Years 1619–1621 by John Philipot*, Hoveden, R., ed. (1898).

*The Visitation of London in the Year 1568 Taken by Robert Cooke, Clarenceux King of Arms*, Howard, J.J. and Armytage, G.J., eds (1869).

*The Visitation of the County of Lincoln in 1562–4*, Metcalfe, W.C., ed. (1881).

*The Visitations of the County of Surrey Made and Taken in the Years 1530 by Thomas Benolte, 1572 by Robert Cooke, and 1623 by Samuel Thompson and Augustin Vincent*, Bannerman, W.B., ed. (1899).

*The Visitation of the County of Worcester Made in the Year 1569*, Phillimore, W.P.W., ed. (1888).

Vivian, J.L. and Drake, H.H. (eds), *Visitation of the County of Cornwall in the Year 1620* (1874).

*Warkworth's Chronicle*, an extract printed in Dockray, K. (ed.), *Edward IV: A Source Book* (Stroud, 1999).

Warner, R. (ed.), 'The Great Feast at the Intronization of the Reverende Father in God George Nevell, Archbishop of York, and Chauncelour of Englande in the VI Yere of the Raigne of Kyng Edwarde the Fourth, and First the Goodly Provision made for the Same' in *Antiquitates*

*Culinariae or Curious Tracts Relating to the Culinary Affairs of the Old English* (1791).
Williams, C.H. (ed.), *English Historical Documents*, vol. V (1967).
Willis, B. (ed.), *Notitia Parliamentaria: Containing An Account of the First Returns and Incorporations of the Cities, Tows, and Boroughs, in England and Wales, That Send Members to Parliament* (1750).
Wood, M.A.E (ed.), *Letters of Royal and Illustrious Ladies*, 3 vols (1846).
Wright, T. (ed.), *Churchwarden's Accounts of the Town of Ludlow in Shropshire, from 1540 to the End of the Reign of Queen Elizabeth* (1869).
Wriothesley, C., *A Chronicle of England During the Reigns of the Tudors,* 2 vols, Hamilton, W.D., ed. (1875–78).
Wyatt, T., *The Poetical Works of Sir Thomas Wyatt*, Gilfillan, G., ed. (1858).
'The Young Children's Book' in Furnivall, F.J. (ed.), *Early English Meals and Manners* (1868).

SECONDARY SOURCES

*A Guide and History of the Parish Church of St Peter Astley Worcestershire.*
*Antiquarian Researches of the Archaeological Institute* (The Gentleman's Magazine vol. 30 new series, 1848).
Adams, S., *Leicester and the Court: Essays on Elizabethan Politics* (Manchester, 2002).
Anderson, J.C., *Shropshire: Its Early History and Antiquities* (1864).
Armstrong, D.L., *The Ivor Taillebois Dynasty – Raithby Old Church Yard* (Horncastle, 2008).
'Ashburnham Sale Prices' (New York Times, 25 December 1897).
Ashmole, E., *The History of the Most Noble Order of the Garter* (1715).
Backhouse, J., 'Illuminated Manuscripts Associated with Henry VII and Members of his Immediate Family' in Thompson, B. (ed.), *The Reign of Henry VII* (Stamford, 1995).
Bagley, J.J., *The Earls of Derby 1485–1985* (1985).
Baldwyn Childe, F.C., 'Kinlet Introduction', in Fletcher, W.G.D. (ed.), *Shropshire Parish Registers Hereford Diocese*, vol. XVII (Shropshire Parish Register Society, 1920).
Barnard, E.A.B., *New Links with Shakespeare* (1930).
Barrett, M.N., 'Bewdley Bridge' in Snell, L.S. (ed.), *Essays Towards a History of Bewdley* (Bewdley Research Group).
Becker, L.M., *Death and the Early Modern Englishwoman* (Aldershot, 2003).
Bernard, G.W., *The Rise of Sir William Compton, Early Tudor Courtier* (English Historical Review 96, 1981).
Betham, W., *The Baronetage of England*, vol. II (1802).
Bindoff, S.T., *The House of Commons 1509–1558*, vol. III (1982).
Blakeway, J.B., *Notes on Kinlet by the Rev. J.B. Blakeway, M.A., F.S.A., Vicar of Kinlet*, Baldwyn Childe, Mrs, ed. (Transactions of the Shropshire Archaeological and Natural History Society, third series, vol. VIII, 1908).
Blumenfeld-Kosinski, R., *Not of Woman Born* (Ithaca, 1990).
Blunt, R., *Memoirs of Gerald Blunt of Chelsea* (1911).
*Book-Prices Current: Records of the Prices at Which Books have been Sold at Auction, From December 1897, to the Close of the Season 1898*, vol. XII (1898).
Bond, F., *Westminster Abbey* (1909).
Brayley. E.W., *A Topographical History of Surrey*, vol. II (Dorking).
Bridgeman, G.T.O., *The History of the Parish of Church Eaton and its Members, Wood Eaton, Orslow, High Onn, Shushions, and Marston* (Collections for a History of Staffordshire vol. IV, 1883).
Brooke, C., *A History of Gonville and Caius College* (Woodbridge, 1985).
Brooks, F.W., *The Council of the North* (1966).
Brown, S.I., 'Markets and fairs of Bewdley and some relevant information on trading' in Snell, L.S. (ed.), *Essays Towards a History of Bewdley* (Bewdley Research Group).
Burke, B., *A Genealogical History of the Dormant, Abeyant, Forfeited, and Extinct Peerages of the British Empire* (1866).
Burke, J., *A Genealogical and Heraldic History of the Commoners of Great Britain and Ireland*, vol. I (1834).
Burke, J. and Burke, J.B., *A Genealogical and Heraldic Dictionary of the Landed Gentry of Great Britain and Ireland*, vol. II (1847).
Burke, J.B., *A Genealogical and Heraldic Dictionary of the Peerage and Baronetage of the British Empire* (1852).
Burke, S.H., *Historical Portraits of the Tudor Dynasty and the Reformation Period*, vol.

III (1883).

Burton, J.R., *A History of Bewdley* (1883).

Butterfield, A., 'Confessio Amantis and the French Tradition' in Echard, S. (ed.), *A Companion to Gower* (Cambridge, 2010).

Carley, J.P., *The Books of King Henry VIII and His Wives* (2004).

Chappell, W., *Some Account of an Unpublished Collection of Songs and Ballads by King Henry VIII and His Contemporaries* (Archaeologia, vols 1–50, 1867).

Childe-Pemberton, W.S., *Elizabeth Blount and Henry VIII* (1913).

Churton, R., *The Lives of William Smyth Bishop of Lincoln and Sir Richard Sutton, Knight, Founders of Brasen Nose College* (Oxford, 1800).

Cockayne, G.E., *The Complete Peerage of England, Scotland, Ireland, Great Britain*, vol. 12, pt I (1910).

Collins, A., *The Peerage of England*, vol. IV (1768).

Collins, A., *The Peerage of England*, vol. II, Brydges, E., ed. (1812).

Colvin, H.M., *The History of the King's Works*, vol. IV (1982).

Craik, A.R., *Annals of Our Ancestors* (Edinburgh, 1924).

Cranage, D.H.S., *An Architectural Account of the Churches of Shropshire* (Wellington, 1900).

Crane, R.S., *The Vogue of Medieval Chivalric Romance During the English Renaissance* (Menasha, 1919).

Creasey, J., *Sketches Illustrative of the Topography and History of New and Old Sleaford in the County of Lincoln* (Sleaford, 1825).

Croke, A., *The Genealogical History of the Croke Family, Originally Named Le Blount*, 2 vols (Oxford, 1823).

Cule, J., *A Note on Hugo Glyn and the Statute Banning Welshmen from Gonville and Caius College* (The National Library of Wales Journal 16, 1969–70).

Denny, J., *Katherine Howard* (2005).

Derrett, D.J., *Henry Fitzroy and Henry VIII's 'Scruple of Conscience'* (Renaissance News 16, 1963).

Dewhurst, J., *The Alleged Miscarriages of Catherine of Aragon and Anne Boleyn* (Medical History, 1984).

Dodds, M.H. and Dodds, R., *The Pilgrimage of Grace, 1536–1537 and the Exeter Conspiracy, 1538*, 2 vols (Cambridge, 1915).

Dowden, A., *The Return of Lady Blount* (Transactions of the Monumental Brass Society vol. XIV pt 5, 1990).

Echard, S., 'Gower in Print' in Echard, S. (ed.), *A Companion to Gower* (Cambridge, 2010).

Elton, G.R., *Presidential Address: Tudor Government: The Points of Contact. III. The Court* (Transactions of the Royal Historical Society, fifth series, vol. 26, 1976).

Emery, A., *Ralph, Lord Cromwell's Manor at Wingfield (1439–c.1450): Its Construction, Design and Influence* (The Archaeological Journal 142, 1985).

Eyton, R.W., *Antiquities of Shropshire*, vol. IV (1857).

Fiddes, R., *The Life of Cardinal Wolsey* (1726).

Fleming, P., 'Politics' in Radulescu, R. and Truelove, A. (eds), *Gentry Culture in Late Medieval England* (Manchester, 2005).

Fox, J., *Sister Queens: Katherine of Aragon and Juana, Queen of Castile* (2011).

Fraser, A., *The Six Wives of Henry VIII* (1993).

Freeth, S., *The Brasses of the British Museum: A Historical Survey* (Transactions of the Monumental Brass Society, vol. XVI pt 4, 2000–2001a).

Freeth, S., *A List of Brasses in the British Museum* (Transactions of the Monumental Brass Society, vol. XVI pt 4, 2000–2001b).

Fuller, T., *The History of the University of Cambridge, and of Waltham Abbey*, Nichols, J., ed. (1840).

Fuller, T., *The Church History of Britain*, vol. III, ed., Brewer, J.S. (Oxford, 1845).

Gill, L., *Richard III and Buckingham's Rebellion* (Stroud, 1999).

Gillespie, A., *Print Culture and the Medieval Author: Chaucer, Lydgate, and Their Books 1473–1527* (Oxford, 2006).

Gordon, M.A., *Life of Queen Katharine Parr* (Kendal).

Greenslade, M., *Catholic Staffordshire* (Leominster, 2006).

Griffiths, R.A. and Thomas, R.S., *The Making of the Tudor Dynasty* (Stroud, 1998).

Gunn, S.J., *Charles Brandon, Duke of Suffolk* (Oxford, 1988).

Guy, J., *Henry VIII and the Praemunire Manoeuvres of 1530–1531* (English Historical

Review 97, 1982).

Hall, J.H., *Genealogical Notices Upon the Family of Tailbois* (Transactions of the Leicestershire Architectural and Archaeological Society vol. II, 1870).

Hanham, A., *Home or Away? Some Problems with Daughters* (The Ricardian 13, 2003).

Harris, B.J., *Women and Politics in Early Tudor England* (The Historical Journal 33, 1990).

Harris, B.J., 'Sisterhood, Friendship and the Power of English Aristocratic Women, 1450–1550' in Daybell, J. (ed.), *Women and Politics in Early Modern England, 1450–1700* (Aldershot, 2004).

Hart, K., *The Mistresses of Henry VIII* (Stroud, 2009).

Harwood, T., *The History and Antiquities of the Church and City of Lichfield* (Gloucester, 1806).

Hayward, M., *Gift Giving in the Court of Henry VIII: The 1539 New Year's Gift Roll in Context* (The Antiquaries Journal 85, 2005).

Hazlitt, W.C., *The Book-Collector* (1904).

Hellinga, L., *William Caxton and Early Printing in England* (2010).

Herbert, E., *The History of England Under Henry VIII* (1870).

Hewitt, J., *Stanley Monuments in Lichfield Cathedral* (The Archaeological Journal 24, 1867).

Hill, J.H., *Genealogical Notices upon the Family of Tailbois* (Transactions of the Leicestershire Architectural and Archaeological Society, vol. II, 1870).

Hindley, G., *England in the Age of Caxton* (St Albans, 1979).

*The History of the County of Lincoln*, vol. II (1834).

Hitchins, F., *The History of Cornwall*, Drew, Mrs S., ed. (Helston, 1824).

Hobden, H., *Tudor Bastard: Henry Fitzroy Duke of Richmond and Somerset and His Mother Elizabeth Blount* (2001).

Hodgson, J., *A History of Northumberland*, Part II vol. I (Newcastle upon Tyne, 1827).

Hole, C., *Haunted England: A Survey of English Ghost Lore* (1941).

Hoskins, A., *Mary Boleyn's Carey Children: Offspring of Henry VIII?* (Genealogists' Magazine, vol. 25, March 1997, no. 9).

Hume, M., *The Wives of Henry VIII*, n.d.

James, M., *Society, Politics and Culture* (Cambridge, 1986).

James, S., *Catherine Parr* (Stroud, 2008).

Jewitt, L.F.W., *A History of Plymouth* (1873).

Johnson, M., *Behind the Castle Gate* (2002).

Jones, M.K. and Underwood, M.G., *The King's Mother* (Cambridge, 1995).

Klein, P., *Ludlow Parish Church and Its Clergy at the Reformation* (Transactions of the Shropshire Archaeological and Historical Society 73, 1998).

Leach, T.R., *Lincolnshire Country Houses and Their Families*, 2 parts (Gainsborough, 2009).

Lehmberg, S.E., *The Reformation Parliament 1529–1536* (Cambridge, 1970).

Leighton, S., *Shropshire Houses Past and Present* (1901).

*The Leominster Guide* (Leominster, 1808).

Lewis, K.J., 'Model Girls? Virgin-Martyrs and the Training of Young Women in Late Medieval England' in Lewis, K.J., Menuge, N.J. and Phillips, K.M. (eds), *Young Medieval Women* (Stroud, 1999).

Loach, J., *Edward VI*, Bernard, G. and Williams, P., eds (New Haven, 1999).

Maclean, J., *Remarks on the Barony of Tailboys* (Proceedings of the Society of Antiquaries of London 3, 1856).

Madan, F., *The Gresleys of Drakelowe* (Collections for the History of Staffordshire, vol. I, new series, 1899).

Maddern, P., 'Gentility', in Radulescu, R. and Truelove, A. (eds), *Gentry Culture in Late Medieval England* (Manchester, 2005).

Maddison, A.R., *Domestic Life in the Sixteenth and Seventeenth Centuries, Illustrated by Wills in the Registry at Lincoln* (Associated Architectural Reports and Papers vol. 17 pt 1, 1883).

Marshall, P., 'Crisis of Allegiance: George Throckmorton and Henry Tudor', in Marshall, P. and Scott, G. (eds), *Catholic Gentry in English Society: The Throckmortons of Coughton from Reformation to Emancipation* (Farnham, 2009).

Mattingly, G., *Catherine of Aragon* (1944).

May, L.M., *Charlton: Near Woolwich, Kent, Full and Complete Copies of all the Inscriptions in the Old Parish Church and Churchyards Together with Notes of the*

*Families Connected with the Place* (1908).

McPherson, K.R., '"My Deare Sister": Sainted Sisterhood in Early Modern England' in Miller, N.J. and Yavneh, N. (eds), *Sibling Relations and Gender in the Early Modern World* (Aldershot, 2006).

Meyer, K., *John Gower's Beziehungen zu Chaucer und Konig Richard II* (Bonn, 1889).

Mitchell, R., *The Carews of Beddington* (Sutton, 1981).

Morant, P., *The History and Antiquities of the County of Essex*, vol. II (1768).

Morgan, M.M., *Pynson's Manuscript of Dives and Paupers* (The Library, fifth series, vol. VIII, 1933).

Moule, T., *The English Counties Delineated; or a Topographical Description of England*, vol. II (1837).

Murphy, B.A., *Bastard Prince: Henry VIII's Lost Son* (2002).

Naunton, R., *Fragmenta Regalia: Memoirs of Elizabeth, Her Court and Favourites* (1824).

Newton, M., *South Kyme: The History of a Fenland Village* (South Kyme, 1995).

Nicholson, C., *The Annals of Kendal* (1861).

Nicolas, N.H., *The History of the Town and School of Rugby* (Coventry, 1826).

Noake, J., *The Rambler in Worcestershire, or Stray Notes on Churches and Congregations* (1851).

Noble, M., *History of the Beautiful Elizabeth Blount* (The Genealogist vol. II, 1878).

Norton, E., *Jane Seymour, Henry VIII's True Love* (Stroud, 2009a).

Norton, E., *Anne of Cleves, Henry VIII's Discarded Bride* (Stroud, 2009b).

Norton, E., *Catherine Parr* (Stroud, 2010a).

Norton, E., *Margaret Beaufort* (Stroud, 2010b).

Norton, E., *England's Queens: The Biography* (Stroud, 2011b).

Norton, E., *Elizabeth Blount of Kinlet: An Image of Henry VIII's Mistress Identified* (Transactions of the Shropshire Archaeological and Historical Society, 2011c, forthcoming).

*Notes and Queries*, vol. I (1850)

*Notes and Queries*, vol. XI, fifth series (1879).

Oliver, G., *History of the Holy Trinity Guild, at Sleaford* (Lincoln, 1837).

Orme, N., 'Education and Recreation', in Radulescu, R. and Truelove, A. (eds), *Gentry Culture in Late Medieval England* (Manchester, 2005).

Owen, H., and Blakeway, R., *A History of Shrewsbury*, vol. II (1825).

Oxley, J.E., *The Reformation in Essex* (Manchester, 1965).

Page, W. (ed.), *The Victoria History of the Counties of England: Durham*, vol. III (1928).

Palmer, C.J., *The History of Great Yarmouth* (Great Yarmouth, 1856).

Parkyns, G.J., *Monastic and Baronial Remains, With Other Interesting Fragments of Antiquity, in England, Wales, and Scotland*, vol. II (1816).

Parmiter, G. de C., *The King's Great Matter* (1967).

Parshall, H.F., *The Parshall Family AD 870–1913* (1915).

Parshall, J.C., *The History of the Parshall Family* (1903).

Pearsall, C.E., Pearsall, H.M. and Neall, H.L., *History and Genealogy of the Pearsall Family in England and America*, vol. II (1928).

Pearsall, D., 'The Manuscripts and Illustrations of Gower's Works' in Echard, S. (ed.), *A Companion to Gower* (Cambridge, 2010).

Phillips, K.M., 'Maidenhood as the Perfect Age of Women's Life' in Lewis, K.J., Menuge, N.J. and Phillips, K.M. (eds), *Young Medieval Women* (Stroud, 1999).

Pfander, H.G., *Dives et Pauper* (The Library, Fourth Series, vol. XIV, 1933).

Plomer, H.R., *The Lawsuits of Richard Pynson* (The Library, New Series, vol. X, 1909).

Plomer, H.R., *A Short History of English Printing 1476–1900* (1927).

Pogue, K.E., *Shakespeare's Friends* (Westport, 2006).

Pollard, G., *The Names of Some English Fifteenth Century Binders* (The Library, Fifth Series, vol. XXV, 1970).

Polwhele, R., *The History of Cornwall*, vol. IV (1816).

*Proceedings of the Society of Antiquaries of London, 17 November 1864 – 20 June 1867*, Second Series vol. III (Report of 16 March 1865 by O. Morgan).

Purton, W., *Stottesdon Church* (The Journal of the British Archaeological Association, vol. 24, 1868).

Quinn, D., *Henry Fitzroy, Duke of Richmond, and his Conexion with Ireland, 1529–30* (Bulletin of the Institute of Historical Research 12, 1935).

Richardson, W.C., *The Surveyor of the King's Prerogative* (English Historical Review 56, 1941).

Richmond, C., *The Paston Family in the Fifteenth Century: Fastolf's Will* (Cambridge, 1996).

Sanderman, J.G., *The Spears of Honour and the Gentlemen Pensioners* (Hayling Island, 1912).

Seacombe, J., *The History of the House of Stanley, From the Conquest to the Death of the Right Honourable Edward, Earl of Derby, in 1776* (Manchester, 1821).

Seaton, E., *The Devonshire Manuscript and Its Medieval Fragments* (Review of English Studies VII, 1956).

Senderowitz, J., *'Plate, Good Stuff, and Household Things': Husbands, Wives, and Chattels in England at the End of the Middle Ages* (The Ricardian vol. XIII, 2003).

Shaw, T., 'Music' in Radulescu, R. and Truelove, A. (eds), *Gentry Culture in Late Medieval England* (Manchester, 2005).

*The Shropshire Gazeteer, with an Appendix, Including a Survey of the County* (Wem, 1824).

Sims, R., *Handbook to the Library of the British Museum* (1854).

Smart, T.G., *Genealogy of the Descendants of the Pritchards, Formerly Lords of Llanover, Monmouthshire* (Enfield, 1868).

Somerset, A., *Ladies in Waiting* (1984).

Southall, R., *The Devonshire Manuscript Collection of Early Tudor Poetry, 1532–41* (Review of English Studies vol. XV no. 58, 1964).

Southern, H., and Nicolas, N.H. (eds), *Biographical Memoirs of Sir James Croft, Privy Counsellor and Comptroller of the Household of Queen Elizabeth* (The Retrospective Review, and Historical and Antiquarian Magazine, Second Series vol. I, 1827).

Spelman, H., *The History and Fate of Sacrilege, Discover'd by Examples of Scripture, of Heathens, and of Christians, From the Beginning of the World, Continually to this Day* (1698).

Starkey, D., *Six Wives* (2004).

Stephenson, M., *Monumental Brasses in Shropshire* (The Archaeological Journal, vol. 53 second series, 1894).

Stephenson, M., *A List of Monumental Brasses in the British Isles* (1926).

Strype, J., *Annals of the Reformation and Establishment of Religion, and Other Various Occurrences in the Church of England During Queen Elizabeth's Happy Reign*, vol. II pt I (Oxford, 1824).

Strype, J., *Ecclesiastical Memorials, Relating Chiefly to Religion, and the Reformation of it, and the Emergencies of the Church of England, Under King Henry VIII, King Edward VI and Queen Mary I*, vol. II pt II (Oxford, 1822).

Thompson, P., *The History and Antiquities of Boston* (Boston, 1856).

Tremlett, G., *Catherine of Aragon: Henry's Spanish Queen* (2010).

Tucker, M.J., *The Ladies in Skelton's 'Garland of the Laurel'* (Renaissance Quarterly Winter 1969).

Turk, W.A.C., *Beatty-Asfordby: The Ancestry of John Beatty and Susanna Asfordby With Some of their Descendants* (New York, 1909).

Vaughan, H.F.J., *Donnington Church and Lordship* (Transactions of the Shropshire Archaeological and Natural History Society vol. VI, 1882).

Warton, T., *The History of English Poetry, From the Close of the Eleventh to the Commencement of the Eighteenth Century*, vol. III (1824).

Watt, D., 'Gender and Sexuality in Confessio Amantis' in Echard, S. (ed.), *A Companion to Gower* (Cambridge, 2010).

Welch, C., *Pynson's Dealings with John Russhe* (The Library, Third Series, vol. IX, 1918).

Whiting, R., *The Blind Devotion of the People* (Cambridge, 1991).

Wilkinson, J., *Mary Boleyn* (Stroud, 2009).

Williamson, J.A., *Sir John Hawkins: The Time and the Man* (Oxford, 1927).

Wright, T., *The History and Antiquities of the Town of Ludlow, and its Ancient Castle* (Ludlow, 1826).

Wrottesley, G., *The Parish of Church Eaton: Little Onn* (Staffordshire Historical Collections vol. 4, 1883).

Wrottesley, G., *History of the Family of Wrottesley, County Stafford* (Collections for a History of Staffordshire vol. 6 pt 2, 1903).

UNPUBLISHED PhD THESES

Bundesen, K., *'No Other Faction But My Own': Dynastic Politics and Elizabeth I's Carey*

*Cousins* (University of Nottingham, 2008).

Murphy, B.A., *The Life and Political Significance of Henry Fitzroy, Duke of Richmond, 1525–1536* (University of Wales, 1997).

Roberts, R.S., *The London Apothecaries and Medical Practice in Tudor and Stuart England* (University of London, 1964).

Rowley-Williams, J.A., *Image and Reality: The Lives of Aristocratic Women in Early Tudor England* (University of Wales, Bangor, 1998).

Rowney, I.D., *The Staffordshire Political Community 1440–1500* (University of Keele, 1981).

Samman, N., *The Henrician Court During Cardinal Wolsey's Ascendancy c.1514–1529* (University of Wales, 1988).

Williams, J.J., *Hunting in Early Modern England: An Examination with Special Reference to the Reign of Henry VIII* (University of Birmingham, 1998).

# LIST OF ILLUSTRATIONS

16. Sir John Blount from his tomb in Kinlet Church. Bessie's father received little benefit from his daughter's relationship with the king and struggled to obtain his inheritance from his father. © Elizabeth Norton.

17. Katherine Pershall from her tomb in Kinlet Church. Bessie's mother was an heiress and often found herself in court defending her claims to her inheritance. © Elizabeth Norton.

18. & 19. Pages from the fifteenth-century Beauchamp Pageant showing the birth and baptism of Richard Beauchamp, Earl of Warwick. The images provide useful information on childbirth and baptism in the late medieval period. © Jonathan Reeve JR1815b90fp1c 14001500 and © Jonathan Reeve JR1861b90p4c 14001450.

20. Bessie Blount from the side of her parents' tomb. © Elizabeth Norton.

21. Bessie was depicted with a demure expression on the side of her parents' tomb. © Elizabeth Norton.

22. Anne Blount from the side of her parents' tomb. © Elizabeth Norton.

23. The third sister depicted on the side of John Blount and Katherine Pershall's tomb. This is likely to be Rose, the sister to whom Bessie was closest. © Elizabeth Norton.

24. Bessie's younger sister, Anne married twice and was prominent in Shropshire. © David Sawtell.

25. The fourth sister depicted on the side of John Blount and Katherine Pershall's tomb. This is likely to be Isabel, who married a gentleman of Surrey and died young. © Elizabeth Norton.

26. Albora Blount from the side of her parents' tomb. Bessie's youngest surviving sister never married but was popular within the family, with her sister Anne naming one of her daughters after her. © Elizabeth Norton.

27. The three eldest sons of John Blount and Katherine Pershall depicted on the side of their tomb. The eldest two, who were the siblings closest in age to Bessie died young. The third was her brother, George Blount. © Elizabeth Norton.

28. Bessie's brothers, William and Henry, depicted on the side of their parents' tomb. Bessie had already left for court by the time that her brothers were born, although she took an interest in their early lives and advancement. © Elizabeth Norton.

29. Sir George Blount. Bessie's eldest surviving brother was a prominent Shropshire gentleman during the mid-Tudor period. © Elizabeth Norton.

30. The sixth sister depicted on the side of John Blount and Katherine Pershall's tomb. Claims that this sister was named Margaret and married into the Pigott family are false and it appears she died in infancy. © Elizabeth Norton.

31. The tomb of Sir George Blount at Kinlet Church. George chose to bequeath his estates to his nephew, Rowland Lacon, who paid for his elaborate tomb. © Elizabeth Norton.

32. Bessie's brother, George, from his tomb in Kinlet Church. George enjoyed a turbulent reputation, with local legends claiming that he haunted Kinlet after his death. © Elizabeth Norton.

33. Constance Talbot, wife of Sir George Blount. Bessie's sister-in-law was a kinswoman of the Earl of Shrewsbury and Katherine Pershall took great pains to secure the match for her son. © Elizabeth Norton.

34. Bessie's nephew, John Blount, from his father's tomb at Kinlet. John was George Blount's only son but died in childhood, reputedly dying after choking on an apple. © Elizabeth Norton.

35. Bessie's niece, Dorothy Blount, from her father's tomb at Kinlet. George Blount's only surviving child married beneath her. She was disinherited by her father but retained good relations with her cousins, the Lacons, who took the Blount estates in her place. © Elizabeth Norton.

36. A memorial brass to a member of the Lacon family at Harley Church in Shropshire. Bessie's sister, Anne, married Richard Lacon, a man who had almost certainly been previously intended for Bessie herself. © Elizabeth Norton.

37. Bessie's uncle, Walter Blount, from his tomb in Astley Church. © Elizabeth Norton.

38. Joyce Blount of Astley from the side of her father, Walter Blount's, tomb. Joyce's family moved to Stratford upon Avon and were close friends of William Shakespeare. © Elizabeth Norton.

39. Bessie's cousin, Robert Blount, from his tomb in Astley Church. © Elizabeth Norton.

40. The tomb of Bessie's cousin, Sir Thomas Blount, in Kidderminster Church. Thomas' father, Edward, was a favourite of his father, who attempted to disinherit his eldest son in his favour. © Elizabeth Norton.

41. The tomb of Sir Edward Blount with his two wives, in Kidderminster Church. Edward was the grandson of Bessie's uncle, Edward Blount. The Kidderminster Blounts became the most

prominent branch of the Blount family in the seventeenth century. © Elizabeth Norton.

42. and 43. Two views of London by Anthony von Wyngaerde in *c*.1550. Bessie's family had connections to London and she would have arrived in the capital shortly before her appointment to the queen's household. © Jonathan Reeve JR1873b46fp2215001550 and © Jonathan Reeve JR1874b46fp28 15001550.

44. Henry VIII shown in a later copy of the parliament roll of 1512. This was the year that Bessie first met Henry. He had only turned twenty the year before. © Jonathan Reeve JR971b54p363 15001550.

45. Great Tournament Roll of Westminster depicting the king taking part in a joust to celebrate the birth of his eldest son by Catherine of Aragon. Sadly, the prince lived only a few short weeks. © Jonathan Reeve JR1098b2fp204 15001550.

46. King Henry VIII from King's College, Cambridge. Henry VIII quickly took an interest in Bessie following her arrival at court. © Elizabeth Norton.

47. 'Pastyme with good companye', a song composed by Henry VIII in his youth. During his relationship with Bessie, the king was in his prime. He was reputed to be the most handsome prince in Europe. © Jonathan Reeve JR1176b2p149 15001550.

48. Catherine of Aragon. Bessie's appointment to serve Henry VIII's first wife was a prestigious one, and brought her to the attention of the king. © Ripon Cathedral.

49. Richmond Palace, another palace that Bessie visited with the king. © Jonathan Reeve JR1112b67plviii 16001650.

50. Henry VIII's lock for his private apartments. The Tudor royal court was highly mobile, with courtiers constantly being forced to pack and unpack their belongings. Henry took his own lock with him on his travels, keeping the master key himself. © Jonathan Reeve JR976b61p709 15001600.

51. Greenwich Palace, one of Henry VIII's favourite palaces and one of the residences in which he conducted his love affair with Bessie. © Jonathan Reeve JR1882b46fp186 14501500.

52. Henry Fitzroy. Bessie's eldest son bore a strong resemblance to his royal father, who delighted in him. © Elizabeth Norton.

53. Princess Mary in childhood. Catherine of Aragon's daughter was a rival to Bessie's son, with the Imperial ambassador commenting after his death that it was no bad thing for the princess. © Elizabeth Norton.

54. An allegorical representation of the betrothal of Princess Mary to the Duke of Orleans in 1527. In spite of the king's elevation of Henry Fitzroy, Princess Mary remained the king's heir presumptive until the divorce of her parents. © Jonathan Reeve JR2298b4p645T 15001600.

55. Mary Boleyn, the woman who supplanted Bessie as the king's mistress. © Hever Castle.

56. The tomb of Catherine Carey in Rotherford Greys Church. Catherine was the daughter of Mary Boleyn and it has been suggested that she was also the daughter of the king. Even stronger evidence suggests that Bessie's own daughter, Elizabeth Tailboys, was the daughter of Henry VIII. © Elizabeth Norton.

57. The tower at South Kyme. These are the only surviving remains of Bessie's marital home. © Elizabeth Norton.

58. South Kyme Church. The church was remodelled during the early nineteenth century and is now considerably smaller than it would have been in Bessie's time. © Elizabeth Norton.

59. Interior of South Kyme Church. Bessie's husband, Gilbert, was buried inside the church following his death in 1530. © Elizabeth Norton.

60. Bessie's replica memorial brass in South Kyme Church. © Elizabeth Norton.

61. The remains of the memorial brass commissioned by Bessie for Gilbert at South Kyme Church. The brass depicting Bessie is a replica of the original which is now in the British Museum. © Elizabeth Norton.

62. The early twentieth-century memorial marking the site of Gilbert Tailboys' grave in South Kyme Church. © Elizabeth Norton.

63. Lincoln Cathedral. The Tailboys family were prominent in Lincolnshire, with Bessie's parents-in-law founding a chapel in the cathedral. © Elizabeth Norton.

64. The tomb of Bessie's parents-in-law, Sir George Tailboys and Elizabeth Gascoigne in Lincoln Cathedral. © Elizabeth Norton.

65. Wolsey in his last days at Leicester Abbey, 1530. Cardinal Wolsey arranged Bessie's marriage, as well as ordering the upbringing of her son and she and her family depended on his favour. © Jonathan Reeve JR1094b20fp904 15001550.

66. The tomb of William Tailboys, Gilbert's brother, which lies beside his parents' tomb in Lincoln Cathedral. © Elizabeth Norton.

67. Anne Boleyn. At one time Bessie was considered a potential rival to Anne for the king's affections. © Elizabeth Norton.

# Tudor History from Amberley Publishing

## THE TUDORS
Richard Rex

'The best introduction to England's most important dynasty'
**DAVID STARKEY**

'Gripping and told with enviable narrative skill... a delight'
**THES**

'Vivid, entertaining and carrying its learning lightly'
**EAMON DUFFY**

'A lively overview' **THE GUARDIAN**

£9.99    978-1-4456-0700-9    256 pages PB  143 illus., 66 col

## CATHERINE HOWARD
Lacey Baldwin Smith

'A brilliant, compelling account' **ALISON WEIR**
'A faultless book' **THE SPECTATOR**
'Lacey Baldwin Smith has so excellently caught the atmosphere of the Tudor age' **THE OBSERVER**

£9.99    978-1-84868-521-5    256 pages PB  25 col illus

## MARGARET OF YORK
Christine Weightman

'A pioneering biography of the Tudor dynasty's most dangerous enemy'
**PROFESSOR MICHAEL HICKS**

'Christine Weightman brings Margaret alive once more'
**THE YORKSHIRE POST**

'A fascinating account of a remarkable woman'
**THE BIRMINGHAM POST**

£10.99    978-1-4456-0819-8    256 pages PB  51 illus

## THE SIX WIVES OF HENRY VIII
David Loades

'Neither Starkey nor Weir has the assurance and command of Loades' **SIMON HEFFER, LITERARY REVIEW**

'Incisive and profound. I warmly recommend this book'
**ALISON WEIR**

£9.99    978-1-4456-0049-9    256 pages PB  55 illus, 3

## MARY ROSE
David Loades

£20.00  978-1-4456-0622-4
272 pages HB  17 col illus

## THOMAS CROMWELL
Patrick Coby

£20.00  978-1-4456-0775-7
272 pages HB  30 illus (20 col)

## MARY BOLEYN
Josephine Wilkinson

£9.99  978-1-84868-525-3
208 pages PB  22 illus, 10 col

## ANNE BOLEYN THE YOUNG QUEEN TO BE
Josephine Wilkinson
£9.99  978-1-4456-0395-7
208 pages PB  34 illus (19 col)

## JANE SEYMOUR
Elizabeth Norton

£9.99  978-1-84868-527-7
224 pages PB  53 illus, 26 col

## ELIZABETH I
Richard Rex

£9.99  978-1-84868-423-2
192 pages PB  75 illus

## HENRY VIII
Richard Rex

£9.99  978-1-84868-098-
192 pages PB  81 illus, 48 co

## ANNE OF CLEV
Elizabeth Norton

£9.99  978-1-4456-0183-0
224 pages HB  54 illus, 27

# More Tudor History from Amberley Publishing

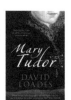

Available July 2013 from Amberley Publishing

The Tudor femmes fatales
who changed English history

B

*The* Boleyn
Women

ELIZABETH
NORTON

**Also available as an ebook**
Available from all good bookshops or to order direct
Please call **01453-847-800**
**www.amberleybooks.com**

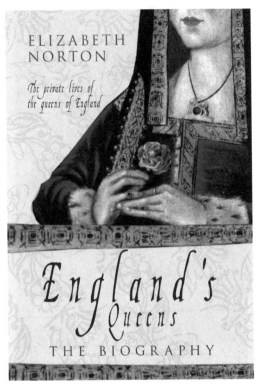

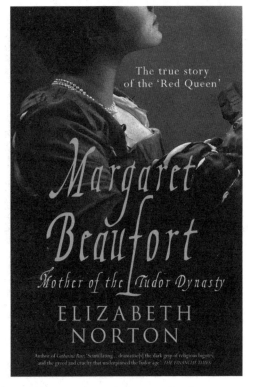